The Gaullist Attack on Canada 1967–1997

What lay behind Charles de Gaulle's "Vive le Québec libre!" speech in Montreal on 24 July 1967, Philippe Rossillon's activities in New Brunswick, Belgium, and Africa, and the sinking of Greenpeace's *Rainbow Warrior* in New Zealand in 1985? J.F. Bosher argues that the motivation behind all these incidents was a policy of underhanded imperial ambition on the part of France. In *The Gaullist Attack on Canada* he contends that behind the screen of harmless fraternizing of international francophonie, French nationalists have been at work to stimulate French revolutionary nationalism in Quebec and elsewhere. He argues that the Gaullist ideology behind these attempts rests on a set of myths about past events, age-old resentment of the English-speaking nations, and a deep-rooted belief in the superiority of France, its language, and its culture.

The French imperialism revealed in *The Gaullist Attack on Canada* poses a threat to Canadian Confederation. Since the 1960s, Bosher argues, de Gaulle and his followers have conspired to stimulate Quebec separatism as part of their larger goal to revive France's role as a great power. He bases his case on the evidence of France's actions in other former French colonies, especially in Africa, as well as the writings of such leading Gaullist conspirators as Bernard Dorin, Pierre-Claude Mallen, Pierre de Menthon, and Philippe Rossillon, who have boasted about their efforts to win Quebec away from Canada for France.

Bosher criticizes the Canadian government for its failure to respond to, or even to recognize, the Gaullist threat. Marcel Cadieux, the under-secretary of state for External Affairs in the 1960s, wanted to take vigorous steps against the Gaullist mafia but was overruled by his political superiors. Bosher argues that, even now, by standing up to French aggression the government might weaken the separatist movement in Quebec, or at least turn the tide of political support for it.

J.F. BOSHER taught the history of France and New France for forty years at King's College London, University of British Columbia, Cornell, and York University. Among his other books are *Business and Religion in the Age of New France*, *The French Revolution*, and *The Canada Merchants 1713-63*. In 1993 the Académie des belles-lettres, sciences et arts de La Rochelle (France) awarded him their prize/medal for *Négociants et navires de commerce avec le Canada de 1660 à 1760: dictionnaire biographique*.

The Gaullist Attack on Canada 1967–1997

J.F. BOSHER

McGill-Queen's University Press
Montreal & Kingston · London · Ithaca

© McGill-Queen's University Press 1999
ISBN 0-7735-1808-8 (cloth)
ISBN 0-7735-2025-2 (paper)

Legal deposit first quarter 1999
Bibliothèque nationale du Québec

Printed in Canada on acid-free paper
First paperback edition 2000

This book was first published with the help
of a grant from the Humanities and Social
Sciences Federation of Canada, using funds
provided by the Social Sciences and Humanities
Research Council of Canada.

McGill-Queen's University Press acknowledges
the financial support of the Government of
Canada through the Book Publishing Industry
Development Program (BPIDP) for its activities.
We also acknowledge the support of the
Canada Council for the Arts for our publishing
program.

Canadian Cataloguing in Publication Data

Bosher, J.F. (John Francis), 1929–
The Gaullist attack on Canada, 1967–1997
Includes bibliographical references and index.
ISBN 0-7735-1808-8 (bound)
ISBN 0-7735-2025-2 (pbk)
1. Quebec (Province)–History–Autonomy and
independence movements. 2. Gaullism.
3. France–Relations–Canada.
4. Canada–Relations–France. I. Title.
FC247.B68 1998   971.4'04   C98-901094-5
F1029.5.F8B68 1998

Typeset in 10/12 Sabon by True to Type

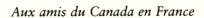

Aux amis du Canada en France

Contents

Contents

Preface

After twenty-five years of research, writing, and teaching in French history, I came back to the study of Canada's links with France, which had been my main reason for going to Paris and London in 1953. But since the late 1970s I have lingered in the seventeenth and eighteenth centuries, turning only recently to Charles de Gaulle's assault on Canada. This subject will arouse indignation in any patriotic Canadian. I am therefore eager to begin by saying that I have come to love and admire France during many years of residence there. These feelings and some of the reasons for them must be expressed at once to show that the following chapters are not the work of an enemy and not written out of mere prejudice. I am not thinking of France as a whole when writing about the Gaullist movement that has been trying to destroy Canada. Whatever Charles de Gaulle may have claimed during the Second World War, he never was France. The faith and obedience he required of his followers tended to confuse them about his hawkish views and to lead them into sharing a foreign policy that not many were fully aware of or could defend on their own. Those few involved in his assault on Canada are not France, any more than their leader was.

I first saw him in November 1953 in an armistice day parade, riding along the Champs Élysées in what looked like a military invasion of armoured vehicles and machine-guns. Fresh from Canada by way of England, where armistice day was remembered with hymns, a minute of silence, a single bugle call, and the red poppies of Flanders fields, I was puzzled by such a brave show of force in a country that had collapsed in June 1940 and been rescued by our soldiers. Nearly half a century in the study of French history has only begun to clear up the puzzle.

When I think of France, many images drift into mind. I think of a

September evening in a courtyard in Saint-Mandé near Paris, blvd du commandant René Mouchotte, with men and women playing *à la pétanque* with steel balls, benevolent, joking, patient with a foreigner. A pocket diary of c. 1958 reminds me to telephone "Jacques Parizeau à l'ELY 88–81." Another note, of the address "15 ave. Ledru-Rollin," recalls how student poverty was relieved now and then by heavenly days that began with pink Veuve Clicquot in tumblers at breakfast, cascades of Chaminade sounding on a distant piano, and ended with the cinema of Louis Jouvet, Jean Gabin, and Marcel Pagnol (*César, Fanny, La femme du boulanger*). Sometimes ancient streets in La Rochelle, Bordeaux, or Paris suddenly spring into memory as I saw them in the 1950s, with a glazier, panes of glass on his back, sauntering by shouting "Vitrier!" in the time-honoured way of his craft. Wonderful, too, was the cry "allez aux ceps!" by the mushroom merchants in a Bordeaux market late in the summer.

Here in my room is a pair of wooden shoes made of poplar wood by a *sabotier* in the Limousin who solemnly fitted me with them, carving out bits here and there until they fitted; I wore them once to the Reading Room of the British Museum during my silly student days. Wooden shoes may be a shameful sign of backwardness and poverty to many French people, as they were to my Lancashire grandmother when she recalled her youth near Salford, but no historian of early modern times could fail to be stirred by the sight of peasants in wooden shoes, red-faced and merry as they harvested grapes in a vineyard near the Garonne, tipsy enough not to mind being photographed by a shameless passing foreigner. I still have the picture to prove it!

If all this seems hopelessly sentimental, at least it was real, as was the nightingale that sang morning and evening for weeks near Paris's Jardin des Plantes, where we listened for it daily at 5 rue Guy de la Brosse while the concierge's aged turtle tottered about slowly in the courtyard. From there I could walk westward to the Clavreuil bookshop in fifteen minutes or northward to the Archives nationales, across the Seine, through the Île Saint-Louis, past the house where Frédéric Chopin was said to have lived, and into the Marais before it had been tarted up.

Many a lunch with Richard Cobb I seem to recall *Chez Madame Alice*, where he had an habitué's linen napkin on a shelf, and sometimes with George Rude, too, or with other passers-by, such as Kåre Tønnesson from Oslo or Paul Bamford from Minnesota. Among the fifteen or twenty readers at the Archives in the 1950s were a M. Larocque de Rochebrune, working for the Public Archives of Canada and helpful to fellow Canadians; Maître Robert Le Blant, so original on the early history of New France; and Professor Jean Meuvret, won-

derfully willing to hold forth for hours to an ignorant foreigner, and
even to invite him occasionally to dinner at his apartment on the Île de
la Cité, where Mme Meuvret would snooze quietly at the table through
her husband's learned monologues. Do all foreign historians of France
have such memories?

With these recollections I would like to send good wishes to friends
in France who spent hours, sometimes days, in conversation. The chapters of this book are not directed at them or at others like them. It is
the Gaullist régime, its servants, and their predecessors, studied in print
and occasionally in the flesh, who have driven me to write the tense
and ruthless pages herein. French bureaucracy, the French Revolution,
and various aspects of the Bourbon monarchy and the Fifth Republic
have preoccupied me in one way or another for forty years. Against
that background, the gratuitous Gaullist assault on the Canadian
confederation appears as one of the more sinister aspects of a world-
wide policy of prestige reminiscent of the Bonapartes and of the Bourbons before them. It is time that Canadians became acquainted with
some of the darker sides of France that Englishmen have known for
centuries.

I owe a debt of gratitude to many people for assistance. Their kind
efforts have much improved this book, and its faults are not theirs. In
particular, Mme Anita Cadieux has allowed me to read through many
volumes of the papers of her husband, Marcel Cadieux. Eldon Black,
Georges Blouin, Mme Cadieux, Joseph Ferraris, Dan G. Loomis,
Charles Lussier, Peter Marwitz, John Ross Matheson, Pauline
Sabourin, and Max Yalden have granted me interviews, answered
questions, and offered suggestions with care and patience. Various
chapters have been read by George Cowley, Naomi Griffiths, William
Irvine, Dan Loomis, R.M. Middleton, H. Blair Neatby, R.H. Roy,
Hubert Watelet, and Max Yalden, all of whom offered encouragement
and useful criticisms. John Starnes did all these things and watched
over my project with benevolent and unflagging interest. Carlos
Roldan and Pierre Savard gave me some useful hints. Thanks to Mimi
Benoît's kindness I was able to read through the entire run of Philippe
Rossillon's obscure Paris journal, *Les Amitiés acadiennes*. Ottawa's
libraries – the national, the municipal, and those at the universities of
Ottawa and Carleton – have been most obliging. York University has
been generous with support. I am grateful for John Parry's patient,
experienced editing. My daughter, Kate, interrupted her study of
ancient Greek to obtain rare articles by inter-library loan. My wife,
Cecil, has been, as ever, intelligently here and full of affectionate
responses.

Preface to the 2000 Reprint

Since this book went to press in 1998 other students of French interference in Canada have reached the same conclusions: Charles de
Gaulle and the Fifth Republic he founded in 1958 have been supporting Quebec separatists and preparing to launch an independent
Quebec the moment an acceptable "Yes" vote is extracted from the
province's population. More and more evidence has come to light.
"Since 1961," Alain Peyrefitte declared on French radio on 17 March
1999, "[de Gaulle had been] preparing for this event, whose progress
he was following ... the liberation of Quebec."[1] And since then, young
Swiss-educated journalist Frédéric Bastien has written, "Links with
Quebec weigh more heavily [in France] than links with Canada ... If
the Québécois were to vote finally for independence, there can be no
doubt that France would accompany them. In the meantime, faithful
to her Gaullist heritage, she will pursue the development of her special
relations with Quebec in the footsteps of the General."[2]

From other sources than mine, notably scores of interviews in
France, Bastien stresses the evil intentions of the many figures in
French public life who have been working for Quebec's independence.
Robert Bordaz, Raymond Bousquet, and Pierre-Louis Mallen were in
Montreal on 24 June 1963, applauding the nationalist demonstrators.
Thereafter all three of them worked hard for the cause, founding
support movements in France, lobbying the French government,
finding audiences for visiting separatists from Quebec, and raising
funds.[3] Philippe Rossillon, acting on orders from Michel Jobert to
agitate in Quebec, gave thousands of dollars to the cause through
secret routes. Gilbert Pérol, general secretary at Air France, managed
to arrange for free travel between Quebec and Paris for PQ leaders.[4]
Once there, they were funded, assisted, and encouraged in every possible way by those in the French Quebec mafia, such as Régis Debray,
Xavier Deniau, Janine Gravelin (Mallen's sister-in-law), Jean-Daniel
Jurgensen, Philippe Séguin, and Auguste Viatte.

Bastien identifies several more *mafioso* than I did, including – to my
astonishment and regret – the late Michel Bruguière. From 22 January

1984, when Bruguière knocked on my door in Toronto to discuss our common interest in the French financial officials of the 1780s and 1790s, we spent weeks together immersed in the history of the French revolution. Intelligent, hard-working, and generous, he soon became a good friend and, indeed, dedicated his next book to me.[5] The Fifth Republic, then on my back burner, never came up in the conversation. I knew that he had been one of President Pompidou's personal assistants but not that his job had been to advise on policy towards Canada and Quebec, not that in 1968 he had been one of the eight Gaullist founders of the *Association France-Québec*.[6] At Pompidou's death in 1974 Michel became a professor at the *École pratique des hautes études* in Paris. I assumed that his many foraging expeditions across Canada were innocent efforts to collaborate with various branches of the *Alliance française* and a way of passing the time while his wife was away on scholarly expeditions to China.

In short, during that time I went bumbling along, much the way most Canadians still seem to be doing, not noticing how Bruguière and other Frenchmen were working for the independence of Quebec – or assuming that if they were it didn't matter. The letter of protest I had written to the Montreal daily *Le Devoir* just after de Gaulle's "Vive le Québec libre!" speech in 1967, and which they published on 12 August, shows that I did not understand all the issues. Hindsight is all too easy, of course, but it is the historian's business. Just how oblivious most of us have been will come home to anyone who reads Bastien's *Relations particulières*, which adds usefully to the present volume and comes to much the same conclusions.

Bastien writes about politicians, diplomats, and other officials. On the subject of French secret agents agitating in Quebec, valuable information was compiled by Canadian journalist Robert Reguly, whose work I discovered only when my book had gone to press. After several years of investigation in Canada and abroad, Reguly was able to publish the names and activities of a dozen French *barbouzes* (thugs) working out of a bookshop in Montreal under the French government's Octogon Plan and Ascot Operation, master-minded by the SDECE (secret service).[7] On 4 June 1999 my wife and I invited Reguly home for lunch and in several hours of conversation found him tough, level-headed, intelligent, and well versed in what he writes about. Face to face he revealed details that he hesitates to publish for fear of the libel laws or other retribution. And, like us, he is bewildered at the general indifference of the Canadian public.

Reguly was well acquainted with Philippe Thyraud de Vosjoli, the SDECE agent who fled from his post in Washington to Mexico in 1963 for fear of being asssaulted by his own agency but refused to come to Canada because "of the presence of numerous Gaullist agents charged with organizing subversive activities in the French-speaking provinces."[8] Like me and others, Reguly holds Thyraud in high regard. My opinion was formed partly in a long telephone conversation with Thyraud on 29 May 1998, thanks to the good offices of another Toronto journalist, Peter Worthington, who visited and befriended Thyraud, as Reguly did. These men all know, as Bastien does, that the French government, driven by a powerful lobby, has long been committed to breaking up Canada by fair means or foul.

When this book was published a year ago, it reached a number of people who had witnessed some aspect of French aggression and wanted to tell me about it. Most of them held responsible posts of one kind or another. A Canadian official was eager to describe a French proposal to have the communication room in the basement of the Canadian embassy in Paris moved up to a higher floor near an outside wall, where sensitive spying devices might pick up messages. Another told me how his father and others had tried in vain to persuade Prime Minister Lester Pearson to have de Gaulle arrested and removed from Canada in July 1967. From Montreal came a first-hand report of a file showing that forty-eight hours before the 1995 referendum Jacques Parizeau had set aside five million dollars at the Quebec treasury to pay for a French ship that was bringing four regiments of French troops to the island of Saint-Pierre, a file that Parizeau took away with him when he resigned. This seemed all the more plausible when combined with a report from an M.P. in Ottawa that Monsieur Parizeau had arranged with General Armand Roy to take command of the revolutionary Quebec army that was to be formed of those French-speaking soldiers expected to respond to the infamous fax message sent out by Jean-Marc Jacob just before the referendum.[9] A group in Quebec City telephoned to say that in 1963 they had met an unhappy young Frenchman in Paris who complained that he was being sent to Canada as one of fifteen hundred *agents provocateurs*.

Several new books have thrown light on other subjects treated in this book. In *The Mitrokhin Archives: The KGB in Europe and the West* Christopher Andrew and Vasili Mitrokhin confirmed Thyraud de Vosjoli's claims by showing that the Soviet Union had about fifty agents in France, some even in the Élysée Palace. In 1974 there were at least fifty-five, some in close contact with major figures such as Georges Pompidou and Pierre Messmer. A wealth of detail shows that the Fifth Republic was riddled with so many KGB agents because France could be penetrated more easily than any other western country. "After the compromise of the British Magnificent Five in 1951, France became for the remainder of the decade the KGB's most productive source of intelligence on Western policy to the Soviet Bloc."[10] At the French embassy in Moscow during the early 1960s "Both the ambassador, Maurice Dejean, and the air attaché, Colonel Louis Guibard, were seduced by KGB "swallows" [state prostitutes trained to seduce foreign officials] after elaborate 'honey trap' operations directed by the head of the Second Chief Directorate ... with the personal approval of Krushchev. Dejean was beaten up by a KGB officer posing as the enraged husband of the swallow.[11]

Perhaps the most successful Soviet recruitment was of a politically active Gaullist businessman, François Saar-Demichel, who gained access to the Élysée during de Gaulle's presidency and supplied Moscow with regular reports on French foreign policy. Through its many agents and friends in Paris, the Soviet government had considerable influence on public opinion, secretly maintaining its own news agency, manipulating Pierre-Charles Pathé, son of the film magnate, and reinforcing the Gaullists' anti-American inclinations and their opposition to the reunification of Germany. Until the early 1980s it was through France that the KGB had its greatest success in penetrating NATO.[12] There is undoubtedly more to be learned, but already *The Mitrokhin Archive* provides strong reinforcement for parts of chapters 3 and 9 below.

Other books, new and old, add to what I wrote in chapter 13 about the part the Fifth Republic played in the Rwanda massacre in 1994. Such studies as *Un génocide secret d'État, la France et le Rwanda, 1990–1997* (Paris: Éditions sociales, 1998) by Jean-Paul Gouteux and *Rwanda 1959–1996, le génocide* (Paris: Dagorne, 1998) by Gérard Prunier have not been able to take the full measure of French involvement in that dreadful massacre, but they have brought more evidence in the case against the government of the Fifth Republic. The general issues I raised in chapters 14 and 15 have been taken up by Nicolas Tenzer, a high-ranking French official, who in the 329 pages of his book *La face cachée du gaullisme* (Paris: Hachette, 1998) analyses the harm that Charles de Gaulle and his influence have done in France these past thirty years. The aggressive ethnic nationalism that lies behind French policy towards Quebec appears all the more clearly, as I have argued, to be Gaullist in its inspiration.

A related point of a general nature needs to be stated over and over again: the revolutionary tradition is one of the least understood of French contributions to the separatist movement in Quebec. This tradition, developed over the last two hundred years, assumes that a nation is defined by its language, culture, and history, but holds that political independence or sovereignty is essential to its very existence. The nation has a fundamental right and duty to free itself from all outside authority and to "constitute itself" (*se constituer*) in writing. It is in that tradition that the French nation has adopted fifteen constitutions over the past two centuries, each the result of a revolution. And that revolutionary tradition has been absorbed by the governing élites in Quebec as an inevitable part of *la francophonie*.

Many recent members of the French-speaking club, notably Algeria and other north African countries, were born in French revolutionary processes. Cambodia, Vietnam, and others in Asia have similar histories. Belgium was born in a revolution against the Kingdom of the Netherlands in 1831. This being so, membership in *la francophonie* cannot help but encourage Canada to cut all ties with the British monarchy and Quebec to cut all ties with Canada. We seem to be almost defenceless against these insidious influences. Explaining the French revolutionary tradition in English-speaking Canada is almost as difficult as trying to make our constitution clear in a Paris café. Incredulity strains courtesy at every point in the conversation. It is our misfortune that the French revolutionary tradition plays a bigger part in Quebec than Canadian federal authorities seem to think and makes nonsense of Ottawa's efforts to formulate and organize the separation process by laying down rules and conditions.

Ottawa's weak and misguided defences, now almost a tradition, were visible again in the Spring of 1999. Early in March the French government invited the Quebec minister of culture, Agnès Maltais, to an official meeting in Paris without so much as informing the Canadian government.[13] Officials in Ottawa were in no doubt that President Chirac and Prime Minister Jospin supported their colleague Catherine Trautman, who had issued this invitation. Treating Quebec as an independent state seemed all the more blatant on this occasion because Premier Bouchard was then in Barcelona opening a provincial trade centre almost as if he were establishing the delegation of a sovereign state, and trading declarations with the leader of Catalonia about the rights of peoples to express themselves on the international stage.[14] On 13 March Bouchard and a large official party were due to arrive in Paris as special guests at the Salon du Livre – the first non-sovereign government group to be so honoured.[15] All this was too much even for Ottawa. The Canadian government showed enough spunk to lodge a protest and declare that the federal minister of culture, Sheila Copps, would boycott the cultural meeting. Prime Minister Chrétien spoke out against Bouchard and Trautman for their transgressions.[16] He even asked how France would regard Canadian encouragement for Corsican independence. But Canada was already backing down, as usual, with Canadian Ambassador Jacques Roy declaring that no such insult had occurred before or was ever likely to occur again.[17] Paris and

Quebec City went on refusing to retract or apologize, pointedly sneering at the Canadian government's protests.[18]

At the Salon du Livre, French authorities lavished unfair attention on Quebec and ignored Canada altogether. President Chirac, with Premier Bouchard at his side, paraded down the aisles past the publishers' book stands until he arrived at the huge exhibition funded by the Quebec government, where he declared the fair open. Jacques Parizeau, Louise Beaudoin, and other cultural officials from Quebec were on hand, along with all the invited authors and publishers from the province. Nothing in the opening ceremonies marked the presence of Canadian exhibits, publishers, and authors – including francophones from outside Quebec – or the Canadian ambassador, Jacques Roy. Radio Canada and other media telecast the fanfare around the Quebec stand and filmed the Canadian stand at the end of the festivities when it was deserted and the Canadian ambassador happened to be there to pick up his briefcase. "L'ambassadeur du Canada est seul," the announcer commented, and this unfair picture of events was repeated next day on TV5. At his residence the next night, the ambassador gave a hugely successful reception for Quebec and Canadian writers, artists, and publishers at the fair, but neither Radio Canada nor any other media were around to report on this event. Jacques Roy was naturally indignant at Radio Canada's distorted reporting of the reception and the Salon du Livre.

At the Salon, books by Quebec publishers who publish in English – including twelve copies of my Gaullist Attack on Canada – were missing from the shelves of the Quebec stands; they were kept in the storage rooms well hidden from the crowds. The organizers explained this with the unconvincing excuse that they had not had time to unpack the boxes holding those titles. In fact, the organizers were unwilling to present Quebec as also having an English fact and face. This situation was rectified on the second day of the Salon but only after the executive director of McGill-Queen's University Press and the rights manager for the French publisher Gallimard, Anne-Solange Noble – a former Montrealer – threatened to make the situation public. Following these interventions, books in English, at least the few that were there, were immediately placed in public view. (This small example shows the value of denouncing and opposing the machinations of the French Quebec mafia and their friends.)

Near the end of November 1999, Prime Minister Chrétien began to denounce and oppose the referendum policy of the Quebec government so as not to be caught unprepared as he was on 30 October 1995. At first he had to overcome the resistance of the Liberal establishment in Ottawa, inclined as they are to appease the PQ government and to tiptoe around the referendum issue in the hope that it will fade away, as recent polls have been suggesting it might. He showed commendable courage in facing criticism from all federal political parties except Reform, as well as from Liberals and the PQ in Quebec. Pressing on with his intention of setting rules and limits for any future referendum, he has at least succeeded in provoking the PQ to state its sinister revolutionary policy more clearly than usual. Premier Bouchard and his colleagues, educated in France and encouraged by the French Quebec mafia, will undoubtedly go on ignoring any constitutional laws – and Supreme Court decisions – made in Ottawa. After all, Big Brother in Paris is still there, repeating the mantras of popular sovereignty that have been chanted throughout the francophone world since the revolution of 1789.

NOTES

1 Campbell Clark, "Explosive Statement Planned, de Gaulle Minister Insists," *National Post*, 18 March 1999, A10.
2 Frédéric Bastien, *Relations particulières: la France face au Québec après de Gaulle* (Montreal: Boréal, 1999), 358.
3 Ibid., 99.
4 Ibid., 104–7.
5 See Michel Bruguière, *Gestionnaires et profiteurs de la Révolution: l'administration des finances françaises de Louis XVI à Bonaparte* (Paris: Olivier Orban, 1986), 9, "A John Bosher," to which he scribbled in my copy "qui n'a pas seulement ouvert des voies nouvelles à l'histoire financière, mais a très généreusement accueilli l'importun qui s'y engageait à son tour, et partagé un biscuit toujours croustillant. En très fidèle et amical hommage, Michel Bruguière."
6 Bastien, *Relations particulières*, 96.
7 See Robert Reguly, "The French Connection," *Sunday Sun* (Toronto), 15 October 1978, 3.
8 Philippe Thyraud de Vosjoli, *Lamia, l'anti-barbouze* (Montreal: Les Éditions de l'homme, 1972), 423, and see page 24 of the present book.
9 See *The Hill Times*, 334 (22 April 1996).
10 Christopher Andrew and Vasili Mitrokhin, *The Mitrokhin Archive: The KGB in Europe and the West* (London, Allen Lane, 1999), chapter 27.
11 Ibid., 603–4.
12 Ibid., 605–6, 609.
13 Gilles Toupin, "Sheila Copps boycotte une réunion à Paris parce que Québec y est invité," *Le Devoir*, 10 March 1999, B1; "Paris Froisse Ottawa," *France-Amérique* 20–26 March 1999, 4.

14 Kate Jaimet, "Separatism's Quiet Evolution," *Ottawa Citizen*, 13 March 1999, A1–A2.

15 Campbell Clark, "Hundreds Join Quebec Premier on Trip to Paris," *National Post*, 13 March 1999, A8.

16 David Gamble, "No New Powers, PM Tells Quebec: Chrétien says Quebec Will Not Represent Canada's French Culture," *Ottawa Citizen*, 17 March 1999, A4; Bernard Descôteaux, "La Corse de Jean Chrétien," *Le Devoir*, 12 March 1999, A8.

17 Robert Fife, "Canadian Envoy Confident France Won't Err Again," *National Post*, 12 March 1999, A11.

18 Campbell Clark, "No Regrets about Inviting Quebec, French Official Says," *National Post*, 19 March 1999, A6; Sean Gordon, "Quebec Has Right to 'Express Itself'," *Ottawa Citizen*, 19 March 1999, A5; Sean Gordon, "Quebec Insists on Its Own Voice in World Trade," *Ottawa Citizen*, 26 March 1999, A3; Christian Rioux, "La France ne regrette rien," *Le Devoir*, 19 March 1999, A10; Mario Cloutier, "Le Gouvernement Bouchard en fait un élement de sa politique officielle," *Le Devoir*, 25 March 1999, A5; Françoise Lepeltier, "Lucien Bouchard: «Le Canada et le Québec divergent de plus en plus»," *France-Amérique*, 27 March–2 April 1999, 4.

PART ONE

Gaullist Assaults on Canada

– 1 –

Introduction

All through the spring of 1997, the French government was intending to issue a postage stamp commemorating the fourth visit of General de Gaulle to Quebec thirty years earlier.[1] The government of Quebec was planning to celebrate the event by unveiling a statue of de Gaulle near the Plains of Abraham. It was during his visit, on 24 July 1967, that he caused a diplomatic row by shouting the slogan, "Vive le Québec libre!" from the balcony of the Montreal city hall. The whole affair – which more than any other event made public the connection between Quebec nationalism and Gaullist designs – still arouses emotions and brings up unexplained or debatable aspects and strange coincidences. One of the most immediate is that the person who was promoting and preparing the anniversary postage stamp, Pierre-Louis Mallen, spent six years in Quebec, at first preparing for General de Gaulle's impending visit of 1967 and then working to maximize its effects.[2] He arrived at Montreal on 21 June 1963, four years before the visit, having been sent to represent the *Office de la radio-diffusion télévision française* (ORTF), and he evidently functioned from the very first as an ardent "separatist" or "sovereigntist". Whether or not his stamp ever appears, he will be working for the separation and independence of Quebec until his dying day.

He told us nearly twenty years ago what he did and in what spirit, in his book, *Vivre [sic] le Québec libre* (Paris: Plon, 1978), and in a preface the premier of Quebec, René Lévesque, wrote, "When I first saw Pierre-Louis Mallen, in 1963, I sensed that this Frenchman arriving among us was going to understand this country. As he was to write later, he had 'his eyes open and his heart also.'" During the next four years, Mallen did his best to stimulate Quebec separatists with assurances of French interest in their cause and to promote that cause in France. These efforts were, indeed, what he had been sent to do. Later,

in 1979, he published a tract in Montreal full of arguments for a separate sovereign republic of Quebec.[3] In 1983 he joined a committee
formed at the Quai d'Orsay, with Philippe Rossillon's encouragement,
to support the Acadians "with vigilance."[4] Today, an aged Mallen is
still working for the separatist movement as a member of the prestigious Institut de France. He is only one of more than thirty French
politicians and officials of the middle and upper ranks who have been
likewise devoted to the cause of Quebec's independence from Canada.
They have also been making converts to that cause in France. In 1995,
just before the Quebec referendum, Mallen was one of the forty French
writers, journalists, and politicians who signed a letter of public
support for the Quebec separatist movement.[5]

One of the remarkable aspects of Mallen's sojourn in Quebec during
the 1960s is that he came just as the terrorists of the *Front de libération du Québec* (FLQ) were beginning their bombings and other activities. Whether or not this was coincidental, early in 1963 the FLQ had
just begun setting fires in rural stations of the Canadian National Railways Company and in March had destroyed the statue of General
James Wolfe standing on the Plains of Abraham in the provincial
capital.[6] In April and May it launched a series of bombings of federal
institutions such as the Royal Canadian Mounted Police, the provincial
headquarters of the federal revenue department, the Canadian army,
and radio and television stations. There was a lull in this first wave of
terrorist attacks at about the time Mallen arrived, broken only by the
explosion of a bomb on a monument to Queen Victoria in July; the
second wave did not begin until September, with a hold-up at a branch
of the Royal Bank of Canada in Montreal.

The FLQ terrorists kept up their campaign in a total of five series of
attacks that did not end until October 1970 with the dramatic events
of what has become known as the October Crisis. In the meantime, de
Gaulle had made his visit, and in 1969 Mallen had returned to France,
well satisfied with these events and the part he had played in them, as
he told us at length in his book, though exactly what he did, if anything, in relation to the terrorists' campaigns is not explained. It was a
series of coincidental political activities that he was eager to report. But
was it he who saw to it that there were two French civil liberties men
in Montreal in September 1968 arguing that the proceedings against
the terrorists Vallières and Gagnon were political trials?[7]

Mallen was one of the more outspoken Frenchmen in a movement
within the Fifth Republic that is half-hidden like a fifth column.
Careful investigation leads to the discovery of more and more French
diplomats, politicians, and state officials active in the cause of Quebec
separatism during the past thirty-five years. Considering only the

middle and higher ranks, I now have information about some three dozen, and many more can be discerned in the shadows behind them. For every enemy like Mallen, however, openly working for the success of the Quebec separatist movement, there is another French person ready to deny that France is hostile towards the Canadian confederation. Thus, two sets of attorneys, like the prosecution and the defence in a court of law, clamour for the historian's attention as he or she accumulates evidence of French interference and tries to assess it. The essential point is that Mallen has not been an eccentric, isolated crank but has had influential collaborators and supporters.

The thirty-five years of Mallen's hostile activity is more or less the span of the Gaullist cold war with Canada. The first assault began in 1963 and is described below in chapter 3. There is a prior question, however, about why General de Gaulle and his advisers thought it worthwhile to send Mallen to Quebec, and I attempt to answer it in chapter 2. It is a matter that concerns mainly the five years between the coup d'état of 13 May 1958 that brought de Gaulle to power, at the head of what became the Fifth Republic, and June 1963, when he dispatched Mallen to Montreal. During those five years, which followed the collapse of the Fourth Republic in the Algerian War of Independence, de Gaulle was preoccupied mainly with consolidating his régime. In July 1962 he brought the Algerian war to an end, and in October that year he established his presidential supremacy over the elected National Assembly. By 1963 he had control over French foreign policy. Ready then to give full attention to imposing himself on the rest of the world, he was particularly drawn towards the French-speaking population of Canada, the most numerous outside France.

By 1967, when de Gaulle made his notorious fourth visit to Canada on 23–6 July, he had already worked out a general plan of attack. That visit was controversial, and still has debatable aspects, and chapter 4 is an effort to establish and assess the facts about it. Having launched a cold war campaign in Quebec, de Gaulle then turned his attention to the smaller French-speaking community of Acadians in the Maritime provinces, and chapter 5 summarizes what he and his followers did there. There was no mistaking his hostility to the Canadian confederation, but as a master of ambiguity he refrained from making clear statements about his objectives. Confusion and uncertainty remained, too, on the question of who in his services – administrative, diplomatic, and political – shared his enthusiasm for interfering in Canada. That subject fills the concluding chapter of part I.

People in Canada responded to Gaullist intervention in various ways. Officials in the Department of External Affairs were aware of

French hostility from 1963 but disagreed about its significance and about how best to meet it. Marcel Cadieux, under-secretary of state from 1964 to 1970, was probably the most determined opponent of the Gaullists, and he kept a daily record of events and what he thought about them. His responses and his colleagues', as they appear in his diary, are the subject of chapter 7. Cadieux's views were important because political changes in 1967–8 brought a change of government: Pierre Trudeau replaced Lester Pearson as prime minister, and the new cabinet needed time to understand the issues. Chapter 8 reviews the diplomatic struggle between Trudeau and de Gaulle and his successors.

Diplomats' trails are easier to follow than policemen's. This was particularly true in the 1960s, 1970s, and 1980s, while the Soviet Union and the Communist bloc were behaving like enemies during the Cold War. Anxiety about Gaullist agents working secretly in Canada was therefore grafted onto the older concern about Communist agents. Unfortunately for Canada, the public debates and disagreements that are essential to liberal democracy happened to be especially lively concerning the Canadian intelligence services during those years. Should intelligence work continue to be left to the RCMP? Or should Canada have a civil intelligence service like those in England and France or like the Federal Bureau of Investigation and the Central Intelligence Agency in the United States? These issues filled the public discussions and confused the Canadian police response to the Gaullist threat, as I try to explain in chapter 9. Part II concludes with an account in chapter 10 of secret military preparations, devised by Pearson and implemented by Trudeau, to meet the threat of a war of liberation in Quebec, which seemed likely to involve French and other foreign forces.

Gaullist support for Quebec's independence can best be explained in a comparative and historical context as in part III, which tackles several themes. First, Chapters 11 and 12 broach the subject of what the international club of French-speaking countries (*la francophonie*) means to Canada, Quebec, and France. Second, though they may seem irrelevant at first sight, the aggressive adventures of Gaullist forces in New Zealand, the Pacific, the European Union, and Africa, as sketched in chapter 13, throw a useful, indirect light on the interference in Canada. An aggressor's victims can learn much by comparing notes. Finally, a historical perspective is essential if we are to probe the Gaullist motives. The general himself formed policies according to his own interpretation of modern history. He and his followers continually referred to past events. Without looking back two centuries or even farther, as in chapters 14 and 15, it is impossible to have more than a superficial idea of why de Gaulle and his followers have been so hostile. The two world wars of this century had the strongest influence on the Gaullist mind. But behind their impact lies the imperial tradition established by Napoleon and followed by his nephew, Napoleon III, who ruled the Second Empire (1851–70). Even farther back, but no less vital, is the imperial tradition of the Bourbons. Not for nothing did the satirical French weekly *Le Canard enchaîné* run a series of cartoons in the 1950s and 1960s representing de Gaulle with a crown on his head uttering grand imperial pronouncements, like Louis XIV, who had ruled France from 1661 to 1715.

– 2 –

Why Quebec Attracted de Gaulle

Even before he was firmly in command of the Fifth Republic, Charles de Gaulle arrived in Canada on 18 April 1960 for four days in Ottawa, Toronto, Quebec City, and Montreal, in that order. This was his third visit to Canada – he had come briefly in 1944 and again in 1945 – and his speeches this time expressed some of his wartime ideas about the fellowship of free peoples defending their liberty against tyrants. By 1960 the principal threat to liberty was the Soviet Union, which had seized Hungary in 1956, and de Gaulle was fully alive to the Soviet Communist danger. After all, the Communists remained strong and hopeful of political success in France. But for his own reasons, discussed below, de Gaulle saw another danger in the growing power of the English-speaking countries, particularly the United States, and the left-leaning part of the French public tended to be strongly anti-American.[1] He remarked in Canada how French the people of Quebec seemed and yet how threatened with assimilation by the United States and the English-speaking parts of Canada; and he told John Diefenbaker's government that the peoples of the earth ought "to dispose freely of themselves."[2] He was able to tap into several common interests examined in this chapter – anti-Americanism, rationalism, closer postwar relations, common social changes, and a shared bureaucratic instinct.

RESISTING ASSIMILATION TOGETHER

In the field of economic development, France and Quebec were drawn together in a common desire to modernize without falling prey to the cultural, social, and linguistic side-effects of Anglo – American leadership. This struggle had been going on in France ever since the eighteenth-century industrial revolution, which began in England and spread slowly to the European continent.[3] British industrial and commercial leadership had never been in doubt. "The most chauvinistic of Frenchmen must recognize," writes François Crouzet, "that, since the seventeenth century, France (all the while protesting) has received from Great Britain more than she has given back in technical matters, in political and economic ideas and examples."[4] The steam-driven, pumping, weaving and spinning machines that had revolutionized manufacturing had been built in France mainly by British technicians or in imitation of their inventions.[5] The first French railways were built in the nineteenth century either by British firms or under their direction.[6] Threatened by competition across the Channel, French businessmen had often followed British examples, too, in the development of banks, insurance firms, public finance and many of the paraphernalia that constitute modern life.[7]

The vocabulary of war had entered the English language from French – words such as "colonel," "lieutenant," "regiment," "bayonette," and "assault" – but the vocabulary of industry, business, and technology moved in the opposite direction. Long lists of English words have been drawn up by the official French commissions appointed in recent years to invent and enforce French substitutes.[8] But some have been used so long as to render the exercise a farce: for instance, the key term "budget" and the financial institution to which it referred were both imported from England in the eighteenth century.[9] The dimensions of the problem, as Pierre Chaunu remarks, appear in the fact that in 1790 four people on the globe spoke French for every one who spoke English, but in 1939 four people had English as their mother tongue (not to mention huge numbers learning it as a second language) for every one brought up to speak French.[10]

De Gaulle was acutely conscious of the twentieth-century phase of the French struggle against the effects of economic leadership by the English-speaking countries. After the two world wars had exhausted British investments abroad and conferred economic leadership on the United States, he was determined to carry on the same old struggle by fighting against American influence while at the same time transforming France into a modern industrial and military power. Under his leadership, the Fifth Republic made enormous and expensive efforts to build nuclear generators and weapons, electric railway and energy systems, television and other electronic technology, and fighter aircraft and naval craft, all the while opposing American leadership and cultural influences in the world whenever possible.[11]

Quebec fitted into de Gaulle's vision of the world as a place where a similar struggle was going on. During his visit at the end of April 1960 he could catch a stimulating view of future nationalist battles in the

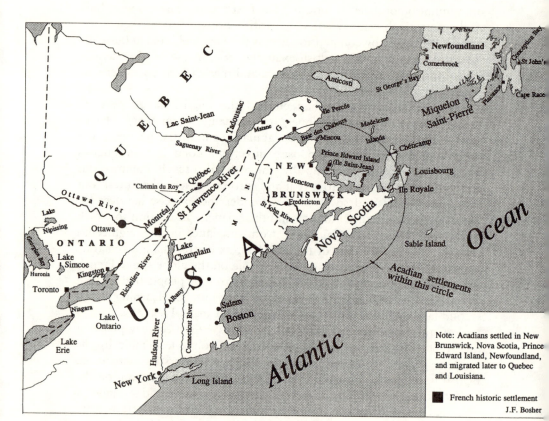

Map 1   Eastern Canada

electoral platform of Jean Lesage's Liberal party, which was being drawn up on the basis of Georges-Émile Lapalme's sweeping ideas. It was publicly endorsed by the party only a week after de Gaulle had returned to Paris and it took the party to power six weeks later on 22 June.[12] The Lesage government was "the most interventionist that the province had known since Confederation."[13] For de Gaulle, Quebec nationalists were allies of France, whether or not they saw their efforts in the same light. The Montreal papers during his visit were complaining about French Canadians controlling no more than 10 to 15 per cent of the Canadian economy; and *La Presse* ran a headline on 20 April: "L'AUTONOMIE: THEME NO 1 DE LA CAMPAGNE ELECTORALE."[14]

There were differences between France and Quebec of which de Gaulle was well aware. A fundamental one was the social struggle of the Québécois to win control of urban life, and all that went with it, from the English-speaking middle class that had brought the elements of modern development to Quebec and continued to direct and control them – railways and factories, banks and investment companies, retail chains and insurance firms and public services. The industrial revolution had come to Montreal with British immigrants either directly across the Atlantic or indirectly from the United States, where it had taken root in the last quarter of the nineteenth century. Quebec nationalists believed that winning control of modern life and all that went with it was essential, because merely to claim a share of it, merely to rise up to leading positions in it, would result in assimilation into English-speaking Canada.

Lesage's newly-elected Liberals proposed a set of reforms removing authority in many fields from the federal government in Ottawa and from the English-speaking minority in Quebec that had been in place since the Conquest of 1759–63. Pierre Arbour tells from first-hand experience how provincial officials and their nationalist friends used the *Caisse de dépôt* (deposit bank) to take control of big business.[15] Efforts to promote the French-speaking population went on for many years, and not only in government. The city of Montreal was slowly won back from the English-speaking minority that had dominated it for so long.[16]

NATIONALISM IN FRANCE AND QUEBEC

Already in 1960 de Gaulle could observe a reviving nationalist movement in Quebec. Political movements for the independence, or sovereignty, of Quebec can be traced back into the 1950s, but the first with any permanence and influence was the *Rassemblement pour l'Indépendance Nationale* (RIN), established in September 1960.[17] Its founders

founders were Raymond Barbeau, who in 1957 had launched a similar but short-lived movement called the *Alliance Laurentienne*; Raoul Roy, who earlier in 1960 had drawn some friends into what he named the *Action socialiste pour l'indépendance du Québec*; André d'Allemagne, who became the RIN's first president; Marcel Chaput, its first vice-president and future president; and a few others. After a preliminary round of consultations they arranged a founding meeting on 10 September at an inn (*auberge*) at Morin Heights in the Laurentians. About thirty people were there, most of them from Hull, Ottawa, or Montreal. For the next two and a half years, until March 1963, they worked to spread the idea that Quebec ought to become an independent republic, "free, French and democratic."[18] They proceeded openly by the democratic methods of public meetings, demonstrations, pamphlets, and subscriptions differing in this and other respects from the traditional or conservative nationalists.

The latter had not been committed to the separation of Quebec and had not organized in an open and forthright manner. A good example of their attitudes and methods was the secret *Ordre de Jacques Cartier*, popularly known as "*la Patente*," formed in Ottawa in 1926. Its main purpose was to advance French Canadians in the dominion and provincial civil services and in the professions and to promote the use of French as far as it could. Gaston Cholette, an ardent nationalist and separatist, acknowledges the influence of this order in the circles of his youth.[19] Deeply Roman Catholic in its membership, *la Patente* saw its enemies as, first, the Protestant movements of Orange Lodges and Freemasons and, second, the English-speaking Catholic Irish in Quebec and Ontario. Beginning in a parish in Vanier (then called Eastview) on the outskirts of Ottawa, it had spread rapidly throughout Quebec and the French parts of Ontario. During the 1930s branches had emerged in New Brunswick at Campbellton, Edmunston, Moncton and Shippegan, and these threw their weight, with discretion, into advancing French-speaking candidates in elections.

Until it dissolved itself on 27 February 1965, *la Patente* coordinated the efforts of various groups and institutions to promote their cause in Quebec, New Brunswick, and other parts of Canada, especially Ottawa.[20] Its membership reached several thousand by 1964: some 3,741 in Quebec, 905 in Ontario, 377 in the Maritime provinces, and 54 in western Canada.[21] These people, all men, were organized in secret cells and undertook, among other things, not to tell their wives and families what they were doing. With a characteristic paranoia or xenophobia, they were hostile to English-speaking people, Jews, and Protestants.[22] The *Ordre de Jacques Cartier* was naturally sympathetic to the semi-fascist Vichy régime in wartime France, shared the views of two nationalist Quebec historians, abbé Lionel Groulx and Robert

Rumilly, on many subjects, and had no use for de Gaulle's Free French. They played a leading part in opposing national conscription during the Second World War and influenced public opinion in French Canada on many issues. The list of members included a number of political leaders later active in the Parti Québécois.[23]

By 1960, when de Gaulle made his visit to Canada, the Lesage Liberals, the RIN, and other nationalists were forming a neo-nationalist movement that was quite different. They were distancing themselves from the *Ordre de Jacques Cartier*, the old *Société Saint-Jean-Baptiste*, and other such strongly Catholic organizations. An outstanding example of a neo-nationalist group consisted of the staff and supporters of the Montreal daily *Le Devoir*, directed from the late 1940s by a committed neo-nationalist, Gérard Filion; edited by another, André Laurendeau; and financed through the 1950s by a like-minded group calling themselves *Les Amis du Devoir*.[24] Observers in France, including de Gaulle, kept abreast of developments in Quebec by reading *Le Devoir*, which was stocked by certain news stands in central Paris from early in the 1950s. The fervently Gaullist reports and columns by Jean-Marc Léger made good reading at the Élysée Palace.

Léger was only one of *Le Devoir*'s editorial team of conscientious and competent nationalists, which also included Pierre Laporte, Paul Sauriol, and Pierre Vigeant, some of whom were also contributors to the nationalist monthly, *L'Action nationale*. Their editorial chief, Laurendeau, had been much influenced as a student in Paris during the 1930s by progressive Catholic thinkers such as Jacques Maritain, Etienne Gilson, Emmanuel Mounier, and Daniel Rops, and some of the others had likewise been educated in France. During the 1950s *Le Devoir* became an organ of Catholic neo-nationalists, independent of political parties but with a strong belief in political action and constitutional reform. This was abundantly clear in their support for the recommendations of the Thomas Tremblay Commission when they appeared, after a three-year inquiry, in 1956.[25]

Arthur Tremblay, consulted by that commission, was one of the leaders in reforming education in Quebec and removing it gradually from the hands of the clergy. He had studied education at Harvard University and in Paris. The Tremblay Commission spent much time on higher education in the province, on which subject it was very influential, notably in opposing the effects of the federal Massey Commission, which pressed for federal funding and interference in education. It was partly as a result of the Tremblay Commission that Quebec fought for the constitutional right of the provincial government, under section 92 of the British North America Act, to control education.[26] Defended in this way as strictly a provincial concern, education was to be one of the

channels by which French influence poured into Quebec from the
1960s, as explained below in chapters 8 and 11. In 1960 Tremblay
became executive assistant to Paul Gérin-Lajoie, the minister of youth
and education in the new Liberal government, and in May 1964 he
rose to the post of deputy minister in the newly created Ministry of
Education.[27]

The neo-nationalists were typical of what has become known as the
Quiet Revolution, an omnibus term for the many changes that began
to transform Quebec during the 1960s.[28] In its narrowest meaning, the
term applies to a series of reforms carried out by the Lesage government, but these were, in a broader sense, manifestations of the troubled
1960s which shook most Western countries in one way or another.
Quebec was feeling the spirit of the 1960s when de Gaulle visited
Canada a few months after the death, on 6 September 1959, of the
powerful, somewhat oppressive premier, Maurice Duplessis, who had
governed the province 1936–39 and 1944–59. Duplessis had presided
over an informal but old and powerful coalition of politicians, business
leaders, and Roman Catholic clergymen which had ruled the province
for more than a century.

When Duplessis died, Quebec was seized with an outburst of liberal
and national sentiments that led to changes so profound that they may
justly be described as revolutionary.[29] Educated Frenchmen, such as
Charles de Gaulle and his staff, were immediately at home amid the
liberal and national aspirations of the Quiet Revolution in Quebec.
Every French republic, even the Fifth, is founded on liberal and nationalist ideas that are an ideological legacy of the French Revolution. The
transfer of education from the hands of the clergy to a new ministry of
public education, accomplished in Quebec during the 1960s, had been
carried out in France during the 1790s and again in the first decade of
the twentieth century. French republics had likewise established min-
istries to take hospitals, charities, and old-age homes from the church,
just as Quebec was doing in the 1960s.

As for the strong national sentiments in the province, they found an
echo in any French heart that was imbued with the legacies of the
French Revolution and Napoleon. De Gaulle never missed an opportunity to embroider on the history of the approximately six million
Québécois who, except for a small minority, descend from about sixty-
five thousand French people remaining in the St Lawrence valley after
the British conquest of 1759–60. In his mind Quebec families who
trace their ancestry back to their French seventeenth-century origins –
Lucien Bouchard, for instance, to a stone mason who reached Quebec
in 1650 – were wonderfully and miraculously French. He could see no
sense in describing them as Canadian if that meant belonging to a con-

federation of English-speaking people. The Canadian multicultural idea, though not yet publicly adopted in 1960, was utterly alien to him.

OLD TIES RENEWED

De Gaulle's visit in April 1960 was one of a series of transatlantic exchanges that were part of a mutual curiosity rekindled after the Second World War. French emigration to Quebec, never very sizeable, slowly increased, and from 1953 the *Union française de Montréal* published a journal, *Le Courrier français*, devoted to keeping French immigrants in touch with France. De Gaulle spoke to "la colonie française de Montréal," as *La Presse* called it, during his brief visit on 21 April.[30] During Maurice Duplessis's long régime, contacts with France had grown stronger and more frequent. Duplessis had no love for the French, but more and more leading Québécois were spending time in France and making friends there. Two who influenced Duplessis were Roger Maillet, one of his political supporters, and Jean Désy, a friend who served for a time as Canadian ambassador in Paris, where he wasted no opportunity for advancing the interests of Quebec. A French cabinet minister, Jules Moch, visited Quebec in 1950, and in April the next year President Vincent Auriol came over.[31] In March 1957 it was the turn of Prime Minister Guy Mollet and his foreign minister, Christian Pineau. In March 1958 Gérald Martineau, treasurer of Duplessis's party, the Union Nationale, went to France with a message for Désy that he might perhaps represent Quebec there when he retired as Canadian ambassador later that year.

The idea for representation in Paris by a *Délégation générale* interested Duplessis and delighted his francophile friends, especially Désy, Maillet, and Pierre Dupuy, who was to succeed Désy as ambassador.[32] Duplessis regretfully shelved the idea in March 1959 as being too expensive, but Jean Lesage revived it soon after he was elected on 22 June 1960. That fall, Georges-Émile Lapalme, the deputy premier and attorney-general of Quebec, travelled to France and managed to obtain an audience with André Malraux – his idea of an outstanding minister of culture. When he explained that he hoped to establish closer links with France, the minister revealed that de Gaulle had recently expressed an interest in Quebec and that the French government was disposed to respond to initiatives from that quarter. He suggested that a good beginning might be the founding of a *Maison du Québec* – a sort of cultural office – in Paris.[33]

This being exactly what the Lesage government had in mind, Lapalme engaged Charles Lussier, director of the *Maison canadienne* at Paris's *Cité universitaire*, as first director of what was soon to be

named the *Délégation générale du Québec à Paris*. Lussier had the task
of finding a suitable building and setting up this agency.[34] He accomplished this by March the following year, installing the *Délégation* at
66 rue Pergolèse, opposite the palace of the archbishop of Paris, and
on 4 October 1961 Lesage flew to Paris for its formal inauguration the
next day. In his speech on that occasion he summed up Quebec –
France relations in ambiguous terms worthy of de Gaulle but added,
"We are offering to collaborate with you French people, you first, in
the exploitation of all the wealth which, as we are pleased to observe,
our province is so abundantly provided."[35] He was received with
honours normally reserved for heads of state and enjoyed the enthusiastic attention of the French government.

In a speech of welcome at the Élysée, de Gaulle embroidered elo-
quently on the links that were thenceforth to bind the French of France
and the French of North America. "'I remember!' is the motto of the
province of Quebec. On seeing her in your person, France says the
same to you. ... The general equilibrium of the world can only gain by
the presence and expansion, on the soil of the New Continent, of an
entity that is French by its roots, its culture and its activity."[36] He con-
gratulated the Quebec government on the *Association des universités
de langue française* (Association of French-Speaking Universities)
which it had just established at a meeting in the Université de Montréal. Hundreds of articles in French journals remarked on the warmth
of the occasion, on the strengthening of French ties with Quebec, and
on how the province was growing and modernizing.[37] The entire affair
was deemed a great success.

When the municipal government of Montreal decided in 1960 to
build some kind of modern urban transport system, it turned to France
for advice and then for the construction itself. The mayor, Jean
Drapeau, and his executive committee chairman, Lucien Saulnier, went
to Paris late in the year to see an experimental monorail as well as the
Paris subway – *le métro* – which in the end they both preferred. It was
the model for the twenty-one miles of new underground railway with
twenty-two stations that opened in 1966.[38] When Drapeau's government decided to reform the Montreal police force it hired an adviser
from Paris's *Préfecture de Police*, André Gaubiac, who, with Andrew
Way, an officer from London's Scotland Yard, drew up plans for the
reforms that were put into effect.[39]

Drapeau hired a well-connected Paris wine-dealer, Georges Marchais, to be his agent – his "eyes and ears" – in Europe and with his
help managed to win the designation for the World's Fair that became
Expo 67. The theme for Expo 67, *Terres des Hommes*, came from a
novel by a French writer, Antoine de Saint-Éxupéry. Drapeau then

induced Prime Minister Lester Pearson to appoint Pierre Dupuy, Mme Drapeau's francophile cousin who had long represented Canada in France, as the commissioner-general of Expo 67.[40] Drapeau even thought of renting and bringing over the Eiffel Tower which had been built for the Paris Exhibition of 1889, but had to give up that idea. Opposition and spiralling costs also forced him to abandon a project for a special Montreal tower for which he had hired a French architect, J. Robert Dalb, on Marchais's advice. Whether his projects failed or succeeded, however, Drapeau turned to France for examples, inspiration, and occasional assistance.

PARALLEL SOCIAL CHANGES

The French pavilion at Expo 67 was intended to convey the image of a progressive France, alive with industrial, technological, and scientific progress, no longer moved by an economy of wines, perfumes, and *haute couture*. Such had been the message, too, of the technological exhibition opened in Montreal by de Gaulle's minister of culture, André Malraux, on 12 October 1963. Both of these exhibitions, and others like them, expressed de Gaulle's enthusiastic endorsement of postwar efforts to modernize, industrialize, and urbanize his country. In this too he found himself at home in Quebec.

France and Quebec had postwar experiences in common that seemed vital to observers such as de Gaulle who were prepared to understand them. Long obsessed with demographic trends because of a relatively falling population, in 1946 the French government established an *Institut d'études démographiques* under the distinguished direction of Alfred Sauvy, who published data on population trends at home and abroad. He kept the government and reading public aware that until the war France had had a remarkably large peasant population engaged in subsistence agriculture, in spite of earlier industrialization, and had been economically less developed than Great Britain, Germany, and the United States. But in the twenty-five years since the war, enormous numbers of French peasants had been leaving their villages and their age-old occupations and moving into cities. During the 1950s and 1960s, peasants fell from 46 per cent of the population to 34 per cent.[41] This trend has continued. But these changes in France resembled exactly the postwar prelude to the Quiet Revolution in Quebec. In the fifteen years 1945–60 towns in the province grew by about 15 per cent and the rural population fell proportionately to less than 30 per cent of the total. "By the mid-1950s, whole families were abandoning farming in pursuit of occupations that would ensure them a higher standard of living."[42] French-speaking observers on both sides

of the Atlantic agreed that "urbanization ... is one of the characteristics of our time."[43] An unprecedented social revolution was occurring
in both of these French-speaking societies.

As people moved into the cities, they tended to turn away from the
Roman Catholic church and to come under the influence of the government. De Gaulle's régime in France and Jean Lesage's neo-nationalist government in Quebec had a common desire to use the social revolution of their time to transform their societies into progressive modern
communities, with all that that implied in the 1960s. Both were invest-
ing or planning – or hoping – to invest in regional development, new
factories, electrical and nuclear power plants, airports and seaports,
aircraft industries, railway and telephone systems, highways, mass
housing projects, and the other accoutrements of modern life. In the
circumstances of the time it was natural for them to collaborate, on the
basis of their common language and culture. Already, Quebec neo-
nationalists saw in their joint efforts a way to achieve independence.

De Gaulle for his part saw collaboration as a means for promoting
the power and influence of his country and expanding French civilization in the world. From its very beginning, the Gaullist Fifth Republic
built on the Fourth Republic's efforts to change the official program of
world-wide cultural indoctrination that had long been conveyed by the
Alliance Française in terms of language, literature, and history. The
new stress was on technological, industrial, and scientific development.
Accordingly, the Gaullist régime made serious efforts to promote
French industry, technology, and science abroad. Its own modern
progress became a permanent theme of the Fifth Republic. "French
Canadiens, together we shall make Atlantic civilization," said André
Malraux at the inauguration of the enormous French technological
exhibition in Montreal on 12 October 1963.[44]

A COMMON BUREAUCRATIC INSTINCT

The ruling élites in France and Quebec found it easy to collaborate in
economic development and social reform because they were both prepared to act via powerful government leadership. And in these fields
Quebec adopted French models already widely known and admired.
Masterplans had been launched with great fanfare by the French government immediately after the Second World War. In particular, four-
year economic plans had been guiding the development of France by a
system of collaboration between public and private organizations. The
public sector of the French economy being very large by Western standards, the government had the means to impose its policies more forcefully than most, and the French public accepted the situation all the

more readily because it had been the case almost throughout French history. The French economy has always had a huge public sector and a state that leads, controls, and intervenes more than the governments of Canada, Great Britain, or the United States.

The first two plans, for 1947–50 (extended to 1952) and for 1954–57, were largely the work of Jean Monnet, and he saw them as a way of using Marshall Aid from the United States. Under the general guidance of Pierre Massé's official planning commission, mixed committees of civil servants and corporate managers worked at removing obstacles to growth and set goals for such things as the production of cement, steel, and electrical power. The third plan, for 1958–61, concentrated on promoting foreign trade, encouraging investment, and developing backward regions of the country. De Gaulle spoke of it more than once during his visit to Canada in April 1960.

As the guiding hand in the Fifth Republic from May 1958, and its president from 9 January 1959, de Gaulle took up the official planning process with a will, and so the fourth plan, for 1962–65, was more ambitious. It aimed to maintain an annual increase of 5 per cent in gross national product (GNP), along with full employment, a rising standard of living, and increasing investment, all this in conjunction with economic stability. The fifth and sixth plans were even more ambitious. Although this is hard to explain in our own age of frenetic privatizing, the early French plans seemed immensely successful and were widely admired abroad. Leaders in Quebec were sufficiently impressed to imitate the Gaullist example in many respects, as Pierre Arbour shows in detail. Looking back a generation later on the efforts of the Quebec government, he concludes that its following the French example was an expensive mistake: "This economic intervention (*dirigisme*) was influenced by French experience that has been even more unfortunate than our own."[45] But if such it was, its faults were not yet visible in the early 1960s.

Quebec soon had some of the powerful bureaucratic institutions familiar to French statesmen accustomed to the French bureaucratic tradition. They grew partly from Duplessis's stubborn resistance to the postwar federal government, with its centralizing instincts expressed in social welfare programs and the taxing arrangements needed to pay for them. They developed even more, after Duplessis's death, from neo-nationalist pressure for control over provincial resources. Intellectuals, such as the group at *Le Devoir*, tended to be strongly in favour of government leadership and intervention, all the more after Pope John XXIII recommended state intervention in his encyclical *Mater et magistra* (1961). Lesage set up a *Conseil d'orientation économique du Québec* (COEQ), which put forward a set of typically French ideas for major economic projects to be managed by mixed public and private agencies just like the postwar French plans. The COEQ rapidly became the spearhead of the province's state-run economic enterprises.[46]

Several more state-controlled agencies were soon created, and two of the most influential attracted interest at home and abroad in 1962. The *Société générale de financement* was founded in that year to encourage and finance business ventures. With a more-or-less-secret mandate to buy firms that seemed likely to be taken over by foreign or English-language interests, it eventually took control of Marine Industries and Domtar and invested heavily in the aluminum and petro-chemical industries.[47] By 1964 it had begun to draw up economic plans for the province following the French example.[48] It was also in 1962 that *Hydro-Québec*, a public corporation created in 1944, took charge of all electrical power, which Lesage's minister of natural resources, René Lévesque, was keen to nationalize.[49] There was a good deal of noisy resistance to this authoritarian step, but it gave substance to the phrase *"Maîtres chez nous,"* which Lévesque and his supporters invented during the struggle. One of these supporters active in building up *Hydro-Québec* in 1962 was Jacques Parizeau, employed as a special adviser to the government.[50] *Hydro-Québec* became a symbol as well as a force for government initiative in controlling the destiny of the province. Once launched with the government's blessing, it grew to become what many think of as the flagship of Quebec's state economic enterprise.

More such government corporations emerged within the next few years – notably the *Sidérurgie du Québec* (1964–69) set up to found a steel industry, the *Société québécoise d'exploration minière* (1965), and the *Caisse de dépôt* (1965) founded so that financial capital in the province would be directed into economic uses. Naturally all these ambitious projects were followed with interest by the planning authorities in France and the government that patronized them. More important, officials in Quebec were often anxious to consult French authorities or to follow their example.[51] Thus in 1962 the French *Institut de recherche de la sidérurgie* was brought in to recommend ways and means for creating a provincial steel industry, and the *Sidérurgie du Québec* was a result of French advice.[52]

If, in the last thirty-five years, French influence in the development of Quebec has not grown as de Gaulle might have hoped in the early 1960s, this may be the result of the rigid bureaucratic agencies that dominate both economies. These agencies were created to achieve political objectives; their economic activities were only instrumental. The twenty-seven public organizations listed by Pierre Arbour – *Société de développement de la Baie-James, Société nationale de l'amiante,*

Société des industries culturelles, and others such as the *Société de développement des périodiques culturels québécois* (SODEP), are political engines dressed up as economic, cultural or social services.[53] If this were not the case, most of them would have disappeared long ago, for they have seldom been profitable. But then, the *Parti québécois*, like Charles de Gaulle, has had political purposes destined to be pursued at any cost. Arbour has lost faith in state-directed enterprise; so has Jean-Luc Miqué, professor of economics at Quebec's *École nationale d'administration publique*, but the *Parti québécois* still continues to believe in it.[54]

Gaullist Aggression before 1967

During the early 1960s the Royal Canadian Mounted Police (RCMP) learned from the U.S. Central Intelligence Agency (CIA) that French secret services had been infiltrated by Soviet spies. Since then, fresh revelations have been proving that this was indeed the case. Georges Pâques, for example, spied for Moscow for nineteen years beginning in 1943. He and other high officials supplied the Soviet Union with a flow of documents and information about NATO and French defences, particularly after Charles de Gaulle took power in 1958.[1] Charles Hernu, French minister of defence from 1981 to 1985 and a close friend of President François Mitterrand, spied for the Bulgarian, Romanian, and then the Soviet secret services for at least ten years beginning in 1954.[2] When Anatoli Golitsyn defected in 1961, he revealed Soviet penetration of the *Service de documentation extérieure et de contre-espionnage* (SDECE) achieved via a network code-named "the Sapphire Ring," and this revelation made Western governments suspicious of French intelligence.

Watched at first by the intelligence services of the English-speaking countries for its vulnerability to Soviet penetration, France soon became doubly suspect because of Gaullist support for Quebec nationalist movements. The first part of this chapter deals with clandestine assistance, and the second with official, formal activities.

UNDER-COVER ACTIVITIES

There were signs of French hostility to Canada soon after the founding of the Gaullist Fifth Republic in 1958. Attentive observers might have seen black clouds on the horizon when André Malraux and Pierre-Louis Mallen arrived in Quebec in 1963, particularly as the terrorist activities of the FLQ were increasing. In short, well before de Gaulle's visit in July 1967 observers in the Security Intelligence Branch (SIB) of the RCMP had begun to regard France as a target for surveillance.[3] Monitoring the activities of the separatists and their French friends was thus grafted at first onto the established surveillance of international communism.

What Canadian authorities found out about French under-cover activities in Quebec and elsewhere during the first ten years of the Fifth Republic remains unclear. Security service files, whether compiled by the RCMP or, since 1984, by the Canadian Security Intelligence Service (CSIS), are still secret, not yet accessible even under the Access to Information Act of 1989. Most of those that have been released and deposited in the National Archives of Canada are so heavily censored as to be almost useless, hardly worth the trouble of being gone through. Employees of those two organizations, whether still active or retired, are sworn to secrecy, trained to resist every inquiry and to suspect every researcher. The few who are willing to share their memories cannot, in all fairness, be named. But what they say leaves an impression of serious French penetration when it is considered together with the published remarks of others active at the time.

Mention "les coopérants" to a retired SIB officer: he may recall something about these young Frenchmen sent to Quebec and New Brunswick in one of the alternative government services open to men called up for the obligatory military service. The purpose in sending them was to promote national interests abroad. "There were two of them working with Évangéline [an Acadian newspaper sponsored from 1967 by the French government], and a bunch placed in various business firms," one officer recalled, but he would then say no more.[4] However, the French government spent some $300,000 on the coopérants sent to help L'Evangéline, one of whom, Alain Gheerbrant, did his best from his arrival in 1967 to stimulate a radical student revolt in and near Moncton.[5] Some observers, such as Max Yalden, believe that they were harmless and without political significance, but there are ex-RCMP officers who do not share that belief.[6] Avoiding military service as the coopérants did, many of them were no doubt hostile to their government's policies; but others were sympathetic with the liberation movements of the time. There may have been no paid French secret-service agents in Quebec, but there were certainly enthusiastic French and Canadian informers who were royally entertained in France and offered the best of hotels, restaurants, and holidays on the Côte d'Azur.

In Quebec during much the same years, another Frenchman, Pierre-Louis Mallen, offered vigorous support for separatist movements. For six years beginning in June 1963 he worked there as an agent of the

Office de la radio et télévision française (ORTF), and he later published a long, somewhat pugnacious description of his activities at Quebec.[7] But he was by no means a pioneer in the field. In October 1963, a French agent of the SDECE, Philippe Thyraud de Vosjoli, decided to flee abroad from his posting in Washington, DC, because of a disagreement with his superiors in the French government. At first, he thought of taking refuge in Canada, "but I rejected the idea of going to that country by reason of the presence of numerous Gaullist agents charged with organizing subversive activities in the French-speaking provinces."[8] He was well placed to know what he was talking about.

Before publishing his own account of events, Thyraud de Vosjoli told others about Soviet penetration of French intelligence services, and the novelist Leon Uris published the story in fictional form. This was the novel *Topaz*, which appeared in English in 1967, and in French in 1968 and was ultimately made into a film. As an officer of the French SDECE based in Washington, DC, and in touch with the CIA, the U.S. Federal Bureau of Investigation (FBI), and possibly also the RCMP, Thyraud seemed well informed. After *Life* magazine had made a story of his allegations about the Soviet side of his story, he was interviewed for the Toronto *Telegram* by Peter Worthington, who stressed Gaullist activities in Quebec.[9] Some members of the RCMP's SIB took all this seriously: Raymond Parent showed Uris's novel to Claude Morin in 1969 as though it were a revelation and asked him to read it.[10] Suspicions thus aroused were reinforced in 1970 by Thyraud's own book, *Lamia* – also his official code name – which he himself published to explain why he had quit the French service in October 1963.[11]

One of the French secret services was active in Canada in these years, in the opinion of two Canadian historians – the SDECE, which was attached directly to the office of the French president and directed by a Gaullist of long standing, Jacques Foccart, who was particularly busy with French intelligence-gathering in Africa.[12] Being elusive by their very nature, secret services can rarely be traced in their activities, but it appears that French intelligence forces working in Quebec were directed from the late 1950s by the consul general in New York City, Jacques Hervé, who had been a French military attaché in Ottawa in 1948. There is a suspicion that these forces were somehow in touch with the terrorists of the FLQ. A former French secret agent, Patrice Chairoff, alleges that "Philippe Rossillon, former student at the École nationale d'administration, leader of the group of 'planners' of 'Patrie et Progrès' had been charged by the [secret] services of Jacques Foccart to maintain tension in Canada by using the separatist movements in Quebec. Rossillon went through the various Canadian provinces with other Foccart agents, like Edgar Chaumette, Jean-Luc Gaillardère and

Tom Bailby. He established very close contacts with the Front de Libération du Québec, and with other movements such as that of Adrien Arcand. In 1968, Philippe Rossillon was arrested by the Canadian police services and immediately disavowed by his employers."[13]

Louis Fournier believes that "[Philippe] Rossillon was put in contact with a militant member of the FLQ named Gilles Pruneau, whom he seems to have assisted to take refuge in Algeria."[14] Certainly in September 1968 Gaullist enthusiasts, particularly Rossillon, were found wandering about making contact with Quebec nationalists and gathering information in Canada on such a scale that Prime Minister Trudeau was alerted by the RCMP and made at least one international incident in protest.[15]

It may be suspected that such French prying or spying began earlier. Two Quebec nationalists, Gilles Grégoire and Pierre Bourgault, were reported to have been directed to contact Rossillon when in France.[16] Information was certainly being gathered in Ottawa and Quebec City through French diplomatic channels. Hand-picked for their pro-Quebec, anti-Canadian views, some of the diplomatic and consular personnel sent to represent France seem to have behaved like enemy agents. The RCMP thought so, as it shadowed them carefully for long periods.[17] Until de Gaulle's visit in July 1967, the RCMP was interested in French spying mainly because Soviet agents had notoriously penetrated French intelligence networks and the Soviet Union was the principal danger to Canada.[18] However, after de Gaulle's hostile speech on 24 July 1967 and his unrepentant comments next 27 November, the Gaullist French also came to seem like enemies, as indeed they proved to be.[19] De Gaulle and certain high officials were openly hostile to the Canadian federal government.[20]

Opinions of officers in what was then called the Department of External Affairs are contradictory. Eldon Black and Max Yalden both assured me that tales about French secret agents in Canada have been invented, and then exaggerated, on the basis of nothing more than rumours – people are too ready to listen to "spooks." This view seems consistent with the reticence of two French students of French espionage on the subject.[21] Sources in France, Quebec, and Belgium, however, convinced Marcel Cadieux in the late 1960s that Jacques Foccart's agents were active in Quebec. Indeed, the Paris weekly *Le Canard Enchaîné*, known for its journalistic sleuthing as well as its satirical humour, was certain of it. Cadieux as under-secretary of state at External Affairs passed on to the RCMP the information "that I found in *Le Canard Enchaîné* about the intrigues in Canada of barbouzes sent in by the French government, their pockets filled with money for purposes that certainly had nothing to do with the interests of our country."[22] A few years later, when Cadieux was posted as Canadian ambassador to Washington, he telephoned the director of the RCMP intelligence service, General Michael Dare, to ask him whether "he had observed a reduction in the activities of French agents in Quebec. He tells me," Cadieux recorded the next day, 10 September 1974, "that up to the present there is no sign that French activities have eased. In his opinion, however, it is possible that a change has occurred, but the orders [for it] would not take effect for awhile. In the case of Quebec agents in French pay, their turn of mind and natural enthusiasm might incite them to continue along the lines of the former policy rather than change their approach and follow a different path."[23]

Among the foreign trouble-makers active in Quebec before 1967 were various guests of the French network of the CBC. Known to be riddled with Quebec nationalists, as John Matheson recalls, the francophone network invited socialist and separatist sympathizers from France, Belgium, Cuba, and the Soviet Union to speak in support of the separatist movement.[24] A prominent example is a French writer, Jacques Berque, a professor at the prestigious Collège de France, whom the CBC asked over in 1964. He was a specialist in Arab, Muslim, and North African affairs who was promoting the Quebec separatist cause in a well-known French left-wing weekly, *France Observateur*. These CBC invitations were denounced in the House of Commons, by Réal Caouette in particular.

It is all very well to cite official French inquiries that found no underhand French activity in Canada. Official denial is standard Gaullist procedure. After the French government in summer 1985 had denied all knowledge of the *Rainbow Warrior* affair in New Zealand, the local police proved French guilt beyond a doubt.[25] Official denials that France was developing methods of chemical warfare have likewise been proven false.[26] It is proved beyond a doubt that Philippe Rossillon was busy in French-speaking communities in Canada from time to time in the 1950s and 1960s.

But other, less well-known French people were similarly engaged. There have been too many leaks from too many sources to be mopped up by the denials that come naturally to those fair-minded Canadians who are temperamentally inclined to reject all clues and evidence short of ironclad proof.[27] Jean-François Lisée reports his own extensive findings that suggest French interference.[28] And after all, the Department of External Affairs received a report from the RCMP early in December 1966 that gave cause for alarm: "We received a most worrying report from the RCMP yesterday (the Under-Secretary of State wrote in his personal journal on 8 December 1966) about the sepa-

ratist movement in Quebec. It appears that the Office of the Prime
Minister of France includes a section charged with stimulating agitation in the French-speaking countries outside France. One of the chiefs
of that section is proposing to recruit and train some fifteen French-
Canadians in the handling of explosives and sabotage procedures in
general. The report also provides us with information no less alarming about the activities of the deputy [of the French National Assem-
bly] Xavier Deniau."[29]

Investigations in France showed that a handful of FLQ members had
been trained in guerrilla warfare by the *cadre* of the Palestine Liberation Organization in Algeria and Lebanon and that the FLQ had some
support in Paris. There a group called the *Comité international pour
l'indépendance du Québec* was giving encouragement and collecting
funds for a Quebec body calling itself the *Délégation extérieure du
front de libération du Québec.*[30] More than one investigator has suspected that the mysterious Henri Curiel (1914–1978), an Egyptian in
Paris who provided services for terrorist groups, was helping the FLQ,
certainly by sheltering some of those who had kidnapped James Cross
in 1970, and perhaps in other ways, too.[31] It is easier now to view the
Gaullist aggression of the past thirty-five years, even through the haze
of clues that can be gathered, than it was to anticipate it at the beginning of the period.

The *Comité international pour l'indépendance du Québec* was
founded on 10 February 1963 under its first name, *Comité français
pour l'indépendance du Québec,* in an apartment building in the
Pigalle district of Paris. Begun with the equivalent of a mere $5,000, it
rapidly gained a membership of four hundred, mostly French citizens.
They had elaborate plans to solicit diplomatic and public support,
especially in French-speaking parts of Africa, for an independent
republic of Quebec. Algeria and Sénégal were said already to have
promised such assistance. By the end of 1963 the directors of this
Comité claimed to be in touch with sympathizers in forty-four countries, including Belgium and the Switzerland. A magazine, *Québec
libre,* was being published to assist in the cause. A clear, factual
account of this group, evidently written by someone who had direct
knowledge of it, appeared as an anonymous editorial on the first page
of *Maclean's* magazine on 14 December 1963.[32]

The *Comité* had two founding directors, Bernard Cloutier and Pierre
Gravel, both Canadian. Cloutier, a petroleum engineer from Ottawa,
was the thirty-year-old son of a former Queen's Printer in Ottawa, and
his sister was married to the actor Peter Ustinov. Gravel, aged twenty-
eight, was described as "an intense, dapper journalist" originally from
Trois-Rivières and a member of the *Parti républicain de Québec.* Six

months later he was cited in an incendiary underground monthly of Montreal as "our permanent delegate in Europe."[33] He is now a middle-aged and balding editor with the Montreal daily *La Presse*. Around these founders were gathered an organizing committee of twenty French and French-Canadian enthusiasts who had set up three "study groups," evidently for the indoctrination of French politicians, businessmen, and academics.

The first of these study groups consisted of eighteen Gaullist deputies in the National Assembly, including Martial de la Fournière, a diplomat and former colonial administrator then employed in the ministry of defence who had been to Canada in the 1930s with Philippe Rossillon as a delegate to student conferences; and Xavier Deniau, a member of the Conseil d'État who had recently spent three weeks in Quebec, had married a Canadian, and was planning to visit Quebec again the following spring (1964) as a member of a committee of the National Assembly.[34] Later, on the weekend of 3–4 October 1964, Deniau was honorary chairman (*président d'honneur*) of a Quebec nationalist gathering held at Trois-Rivières by the *Société de Saint-Jean Baptiste*, where he spoke in favour of independence. This provoked a question in the House of Commons, which is not surprising as he was reported to be deputy for Loiret in the French National Assembly, *rapporteur* for that assembly's foreign affairs commission and president of the board (*Comité*) of France-Québec.[35] Martial de la Fournière and Deniau, and some of the other politicians in their study group, have remained lifelong supporters of Quebec separation. They thought their leader, President Charles de Gaulle, shared their views, and, as things turned out, there seems to have been some evidence for their belief.

The second study group, for businessmen, was under the chairmanship of Alain le Bobinec, a director of the *Banque de Paris et des Pays-bas*. His particular interest was in planning to replace American and British capital in Quebec by investments from France and other countries of the European Economic Community (EEC). Britain was not a member of the EEC at that time, and de Gaulle had just vetoed the first British bid to join it. In respect of French investments, the businessmen's study group was involved in French protests over the reluctance of Trans-Canada Airlines (TCA) to buy French Caravelle jet aircraft – a subject that it was preparing to discuss in a forthcoming number of *Québec libre*. In September that year the French ambassador, Raymond Bousquet, had already threatened to cancel the planned Peugeot car-assembly plant in Montreal unless the Canadian government persuaded TCA to buy Caravelles instead of the American DC-9s it preferred. This "naked blackmail" was widely supported in Quebec, and already External Affairs Minister Paul Martin was finding that "coping with the Gaullists was almost a full-time job."[36]

The study group for academics and intellectuals was the most outspoken, as might be expected. Prominent among its members were a writer, Jean Cathelin, and his wife, Gabrielle Gray, who had visited Canada twice and had published a book the previous September entitled *Révolution au Canada*, which touches on Quebec's independence.[37] It is mainly an account of their journey across the country, but in chapter 5, on Quebec province, they professed to see a new vigour likely to lead to the emergence of a sovereign republic. The Cathelins laid out all the now-familiar reasons for favouring independence and discussed French support for it. Perhaps the book's title invites unwarranted conclusions about its nature, for it is in fact more moderate, careful, and intelligent than the editorial staff at *Maclean's* suggested. One wonders whether they bothered to read it.

This book sold no fewer than four thousand copies in France during its first three weeks, and the authors claimed that General de Gaulle had written to congratulate them on it.[38] Indeed, he said that he had personally profited by reading it. What it had taught him was that Canada was ripe for Gaullist intervention, the movements for Quebec's independence having obtained an encouraging measure of vigorous support. *Révolution au Canada* even quoted "young Anglo-Canadian intellectuals resident in Montreal" as supporters of the movement: "We are in the same situation as the French North Africans [pieds-noirs]; but as good realistic Anglo-Saxons we reckon that, just as the French North Africans have chosen Ben Bella's Algeria rather than de Gaulle's France, we shall choose Quebec citizenship rather than go to live in English Canada which, once Quebec has been liberated, will be rapidly absorbed into the United States."[39] As a member of the *Comité international pour l'indépendance du Québec*, Cathelin himself was evidently becoming more militant than his book revealed. According to *Maclean's*, he believed that part of de Gaulle's foreign policy was to promote an independent French-speaking republic in North America.

The cause of Quebec's independence aroused much interest in France from the early 1960s on, if articles in the press are any guide. This was due not only to the efforts of the *Comité* and to reports of FLQ terrorism, but also to other transatlantic contacts. In Montreal the socialist *Parti pris* movement was more and more active, and some of its members, such as Pierre Maheu, were strongly influenced from France.[40] The nationalist RIN announced its founding in 1960 by demonstrations before the French consulates in Montreal and Quebec and at the new *Maison du Québec* in Paris, and it made itself known by the activities of its Paris branch, founded in 1962, and by the visits to France of one of its founders, André D'Allemagne.[41]

As Jean Cathelin observed in mid-1963, "Already *Le Monde* and *Combat* devote articles each week approving of the Quebec nationalists: this can only encourage the terrorists who have chosen to risk losing the comfort of refrigerators in order to succeed where those who revolted in 1837 had failed. ... On the left as on the right, in *France-Observateur* as in *Patrie et Progrès*, there is support for the [Quebec revolutionary] movement, as is proven by a recent conference [colloque] held in the centre of Paris at the Chambre de Commerce France-Canada (9–10 May 1963) between French and Canadians of every political stripe."[42] There cannot be much doubt that Gaullists were the leaders in this French campaign to support Quebec, in their own journal, *La Nation*, as well as in many others, but sympathetic accounts of Quebec's national aspirations appeared in journals of every political persuasion.

This was, of course, only one of the causes championed by the international brotherhood of writers caught up in the euphoria aroused by the idea of world-wide liberation that was to reach its climax in the French "student" uprisings of May 1968. They and the Quebec "liberation" movement were encouraged by the success of the French African colonies in winning their independence in the early 1960s, particularly Algeria, at last in June 1962, after a bitter war that racked France for years. French-speaking parts of the world, educated in traditions of the French Revolution, were particularly moved. In summer 1964 Gravel attended a demonstration of Walloons in Brussels that "brought tears to his eyes" by chanting "Vive le Québec libre!" as was enthusiastically reported in Montreal.[43] In 1965 the cause of Quebec's independence was still being discussed in journals throughout France, and here and there throughout Europe. Among the French proponents was another member of the *Comité international pour l'indépendance du Québec*, Jacques Berque, introduced above, an expert on Arab, Muslim and North African affairs, whose reasoning was that the Canadian federal government practised an insidious form of imperialism by putting economic pressure on Quebec and exploiting it financially, all the while making much of a false or fake bilingualism. He thought that Canadian immigration policy was intended to submerge the Latin element in Canada as quickly as possible.

The transatlantic network of radical journalists and "intellectuals" inevitably brought French people to Canada in addition to the above-mentioned Deniau and Rossillon. Many incendiary articles in the Montreal radical journal *Québec libre* were written by one Jacques S. Lucques, who had been born in France in 1930 and was fond of comparing Canadian police with the wartime *gestapo* that he claimed to have seen during his childhood under the German occupation of France.[44] Lucques gave occasional lectures, in English as well as in French, and wrote on many subjects, all apparently intended to further the cause of world-wide liberation of peoples from "capitalists," "fascists," "imperialists," and so on.

A younger French immigrant who joined the incendiary movements in Quebec was François Dorlot, a naturalized Canadian, aged twenty-six in 1968 at about the time he was discovered to be one of Philippe Rossillon's contacts in Canada.[45] Dorlot was employed then by the Canada Council and had obtained one of its grants, which he planned to use in France in autumn 1968, for a study of shipping from French ports on the English Channel to the St Lawrence in the seventeenth and eighteenth centuries. He soon became part of the international liberation movement and was one of those who took charge of René Lévesque's program during an official visit to France in 1972. His ability to assist in the cause was much increased when he married Louise Beaudoin, the present Quebec minister of culture, on 11 August 1973.[46]

OFFICIAL TRANSATLANTIC RELATIONS

General de Gaulle began to take an interest in Quebec soon after he took office as president of the new Fifth Republic in January 1959. He received Premier Jean Lesage enthusiastically during his visit in autumn 1961. Reflecting on that encounter, de Gaulle observed: "[Lesage's] government and the one in Paris are settling between them, and without any intermediary, the beginning of the assistance that France is henceforth to devote to the French of Canada."[47] The news of de Gaulle's intention to negotiate with Quebec "without any intermediary" does not seem to have reached Ottawa immediately, and in the early 1960s Franco-Canadian relations remained as amicable as they had been ever since Canada had played its generous part in the liberation of France from the Nazi German occupation. In July 1962 the French government settled some of the debts it had contracted with Canada in 1946 under the terms of the Marshall Plan. At the end of 1962 a French economic mission under Wilfrid Baumgartner, a former governor of the Bank of France, visited Canada, and a commission of the French National Assembly arrived the following February. The year 1962 was a troubled one, with the crisis of the Algerian war and all of its incidental conflicts in France, but these began to die down after Algerian independence was negotiated in June.

It was in 1963 that the first rumblings of aggression to come could be heard, and students of French history might have anticipated trouble. This is because 1963 was the two-hundredth anniversary of the Treaty of Paris, by which France had ceded Canada to Great Britain, and therefore a key date that was not to be missed by Charles de Gaulle. History and symbolism play important parts in French political thinking. Most Canadians tend to suppress the patriotic emotions of their British past, even when they happen to have a British past, which fewer and fewer do. But in Quebec and Acadia, many people tend to respond with strong feelings to evocations of their French past. De Gaulle's speeches in Canada or to Canadians in France played rhetorically on Quebec nostalgia for New France and its French roots; that is how he aroused such emotional responses during his visits. The remembrance of 1763 in 1963 was certain to touch a chord in the feelings of a people who live with the motto "Je me souviens." As a symbol, this anniversary had value in the Gaullist campaign, and two principal agents were sent to Quebec with it in mind. The first of them, Pierre-Louis Mallen, was aware of it when he received the instructions that sent him to Quebec in June as a permanent representative of the ORTF.[48]

Mallen's task was to prepare French and Canadian opinion for the Gaullist message and political initiative – a task that can be appreciated only in terms of the total monopoly that the ORTF had exercised in France since the Second World War. There were no private stations in France, either for radio or for television. Of course, most French people could listen to broadcasts in French from Andorra, Belgium, Luxemburg, Monaco, or Switzerland, but the only domestic broadcasts came from three AM radio networks and one FM network, all maintained by the ORTF, a state monopoly, from its gigantic round building on the Seine at the western end of the Quai de Passy. There was only one television channel, and a second was to be added in 1964, but both were also controlled by the ORTF. Nominally an independent state agency, the ORTF was in fact an instrument of the cabinet, directed at that time by Robert Bordaz or his deputy, Jacques-Bernard Dupont, according to policies set by de Gaulle or his minister of information, Alain Peyrefitte – and the French public knew this.[49] Soon after Mallen arrived in Quebec in June 1963, the Gaullist version of Quebec's plight began to be broadcast more and more loudly in France. I lived in Paris for about nine months in 1964–65 and recall with horror, even now, the twisted message, frequently repeated in the news media, sometimes mildly, sometimes bluntly, about the oppression of the brave, patient French people in Quebec, victims of "les Anglo-Saxons" who had conquered them two centuries earlier.

About four months after Mallen's arrival in Montreal, there came a much more distinguished French visitor, the writer André Malraux, a communist whom de Gaulle had managed to recruit by playing on his patriotism. The visit to Canada in October 1963 was not his first; indeed, he came once before the Second World War to promote the republican cause in the Spanish Civil War. In the week of 7–15 October 1963, however, he arrived to open a French technological exhibition in Montreal and to make speeches in those high-pitched, rhetorical tones that in some ways resembled the keening at a Gaelic funeral. De Gaulle called on Malraux whenever he felt the need to generate maximum emotional effect. For instance, when on 19 December 1964 the remains of a famous hero of the wartime *résistance*, Jean Moulin, were ceremonially taken to the Panthéon in Paris, the tomb for all the great in the French past, I witnessed waves of public emotion, hundreds of people all weeping in the blvd Saint-Michel, in response to a speech delivered outdoors by André Malraux after General de Gaulle had come striding up the avenue in the winter sunshine with his wartime companions in battle-dress.

The purpose was different in Quebec City and Montreal in October 1963, but Malraux's speeches were similarly effective, in some quarters at least. Jean-Marc Léger responded with francophile editorials in *Le Devoir* that must have warmed Gaullist hearts. In Léger's mind, the occasion was evidently full of promise for an independent future for Quebec; he seemed to be giving a political interpretation to what was supposed to be a purely cultural and technical occasion. It has been usual among English-speaking Canadians to minimize the political effects of occasions such as Malraux's visit. Dale Thomson, a specialist in the subject, thought in November 1986 that Malraux had "systematically avoided being drawn onto political ground" during his visit in 1963.[50] Shortly after this visit, on 25 March 1964, I drew a similar conclusion in a program for the Canadian Broadcasting Corporation (CBC) from Vancouver, arguing that such emotional Franco – Quebec gatherings would have no political effect; but now, more than thirty years later, I believe that I was mistaken. There were political effects, there have been since, and worse ones seem likely to follow.

The problem for all observers was that the political developments were neither clear nor explicit. They were easily confused, as they still are in part, with a policy of cultural exchanges and cultural events. What was the purpose, for example, of sending a party of no less than 140 French senators, bankers, industrial leaders, and politicians to Montreal to coincide with Malraux's visit?[51] Their presence seemed natural enough in conjunction with the French technological exhibition that opened on 11 October 1963, but a French Caravelle aircraft arrived at the same time and René Lévesque announced that Quebec would be pressing the federal government to buy Caravelles for Air Canada.[52] In speech after speech Malraux hammered home the same themes about France and Quebec as leaders of civilization and Jean-Marc Léger kept harping on the political implications of these speeches, announcing "a new era in France – Canada relations and France – Quebec relations".[53]

Meanwhile, the *Société Saint-Jean Baptiste of Quebec* – some 65,000 strong – was urging at its twenty-seventh annual congress that French should be the only official language in the province; Bona Arsenault was telling a conference in Ottawa that Quebec should have a special constitutional status; and Marcel Chaput assured students at the University of Sherbrooke on 9 October that "the present generation will see the independence of Quebec."[54] Chaput and two cameramen from the British Broadcasting Corporation (BBC) were arrested in Montreal on 9 October 1963 and fined fifty dollars each for crossing a police barrier around striking dockworkers; Chaput had been trying to help his two guests to make a documentary film about Quebec separatism.[55]

By that time, the federal government was beginning to assert its constitutional right to the management of foreign relations, and Jules Léger made this clear when he presented his credentials as Canadian ambassador to the French government on 1 June 1964. On that occasion de Gaulle replied in one of his condescending speeches that ended as follows: "France is present in Canada not only through its representatives, but also because many Canadians are of French blood, French language, French culture and French mind. In short, they are French except in matters concerning the realm of sovereignty."[56] How insulting this must have been to a cultivated French Canadian such as M. Léger!

But there was more in de Gaulle's speech than merely personal insult to a Canadian ambassador representing the federal government. Whither de Gaulle's thoughts were tending may be seen from a note that he made between the time of this incident and his own visit to Quebec three years later: "There can be no question of my sending a message to Canada to celebrate its 'centenary'. ... We do not have to congratulate the creation of a 'State' founded upon our former defeat and on the integration of a part of the French people in a British *ensemble*. For that matter, this *ensemble* has become most precarious ... C. de Gaulle."[57]

It must be clear, even to the most cautious and sceptical observer, that de Gaulle and his staff had political purposes in their dealings with Quebec, purposes that were firm, though not perhaps precisely formulated, long before he shouted "Vive le Québec libre!" in Montreal. Jean Chapdelaine, at least, seems to have realized as much when he was invited to a reception at the Élysée Palace even before 30 December 1965, when the Canadian embassy notified de Gaulle of his appointment to the post of *Délégué général* in Paris. Chapdelaine certainly saw the political implications of France's treating the *Délégation général du Québec* as if it were the embassy of an independent, sovereign country and signing with it (on 27 February 1966) an entente for the promotion and expansion of French in the world.[58]

That the arrivals of Mallen and Malraux were not fortuitous events may be surmised from a note that de Gaulle wrote to the secretary general of the Élysée on 4 September concerning Prime Minister Pearson's impending visit to France. It concluded with the ominous line, "Besides, French Canada will inevitably become a State and it is in that perspective that we must act."[59] This was followed on 7 November with a friendly, indeed eager, reply to a letter from Premier Jean Lesage. "You know well enough the interest that I bear myself in the development of French Canada, linked with France," he wrote, but he couched his intentions and hopes in his usual ambiguous but ominous phrases.[60]

Thanks to Paul Martin's determination to carry on as usual, there was as yet little strain in diplomatic relations, but de Gaulle, who directed foreign policy entirely himself and from the Élysée, seemed bent on creating trouble. From mid-1964 he systematically snubbed the new Canadian ambassador, Jules Léger, as Eldon Black relates in detail. By October the story had reached the pages of *Québec libre*, published monthly by a group of young separatist radicals in Montreal, who told it in a sneering article entitled, "Les frasques d'un fédéraste [!!] à Paris: la vieille Conf[édération] a des difficultés avec son Jules."[61] The French foreign minister, Couve de Murville, insulted Paul Martin himself on 6 May 1965 by sending a junior official to meet him at Orly airport and making careless arrangements for his arrival. His RCAF Yukon waved away to a distant parking bay, Martin had to take the airport bus along with his staff and their luggage.[62] Again, when in 1965–66 the Canadian government proposed that Governor General Georges Vanier, as Canada's de facto head of state, make an official visit to Paris, de Gaulle refused on the grounds that the governor general was not a head of state but only the Queen's representative. Interpreting our constitution in this way was an insulting and outrageous interference in our affairs.[63] The mayor of Montreal and his travelling companions, however, were honoured in 1966 at a special private dinner at the Élysée. Meanwhile, the Canadian government managed to draw de Gaulle into a cultural treaty – *un accord-*

cadre – that Martin signed with the French ambassador at Ottawa on 17 November 1965. On this occasion, the Canadian government was trying to make direct arrangements with France before the Franco – Quebec cultural entente could be fixed independently. The French government allowed this to happen but ominously refused to bind itself to respect Ottawa's interpretation of the Canadian constitution.[64]

The government of the Fifth Republic was also gathering information in the course of increasing transatlantic exchanges, which took place as a series of events with a different significance. More and stronger links were being forged between Quebec and the old mother country. They seemed to be purely cultural, but an attentive observer with a knowledge of Gaullism and French history might have seen their political undercurrent. In 1963 a mission of the Organization for Economic Co-operation and Development (OECD) was instructed in Paris by Roger Grégoire, a French *secrétaire d'État* advising the secretary-general of the OECD, to visit Quebec in spite of formal objections by the Canadian government. Gaston Cholette, who met the members of this mission, tells as a joke how they spent an evening with Paul-Gérin Lajoie, Arthur Tremblay, and other Quebec officials at a dinner in Quebec City, at which the federal government's representative could not speak French and understood only what the British representative on the mission translated for him.[65] The point of this story was that Quebec was already going its own way with French encouragement and thumbing its nose at the government of Canada. A different example: in May 1964, Georges-Émile Lapalme was again in Paris discussing with André Malraux how the Quebec *Délégation générale* might be given increased diplomatic powers, or even the status of an embassy, as if it were representing an independent state.[66] Already, four months earlier, the French Ministry of Youth had set up an External Cooperation Service to administer a system of short-term training programs in France for Quebec officials and others.

In June 1964, Xavier Deniau, an active member of what is often termed the "Quebec mafia" in France, made one of his many trips to Canada, this time as president of the National Assembly's study group on Quebec; he was followed a few weeks later, on 13 July, by that assembly's *Commission des affaires culturelles, familiales et sociales*, intent on arranging a program of exchange and cooperation with Paul Gérin-Lajoie in education. In November, Jean Basdevant, *Directeur général des Affaires culturelles et techniques* at the Quai d'Orsay, arrived for a visit, and Jean Lesage then went over to Paris to discuss these matters with General de Gaulle and his government. A formal agreement on educational cooperation was signed in Paris a few months later, on 27 February 1965; and on the following 24 November a broader Franco – Quebec cultural agreement was signed.[67] Already the new *Commission permanente de coopération franco–québecoise* had had the first of its biannual meetings, to be held alternately in Paris and Quebec City, and it gathered for the second time on 1 December 1965 in Paris.

"Vive le Québec libre!"

Before 1967, Charles de Gaulle and his government were gathering information and strengthening ties with Quebec.[1] Early in September 1966 the French minister of education, Christian Fouchet, a Gaullist of long standing, visited Ottawa and Quebec City, and Maurice Couve de Murville, the minister of foreign affairs, was there at the end of that month. In October Louis Joxe, one of the Gaullist "barons," visited Quebec on the occasion of the opening of the partly-French metro (subway) in Montreal. Already, on 13 September, Premier Daniel Johnson had written to de Gaulle proposing that they visit one other. He invited the French president in particular to attend the opening of Expo 67, the World's Fair at Montreal. When de Gaulle finally agreed, it was Johnson's invitation rather than Prime Minister Lester Pearson's that he had in mind. He saw the journey as an opportunity to assist the nationalist movements of Quebec. In this chapter I look first at de Gaulle's trip to Canada, then at responses in France and in Quebec to the events of that fateful expedition, and finally, at its long-term effects.

THE JOURNEY

As usual, de Gaulle let a cloud of ambiguity grow up about his intentions on his impending trip, but any detailed study of the man and of this period will show that he travelled with mischief in his mind. There can be no doubt that sending Mallen and Malraux to Quebec in 1963, the bicentennial of the Treaty of Paris, was an early step in the preparation of a Gaullist imperial campaign. Reflecting on his next step, and on Pearson's forthcoming visit to Paris in January 1964, de Gaulle had made a note to the effect that "French Canada will necessarily become a State, and it is in that perspective that we must act."[2] The next move was naturally to be made in 1967, the centenary year of the Canadian confederation, a symbol that might be used in another way.

De Gaulle's journey to Quebec in July 1967 was carefully planned. He appreciated the year's symbolic value, when insults to Canada would have all the greater effect. Another symbolic part of his plan was to make a voyage across the Atlantic in a warship named *Le Colbert*, after the minister of Louis XIV who had presided over the first great French migration to Canada. For one thing, approaching Canada by sea allowed de Gaulle to visit the old French colony of Saint-Pierre and Miquelon, which his Free French forces had seized from the Vichy French on 24 December 1941.[3] By air, the only convenient way of reaching these islands was through Newfoundland, because the airfield at Saint-Pierre was too small (it has been enlarged since), and he was determined not to do this. True, he had landed at Gander on 20 August 1945 – one of those occasions when he pretended to have been greeted by French-speaking admirers[4] – but since then Newfoundland had become a province of Canada.

This brings up a second matter: he wanted to avoid all the English-speaking parts of Canada, such as Newfoundland. The approach by sea allowed him to make an impressive, traditional landing at Quebec City without any possibility of going first to Ottawa. Stubbornly insisting that French-speaking Canadians were part of the French nation – "les Français du Canada" – de Gaulle wanted to be able to encourage and patronize them without deferring in any way to the Canadian government. The result of his careful planning was a kind of historic, almost imperial voyage to places that de Gaulle thought of as French. It has been said that the *Colbert* arrogantly refused to return the customary salute by a small flotilla of the Canadian navy that met it inside territorial waters, but Captain Hugh Plant, a naval officer assigned to meet de Gaulle at sea, assures me that this was not so. "The French cruiser *Colbert* did reply, returning a National salute of the HMCS *Terra Nova*. I was aboard the latter and transferred to the former shortly after the acknowledgment.[5]

The Gaullist charade continued, however, with an imperial progress from de Gaulle's landing at the Anse-au-Foulon, where General Wolfe's conquering army had scaled the cliffs of Quebec City in 1759, to the Citadel, and eventually to Montreal along the so-called *Chemin du Roy* on the north shore of the river, allowing for addresses in towns along the way. In one much-quoted speech, de Gaulle said that the journey had reminded him of his trip to liberate Paris in 1944.[6] No one there missed the implication that Quebec ought somehow to be freed from the conquering English. The French-language press in Montreal made the most of this idea.[7] Wolfe's statue on the Plains of Abraham had conveniently been destroyed by FLQ terrorists in 1963 and was to be replaced in due time by statues of Montcalm and, as we see below, de Gaulle.[8]

There are still people who object that de Gaulle was also planning to visit Ottawa; after all, he and others said so before he sailed. However, given his policies, beliefs, character, and usual behaviour, it is reasonable to conclude that he had no intention of visiting the capital of Canada. First, the sixteen speeches that he made during his visit were full of allusions to the essential Frenchness of each occasion and of Quebec itself.[9] All of them were tinctured with hostility to Confederation and fully in tune with a rebuff to the federal government. The infamous speech from the balcony of Montreal's city hall was only the most blatant, not really out of character with the rest. To have gone on to visit the Canadian capital and exchange cordial remarks with representatives of the federal government would have weakened, or even undermined, the political effect of those sixteen speeches and the policy they expressed. More than one of the guests at the dinner for de Gaulle following the balcony speech came away convinced that he would not visit Ottawa.[10]

Second, the discourtesy of not visiting the national capital was entirely consistent with the ensuing hostilities between Ottawa and Paris. These were largely results of French policy, made brutally clear in the cabinet statement that followed de Gaulle's return home, in the letter he wrote to Premier Johnson on 8 September 1967, and in de Gaulle's press conference of 27 November 1967.[11] The Canadian government did its best to smooth things over, to avoid "over-reacting," to patch up a quarrel that was kept alive by a series of French provocations that alternated with the bland denials of Maurice Couve de Murville and other French officials.

Third, it was de Gaulle, not the Canadian government, who made the decision to cut short his visit and return to France on 26 July. True, Prime Minister Pearson had commented sharply on his "Vive le Québec libre" speech, but that was all. The federal government did not, in any other way, cancel or discourage the official visit that had been arranged. Fourth and finally, although it fitted de Gaulle's purposes in Quebec to appear to have deliberately snubbed Ottawa, it also suited his government to pretend that he returned directly to France because of Ottawa's "brutal reaction" to his speech.[12] The chilly diplomatic atmosphere that ensued could thereby be blamed on Canada. An attitude of injured innocence became, indeed, a standard response to the affair among separatists and members of the French Quebec mafia.[13]

This was an example of the denial that has always been part of Gaullist aggression. It is consistent with the instructions to the French ambassador in Brussels, Francis Lacoste, to give his word in the early 1960s that no aggression was intended, when he knew that indignant Belgian accusations of French political interference at Liège were justified.[14] Yet another example occurred in the *Rainbow Warrior* affair in 1985, when the French government at all levels loudly denied all knowledge of the bombing until New Zealand had produced incontrovertible proof of French guilt.

At the same time, students of Gaullist diplomacy will recognize in de Gaulle's intentions in July 1967 a certain ambiguity that was typical of his methods.[15] Bruce Hutchison stressed it in his report on the affair in the *Christian Science Monitor*.[16] There is no proof that de Gaulle did or did not intend to visit Ottawa, but anyone who believes that he did is being, in my opinion, so fair as to be gullible. Some Canadian observers thought so at the time: on 27 July 1967 Peter C. Newman wrote, "Supporting the theory that the stormy course of the de Gaulle tour was premeditated is the fact that canny external affairs officials were insisting as long as three months ago that de Gaulle would never get as far as Ottawa."[17] One of those officials was Marcel Cadieux, whose early grasp of Gaullist hostility is discussed below in chapter 7.

Ambiguity also pervades the matter of whether General de Gaulle's "Vive le Québec libre!" speech was deliberate or a blunder. Ordinary English-speaking Canadians in large numbers are still persuaded that it was not premeditated at all. Even Paul Martin, the minister for external affairs, who ought to have known better, expresses puzzlement and doubt in his memoirs.[18] In Paris, the Gaullist journal, *L'Espoir*, still finds reason to hold debates on whether it was "une intuition ou une politique?"; Gaullists and Quebec separatists love to relive and savour the events of 24 July 1967.[19] In one such debate, Gilbert Pérol, press secretary at the Élysée, recalled that "Vive le Québec libre!" was not in any of the speeches that de Gaulle had drafted in advance. "It would naturally have drawn my attention," Pérol added, to the merriment of his audience of Gaullist enthusiasts.[20] As he sketches the thoughts and habits of de Gaulle at that time, however, he makes clear that the offending phrase was hardly a bolt out of the blue. Pérol and others closest to de Gaulle, including members of the Quebec mafia, had no doubt that the development of Franco-Quebec relations in the years 1960 to 1967 were leading up to a political initiative such as that speech.[21] Only three months earlier, de Gaulle had offered a gratuitous insult to Canada by refusing to attend the fiftieth anniversary of the battle of Vimy Ridge on 9 April 1967 and refusing even to send a guard of honour.[22]

"Far from being improvised," says Xavier Deniau, who accompanied de Gaulle, "his declaration in Montreal had been prepared as a result of the warmth of the Québécois."[23] Edgar Faure, Georges Gorse, Olivier Guichard, Pierre Messmer, and others who knew de Gaulle believed that it would have been quite out of character for him to make the speech he made as a blunder in the excitement of the moment, though not all of his entourage shared that opinion.[24] Jean Touchard concludes that the offending address was deliberate.[25] Stories have gradually emerged, too, showing that men in de Gaulle's circles, whatever they might say in public, believed he set out to do what he did. Roger Vaurs, who had been in the presidential party at the time, had no doubt about it.[26] Nor did Pierre de Menthon, whom de Gaulle sent out to Quebec as consul general with instructions to aid the separatist cause given in a personal audience on 6 January 1968.[27]

Bernard Dorin, who had accompanied de Gaulle to Quebec, declares categorically that the speech was intentional and part of a carefully planned campaign of provocation.

Some have pretended that this voyage, and especially the speech from the balcony at Montréal, had been largely improvised and that de Gaulle had in some sense been surprised and excited by the exceptional welcome accorded him by the people of Quebec. Nothing could be more false! I am well placed to bear witness that this was not true at all and that, on the contrary, the visit, with an analysis of all possible consequences, had been prepared in minute detail. Indeed, from the first fortnight of January 1967, René de Saint-Légier, with whom I had relations of great confidence and friendship, had asked me to send him confidential weekly reports of everything I had been able to gather concerning the situation in Canada and in Quebec, this in view of the voyage in July. ... Of course, no one had foreseen the thunder clap of 24 July but we were convinced that this voyage would be memorable and that it would powerfully advance the national cause whose first movements I had felt in Quebec between 1957 and 1960.[28]

De Gaulle is said to have remarked to one of his followers as he boarded *Le Colbert* at Brest, "They are going to hear me over there; I'm going to make some waves."[29] According to another account, he had a conversation at sea on board *Le Colbert* with Admiral Philippon, in the course of which he proposed to say, "Vive le Québec libre."[30]

Opinion on this side of the Atlantic is divided, but Paul Gérin-Lajoie was convinced that de Gaulle's action was entirely premeditated.[31] This was the assessment of many other attentive observers even at the time. "Words are being chosen carefully," the *Globe and Mail* commented, along with offering a translation of the French cabinet's statement. "They leave little doubt that General de Gaulle, with the support of his Cabinet, intends to continue to interfere in the affairs of Canada."[32] In the same paper, George Bain wrote cool, detailed, anxious reviews of the visit, which stand up well in retrospect.[33] "We must assume," the

Ottawa Journal concluded, "that the French government is bent on gravely dangerous policies towards Canada."[34] By 1 August a few, such as the editor of the *Albertan*, were stressing that Pearson's gentle rebuke was not enough: "A considered but firm reponse is required."[35] The government meekly submitted to another French insult when, early in October, de Gaulle went on to instruct his ministers to avoid Ottawa during visits to Quebec: Peyrefitte and Misoffe had already done so with impunity in September 1967.

RESPONSES

France

Following de Gaulle's speech on 24 July 1967, the response of press and public in France was reported as favourable or critical, according to taste and inclination. Few disinterested, thorough estimates were ever made. The editor of de Gaulle's *Discours et messages*, for example, wrote, "Comments in the French press on General de Gaulle's voyage to Quebec have been almost unanimously in a tone systematically unfavourable."[36] In contrast, a paperback published anonymously in Montreal on 28 August 1967 by *Les Éditions Actualité* declared: "The French government unanimously approved of de Gaulle and announced the total support of France for the emancipation of Quebec."[37] It went on to imply that public opinion in France was similarly disposed. Many such contradictory examples may be found.

The speech brought various responses in Europe. "Everything confirms that Gen. de Gaulle said what he intended to say, and that he was perfectly aware of possible repercussions," Charles Hargrove wrote in the *Times*.[38] The offending phrases were widely denounced at first, even in France. Donald Baker, in France during that summer, observed that "most Frenchmen with whom I had any contact – chiefly professors, students and retired politicians ... – expressed shock and bewilderment at de Gaulle's spectacular endorsement of the separatist cause in Quebec and at the resulting diplomatic flap."[39] *Le Monde* ran an acerbic editorial under the heading "L'excès en tout ...," with lines such as "[de Gaulle's] denunciation extended practically to the entire English-speaking world," and "He passed thus, in twenty-four hours and three hundred kilometres, from patriotism to nationalism, thence to separatism."[40] The writer went on to ask sarcastically what had become of the much-vaunted Gaullist policy of non-interference. The following week, however, French-speaking opinion, even in *Le Monde*, began to come around to the Gaullist view in response to reports of official approval in Paris and general enthusiasm in Quebec. It did not take long to smother and bury the results of a survey by the *Institut Français de l'Opinion publique* showing that only 18 per cent of the French public approved of de Gaulle's speeches at Quebec, while 45 per cent disapproved.[41]

A few days after de Gaulle's return to Paris, the French Council of Ministers issued a communiqué telling people what to think: "France intends to help the French Canadians to reach the goals of liberation they have set up for themselves."[42] They are French people whom France ruled for two and a half centuries [!!]; they were oppressed for a century after the British Conquest; and the Canadian confederation has not assured them, even in their own country, of liberty, equality, and fraternity. Loyal Gaullists soon rallied round: an article by one of them, Michel Habib-Deloncle, under the heading "I was at Montréal ....," described the warm approval that he saw everywhere among Québécois for de Gaulle's "proclamation of their liberty." He went on to develop a range of those superficial conclusions that an outsider, totally unfamiliar with Quebec, might draw: that the English west end of Montreal was prosperous and the French east end poor because of English oppression; that the poor folk were filled with resentment, and that de Gaulle's words on 24 July 1967 had "lanced an abcess" (crevé un abcès).[43] *Le Monde*'s special correspondents began to adopt a similar tone.[44] The most vocal criticism in the French-speaking world was expressed by writers in left-wing journals, such as Hector de Galard, who was scathing about "sa mégalomènie galopante," and by political opponents of the government, such as Gaston Deferre, a socialist leader in the National Assembly, writing in his own newspaper, *Le Provençal*.[45] The usual response in France to those who criticized de Gaulle was, "Well, but they would, wouldn't they."

De Gaulle's views and journalists' reports from Quebec and Montreal, adopted, expanded, and annotated by members of the French Quebec mafia, soon cast the entire visit and its consequences in the heroic light that has been carefully tended ever since. Many books and more articles have been written telling the story of "la journée du 24 juillet 1967," "the General's July days," "origins and preparation of the voyage," or "Quebec a quarter-century after ...." Leading members of the mafia repeat the story over and over, adding details and explanations, like disciples telling the story of His wondrous deeds. A new gospel is being spread far and wide, and defended by the disciples. A fresh version, by Xavier Deniau, who travelled to Quebec with de Gaulle, appeared as recently as summer 1996.[46] Pierre de Menthon, whom de Gaulle named consul general at Quebec City in 1967, says of the infamous speech: "The moment, was it not unique, when he the old man, supremely powerful by the Word [souverainement puissant par le Verbe] was still able to respond to an appeal and to restore to these people the self-confidence they needed."[47] The events of 1967 have been reviewed again and again in books and in journals devoted to glorifying de Gaulle, such as *L'Espoir, revue de l'Institut Charles-de-Gaulle* (Paris), *Études gaulliennes* (Paris, 1973–88), and *Les Amitiés Acadiennes* (Paris). The Gaullist–separatist view, with its cynical attitude to the Canadian government's anxiety, may be read in accounts such as Pierre Godin, *La difficile recherche de l'égalité, la révolution tranquille*, vol. II (Montreal: Boréal, 1991).

Ten years after those events, the Quebec *Délégué général* in Paris, Jean Chapdelaine, poured scorn on hostile interpretations of de Gaulle's voyage: "From [news of his speeches in July 1967] there was only a short step to construct the theory of a Gaullist conspiracy, with the collaboration of Quebec, against the Anglo-Saxon world, United States, England and Canada (ABC: America, Britain, Canada), to have researched a destabilizing of the Canadian state, vengeance for humiliations suffered at the hands of Churchill and Roosevelt during the war."[48]

Yet it turns out, as close observers already knew, that there was indeed a conspiracy, and its motivation was, in part, much as Chapdelaine sketched it in his caricature. As Charles Halary concludes, "For de Gaulle, the historical perspective was clear: the sovereignty of French civilization in North America was to permit the creation [réalisation] of an independent State."[49] By November 1976, when the Parti Québécois won its first provincial election, French newspapers, television, and politicians had somehow become strong supporters of the "emancipation" and "liberation" of Quebec from what a middle-aged lady in a railway carriage between Bordeaux and La Rochelle described to me as "the English occupation."[50]

Now, thirty years later, de Gaulle's visit is being celebrated in Paris and throughout Quebec as a fundamental step forward in the cause of Quebec's independence from Canada. Daniel Johnson, then premier of Quebec, is quoted as saying, "The 'Québec libre' launched by de Gaulle at the town hall in Montreal advanced the cause [of Quebec's separation] by five good years."[51] "I advanced them by ten years," de Gaulle told his entourage in Paris, with characteristic exaggeration, on his return home. Valéry Giscard d'Estaing was critical of de Gaulle, writes Bernard Dorin, but "as for us, obviously we were exultant."[52]

Quebec

Public approval for de Gaulle's aggressive stand, carefully orchestrated from Paris, had a tonic effect on certain sections of opinion in Quebec, as it was intended to do. It encouraged some politicians to take a similarly bold stand in de Gaulle's wake. The first to do so in Quebec political circles was François Aquin, Liberal MPP for Dorion, who left the provincial Liberal party almost immediately and explained his change of mind in a speech to Quebec's National Assembly on 3 August 1967. Contrary to the party, he thought "the president's voyage, the statements he made, the frankness with which he went to the very heart of things, constitute an historic event and a step forward in the realization of our destiny. ... At the cry, 'Vive le Québec libre', it was the soul of an entire people, oppressed and bullied, which rose suddenly as a response to the triumphal acclamation of 24 July."[53] As René Lévesque recalls, Aquin was the first of many "Gaullists" in the provincial legislature.[54]

While the Quebec public proceeded to debate de Gaulle's speech and the English-Canadian reaction to it, several more politicians joined the separatist cause and resigned from the Quebec Liberal party or from offices within it: Yves Bériault, André Brossard, and Pierre Germain in early August, and others later.[55] By no means all flocked to join the separatists, but there was widespread satisfaction at de Gaulle's bold words. Even radical left-wing opinion in journals such as *Parti pris*, normally hostile to de Gaulle and what he stood for, veered around to take tactical advantage of the Gaullist attack on the Canadian confederation.[56]

Quebec increased its already busy contacts with France. High-level visits became ever more frequent. Premier Johnson himself planned to make a state visit to Paris on 11–16 October 1968, and although he died shortly before, on 25 September, the preparations were revealing of his ambitious plans. A couple of days before his death his government paid for a thirty-page newspaper supplement in the Paris financial daily, *Les Echos*, prefaced with a message from the premier. The purpose was to appeal for French investment in Quebec and to make the province seem attractive to French investors.[57] De Gaulle and his government, for their part, were planning to welcome the premier and his party with flattering and encouraging warmth.

Other less obvious forms of encouragement followed de Gaulle's visit of 1967. For instance, French support has strengthened the "two-nations" theory of Confederation, according to which the French nation of Quebec has the fundamental right to withdraw from Confederation by a unilateral declaration. The representatives of Quebec were already expressing this view as a basic principle at the constitutional conferences held by Prime Minister Pearson's government in Toronto in November 1967 and at Ottawa early in February 1968.[58] An idea even more fundamental in Quebec and Gaullist thinking, to the effect that Quebec is a nation but Canada is not, was put forward in the same period by MPP François Aquin: "The anglophone community does not constitute a nation. Half of the Canadian provinces are already sociologically Americanised. Ethnic and regional differences constitute forces of rupture that irremedially mark the Canadian future. We are thus faced with a heterogeneous community that has in common only its perpetual interrogation about the aspirations of the Québécois. *What does Quebec want?*"[59] It is upon this ethnic definition of what constitutes a nation that leaders in the Parti Québécois have been transforming the province into an ethnic state.[60]

The attitude of the Quebec clergy to de Gaulle's 1967 visit was less clear but no longer what it would have been in the past. It was the church that through the best part of two centuries shaped a hostile attitude in Quebec to the "godless" French of the revolutionary republics. It was the clergy who welcomed authoritarian governments such as those of Napoleon III and Maréchal Pétain. What abbé Lionel Groulx would have thought of de Gaulle's visit in July 1967 will never be known, as he died exactly two months earlier, on 23 May. However, it is significant of a change of heart that leading members of the clergy attended on de Gaulle in 1967, and were photographed with him: Maurice Cardinal Roy and Mgr Vachon, vice-rector of Laval University, on 23 July in Quebec City; and Paul-Émile Cardinal Léger on 25 July, the day after the infamous *Vive le Québec libre* speech in Montreal.[62] Léger's meeting with de Gaulle prompted Marcel Cadieux to write: "It must be said that in political matters his brother the ambassador [Jules Léger in Paris] seems to have inherited all of the genius in the family."[63] Among the Acadians, *père* Anselme Chiasson o.f.m. cap. was active in the cause of stronger relations with France and occasionally collaborated with the French mafia.[64] If clerical attendance on de Gaulle and the Parti Québécois (PQ) is any indication, conservative support within the church for political loyalty to Canada appears to have evaporated.

In public statements, too, the bishops of Quebec were willing by 1967, perhaps even earlier, to make guarded statements in favour of the self-determination of their province.[65] Clergymen no longer lead public opinion in Quebec, but they represent one more sector of opinion that has apparently responded to the Gaullist and separatist initiatives. Marcel Cadieux, under-secretary of state for external affairs, was convinced in the late 1960s that the Roman Catholic church, both in Quebec and in France, would support the Canadian confederation rather than the separatist movement, but that may no longer be true.[66] Probably the clergymen, like Quebec society in general, have been divided in their loyalties. But near the end of December 1997 one of Cardinal Léger's successors, Jean-Claude Cardinal Turcotte, pronounced himself in support of Quebec's right to decide on its future by a referendum.[67]

LONG-TERM EFFECTS

The long-term effects of de Gaulle's visit in 1967 are not clear, and there has been much disagreement about them. Many anglophone Canadians might still agree with Stephen Clarkson's estimate in 1987 that even though "it was successful in its immediate goal of dramatizing the cause of independence for Quebec, de Gaulle's famous four words failed in the longer term because of the miscalculations which had inspired them. ... [His aggressive speech] strengthened rather than weakened the Canadian federal state and helped stymie the very thrust towards Quebec's independence it was designed to encourage."[68] There persists widespread opinion that the independence movement is entirely home-grown in Quebec and that French support for it is largely irrelevant. English-Canadian opinion has been inclined to focus on such events as the Quebec referenda and to ignore the French-language press. Has anyone in a major newspaper been digesting and reporting on the contents of the separatist daily, Le Devoir, of the monthly separatist journal, L'Action nationale, and of the quarterly, Études internationales? The alarming results of the second referendum, held on 30 October 1995, have left the public with little more than a vague sense of dismay.

The English-speaking public takes little if any notice of the many French-speaking tributes to de Gaulle's initiatives. Warnings from Quebec watchers, such as those who publish columns in the Financial Post and the Montreal Gazette, seem to arouse less response than the expressions of hope that follow such events as the relatively poor showing of the Bloc Québécois in the federal election of 2 June 1997.[69] When Premier Lucien Bouchard and his party visited France for five days beginning on 28 September 1997, first reports in English-language newspapers were alarming summaries of President Chirac's renewed assurances of French support for Quebec, but on 1 October the press and the federal government announced with relief that Prime Minister Jospin's assurances to Bouchard had been less bold, more perfunctory. Canadian responses to such events were invariably weak and confused. Political leadership in Canada seemed uncertain, many people making brave declarations about the decline of the separatist movement, others planning gloomily for the contingency of an independent Quebec. Few indeed would credit the Quebec lobby in France with any influence on the course of events in Quebec, and this is a measure of Canadian general ignorance about the underhanded Gaullist assault on Canada these past thirty-five years.

It is not widely known, for example, that only a couple of years after de Gaulle's visit the French government supported the PQ with funds as well as words and policies. Marc Lavallée, a member of the party's executive, relates how he travelled to Paris in spring 1969 to ask for donations. Like other Quebec separatists, he was welcomed by Pierre-Louis Mallen's influential Gaullist sister-in-law, Mme Robert Gravelin, at her apartment, 29 rue Cortembert, in Paris's sixteenth arrondissement, where she introduced him and his cause to a wide circle from the reading, writing, and governing classes.[70] Through her good offices, Lavallée was introduced to Jean de Lipkowski, then *secrétaire d'État aux Affaires étrangères*, and passed on to the *chef de cabinet* of prime minister Alain Poher. During a subsequent visit to France, on 6 February 1970, Lavallée met Jean-Daniel Jurgensen (whose name he consistently misspells), who was sufficiently high in the Ministry of Foreign Affairs to promise the $300,000 that Lavallée was asking for on behalf of the PQ.[71] It was about that time that Jacques Parizeau took control of the PQ's financial relations with the French government so that Lavallée is able to express ignorance about the actual payments. However, he echoes the suspicions bandied about in those years that the PQ did collect funds from the French government, suspicions that were noted by the RCMP, reported to the Canadian government, and brought to the notice of the McDonald Commission by John Starnes in 1977.[72] It would be surprising if French funds did not reach the PQ; after all, the Acadians were openly receiving similar aid in those years, though under the rubric of "cultural aid."[73]

"Liberating" Acadia

Having launched his assault on Canada at Montreal in July 1967, Charles de Gaulle and his followers then began a flanking attack on the much smaller French-speaking community of the Acadians in New Brunswick and Nova Scotia. Gaullists had, of course, always been aware of the Acadians as part of *la francophonie*. How could they not be? French plans to influence the Acadians date back to the 1890s, when the *Alliance française*, working through a Canadian senator, Pascal Poirier, sent out information about the efforts of authorities in France to promote the French language in the world and discreetly offered friendship and some financial aid. It sent sums of several hundred dollars to the weekly journal, *L'Évangéline* and to the organizers of congresses, and gifts of books to schools and parishes.[1]

Probably more effective was the *Comité France–Acadie*, with members on both sides of the Atlantic, founded in the 1920s by a rabidly anglophobic French historian, Émile Lauvrière, author of a well-known history of the Acadians, *La tragédie d'un peuple*.[2] Among the French members of this *Comité France-Acadie* were the historian Gabriel Hanotaux, maréchal Émile Fayolle, comte Robert de Caix, several members of the French Academy including René Bazin, and the editor of the *Revue des Deux Mondes*. The Acadian branch was led by prominent Catholic clergymen, magistrates, and politicians. Their most practical accomplishment was to offer two scholarships annually, from French government funds, to support university students. Some distinguished Acadians benefited from these scholarships. Books, films, and records were also sent out from France. But all this activity was quiet, limited, and modest by present standards.

Canada also undertook an early round of activities among the Acadians. Gaston Cholette tells how the federal Ministry of Labour arranged a visit for him in 1962 to the *Centre français de productivité*

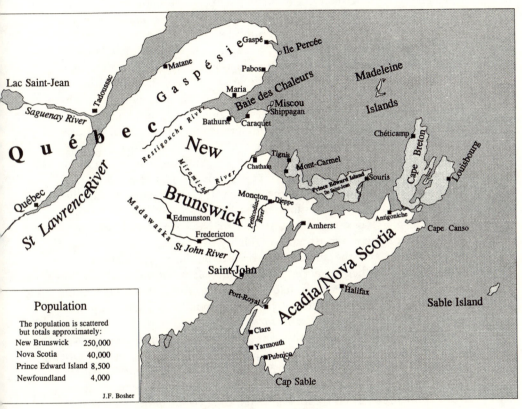

Map 2   Acadian Settlements

Lac Saint-Jean

Saguenay River

Tadoussac

Matane

Gaspé

Ile Percée

Pabos

Maria

Baie des Chaleurs

Miscou
Shippagan

Madeleine

Islands

Québec Gaspésie

Restigouche River

Bathurst   Caraquet

Chéticamp

Québec

St Lawrence River

Miramichi River

New

Tignis

Chatham

Mont-Carmel

Prince Edward Island
Ile Saint-Jean

Souris

Cape Breton

Louisbourg

Brunswick

Madawaska

Edmunston

Moncton   Dieppe

Petitcodiac River

Amherst

Antigoniche

Cape Canso

Fredericton

St John River

Saint John

Port-Royal

Acadia/Nova Scotia

Halifax

Sable Island

Clare

Yarmouth

Pubnico

Cap Sable

Population

The population is scattered
but totals approximately:

New Brunswick   250,000
Nova Scotia   40,000
Prince Edward Island   8,500
Newfoundland   4,000

J.F. Bosher

in Paris preparatory to visiting French-speaking communities in western Canada and in New Brunswick. As an agent of the Canadian *Conseil national de la productivité*, his purpose was to make contact with these communities and to encourage them to assert their right to use French – "les sensibiliser".[3] Although the western journey was a success, the trip to the Maritimes was cancelled because of objections to it raised there by managers of certain large enterprises. He hints at hostility in English-speaking circles.

Much later, in October 1968, he was sent on a mission to Louisiana by the Quebec's *ministère des affaires intergouvernementales*, to make contact with French-speaking communities there whom he thought of as Acadian. His first impressions were of a depressing prevalence of English, but certain survivals of French soon emerged. On 17 October he was one of about a thousand people attending a demonstration at Saint-Martinville to launch a campaign for the preservation of the French language in the state. As a result, Quebec opened a *Délégation* at Lafayette in 1970 and joined with France and Belgium in cultural exchanges and other encouragement of French in Louisiana.[4]

General de Gaulle's first reference to the Acadians came in a radio address in Paris, on 27 November 1967, four months after his visit to Quebec. He mentioned "all of the French in Canada who do not live in Quebec and who are a million and a half. I am thinking in particular of those 250,000 Acadians, settled in New Brunswick and who have, they too, kept a most moving fidelity to France, to her language, to her soul."[5] But the speech was only a public manifestation of a process that had begun more quietly some years before. Early in the 1960s the French government had moved its consulate from Halifax to Moncton to be near the French-speaking population. Then, on 9 September 1967 the *Association France–Canada* sent a party of French people to visit the Acadians; this was its first delegation to them. It was led by the body's faithful secretary-general, Lucien Bertin, but a more influential and interesting member of the party was Philippe Rossillon, one of the leading members of the French Quebec mafia, whose efforts we examine next. Then we look at expanding contacts between France and Acadia, Canada's response, Quebec's response, and the evolving relationship between Acadia and France.

ROSSILLON'S EFFORTS

Philippe Rossillon and his wife had already visited New Brunswick in 1956 and later years as tourists. By October 1979 he could recall ten visits since 1956, even though he had been excluded for six or seven years after the row that Trudeau made over his activities in September

1968.[6] He evidently had a Gaullist purpose in going to Moncton in September 1967, as he was ready to keep in close touch with other members of the Quebec mafia in France, notably Bernard Dorin and Xavier Deniau, the latter being a co-founder of the *Association France–Canada* with Lucien Bertin. According to the accounts of Robert Pichette and Léon Thériault, close students of these events – and active in them, too – Deniau and the others in France swung into action on Rossillon's initiative at Moncton on this occasion. Drawing on local memories and notes from interviews, historians credit Philippe Rossillon with leading the way in the new developments.[7] They present him, and he liked to think of himself, as a free-wheeling, enterprising *franc-tireur*, always ready to stir up the immobile bureaucracies in Paris and in Ottawa, where in 1967 he badgered the French ambassador, François Leduc.

What Rossillon did in 1967 was to seek out four men in Moncton and introduce himself not only as the *rapporteur* of the *Haut Comité de défense de la langue française*, which he was, but also as de Gaulle's personal representative, which he was not, at least not in any formal way.[8] He told them that the general had entrusted him with a special mission to the Acadians and asked them to meet him at the office of one of the four, Gilbert Finn, general manager of the *Compagnie mutuelle l'Assomption*, in the rue Saint-Georges. Speaking to them there as what Robert Pichette calls "a sublime imposter," Rossillon persuaded them that de Gaulle wished to sign a Franco–Acadian agreement and that they should forthwith petition him on that subject. This they were to do with the greatest discretion. These four Acadians were ready to trust Rossillon, incredible though his proposal seemed, because the French minister of education, Alain Peyrefitte, was at that moment in Quebec negotiating a Franco–Quebec agreement. A similar accord with Acadia seemed logical enough.

So they set about drawing up a list of what they thought of as Acadia's most pressing requirements, things that could be included in the terms of a cooperative agreement. Then, with much help from Rossillon, they composed a formal letter to de Gaulle that began: "Monsieur le Président de la République, Please allow the Acadians to tell you that your recent visit to our country has determined us to preserve French culture more than ever in the regions neighbouring Quebec."[9] There followed a brief statement of their history and their recent interest in *la francophonie*.

The letter then laid out ten requests for assistance of the most concrete kind: funds for the Université de Moncton to send professors to France; financial and technical help for the daily newspaper, *L'Évangeline*, through the *Société nationale des entreprises de presse*; the building in Acadia of a cultural centre to be dependent on the Canadian Department of External Affairs; "assistance moral and material" for the establishment in Paris of a General Delegation of the Acadian People; the founding in Moncton of a private French primary school; a film distribution bus (cinébus) for the *Société Nationale des Acadiens*; a French shop in Moncton to sell books, records, and other French goods; scholarships for young Acadians; "a large consignment" (envoi plus considérable) of books for public libraries; and in general an increase in cultural exchanges between France and Acadia. The letter ended with a reference to Peyrefitte's visit to Quebec and a final sentence, "We put all our hopes in you and beg you to accept our assurances of profound respect and of our firm attachment to our fatherland of origin".[10] It was signed by Léon Richard, MD, president of the *Société Nationale des Acadiens*. The four took this letter to Alain Peyrefitte, then in Quebec City, and when he failed to pass it on to de Gaulle, Rossillon sent a copy to René de La Saussaye de Saint-Légier, who did.[11]

Léon Richard, who signed this letter, was one of the four delegates whom Rossillon designated for a forthcoming visit to France. From the viewpoint of Moncton's Acadian leaders and for the purposes of the French Quebec mafia, these four were well chosen. That is, they were already involved one way or another in Acadian cultural matters and were all members of the secret *Ordre de Jacques Cartier*. Adélard Savoie was recteur of the new Université de Moncton. Euclide Daigle was vice-president of the *Association acadienne d'éducation*. Gilbert Finn, general manager of the *Compagnie mutuelle l'Assomption*, had already visited France in June 1966 with a party from the Acadian Historical Society, together with representatives from the Maritime and federal governments.

On 17 June 1966 Finn and his party had been welcomed in Paris at the National Assembly and the Quai d'Orsay with the greatest interest by members of the French Quebec mafia: Lucien Bertin, Marcel Brion, Xavier Deniau, Martial de la Fournière, Jean-Daniel Jurgenson, Raymond Poussart, and others.[12] The French had offered friendship and sympathy and then announced that they were hoping to send a party of some seventy ministers, deputies, and other visitors to Moncton the following summer. Meanwhile, Bertin had asked Gilbert Finn what steps could best be taken to establish regular relations between France and Acadia.[13] This Acadian expedition to France in June 1966 was what led to the French visit to Acadia in September 1967.

In response to the letter from Moncton prompted by Rossillon, de Gaulle replied on 28 October 1967 with enthusiasm and an assurance that the French ambassador to Canada, François Leduc, would soon invite the four signatories of the letter to visit Paris.[14] This moved the consul in Moncton, Jacques Longuet, to take an active part in the arrangements for such a visit, in collaboration with André Bettencourt and Jean-Daniel Jurgensen in Paris. It was thus that Rossillon's four Acadians journeyed to Paris early in January 1968 by way of Montreal for a fortnight's visit at the expense of the French government. They were received with all the lavish and generous attention that French authorities can bestow when it suits them.

Jurgensen and Jean Basdevant awaited them at Orly on the morning of 7 January with champagne in the airport's *salon d'honneur* and then lodged them at the splendid Hôtel de Crillon, Place de la Concorde. Escorted on visits to Versailles, Toulouse, Nice, Lille, Caen, the principal monuments of Paris, a selection of schools and universities, and the nuclear labs at Saclay and elsewhere, they met such distinguished figures as André Malraux, François Misoffe, Alain Peyrefitte, and Jacques Viot. They laid a wreath on the tomb of the unknown soldier at the Arc de Triomphe. On 20 January de Gaulle entertained them at a lunch at the Élysée, along with Philippe Rossillon, René de la Sausaye de Saint-Légier, and four other senior French civil servants.[15] Formal receptions or meals were laid on at the Hôtel de Ville, the Palais de Luxembourg, the Senate, the Canadian embassy, where Jules Léger presided, and the *Délégation générale du Québec*, where they were received by Jean Chapdelaine. The whole experience, as these four Acadians afterwards said in their various ways, was nothing less than dazzling. Plans were laid for closer transatlantic relations and for French assistance.

EXPANDING CONTACTS

The first practical result of this visit, and of Rossillon's initiative in general, was a new and enlarged set of scholarships and exchanges. Fifty-five special scholarships of 750 and 1,500 francs, according to the scholarly level, were established expressly for Acadian students willing to study in France. A mission of thirty-one French experts, including nine doctors and twenty professors, was sent out to New Brunswick, along with a gift of 19,000 books for the Université de Moncton and various other schools. A cultural service was added to the activities of the French consulate in Moncton. A French Trade Office also appeared there and served Rossillon occasionally as a base for his work among the Acadians. The life of the Acadian journal, *L'É-vangéline*, was prolonged (until 1982, it turned out) by an immediate gift of some $500,000 and "une aide en personnel et matériel."[16]

The French government followed this up with further gifts of $125,000 in 1974, $150,000 in 1976–7, and $100,000 in 1980. In addition it spent some $300,000 on "coopérants," or young agents (the "aide en personnel"), sent out to promote French interests abroad instead of doing the usual obligatory military service.[17] There were three French *coopérants* still working in the Maritime provinces at the time the French government recalled two of them in 1994, leaving only the one who was then assisting the journal, *Le Gaboteur*.[18]

Parties of Acadians were welcomed in France again and again in the intervening years – for instance, thirty-six teenagers in March 1978, two more groups of young people in May 1979, a delegation of the *Société nationale des Acadiens* in January 1980, and several parties attending congresses of *Amitiés acadiennes* – the first at Châtellerault on 6–7 December 1980, the second at La Rochelle on 5–6 June 1982, and the third at Chartres on 12–13 November 1983.[19] There was talk of setting up a *Bureau acadien* in Paris and of cultural centres in Moncton and somewhere in the northeast of New Brunswick.

As a result of the Gaullist initiatives, there was more interest in these transatlantic relations in France than in the Maritime provinces. This interest is visible in, for example, the organization of groups of Acadian descendants and sympathizers in western France – at least nine of them by 1994.[20] In addition, the Université de Poitiers established an *Institut d'études acadiennes et québécoises*, and in 1976 a group in Paris headed by Philippe Rossillon and Lucien Bertin founded the assocation *Amitiés Acadiennes*.[21] How that body must have lamented the fact that the quarterly journal it had been publishing since 1977 was not mentioned in, for example, Lise Bissonnette's lecture, "L'importance de la presse écrite dans le développement de l'identité d'un peuple," delivered at the Acadian World Congress at the Université de Moncton in 1994![22] Another example, disappointing from the Gaullist point of view, is that *L'Evangéline* published fewer and fewer articles about France: ninety-one in 1959–60, twenty-four in 1969–70, and only four in 1979–80.[23]

Acadians were not indifferent to the world-wide francophone movement that so engrossed Quebec's attention in the 1960s, but most of them were inclined to remain sturdily independent of outside entanglements, as they had learned to do over the previous two centuries or more. Besides, being divided in various ways, they were not in the habit of acting as a single, unified people.[24] Their response to overtures from France has been marked by the "cupboard love" more often remarked in pet animals and needy students. Subsidies, literary prizes, grants-in-aid, lavish receptions, and gifts of computers and scanners (for example, for the journal *Le Courrier de la Nouvelle-Écosse* in 1990) are what gladden the hearts of most francophile Acadians, as the French consulate in Moncton must be only too aware.[25] Some of the leaders of institutions in and near Moncton are enthusiastic; among the *pure laine* Acadians descended from seventeenth-century colonists are people more or less indifferent to outsiders; and then there are some whose Acadian identity has become a faded family tradition of mainly antiquarian interest to them. Many hold a shrewdly cynical view of what the Gaullist mafia is up to.

The essential point is that members of the Quebec lobby in France extended their activities to Acadia and were the driving force in attempting to spread French influence there. Not only did they sponsor the visit of the four Acadians to Paris, as described above, but they also set up *Amitiés acadiennes*. There were a score of founding members, led by Rossillon and his friend Lucien Bertin, who was also a founder of the *Association France–Québec*. This group drew four distinguished patrons to a *Comité d'honneur*: two professors, Ernest Martin and Auguste Viatte; a writer, Henri Queffélec; and a diplomat, François Seydoux, with the high rank of ambassadeur de France.[26] The latter, be it noted, was Philippe Rossillon's father-in-law. Viatte had visited Acadia soon after the Second World War and was to go again in 1977.[27]

At the association's headquarters on the Quai de Grenelle in Paris these "friends" of the Acadians launched a series of initiatives to stimulate Acadia, to bind it more and more to France, and these have continued to this day. In summer 1983 Pierre Maillard, then recently promoted to ambassadeur de France, founded a committee of a score of French officials, politicians, diplomats, and writers "for the vigilant support" of Acadia.[28] Rossillon supported much of what they did and travelled back and forth to Acadia. Max Yalden recalls meeting him at a party in Halifax in the late 1970s, and his visits to Moncton continued until his death on 6 September 1997.[29]

After the tempestuous francophone conference on education at Libreville, Gabon, early in 1968, the Canadian federal government apparently encouraged the government of New Brunswick, as well as those of other provinces with French-speaking minorities, to think of taking part in the *la francophonie* by placing representatives on Canadian delegations. Claude Morin saw this as a cunning step towards reducing Quebec's independence by inducing it to take part in conferences as only one of several provincial governments represented on a Canadian delegation.[30] However that may be, on 30 March 1968, Premier Louis Robichaud of New Brunswick wrote a personal letter to Premier Daniel Johnson of Quebec to tell him that his government wished to take part in any future francophone conferences on education. He (Robichaud) had already discussed this matter with a visiting official from the French Ministry for Foreign Affairs, Jean Basdevant, who was evidently a member of the French Quebec mafia. Three years earlier, on 27 February 1965, Basdevant had been one of the signatories of the first entente for cooperation between France and Quebec.[31] Early in 1968 he and another member of the mafia, Jean-Daniel Jurgenson, then *Directeur d'Amérique* at the Quai d'Orsay, had taken the opportunity of a visit to Quebec to call on Robichaud in Fredericton. But what Robichaud had in mind when writing to Premier Johnson was to ask for Quebec's support in its bid to take part in francophone conferences on education. Whatever the reason, Robichaud was himself present at the Kinshasa conference in January 1969.

CANADA'S RESPONSE

The Canadian government faced the same problem in dealing with Franco–Acadian relations as in the case of France and Quebec. That is, it was willing to approve and even to support French cultural and linguistic activities, but it could not help being aware of the obvious political dangers. Friendly cultural links can so quickly and easily convey French meddling, especially when managed by a Philippe Rossillon or a Lucien Bertin. Marcel Cadieux heard about this latest French intrusion at the end of 1967 and dispatched an official, Jacques Gignac, to find out what was happening in Moncton.[32]

Gignac returned to Ottawa with news of what has been described above. Rossillon's role in the affair caused Cadieux particular anxiety. "What is very serious in this business," he wrote, "is that [Premier] Robichaud may have trouble, as a result, convincing his English-speaking majority to make concessions to the French-Canadians of New Brunswick and these seem to be carrying on with de Gaulle, the sworn enemy of Anglo-Saxons. ... And to top it all off, the ambassador of France has just declared to a group of western Canadians that France wishes only to develop cultural relations with Canada and has no political objectives."[33]

What was to be done? Cadieux tried to encourage the Canadian Broadcasting Corporation to set up a French-language station at Moncton, for which Acadians were already clamouring. Occasionally there seem to have been signs of official efforts to foster a federal presence there in other ways. For example, Prime Minister Trudeau gave the principal address at the graduating ceremonies of the Université de Moncton on 18 May 1969, and his friend and cabinet colleague Gérard Pelletier did the same on 3 May 1970, both giving strong support to Canada, which Pelletier praised as "un pays fraternel."[34] But such efforts have been only sporadic.

Premiers Louis Robichaud and Richard Hatfield were inclined to encourage Franco–Acadian relations as natural cultural links. They evidently expected some political support from the French-speaking parts of their public, but did they also see political dangers over the horizon? How could they fail to see the political message of discontent and insurrection that Rossillon was continually broadcasting in his society's quarterly journal?[35] Whatever the answer, New Brunswick's provincial government, along with the government of Quebec, soon agreed to sponsor an *Institut d'études acadiennes et québécoises*, created in 1982 at the Université de Poitiers, probably because of an earlier initiative there that had resulted in the creation of a *Comité des Amitiés acadiennes* in 1973. Since June 1992 this institute has had a cooperative arrangement with the Université de Moncton. Meanwhile, a program of exchanges in education, trade, tourism, economic life, and so on has been in place since Hatfield endorsed it in September 1983. The concessions granted to Quebec by the Conservative federal government in 1985, and the resulting thaw in Canada's relations with France and Quebec, also touched Acadia.

Early in December 1985, Prime Minister Brian Mulroney signed an agreement with Hatfield whereby New Brunswick was to take part in francophone summit meetings on the same terms as Quebec.[36] Hatfield even took out membership in the Parti Québécois. When President Mitterrand visited Canada in May 1987, Lucien Bouchard, learning that his return flight was to make a stop at St John's, Newfoundland, arranged for it to touch down at Moncton instead. There at the airport on 29 May, while the plane was refuelling, Mitterrand appeared before a crowd of several hundred in an empty hangar. Premier Hatfield and Lieutenant-Governor George Stanley were there to greet him, as were the four Acadian delegates – Daigle, Finn, Richard, and Savoie – who had been welcomed in Paris by General de Gaulle twenty years earlier. For some Acadians this was an emotional occasion, as Mitterrand was the first French head of state ever to visit them. He himself was moved to call on them a second time, later that year, during the francophone summit meeting at Quebec City.[37]

QUEBEC'S RESPONSE

Relations between Quebec City and Moncton have been perfunctory for long periods, and sometimes the Acadians have been resentful of certain Québécois, such as Jean-Noël Tremblay, provincial minister of cultural affairs, who in January 1968 seemed inclined to manipulate the Acadians for Quebec's advantage.[38] The first electoral victory of the Parti québécois on 15 November 1976 made the Acadians anxious, as they wondered what would be their fate after Quebec quit Confederation.[39] With Rossillon's prompting, Acadian leaders asked Claude Morin, the Quebec minister of intergovernmental affairs, to send a delegation to Moncton, and so a meeting took place in 1980.[40] It was followed by others. In 1984 Premier René Lévesque even addressed an Acadian gathering to celebrate the one-hundredth anniversary of the Acadian flag.[41]

Such encounters do not remove all the difficulties between Québécois and Acadians. Some Quebec separatists have insulted Acadians by suggesting that they would soon cease to be French-speaking: Yves Beauchemin once described them as "corpses still warm," and on 3 October 1997 Gilles Duceppe caused a minor row by advising all Canadian French-speaking artists and writers to settle in Quebec if they did not want to be assimilated into English-speaking communities.[42] "We don't need a second Gaspé," said René Lévesque harshly when some Acadians were reported to be in favour of annexation by Quebec.[43] But occasionally Acadian and Quebec leaders have collaborated. Since 1980 Quebec has maintained a "bureau" at Moncton, which, according to the Paris agency *Amitiés acadiennes*, "plays practically the rôle of a Quebec embassy in the Atlantic provinces and supports, in particular, the promotion of a francophone linguistic policy."[44] In November 1987 a *Fédération acadienne du Québec* was founded to link local Acadian societies. On 17 December 1996 the Quebec National Assembly voted to support the (successful) candidature of Moncton to host the *Sommet francophone* scheduled for 3–5 September 1999.[45]

ONGOING RELATIONS

Meanwhile, French aid to Acadia has continued, in somewhat the same way as French aid goes out to parts of Africa and the Far East, though naturally on a smaller scale. What makes it worthy of note is the French practice of patronage based on the language and culture held in common. Apparently unable or unwilling to resist, the provincial government of New Brunswick copes with this as best it can. When Alain Decaux, the French minister in charge of *la francophonie*, visited Acadians in Caraquet, Moncton, and elsewhere on 7–11 September 1990, he had interviews with Premier Frank McKenna and his deputy, Aldéa Landry, in order "to reaffirm the intention of the French government to maintain its support for the Acadian communities and to announce that he [Decaux] would be presiding over the meeting to be held in Paris at the end of November for the renewal of the cooperation agreements [*accords*]."[46]

It was not the provincial government, however, that was invited to that meeting in Paris: the delegation that went to receive this manna from the French government consisted of people from the *Société nationale des Acadiens*, led by their president, Pierre Arsenault.[47] Two years later, observers of the Acadian communities in Nova Scotia wrote, "Over the past twenty years, the *Société nationale des Acadiens* has acted on behalf of the three provincial associations at the international level. In Nova Scotia, for instance, the Université de Sainte-Anne, [the newspaper] *Le Courrier*, Radio-Canada and the community radio station in Clare all benefit in a variety of ways from French government assistance. Support from France and also from the government of Quebec has greatly strengthened the cultural framework of the Acadians, particularly in Nova Scotia where the francophone minority is small and broken up into several isolated communities."[48]

By then, the French government had appointed a diplomat, Eric Noitakis, its former commercial attaché at Montreal, "to take charge of the files concerning economic exchanges with New Brunswick."[49] It had also founded a French-language institute called "Francoforum" on the nearby island of Saint-Pierre, under the auspices of the Paris chamber of commerce and the universities of Brest, Caen, and Poitiers, to be "a centre for the spreading of French culture to the North American continent."[50] The effect of all this effort is that France supports, patronizes and encourages its former colony in eastern Canada much as it does those in West Africa.

Driven by the enthusiasm of people in France, including members of the French Quebec mafia, *Amitiés acadiennes* has held a series of congresses in French towns – Châtellerault (1980), La Rochelle (1982), Chartres (1983), Belle-Ile (1985), Nantes (1987), and so on – and it has published a monthly newsletter, *Acadie Infos*, and a quarterly journal, named after itself, to keep the French public informed about Acadia. More than eighty numbers of this journal had appeared by the end of 1997. Since 1978 it has offered a prize for a work of literary merit concerning Acadia, which was awarded to twenty-four books in the first thirteen years. Two-thirds of the jury are French, one-third Acadian.

Some members of this essentially French association, such as a certain Roger Chevant, an employee in the French postal service, have worked enthusiastically as militant partisans of the Acadian cause. "If there were a hundred Chevants distributed between France and the Atlantic provinces," writes a friend of Acadia at the Université de Poitiers, "Acadia would be assured of its destiny."[51] It was partly on Chevant's initiative that a square in Paris, in the Latin quarter, was renamed "place d'Acadie" in a ceremony on 8 March 1984 attended enthusiastically by the mayor of Paris, Jacques Chirac, the vice-president of *Amitiés acadiennes*, Lucien Bertin, other dignitaries, and, of course, the association's president, Philippe Rossillon, who is to be seen at the ceremonial microphone in one of Robert Pichette's photographs.[52] At the time of Rossillon's death early in September 1997 he was busy raising money to build a memorial at Grand-Pré, Nova Scotia, to the deportation of the Acadians.[53]

The society's journal, *Les Amitiés acadiennes*, is essentially literary and cultural, but no student of the French Quebec mafia would be surprised to find that it has considerable political content. Many of the articles, and editorials also, have been written by Philippe Rossillon.[54] The satirical tone of many editorials, referring more than once to Premier Hatfield as "M. Chapeauchamps," springs from his pen. "[This tone] is no less passionate and inflamed," one observer comments, "when Philippe Rossillon exercises his verve on explicitly political subjects."[55] And indeed *Les Amitiés acadiennes* has served as a vehicle for him to comment in an inflammatory way on Canadian political matters, under such titles as "Illusions constitutionnelles et réalités politiques" (April 1979, pp. 4–5) and "Les Acadiens, le Québec et la constitution" (October 1981, 3). "For Quebec not to be drowned and anglicized in a Canadian ensemble where French-speakers are rapidly becoming a minority," he said in a speech to the Acadian Congress at Saint-Malo, France, on 8 June 1990, "it must attain an autonomy bordering on independence."[56]

Here, once more, is an example of French cultural and linguistic friendship that seems to have political objectives. For some of the writers in *Les Amitiés acadiennes* the Acadians are French and must be encouraged to stage one of those political and social revolutions that have been so frequent in France since 1789 that people such as members of the French Quebec mafia cannot conceive of a francophone group that is not in a constant state of political rebellion. Rossillon continually exhorted his readers and hearers to take political action. At a celebration of the hundredth anniversary of Charles de Gaulle's birth, Lucien Bertin rejoiced publicly at the effects of his intervention in Canada in 1967–68: "Relations between the Acadians and the French continue at a very high level in various realms including the political."[57] For Rossillon and his friends, a federal country such as Canada is intrinsically evil, for no matter how it behaves it cannot but be oppressive by its very existence. "I offer the complete works of Machiavelli," he wrote in 1986, "to whoever will explain to me why Ottawa encourages the Acadian journalistic muddle."[58] Some Acadians have responded to Rossillon's enthusiasm in their cause: in 1996 the Université de Moncton awarded him an honorary degree.[59]

– 6 –

The French "Quebec Mafia"

The Gaullist attack on Canada was only part of a much larger imperial campaign. Busy as he was in many parts of the world, de Gaulle passed the task of encouraging Quebec on to small groups of French civil servants. These were some of the figures who ignored Ottawa's objections, as he instructed them to, and simply went ahead in dealing directly with the government of Quebec. Claude Morin, a leading figure at Quebec City in the 1960s and 1970s, names the following: Bernard Dorin, Martial de la Fournière, Jean-Daniel Jurgensen, and Philippe Rossillon.[1] Apart from André Malraux, who must be added to the list as the minister of culture who seconded de Gaulle in his Quebec policy, the leader seems to have been Jurgensen who served as *Directeur d'Amérique* at the Quai d'Orsay from 1964. But others, too, were collaborating, such as Xavier Deniau, a *député* in the National Assembly; Jean Charbonnel, *Secretaire général aux affaires étrangères de la coopération* during the critical years 1966–7; Pierre de Menthon, who served as consul general at Quebec city in the years 1968–72; and also, I believe, Alain Peyrefitte, minister of education in 1967–68, and Pierre Messmer, the minister for war.

PERSONNEL

The "Quebec mafia" is an expression first used by historians and members of the Canadian diplomatic service to refer to a variable number of high-ranking officials and politicians in France keen to encourage Quebec separatists and to offer them every possible assistance. There are several groups of them, and their members tend to refer to themselves collectively by the kinder expression, "le lobby québécois en France." The "Quebec mafia" is not a frivolous expression, though somewhat derogatory, and appears in serious, scholarly studies such as those by Eldon Black and Dale Thomson.[2] As they would be the first to admit, however, it applies to French people with a variety of views. Not all members and hangers-on think the same way or have the same objectives. This chapter first distinguishes cultural from political support for *la francophonie* and delineates the mafia by considering types of members within the French government, associates, numbers, common characteristics, and mission, then it examines the rites and symbols that define the organization's mysteries.

Cultural versus Political

Just outside the mafia are people who have a simple desire to promote the French language and culture in the world and are therefore part of the international movement of *la francophonie*. This is a world-wide movement bringing together representatives from French-speaking countries and minorities, usually in annual conferences but also in cultural exchanges and other cooperative endeavours. Quebec separatists easily win the sympathy of French observers whose interests are purely cultural, such as André Fontaine, editor-in-chief of the distinguished Paris newspaper *Le Monde*. He joined in a debate organized by Louise Beaudoin in Paris on 11 February 1980, a few days before a Canadian federal election and a few months before the first Quebec referendum on sovereignty, and he later contributed an article, "La France et le Québec," to a Laval University journal.[3] But he seems to have had no commitment to the political movement of the Quebec separatists and their French friends. Movements for promoting the French language and culture in the world do not necessarily have political objectives, and on that understanding the government of Canada has joined them and continues to play a full part in them. I describe and explain them below, in chapters 11 and 12.

Some of their French members, however, find it hard to draw a line between cultural and political purposes. This is partly because French people, since their revolution of 1789–94, have been taught to believe that language, culture, and history define a nation as a political entity. A French republic – even the Fifth Republic – lives by the revolutionary tradition which claims that it is the political expression of the general will of an independent, sovereign nation. Its citizens find it hard to think of a people with the same language, culture, and history as anything other than independent and self-governing, though they tend to find reasons why this idea does not apply to the Basques, Bretons, Catalans, Corsicans, and Germans in France. In their view, the people of Quebec and Acadia, by virtue of their language, culture, and history, are parts of the French nation, as Charles de Gaulle always said, and ought to be separate from Canada. They have little understanding of a federal political structure such as Canada's and tend to be hostile to it and critical. No doubt Pierre Elliott Trudeau had this type of misunderstanding in mind when, in 1967, he published *Le fédéralisme et la société canadienne française*, expressing such strong thoughts as, "What is retrograde is not the national idea, but the idea that the nation must necessarily be sovereign."[4] He pointed out that there are many minorities in most countries; if every one claimed political independence, the result would be world-wide chaos.

As a result of their political tradition, however, French people who support the world-wide French-speaking community, *la francophonie*, as a purely cultural and linguistic grouping sometimes change their colours – suddenly, like a chameleon – and begin to support Quebec political independence. Such were some of the forty who signed a letter of support for the separatists in January 1995.[5] The fair-minded among these might perhaps have been persuaded to retreat to an unpolitical, purely cultural, idea of francophonie if reminded of the fact that in France a number of groups have their own language, culture, and history but yet remain in France governed, and sometimes oppressed, by Paris. For many centuries a central government in Paris has dominated the rest of the country. This comparison might tend to chasten one part of the Quebec mafia – the unwitting supporters of Quebec separatism – but it would scarcely daunt the more aggressive part.

This other segment of the French Quebec mafia is committed to the separation of Quebec, and if possible Acadia also, from the rest of Canada. It regards the cultural and linguistic francophone movement as a Trojan horse for the forces of political independence. It supports *la francophonie* as part of a campaign to damage the Canadian confederation, which it sees as an English-Canadian device for dominating a part of the French nation conquered in 1759–63. When members visit Quebec they are horrified by the compromises they see on every side – compromises that we think of as both practical and inevitable in a bilingual country. Is this the fate that awaits us in France, they wonder, if we lose the struggle against American pop culture and the English language? They feel the same way when they visit Belgium, but the problem there worries them less because Flemish is hardly a world-wide language and the French-speaking Walloons are proportionately more numerous than the French-speaking Canadians. Still, the mafia gives encouragement to the Walloons just as it does to the Quebec separatists.[6] Occasionally there is even talk of the French-speaking Swiss citizens of the Jura claiming independence and so shaking off German influence. People in Gaullist France who see the world in such terms

often talk as though French-speaking minorities are oppressed and
need encouragement, but their efforts to intervene on their behalf tend
to become aggressive. The truth is that French champions of
"oppressed" minorities are only pretending to be on the defensive and
are in fact engaged in an imperial enterprise that was revived and promoted by Charles de Gaulle.

While most members of the French Quebec mafia cite feelings of cultural fellowship as their explanation for assisting Quebec separatists,
some of them in private conversation will go on to express hatred of
the United States or England, or even of all the English-speaking
peoples – *les Anglais* or *les Anglo-saxons*, as they say. Xavier Deniau,
Bernard Dorin, Jean-Daniel Jurgensen, and Pierre-Louis Mallen have
been openly hostile in this way, some observers would say fanatical.
Gossip has it that Dorin was withdrawn by the French government
from his ambassadorial post in London on 18 October 1993 partly for
this reason. Others, such as Couve de Murville, are more tactful and
reticent about their own anglophobic feelings, which are nevertheless
just as strong. But these ideologues are not the only anglophobes in
France. Anyone who speaks fluent French and lives in France for long
periods of time is likely to meet such people, or become aware of films,
books, and articles expressing uncompromising anglophobia. These
hostile feelings are also widespread in Quebec, as William Johnson has
explained at length.[7] Most people, however, who have little knowledge
of French, or who have not had occasion to live in France or Quebec,
will scarcely credit the strength and persistence of this anglophobia or
the twisted thinking behind it.

There are, then, two kinds of French people promoting *la francophonie*: those who merely wish to give encouragement to the French language and culture, and those who are also committed to promoting the
power of France in the world by doing as much damage as possible to
the English-speaking peoples. The Gaullist movement has attracted
both kinds, and others in between, and it is often difficult to determine
the group to which a particular individual belongs. Charles de Gaulle
himself, in a somewhat sophisticated way, was one of the many educated French people who are hostile to the English-speaking world on
historical as well as political grounds, as I try to explain below in chapters 14 and 15.

Types of Members

People committed to the independence or sovereignty of Quebec are to
be found employed in four spheres of the French government. First,
some of the most active have been diplomats such as Bernard Dorin,

Martial de la Fournière, the late Jean-Daniel Jurgensen, and the late marquis de Saint-Légier. Second, some are parliamentarians who have visited, welcomed, and encouraged separatists from Quebec and Moncton. Prominent among these are Xavier Deniau, Jean de Lipkowski, and also Pierre-André Wiltzer, who was among those receiving a party of six prominent Acadians on a visit to France in November 1992.[8] More recently, Jacques Parizeau's friend Philippe Séguin attended the unveiling of the statue of de Gaulle at Quebec City on 23 July 1997 as Jacques Chirac's representative.

Third, there have been members of the Quebec mafia working for the presidents at the Élysée Palace, including Captain François Flohic and Gilbert Pérol during de Gaulle's time in office. The presidents themselves are somewhat harder to judge, but there is evidence that Jacques Chirac might be counted as a friend of the Quebec separatists. He is the most fervent Gaullist of de Gaulle's successors and seems to be only waiting for the signal from Quebec to recognize a new Quebec republic.

Fourth, there are assorted officials and *franc-tireurs*, loners such as Pierre-Louis Mallen, who, after six years in Quebec from 1963 to 1969, wrote three books expressing contempt for English Canada and support for a separate Quebec. His family in France, particularly sister-in-law Mme Robert Gravelin, has welcomed Quebec separatist leaders, entertained them, and promoted their cause among French officials and politicans.[9] Also in this group were Philippe Rossillon, whom we met above and Robert Bordaz, a devoted supporter of Quebec's independence from the time he served as *commissaire général du pavillon français* at Expo. 67 in Montreal.

These French ideologues – Gaullist zealots working for the independence of Quebec – did not and do not all function together as one conspiratorial team; they busy themselves with different enterprises and in groups that call on one another for assistance from time to time. They surround themselves, too, with allies or willing acquaintances who lend their aid occasionally without devoting themselves wholeheartedly to the cause. It is particularly difficult to judge the motives and the commitment of people on the fringes. But however lukewarm their interest in French-speaking Canada, they are distinct from the normal French bureaucratic personnel who treat public affairs in a routine manner and do not appear to share the zealous enthusiasm of the Quebec lobby, or mafia, in Paris.

Philippe Rossillon explains, for example, that he had the Acadians who wrote to de Gaulle specify exactly what they wanted from France, "which would not allow the accountants in the Ministry of Foreign Affairs to slyly claim that nothing had been asked of them, or else that the matter was being studied."[10] He goes on to say that the French government's troubles after the uprisings in France of May 1968 resulted in just such a bureaucratic obstruction of plans laid down by de Gaulle and what he calls "the francophone clan."[11] It is against the great grey background of French bureaucracy, famous for its delays and confusion, that Rossillon names his collaborators in the struggle to stir up French-speaking people in New Brunswick, Quebec, and Manitoba – notably Lucien Bertin, Yann Clerc (a journalist), Xavier Deniau, Bernard Dorin, Martial de la Fournière, and Sausaye de Saint-Légier. These names appear again, but with many others not mentioned by Rossillon, in Bernard Dorin's account of his activities on behalf of the separatists in Quebec.[12] And the same is true of Pierre-Louis Mallen's account.[13]

The French consul general at Quebec from 1967 to 1972 is a good example of the variety within the Gaullist conspiracy. This was Pierre de Menthon, a career diplomat whom de Gaulle instructed to do his best to encourage the separatists and to strengthen Quebec's links with France. To aid him in this mission and free him from any taint or fetter of federal influence, de Gaulle detached him from the embassy in Ottawa and made him answerable to the Élysée. Budgetary constraints, too, were lifted, and de Menthon proceeded to lease more buildings in Quebec City and to hire additional staff members. As he tells us in an article, his consulate busied itself with public relations and transatlantic initiatives and became very active in the life of the city and the province. He had been warned by the Quai d'Orsay, however, to proceed cautiously, step by step, without visible aggression lest the Canadian government and federalists in Quebec throw obstacles in his path. The foreign minister, Couve de Murville, had personally given him "counsels of moderation, insisting on the General's 'Don't rush things (ne rien brusquer).'"[14] De Menthon understood that he must protect himself "from the overpowering passion of that impatience expressed by a small group of senior French civil servants who would like everything to be done all at once." Entrusted with a major posting in the Gaullist conspiratorial empire, de Menthon was undoubtedly a member of the French Quebec mafia, and yet he felt it necessary to keep himself apart and to proceed differently. The difference, it must be stressed, was one of tactics, not of principle.

Associates

Thus to identify a mafia of Gaullist conspirators is not to suggest that they were all working together in one concerted operation. There seem to have been several conspiratorial groups that occasionally engaged the services of people who were generally sympathetic with Quebec separatism but not devoted to the cause in the manner of the conspirators. We must make a distinction between people actively promoting the separation/sovereignty of Quebec – members of the conspiratorial mafia – and others who were merely carrying out orders or temporarily involved in some compromising manoeuvre of the Gaullist authorities.

For example, it would not be accurate to classify Yvan Bourges together with Dorin, Jurgensen, and Lipkowski. As secretary of state for scientific, atomic, and space affairs, he was intent on getting uranium from Canada in 1965–6 and as a French representative later in Niger and Gabon he was active in French efforts to induce African governments to invite Quebec but not Canada to international conferences; yet he later assured Eldon Black that he had not had full knowledge earlier of what was going on and regretted this.[15] Again, it is possible that Paul Martin, secretary of state for external affairs, was correct in suggesting that the troublesome French ambassador to Canada in 1965–68, François Leduc, was merely obeying de Gaulle's orders and not expressing his own support for Quebec.[16] But Martin's memoirs show that Leduc had done much harm merely by carrying out his instructions.

Others who did not share the mafia's devotion to the Quebec cause but took part in some of the compromising manoeuvres were Joseph-Marie Comiti, French minister for youth and sport, who visited Quebec but not Ottawa in September 1967; Yves Guëna, who was Michel Debré's *directeur de cabinet* in 1958–59 and minister of postal and telegraphic services in 1967–69; and Xavier de la Chevalerie, one of de Gaulle's *directeurs de cabinet*. These were among the many servants of the French government who were merely caught up in the anti-Canadian policy, some of them faithfully carrying out orders, others only doing whatever seemed likely to advance their own careers. Further evidence may remove some of the above from the list altogether, but there are undoubtedly others not yet identified.

Another group may be identified: high-ranking officials and politicians who favoured the independence of Quebec out of a general patronizing benevolence that did not exclude the rest of Canada. With a genuine desire to avoid taking sides, such people did not share the malevolent devotion of the mafia nor the hostile objectives of the Quebec separatists. At worst they may be described as fellow-travellers or sympathizers, whose general collaboration with the mafia qualifies them for dishonourable mention. Such were Gaullist foreign ministers such as Michel Debré and Maurice Schumann, though the latter defended Gaullist views with some firmness in conversation with Mitchell Sharp on 24 September 1969.[17] Some observers profess to see a goodwill and benevolence in the activities of Couve de Murville as a foreign minister who became friendly with Paul Martin in the 1960s and also in those of André Bettencourt, director of the ORTF in the critical years 1962–64 and later secretary of state for foreign affairs responsible for Quebec. But Couve and Bettencourt were party to a cunning plot to encourage French ambitions in Quebec, which came to light only by accident. Early in 1968 they tried to influence the pope to appoint a bishop in Montreal who would be sympathetic to the Gaullist imperial cause.[18] Officials in Canada's Department of External Affairs were horrified at such scheming.

Soon after Cardinal Léger died, in December 1967, two French visitors to Montreal, a politician, Jean-Paul Palewski, and a mathematics professor, Pierre Lelong, suggested to the French foreign ministry that the French presence in Quebec might be fortified by inducing the Vatican to appoint a "suitable" bishop in Montreal. Lelong saw this as a way of checking the threatening advance of the North American obsession with material possessions. He thought that the Catholic church on this continent had all but given up the struggle against it. At all events, Bettencourt promptly asked the French ambassador to the Vatican to sound out any Canadian clergymen there and find out in general how the appointment of Léger's successor might be influenced. The reply from Rome was sent in a dispatch, with enclosures, to Couve de Murville. However, the Canadian ambassador in Paris, Jules Léger, who happened to be Cardinal Léger's brother, somehow obtained a copy of this correspondence and sent it to Marcel Cadieux in Ottawa with a covering note expressing his disgust at this latest Gaullist ploy. Cadieux forwarded it to Prime Minister Pearson on 2 February, together with an assurance that he, Cadieux, was already on friendly terms with the papal legate in Ottawa, Emmanuel Clarizio, whose recommendation was almost certain to determine the appointment in question. Pearson, Cadieux, and Léger all took the view that these activities did not reflect well on Couve de Murville, Bettencourt and the Quai d'Orsay.

In a class by himself was André Malraux, who made grand Gaullist speeches at Montreal in 1963 and in Paris sometimes welcomed French-speaking visitors from Quebec and New Brunswick but did not seem to have clear political objectives. On the occasion of his visit to Montreal the French consul general there described him as a crypto-separatist.[19] He certainly lent his considerable influence to the separatist cause. And yet Malraux thought only occasionally about Quebec and Acadia. For all his damaging activities, he seems to have been devoted to the cause of French culture rather than to the cause of Quebec. Indeed, he assured the *Délégué général du Quebec* in Paris before his visit in 1963 that he was not a supporter of political separation and did not believe that separation/sovereignty would be of benefit to Quebec.[20]

Also in a class by himself is the current president of France, Jacques Chirac, whom Dorin names as one of the politicians "won over to the Quebec cause," who welcomed Quebec leaders on several occasions when he was mayor of Paris, has visited Quebec as president, and in April 1977 wished Claude Morin success in the struggle for independence.[21] Chirac assured Jacques Parizeau in 1995 that France would stand by him in the case of a "yes" vote in the referendum of 30 October that year. Chirac is the most ardently Gaullist president of France since de Gaulle himself. He was involved in some of the most discreditable features of de Gaulle's administration, such as the parallel secret service of Gaullist thugs known as the *Service d'action civique* (SAC).[22] It remains to be seen whether he will show merely a general benevolence towards Quebec in the remaining years of his term – due to end in 2002 – or whether, as seems likely, he will take up de Gaulle's own active role.

Numbers

How many conspirators in this mafia were there, all considered? How many are there today? The first question is easier to answer than the second. Gérard Pelletier recalled that during his time as a Canadian representative abroad, sent out by Prime Minister Trudeau, there were precisely twenty-seven of them.[23] It is not difficult to arrive at a similar figure from other sources. Looking back to 1967, Bernard Dorin names (in addition to himself) twenty-two French officials and politicians as members of a conspiratorial group he calls "le lobby québécois de Paris."[24] His list calls for two qualifications: first, he claims a few whom he found serviceable but who lacked his own malevolent convictions; and second, he says nothing about Jean de Lipkowski, the troublesome secretary of state for foreign affairs, or François Flohic, the anglophobic mariner who accompanied de Gaulle to Quebec in 1967, or Jacques Longuet, erstwhile consul general at Moncton and Halifax. Possibly the latter two were beneath his notice, as perhaps was Robert Bordaz. Others again may have joined the movement so late as to strike Dorin as mere hangers-on: Parizeau's friend Philippe Séguin, for example, or Michel Habib-Deloncle, who wrote so enthusiastically about the reception of de Gaulle at Montreal. Mallen should, of course, be counted with these. Some Canadian diplomats acquainted with Couve de Murville would include him, notwithstanding his tact and discretion.

Most of the above were active during the 1960s and 1970s; many have now retired, and some have died. How many members of the mafia do we face today? A devoted though desultory reading of the French press suggests that much of the higher civil service and much of the National Assembly – nearly all the Gaullists at least – would have to be counted. So at least one may judge by the tone of press reports and the roar of approval that greets Quebec visitors in the National Assembly and in presidential circles. Little by little even many of those who did not, of themselves, form hostile views towards the Canadian confederation have been drawn into a mafia that, in a modest way, has become the newest field of activity wherein faithful Gaullists feel they have won honour and glory – that is, after the Free French adventure of the 1940s, the postwar struggles of the Gaullist political parties in the Fourth Republic, and the founding of the Fifth Republic in 1958–62.

It has to be admitted that much of the hostility towards Canada and the warmth towards Quebec rides on a common assumption among the observant French public that it is only a matter of time before Quebec breaks away from Canada and forms a separate, sovereign state in the time-honoured French revolutionary manner. If in some dramatic way Canadian affairs were to be cast in a different light, many of the mafia's supporters would no doubt drop away or change their opinions. How many would be left it is impossible to estimate, but the original few are ageing. Saint-Légier died late in the 1970s, Jurgensen in 1987, Martial de la Fournière in 1994, Pérol in 1995, Debré and Bordaz in 1996, Foccart, Lipkowski, and Rossillon in 1997. Others too must soon go to their reward in a Gaullist heaven, as Mallen is now eighty-nine; Burin des Roziers, Maillard, and Menthon are all eighty or older. There is, of course, a younger generation in which Chirac and Séguin stand out.

COMMON CHARACTERISTICS

As a group, members of the French Quebec mafia share few discernible characteristics, other than holding high rank in politics or the civil service. They vary widely in age. Some have had long terms as mayors of French towns in which their influence has, of course, been enormous. Thus, Jacques Chirac was mayor of Paris, Alain Peyrefitte of Provins, Jean de Lipkowski of Royan, Philippe Séguin of Épinal, Yvan Bourges of Dinard, Jean Charbonnel of Brive, Philippe Rossillon of Beynac (Périgord), and comte Pierre de Menthon of Choisy. Accumulating posts as mayor of a town and deputy in the National Assembly is an old French tradition, but since 1969 Gaullists have become "notabilized" in this way more than most.[25]

And probably the great majority of the mafia and their allies have been politically inclined to vote for Gaullist parties such as the *Union pour la Défense de la République* (UDR) or the *Rassemblement pour la République* (RPR); socialists such as Jean-Daniel Jurgensen, Pierre Maillard, and Michel Rocard are a rarity in this mafia. It is vital to recognize, however, that French socialists may also be Gaullists at the same time. This is because Charles de Gaulle detested party politics, loftily refused to lead or join the Gaullist parties, and insisted on ruling France with a patriotic coalition drawn from any and all parties, in the manner of the kings and emperors of the past. As long as the people serving in his government were patriotic, capable, and obedient, they could believe whatever they liked. It is therefore misleading to think of the Gaullist movements as normal political parties that can be placed on the usual left–right spectrum.

The French Quebec mafia is fundamentally a Gaullist phenomenon, but this does not mean that a government of another political persuasion could be counted on to quell it. French history in the twentieth century, and earlier, shows that even socialists tend to support nationalist policies. Theoretically international in their outlook, French socialists nevertheless rallied to the national war effort against Germany in 1914. Opposed to rearmament during the 1930s, like socialists in most countries, they did not lack patriotism during the Second World War and the Fourth Republic that followed it. Loyalty to the homeland was always one of the features of French socialism that marked it off from the Communists, whose policies were ambiguous before, during, and after the Second World War. But even Communists were being patriotic as well as anti-fascist in their vigorous contributions to the résistance during the early 1940s, and not a few rallied to de Gaulle, as did André Malraux.

Later, François Mitterrand, during the fourteen years of his socialist presidency, made no visible changes in the aggressive policies of the Fifth Republic, and it was in his time that the *Rainbow Warrior* affair occurred. The graduates of the *École nationale d'administration* (ENA), a prestigious school founded in 1945 by Michel Debré to prepare an élite for high government office, tend towards the left in their politics, even though they are fiercely patriotic and devoted to the greatness of France.[26] Jacques Parizeau regarded Michel Rocard, a socialist who served as prime minister from 1988 to 1991, as a friend of Quebec.[27] In September 1995 another prominent socialist leader, Henri Emmanuelli, said publicly that if he were in Quebec he would vote in favour of separation from Canada.[28] When the thirtieth anniversary of de Gaulle's visit to Quebec was celebrated in July 1997, all five of the major political parties in France sent messages of congratulations and encouragement to the separatist government in Quebec.[29] Among the French visitors who attended the unveiling of the new statue of the general in Quebec City on 23 July 1997 was a member of the Communist party. All the signs are that a majority of left-wing deputies in the National Assembly are unlikely to do anything to stop French patronage of the Quebec separatist movement. Indeed, Lionel Jospin, the new socialist prime minister, together with others in his cabinet, conferred with Premier Bouchard and his party during their visit to Paris from 28 September to 2 October 1997.[30]

Nearly all members of the Quebec mafia in France attended either a university or one of the *grandes écoles*, particularly the *École des sciences politiques* or the *École normale supérieure*, but so have most other French public men. More influential in their education, perhaps, were two other grandes écoles: the ENA, founded in 1945 specifically to form patriotic civil servants, and the *École nationale de la France d'Outre-mer* (ENFO), intended to train colonial civil servants. These institutions have proud records of public service among their lists of graduates, who appear to recognize one another, almost like members of clubs or like graduates of Sandhurst Military College in England or Yale University in the United States. However, the part these schools play in French public life cannot be compared with those of Oxbridge or the U.S. Ivy League, because only a relatively few students pass through them: the ENA accepts only about a hundred students a year, and there are less than five thousand of its graduates in France today.[31] It is therefore significant that one or other of these two schools is listed in the *curriculum vitae* of most members of the French Quebec mafia: this associates them closely with such other ENA graduates as Chirac, Fabius, Jospin, Juppé, and many more, and with General de Gaulle and Debré, who founded the ENA precisely for the purpose of forming a ruling élite.

The ENA is not uniformly Gaullist in the orientation of its graduates, but it implements a Gaullist policy in training an élite for government service and in reinforcing the leadership of officials in national life. In this it is carrying on an old French tradition that can be traced back to Louis XIV and earlier.[32] It is also carrying on some of the principles for forming a national managerial élite that were embodied in the Vichy government's *École nationale des cadres d'Uriage* during the Second World War.[33] The state has always been immensely powerful in France, notwithstanding the post-revolutionary concern for "la Nation" and its liberties. This is the case because the civil and military services are the practical embodiment and general managers of the nation.

National patriotism is the strongest inspiration in the ENA. The directions that it takes can be seen in the choice of names for the grad-

Table 6.1
Names chosen by the first fifty-four graduating classes of the French ENA

1946–47	France combattante	1970–72	Charles de Gaulle
1946–48	Union française	1971–73	François Rabelais
1974–48	Croix de Lorraine	1972–74	Simone Weil
1947–49	Nations unies	1973–75	Léon Blum
1948–49	Jean Moulin	1974–76	Guernica
1948–50	Quarante-huit	1975–77	André Malraux
1949–51	Europe	1976–78	Pierre Mendès-France
1950–52	Jean Giraudoux	1977–79	Michel de l'Hospital
1951–53	Paul Cambon	1978–80	Voltaire
1952–54	Felix Eboué	1979–81	Droits de l'homme
1953–55	Albert Thomas	1980–82	H.F. d'Aguesseau
1954–56	Guy Desbos	1981–83	Solidarité
1955–57	France-Afrique	1982–84	Louise Michel
1956–58	Dix-huit juin	1983–85	Léonard de Vinci
1957–59	Vauban	1984–86	Denis Diderot
1958–60	de Tocqueville	1985–87	Fernand Braudel
1959–61	Lazare Carnot	1986–88	Michel de Montaigne
1960–62	Albert Camus	1987–89	Liberté, Egalité, Fraternité
1961–63	Saint-Just	1988–90	Jean Monnet
1962–64	Blaise Pascal	1989–91	Victor Hugo
1963–65	Stendhal	1990–92	Condorcet
1964–66	Montesquieu	1991–93	Léon Gambetta
1965–67	Marcel Proust	1992–94	Saint-Exupéry
1966–68	Turgot	1993–95	René Char
1967–69	Jean Jaurès	1994–86	Victor Schoelcher
1968–70	Robespierre	1995–97	Marc Bloch
1969–71	Thomas More	1996–98	Valmy

Source: Rafaële Rivais, "ENA, le cérémonial du baptême," Le Monde, 22 Jan. 1998, 14.

uating classes (promotions), listed in Table 6.1; these names are as many clues to the official vision of France. The first duty of ENA graduates, above all else, is to promote the nation's independence and prestige in the world. Among the many consequences of this mission, two stand out in the context of this book. First, the ENA works against any tendency to favour private initiative or to reduce the power of the state. The ENA and the spirit behind it are a powerful bulwark against the privatization so widespread in the 1990s. Second, the ruling élite of Quebec has been learning to imitate this French state of affairs. One evident proof is the creation in 1970 of a Quebec *École nationale d'administration* staffed largely by convinced separatists. It is not too much to say that the separatist/sovereigntist movement in Quebec is sustained by the *cadres* of the provincial government, led more and more by graduates of Quebec's ENA. Quebec is gradually modelling itself in this respect on the Fifth Republic. The liberal forces of an open parliamentary democracy inevitably find it hard to survive in such a régime, and this was one reason why General de Gaulle, for whom parliamentary political life was merely a form of corruption, encouraged Michel Debré to found the ENA.[34] It is not yet clear whether the Quebec public will have more success than the French people in resisting an all-powerful government of zealous ideologues.[35] Here was one of the less obvious but fundamental issues haunting the elections to the French National Assembly and the Canadian Parliament, taking place between 25 May and 2 June 1997.

The flavour of the ENA marks the French Quebec mafia, but some of its members did not attend that prestigious school. A remarkable number have had education and experience in colonial administration, particularly those who might be described as founders. Most have had links with the former colonies of French-speaking Africa in one way or another. The outstanding example is Jacques Foccart (born Jacques Koch), one of the original Gaullist "barons," who after the Second World War headed his own intelligence network active mainly in Africa and in former colonies elsewhere.[36] Gilbert Pérol and Philippe Séguin were both born in Tunis, and Séguin went to school there. Pérol subsequently held various posts in North Africa and in 1983 was appointed ambassador to Tunisia.

Most Gaullist leaders, however, served in the French colonial service in Africa at one time or another. Xavier Deniau was schooled at the ENFO and served for many years from 1944 as a colonial administrator in Indochina, Cameroon, Dakar, and elsewhere. Jacques Larché likewise attended the ENFO and has the *médaille colonial* among his decorations. Yvan Bourges, Étienne Georges Burin des Roziers, and Martial de la Fournière all had experience in North Africa as colonial administrators before their ambassadorial careers.[37] Bernard Dorin spent a year as a lieutenant in Algeria before being posted to the embassy in Ottawa in August 1957. Robert Bordaz, who was sent to oversee the French pavilion at the Montreal World's Fair in 1967, had colonial experience. Alain Peyrefitte was charged from 1962 with repatriation of French Algerians to France, and he has written articles in *Le Monde* on Africa. Philippe Rossillon returned to France from Algeria in 1958 to join the *Patrie et Progrès* movement and was involved in the founding of the *Agence de cooperation culturelle et technique* (ACCT), which began at Niamey.[38] Among the separatist advisers to the PQ government of Quebec, André Patry, a civil servant and professor of international law at Laval University, had a special interest in the countries of the Mediterranean and played parts in what Dale Thomson calls "Power Struggles in Africa".[39]

There is a link between French North African experience and a desire to stimulate Quebec separatism. Profoundly shocked by the force of national movements for independence, particularly in Indochina and Algeria, where France suffered humiliating defeats in the 1950s, the Gaullists, led by the general himself, soon perceived that nationalism might be harnessed to work for France as well as against it. "Decolonizing ought not to be a one-way street," De Gaulle remarked one day to Alain Peyrefitte. "If we are decolonizing our African colonies, there is no reason why the French of Canada should remain colonized."[40] He believed that French patronage might cultivate the ethnic forces of language, culture, and history for their political yield among the French-speaking populations outside France, and the largest of these was in Canada. A commonwealth might be constructed on these unifying forces.

The objective was, of course, not to incorporate all the French-speaking peoples in the French republic but to lead them in a world-wide French league that would begin with exchanges and cooperative ventures of all kinds and move on to whatever common policies might be worked out. De Gaulle carefully refrained from defining these initiatives and spoke of them as "adventures." Gaullist France began to behave somewhat like a multinational corporation, but with a view to acquiring influence and prestige rather than financial profits.

A Vision and a Mission

De Gaulle's much repeated "certaine idée de la France," elastic and ambiguous though it was, emerged fundamentally as an imperial vision. It is an old idea in a new form. The French nationalism that inspires the ideology of Gaullism was a result of imperial thinking from its very beginning in the French Revolution. It was what drove the forces of the French nation that the government of the First Republic unleashed on Europe beginning in April 1792, when it declared war on the Habsburgs of Vienna and the Hohenzollerns of Berlin, and it kept them fighting for a quarter century. The objectives of Gaullist foreign policy have been a modified form of the "gloire," "prestige," or "grandeur" that was the objective of French foreign policy under Napoleons I and III and the Bourbon kings before them, particularly Louis XIV.

There are differences, of course. The long rule of Louis XIV (1661–1715) was devoted to imposing the Roman Catholic religion on the world, as well as French hegemony, whereas Charles de Gaulle and most of his followers have been perfunctory or passive Catholics. Their Catholicism is merely part of a much more powerful ideology of

French nationalism. This ideology is what enabled de Gaulle to appeal
to the latent patriotic feelings of people from all parts of the political
spectrum, even Communist idealists such as André Malraux. "I
replaced the proletariat with France," Malraux said in an interview
with a reporter.[41] "De Gaulle for me," he told another reporter in
Montreal, "is first the honour and justice of France, in France, and
much of the honour and justice of the world."[42]

The French Quebec mafia took on a new lease of life in November
1976 when the PQ was elected. This event gave the francophile Québécois some much-needed dignity in French eyes. The mafia had always
paid particular attention to some of the most vocal and Frenchified
leaders, such as Jean-Marc Léger, whose editorials in Le Devoir were a
kind of bellwether for the Department of External Affairs in Ottawa
and were read with care by de Gaulle himself.[43] When Léger was
appointed secretary-general of the Agence de coopération culturelle et
technique formed at the Niamey conference in 1968, Le Monde published a brief biography of him.[44] Le Devoir, in which he wrote so
many francophile editorials, has become virtually a separatist organ, as
can be seen in its strenuous efforts during the weeks leading up to each
of the referenda to persuade its readers to vote "yes." Other francophile Québécois, too, such as Louise Beaudoin and Jacques Parizeau,
have never ceased to work with their friends in the French Quebec
mafia.

RITUAL, TRADITION AND MYSTERY

More than thirty years ago, Pierre Viansson-Ponté described Gaullism
as a movement based on mystic ties of fidelity to Charles de Gaulle,
like the feudal ties holding together a brotherhood in the Middle Ages:
"Gaullism is first and foremost a compagnonnage."[45] Like an order of
medieval knights, the Gaullists hold a certain fascination for large
numbers of ordinary French citizens, who subscribe to the myths about
de Gaulle's role in the Second World War. There is or was – some have
died – an inner circle of about three dozen men who were with de
Gaulle in London or Algiers during the war, and among them are a few
who have been sympathetic to the cause of Quebec independence:
Burin des Roziers, Michel Debré, Jacques Foccart, Pierre Messmer, and
probably Maurice Schumann. These and their kind are the Gaullist
"barons," deemed to be noblest of all. On ceremonial occasions, a
group of them was to be seen trooping about with their master, as on
19 December 1964, when I saw them striding (not marching) up the
blvd Saint-Michel on their way to move the resistance hero Jean
Moulin into the Panthéon. The sight reminded me irresistibly of a gang

of bandits walking into town, as in an old cowboy film such as *High Noon*.

Not far outside the inner circle is another made up of people who were in the *résistance*, or on the staff of de Gaulle's provisional government, which ruled France from 1944 to 1946, or in the RPF during the Fourth Republic. Among them, too, are a few who, though younger, have entered this second mystic circle by doing much faithful service in Gaullist causes. This second circle includes Jacques Chirac, Xavier Deniau, Captain François Flohic, Martial de la Fournière, Yves Guëna, Michel Habib-Deloncle, Jean-Daniel Jurgensen, Jean de Lipkowski, Pierre de Menthon, Gilbert Pérol, Alain Peyrefitte, and René de la Sausaye, marquis de Saint-Légier.

Some of these men, and others even more distant from the charmed inner circle, such as Dorin, Mallen, Rossillon, and Séguin, are among the most fiercely loyal Gaullists, intent as they are on earning credentials that may allow them to move up in the hierarchy as greater colleagues die off. Their careers show long, arduous service in diplomacy, or in cultural agencies such as the *Haut comité pour la langue française*, or in administration, or even in the intellectual and literary world that had a part to play in de Gaulle's kingdom. He almost invariably sent comments or notes of congratulation to authors who sent him their books, especially books that might in some way add to the glory of France. French authorities have seldom failed to reward agents abroad, formal and informal. Rossillon and his deputy, Lucien Bertin, founding president and vice-president respectively, of the Franco-Acadian association, *Amitiés acadiennes*, were decorated in 1981 by Jacques Chirac, mayor of Paris, with the highest award that the city has to offer – the Médaille de Vermeil – "in recognition of their tireless activity in favour of *la francophonie*."[46] When he died in 1997, Rossillon was given a splendid hero's funeral on 1 October with a mass in Paris at Saint-Louis des Invalides and twenty laudatory memorial speeches in the *Salon d'honneur* of the Military Gallery (Musée de l'Armée).[47]

Honours

The satirical journal *Le Canard Enchaîné* continually wrote of de Gaulle as though he were holding a royal court like that of Louis XIV (1661–1715) and behind the fun there was much truth. The Gaullist hierarchy still resembles the Bourbon. Most members of the inner and second circles have received whatever honours the Fifth Republic has to confer. Probably the highest decoration is the *Croix de la Libération*, which de Gaulle adopted and began to confer in 1940; Viansson-Ponté, a sceptical observer of the régime, counts a total of thirty-nine *Compagnons de la Libération*. Among them at least two, André Malraux and Maurice Schumann, though they might not be counted as members of the Quebec mafia, have certainly been in sympathy with its purposes. The atmosphere in which rising Gaullists become festooned with the republic's many decorations is perhaps best conveyed by listing those held by one of them.

Bernard Dorin is a particularly devoted enemy of the Canadian confederation. His many decorations fall into three main groups: honours and rewards by the French government, courtesies by the governments of foreign countries wherever he had a diplomatic posting, and a miscellaneous group that is mainly of private or non-governmental origin, though the shadow of Gaullist policy can be glimpsed in the background. By 1976 the French authorities that Dorin served had made him *Chevalier de l'ordre national de Mérite*, *Chevalier des Palmes académiques*, *Chevalier du Mérite agricole*, and *Chevalier du Mérite postale*, and he had the *Médaille des opérations de sécurité et du maintien de l'ordre en Afrique du Nord*. By 1997 he was, in addition, *Officier de la Légion d'Honneur*, *Commandeur des Palmes académiques*, and *Officier des arts et lettres et du Mérite agricole* and held the title *Ambassadeur de France*, a distinction not given lightly.

Foreign governments had meanwhile awarded Dorin titles as *Officier des ordres nationaux de la République du Sénégal* and also the same for the *République du Gabon*, *Chevalier de l'ordre national du Tchad*, *Commandeur de l'ordre du Mérite de Malte*, and "*Grand Croix, Grand Officier, Commandeur et Officier des ordres nationaux du Brésil, d'Haïti, de Côte d'Ivoire, du Cameroun, du Sénégal, du Gabon, du Tchad, du Japon, du Mérite, de l'Ordre Souverain de Malte.*" While he was serving as ambassador in London the British government made him an honorary Knight Grand Cross of the Royal Victorian Order (a family order in the sovereign's gift) in July 1993, on the visit of President Mitterrand to England.[48]

Dorin was also keen to list his recognition as *Membre du comité directeur de l'Association de solidarité francophone*, *Conseiller de l'Association France-Québec*, *Membre et président d'honneur du cercle Richelieu-Senghor de Paris*, and *Membre-fondateur de France–Québec*. As the distinguished M. Dorin, who might in England call himself Sir Bernard Dorin, is still only sixty-seven years old and Gaullists tend to live long, he may gather yet more decorations – if there are any. Dorin's vanity is perhaps exceptionally great, but Gaullists tend to dwell in a realm wherein rewards and recognition from higher authority count for a great deal, as they have in the past during the reigns of the Bourbons and the Bonapartes.

Decorations and honours have also been conferred on political leaders from French-Canadian communities, to great effect. For example, on 3 November 1977 Giscard d'Estaing ceremonially named René Lévesque a *Grand Officier de la Légion d'Honneur*.[49] The previous day, when visiting the National Assembly in Paris, Lévesque had been invited, as a rare honour, to pass into the Palais Bourbon by way of a great staircase that no one had used since Louis XVIII in the early nineteenth century. This honour was also conferred on Premier Jacques Parizeau in January 1995, but for him the French government even opened a protective grille that had been kept closed since Woodrow Wilson's visit in 1919.[50] When Parizeau was introduced to the National Assembly by Edgar Faure, all the députés stood up to welcome him. Membership in the Legion of Honour was later conferred upon Jacques-Yvan Morin, former vice-premier of Quebec, and Louise Beaudoin, as *Déléguée générale du Québec* in Paris. Father Léger Comeau from New Brunswick was similarly honoured on 1 December 1988 by Président Mitterrand "for the rôle he has played in the defence of the Acadian people," and so was another Acadian, Gilbert Finn, in 1992.[51] Few ambassadors of Canada have been received with such warmth and such honours.

In March 1998, Premier Lucien Bouchard was decorated with the Grand Cross of the Ordre de la Pléiade, which has also been presented to Jacques Chirac and a former prime minister, Raymond Barre.[52]

Ceremonies and Signs

As General Jean Victor Allard remarked, "in de Gaulle's eyes, decorations had a political character."[53] When de Gaulle proposed to make Allard, who was a senior Canadian officer, a *Grand Officier de la Légion d'Honneur*, it was evidently his intention to count him among the Quebec nationalists so honoured, for he was angry when Allard refused the honour, as Canadian policy required. Allard had thereby shown his Canadian, federalist loyalty. He was immediately treated in Paris as persona non grata; journalists were instructed not to attend his news conference, and several previously planned events were cancelled. It was apparently a matter of total indifference to de Gaulle that Allard had already been made *Chevalier de la Légion d'Honneur* and decorated with the *Croix de Guerre* while fighting with French troops during the Second World War.

Gaullists, like the followers of certain other causes, live in a realm that is full of special ceremonies and mysterious signs. Now, as in de Gaulle's time, much significance is attached to the seating arrangements at dinners and meetings in Paris. These reflect favour as well as rank.[54] Robert Pichette relates with wonder, as in a fairy tale, how four humble Acadians were welcomed and honoured by de Gaulle and his entourage. They were allowed to place a wreath on the tomb of the unknown soldier, a ceremony normally reserved for heads of state, which showed "the importance that General de Gaulle attached to the visit of the Acadian delegates."[55] A special Gaullist emotion is stirred by the story that the general once placed a wreath on the tomb of the unknown soldier on which the ribbon said merely "Québec."[56]

Lucien Bouchard tells in his memoirs how his first meeting as Canadian ambassador with President Mitterrand, in September 1985, was regarded at the Canadian embassy as a triumph because it lasted five minutes longer than the American ambassador's meeting.[57] Similarly, when Marcel Masse replaced Claude Roquet as *Délégué général* of Québec in Paris, his first meeting with Prime Minister Juppé was supposed to last for only fifteen minutes, but Juppé let it go on for half an hour, "which shows the quality and warmth of our relations," Masse declared.[58] Earlier that spring President Jacques Chirac sent a message of congratulations when Bouchard replaced Parizeau – a signal honour, the normal protocol being a message only from the French prime minister. The story is told, with reverence, of how the hat that de Gaulle wore during his visit to Quebec in July 1967 was conveyed to Bernard Dorin by a messenger as a token of presidential gratitude.[59] Such symbols and the emotions they stir in some quarters were the stuff of life at the court of Louis XIV.

De Gaulle and his followers have used historic symbols to good effect. The emotions they evoke among French-speaking people are difficult to estimate but are certainly strong in many quarters. Even when they make fun of symbols, people in France and Canada are not immune to them. Choosing symbolic dates, for example, especially anniversaries, is deliberate and probably effective in moving public opinion: sending Malraux to Montreal in 1963, two centuries after the fatal Treaty of Paris, and making a presidential visit in July 1967, a century after Confederation, are good examples. As early as October 1963 a reporter in *Le Monde* wrote "The visit of M. Malraux will perhaps have contributed to the crystallizing of a movement of liberation, economic, cultural and even political, of French Canada."[60] De Gaulle's visit to Quebec in July 1967 was laden with symbolism, from the voyage in a warship named *Le Colbert*, through the stop at Saint-Pierre, and the landing at Anse-au-Foulon, where General Wolfe's army had made its successful assault on 13 September 1759, to the imperial progress along the *Chemin du Roy* and the *bain de foule* (a bath in the crowd) in Montreal.

The last device was a wonderfully effective piece of demagoguery in which de Gaulle used to dive suddenly into the crowd, to the dismay of his handlers and security men, shake hands, exchange quick remarks, turn this way and that, pat small children, and emerge at last with his clothing rumpled and sometimes buttons missing. It made this bleak, snobbish old officer seem democratic, which he was not; it had the effect of lending him the common touch. In that way he was able to make a sensation wherever he went. And he went nearly all over the world, everywhere in France again and again, as no president had before him, taxing the travelling arrangements of the Élysée to the limit.

Redolent of the monarchy and the empire, the Gaullist régime and its symbols touch the emotions of such French Canadians as join nationalist movements. When the *Rassemblement pour l'indépendance nationale* (RIN) was founded in 1960, it carefully arranged the official founding to be on 13 September, date of the battle of the Plains of Abraham, and adopted a stylized *fleur de lis* as its emblem.[61] Many members were, or had been, also members of the secret Order of Jacques Cartier. Though *la Patente* has gone, the clergy's influence lingers on, and it is alleged that the many branches of the *Club Richelieu* still express the spirit of the older organization. The mentality that it engendered is visible, for example, in the symbolism that touched Acadians and was carefully observed by the Quebec lobby in France when the new place d'Acadie was established in 1984 next to the church of Saint-Germain des Près, where Laval, the first bishop of New France, was consecrated in 1658.

PART TWO

Canada's Responses

Marcel Cadieux Fights Back

The Canadian federal government could hardly avoid becoming aware of Gaullist intervention in Canada in 1963 and the years following. Intended to encourage and assist Quebec nationalism, interference from France touched a perennially sore spot in Canadian political life. For a long time, however – years in some cases – many responsible people in Ottawa believed that the initiative for French involvement came entirely from Quebec and that French activity occurred only in response to appeals from the provincial government. The new vigour in Franco–Quebec relations during the early 1960s seemed like nothing more than part of the Quiet Revolution. English Canadians, as allies of France during the First World War and admirers of Charles de Gaulle's romantic adventure during the Second, were very reluctant to believe that Paris would be hostile in any serious way. As Canadians they were largely ignorant of French history, did not see themselves as heirs of past Anglo–French struggles, and were simply puzzled by Gaullist attitudes towards *les Anglo-Saxons*.

All over English-speaking Canada there were friends of Gaullist France ready to be critical of those in Quebec who espoused a narrow nationalism and for the semi-fascist Vichyite sympathies of some during the recent war. French activities in Canada were widely imputed to the machinations of Quebec nationalists. Even now I meet people who continue to believe that de Gaulle's "Vive le Québec libre!" had nothing to do with French policy and was only a slip of the tongue, merely a proud old Frenchman's momentary response to a moving situation. Quebec might be hostile to Canada, but France could not be. In 1963–64 Professor F.J. Soward at the University of British Columbia, who had strong connections in Ottawa and was a close observer of international events who wrote extensively on Canada in world affairs, told me he thought I had gone badly wrong in my analysis of the Fifth Republic during a series of thirteen radio talks on the CBC in Vancouver. Even so, I had not yet seen Gaullist aggression towards Canada for what it was but had only commented on the violence, dictatorial tendencies, and international ambitions of de Gaulle's government.

In federal government circles one of the most sensitive observers was Marcel Cadieux, who had joined the Department of External Affairs on 21 August 1941, risen to be deputy under-secretary of state in 1960, and served as under-secretary (i.e. deputy minister) from 1964 until 1970, when he went to Washington, DC, as Canadian ambassador. Cadieux was an experienced diplomat with a thorough education in international law – he taught it at the University of Ottawa from 1956 to 1963 – and he had a firm loyalty to Canada, along with an unsentimental attitude towards France and Quebec that was different from the affection of some other French Canadians.[1] Convinced that Quebec's best course was to work for equality within the Confederation, he became, as we see below, more and more anxious as he first watched the manifestations of Quebec separatism and French interference that began with André Malraux's visit in 1963, coped with the events of 1967 and their effects, and then worked under Pierre Trudeau. We go on to consider the policy that he and colleagues worked out behind the scenes to deal with the Gaullists, their responses to the Gaullists, and the attitudes of Canadian ministers.

In his watchfulness, Cadieux was almost alone, at least in higher governing circles. As far as I can discover, Prime Minister Pearson, Paul Martin at External Affairs, and the rest of the cabinet and the senior civil service did not share Cadieux's apprehensions until General de Gaulle had expressed his hostility to Canada at length in his press conference of 27 November 1967. The next day, during a cabinet meeting, Paul Martin had the grace to declare that Cadieux had seen de Gaulle's intentions three years earlier; Pearson and the rest of the cabinet agreed, and they all clapped and beat their desks in approval, according to Canadian parliamentary habit.[2] No tribute could have been better deserved. Yet no worthy civil servant has been more flagrantly ignored by the Canadian press and consequently by the public.

GROWING ANXIETY

Constant Struggle, 1963–66

We find Cadieux almost three years earlier busy with the complex task of persuading French authorities to channel their cultural relations through the federal government in order to reach French Canadians throughout the country and not only in Quebec. He already suspected de Gaulle of systematic hostility towards Canada. After all, from early in June 1964 de Gaulle had virtually turned his back on the new Canadian ambassador to France, Jules Léger, a personal friend of Cadieux's, while treating the *Délégué général du Québec* almost as though he were the ambassador of a sovereign state. The trouble began when Léger, presenting his credentials to de Gaulle, told him that changes taking place in Canada "cannot be made against France; our origins and traditions are opposed to that. It is a question of knowing whether they will take place without France or with France."[3] Putting the worst possible construction on these words, de Gaulle treated our ambassador to a hostile speech about how France was inevitably involved in Canada by virtue of its large minority of "French" people. In November that year Léger was not invited to a luncheon for Premier Jean Lesage held at the Élysée. Throughout the 1960s, Cadieux was able to grasp what was happening by keeping in touch with his opposite numbers in Europe and he also had a well-informed friend in Paris – someone close to Jacques Soustelle in Mme Cadieux's opinion – who kept him discreetly abreast of de Gaulle's intentions.[4]

From the time Cadieux was promoted to under-secretary of state on 7 May 1964, and perhaps earlier, he set out to develop a policy that would prevent Gaullist officials from winning Quebec away from Canada. In this activity he showed unusual insight and a characteristic desire to take the bull by the horns. Observers in Quebec had already marked him as "a mandarin ... who sees red as soon as the couple France–Quebec is mentioned."[5] The Quebec City daily, *Le Soleil*, described him as "in many respects the least diplomatic diplomat possible. He is known for his frank talk."[6]

His colleagues from those years are now divided, I find, in their opinions of his words and his behaviour. Those who see no harm, even now, in French activities in Quebec tend to think that he exaggerated, did not really mean what he wrote in the 1960s, and (some argue) may have been mildly paranoid. In contrast, those who take French interference in Canada, then and now, as a serious threat say that he meant every word of what he wrote. One or two of his surviving colleagues even admit to sharing his views. His personal journal in the form of secret memoranda, written almost daily, suggests that he may have been the only high-ranking official at External Affairs with a sound grasp of the issues. So far I have found no other. Cadieux was, moreover, not only firm but also well-informed, cautious, moderate, and intellectually well-prepared.

By the beginning of 1965 he was already trying to draw the government of Quebec into an agreement on principle that would bring the federal government into Quebec's relations with France. The purpose of this arrangement was to win Quebec's approval for the terms of the proposed *accord-cadre* to be signed with France. Cadieux's official contacts in Quebec City for this purpose were Claude Morin, the minister for intergovernmental affairs, and Paul Gérin-Lajoie, minister of education, though neither of them was a friend or ally. But he had friends in Quebec, as well as in France, who kept him informed. On 20 January 1965 he wrote:

The *accord-cadre* is ready. I must send the draft of it to Morin one day soon. At the next stage, that is when [p. 2] we consult the provinces with federal government approval, my intention is to suggest to Ontario, Nouveau-Brunswick and Manitoba that the three of them set up a programme of cultural relations with France and that they appoint mixed commissions. My intention is to demonstrate to France, if there is some way of doing so, that French life in Canada is not limited to Quebec and at the same time to demonstrate to certain fanatics in Quebec that they are not in a position to manage our relations with France (donner des dimensions valables) on a suitable scale. The operation promises to be difficult but I have high hopes of arranging for the credit of $250,000 allotted for relations with the French- speaking world to be doubled, at least. If I succeed, it will then be easier to prime the pump [of federal funding for this purpose].[7]

Quebec's relations with France were to be brought, if possible, into an expanded federal program of cooperation with the world-wide club of French-speaking countries, *la francophonie*.

The government of the Fifth Republic began to see Cadieux as an opponent at some time in 1965 or 1966, and he was well aware of this. Near the end of a trip to Poland, Russia, Italy, and France in November 1966 he went to receive an honorary degree at the Université de Poitiers. He was astonished to find himself received there with a cold embarrassment and even a touch of hostility. His hosts behaved as though they wished they were somewhere else, and even his gift of 850 books, worth some $5,000, evoked no friendly response.

Reflecting on this occasion, he soon came to the conclusion that the university authorities thought they had made a mistake in inviting a federalist such as he and had been reprimanded by the French government. He had a strong impression that the idea of giving him this degree had come from what he called the friendly "clan Azard et Malaurie," and plans had gone too far by the time the Quai d'Orsay had objected.[8] Unable to back out, the university had gone through with the presentation as though it were a painful duty. Cadieux told this story in a memorandum of 28 November 1966. However, he still did not see the full extent of French hostility. As late as 8 December 1966 he thought that de Gaulle was only trying to encourage Quebec and simply did not realize how the separatists would make use of his efforts.[9]

Centennial Year and After

It was at the turn of the year that the truth dawned on him. During his European tour in December 1966 stories by officials from Luxemburg and Belgium, notably André de Staercke, the astute Belgian representative to NATO, began to make Cadieux anxious, and he heard alarming reports from people at the Canadian embassy in Paris. For instance, James George "assured me that [Robert] Bordaz, commissioner of the French pavillion at Expo ought to be watched. He is apparently in the good graces of the Élysée and Jim George believes that it is he who may have brought [Montreal] Mayor [Jean] Drapeau to lunch at the Élysée and invited a French minister to open the Metro in Montréal. All things considered, we are meeting serious difficulties in putting into effect our policy of *rapprochement* with France. If we do nothing, we shall run the risk of providing arguments for the separatists, we shall give Quebec a good opportunity to take control of *la francophonie* and to use it as a war horse for winning confirmation of its international status. On the other hand, if we leave the doors open, I have the impression that the French villain [le larron français] will get in and may do serious damage."[10] By January 1967 Cadieux was beginning to see the French government as an enemy.

On 12 January he told Governor General Georges Vanier that de Gaulle must have looked for a way to take offence at Ambassador Jules Léger's words on 1 June 1964 in order to insult the Canadian government by ignoring him and courting the *Délégué du Québec* in Paris. His suspicions were confirmed, several months before de Gaulle's visit of July 1967, in stages that we can trace in his personal memoranda. As a result of a long talk with the French ambassador in Ottawa on 25 January, he came to the conclusion that de Gaulle was indeed working for the separation of Quebec.[11] He repeated this conviction on 27 February, with some satisfaction, "now that the General has revealed his game. Earlier, I was wondering with anxiety whether our suspicions about him were justified. I was inclined to believe with the Minister [Paul Martin] that I was seeing Indians behind every tree."

By 12 July Cadieux was lamenting that Martin still refused to believe that the French president had such damaging intentions. De Gaulle's press conference of 27 November 1967 only confirmed his own conclusions. "The General is not content to prophesy [that Quebec will become a separate sovereign state]." he wrote to Paul Martin in a four-page memo. "He is attempting now to influence and speed up the process of Canada's disintegration. In fact, he confidently expects that once Quebec breaks connections with Ottawa it will rush into the arms of France."[12] Even the movement for la francophonie was beginning to seem to Cadieux like a screen for Gaullist aggression. In memos of 13 and 19 February 1968 he wrote in a matter-of-fact way that de Gaulle "wants to destroy our country."

From the beginning of that year he referred angrily to "le vieillard, maléfique et rancunier" (18 January 1968, 3), "ce vieux bandit" (27 June 1968, 3), "ce vieux fanatique" (21 August 1968, 4), and "les intempérances de ce vieux fou" (31 January 1969, 6). This was violent language, thoroughly unprofessional, but no rule of diplomacy says that a man cannot pour his feelings into his secret journal. Frustrated patriotism and a precocious grasp of what was really happening might have driven a weaker person mad. If he had to wait upon short-sighted politicians and an ignorant public, at least his journal as well as his wife and some of his colleagues would know that he was not a complacent, bloodless bureaucrat.

During 1969, notes of anger and bitter irony were sounding in some of Cadieux's memoranda. He saw that General de Gaulle and his servants were behaving brutally, without regard for protocol and legality, evidently bent on intimidating the Canadian government in order to carry on cultivating close relations with Quebec. Their "methods were those of veritable gangsters rather than civilized European statesmen."[13] "The French have decided to play rough," he wrote on 25 October 1969. "Unless it is that the Marseille element at the heart of the Quai d'Orsay (l'élément marseillais au sein du Quai d'Orsay) is now in control of things. At all events, we are now accused, we, of interfering in French affairs. As if it were we who went to shout in Paris "Vive la Bretagne ou Vive l'Alsace Libre". As if it were we who proclaimed in the course of a shattering press conference that French institutions were out of date, that France was an artificial entity and would not survive. The malice in all this is quite plain (cousue de fil blanc)."

During these years Cadieux felt very much alone in his dealings with France and Quebec. Few if any other mandarins shared his gloomy but – as it turned out – sound interpretation of what de Gaulle was up to. In fact, none seems to have done so except possibly Marc Lalonde in the Prime Minister's Office (PMO) and Gordon Robertson in the Privy Council Office (PCO), who recalls that he respected Cadieux's interpretation of French behaviour and agreed with his approach.[14] Cadieux wrote frank personal letters to his old friend Paul Tremblay, Canadian ambassador in Brussels. He also consulted his juniors in the department from time to time, able younger diplomats such as Alan Gotlieb, John Starnes, and Max Yalden, but he despaired of his political masters, Lester Pearson and Paul Martin, as two politicians who thought they knew best, only half understood the French problem, and took foolish steps in spite of expert advice to the contrary.

Pearson was vacillating, in Cadieux's opinion, and inclined to make diplomatic decisions on specious political grounds. This may have been partly because, as Cadieux suspected, one of Claude Morin's friends, Ghislain ("Gerry") Hardy, busied himself trying to discredit Cadieux and his anti-Gaullist projects in the PMO.[15] Whatever the reason, the prime minister made some fundamental mistakes, in Cadieux's judgment. The best example, which haunted Cadieux for years, was Pearson's sudden decision to let Couve de Murville, the French foreign minister, have a private talk with Premier Daniel Johnson in Quebec City on 30 September 1966. As an international lawyer, Cadieux knew that this meeting should not be permitted for any reason at all because it would serve as a precedent, allowing the premier of Quebec to confer thereafter with other French statesmen independently of Ottawa. Cadieux set out to prevent this disastrous precedent either by insisting that Paul Martin should be present at the interview or by cancelling Couve's visit to Quebec. However, at six p.m. on 26 September Pearson told Cadieux "that this problem should not be raised. Couve de Murville should be left to confer as he wished with Johnson because in his [Pearson's] opinion the public would not understand if the federal authorities sought to restrict the right of anyone in Canada and, in particular, the Premier of Quebec to interview whomever he wished."[16] And indeed this hasty, unwise decision contributed not a little to Quebec's growing independence in its relations with France.

A second devastating decision by Pearson was to allow de Gaulle to visit Quebec City first and then Ottawa later by way of Montreal, in July 1967. The Canadian government began by insisting, early in 1967, that the visit must begin at the capital of Canada, according to sound and established diplomatic principle. Cadieux had once again mobilized External Affairs to defend this principle. However, two months before the event Pearson gave way to pressure from France and Quebec. This careless concession left Cadieux angry and nearly ill with despair: "Yesterday, [Jack] Hodgson in the Prime Minister's Office, gave me some very bad news. According to him the PM had seen Mr. Johnson the previous day and told him that if he insisted on having Général de Gaulle begin his visit to Canada at Quebec, he, Mr. Pearson, would have no objection. I explained to Mr. Hodgson as well as to Mr. Gordon Robertson that once again, if this were true, the PM had cut the ground from under the feet of his federal advisers. I said frankly that if the PM continued to grant concessions and to make us look ridiculous in the eyes of Quebec, he would end by having no French-Canadian advisers. He would find himself at last with the separatists whom he seems to favour in all circumstances and with the relentless enemies of French-Canadians.[17] If we can manage to save anything, Cadieux reflected a few months later, history may say that Pearson rescued the furniture but sacrificed all the outbuildings and left the main house seriously shaken. If we fail, history will surely relate that he was too weak and that he ought to have had the courage to resist much earlier. We need a prime minister "who has something other than holy water in his belly."[18] Cadieux knew nothing, of course, about Pearson's strategy in providing for the Mobile Command that was to deal so successfully with the revolutionary crisis in October 1970, as explained below in chapter 10.

In general, Cadieux came to the conclusion that Pearson had a poor understanding of Quebec, was unfair in his dealings with French Canadians such as Favreau, Lamontagne, Tremblay, and even Trudeau, and took too much advice from his wife, who was stronger than he and whom he consulted frequently over the telephone from his office. A furious and somewhat unfair memo of 25 July 1967 (three pages), written immediately after de Gaulle's "Vive le Québec libre!" speech, and another of 21 February 1968, gave vent to Cadieux's feelings: "M. Pearson has never understood the French-Canadians. Besides, he and his wife detest them, and it is in times of crisis like the one we are presently going through that his ignorance of the French presence (la réalité française) in this country and his feebleness as the leader of the government does disservice to the vital interests of our country." Pierre Trudeau, then minister of justice, was likewise angry about Pearson's needless concession on this occasion, and the next year, in June 1968, Gordon Robertson told Cadieux that Trudeau (recently installed as prime minister) had a clearer mind and a better approach to diplomacy and would deal with Canada's Franco–Quebec problem more effectively.[19]

Cadieux lamented Pearson's weakness again and again, but Paul Martin filled him with a deep sense of dismay as a politician apparently indifferent to matters of foreign policy, the perpetrator of an unending series of blunders and misjudgments. "Encore une perle pour la collection" was Cadieux's usual introduction to another incident showing Martin as ambitious, ignorant, shallow, or dishonest. He lavished too much time and attention on his riding in Windsor and not enough on departmental business; he did not read essential memoranda; he put too much trust in his own ability to settle matters by speaking with "his friend" Couve de Murville; he refused to see de Gaulle's intentions even as late as mid-July 1967; he criticized Pearson disloyally and openly; he gave different versions of events to different people – told barefaced "lies," in Cadieux's opinion. When Jules Léger was to be replaced as ambassador in Paris, Martin had the dubious idea of appointing Jean Chapdelaine, whose judgment, in the opinion of some of his superiors, was not reliable and who was already suspected of being a Quebec separatist.

Cadieux agreed with Martin on few matters of policy. And as early as March 1965 he was satisfied that the cabinet had taken Martin's measure, too, and held an equally low opinion of him.[20] Cadieux's exasperation turned to contempt during the months in 1967 and early 1968 while Martin was widely regarded as a strong contender for the leadership of the Liberal party, Pearson having decided to retire. The last straw for Cadieux was when Martin, informed of Norman Robertson's sudden death, remained unmoved, almost indifferent, changed the subject, and carried on discussing the affairs of the day. "And to think that this brute is probably going to become our next prime minister!," Cadieux wrote in his journal on 30 December 1967.

WORKING WITH TRUDEAU, 1968–70

Great was his relief, therefore, when Pierre Elliott Trudeau won the leadership contest. Before this happened, a letter to Paul Tremblay on 28 February 1968 shows that Cadieux was hoping for a prime minister who could face the French with vigour and understanding. "My conclusion is that the Canadian government may possibly decide six months hence to have a major confrontation with Quebec and may decide that this confrontation should be about our relations with France." In March, Trudeau showed his mettle by speaking out firmly against Gabon's unilateral invitation to Quebec to attend an international conference. He began to take a courageous stand against Quebec, and sometimes against France, even before succeeding Pearson, but as prime minister he worried Cadieux and his department in another way.

Trudeau surrounded himself with a set of advisers, some of them personal friends, and seemed to turn his back on the Department of External Affairs. Cadieux noticed this situation in June 1968 and wrote a long, detailed account of it in a secret memorandum of 8 July. Mitchell Sharp, secretary of state for external affairs since April 1968, saw it too.[21] Gordon Robertson agreed with their observation and recalls that Trudeau tended to ignore External Affairs because of an old resentment for its haughty treatment of him when, as a student, he got into difficulties travelling abroad.[22] The people to whom Trudeau was listening were Edgar Benson, Donald Macdonald, Gérard Pelletier, Michael Pitfield, and others in the PMO. Furthermore, they and some of the men in the PCO, notably Hume Wright, Gerry Stoner, even Gordon Robertson, were inclined to take it on themselves to tell External Affairs what the prime minister wanted or intended. The trouble was that they gave various, sometimes contradictory accounts of Trudeau's thinking.

Mitchell Sharp, Martin's successor as minister, was kept at arm's length by the prime minister, possibly because he was not in agreement with Trudeau's plan to review and revise Canadian foreign policy.[23] Sharp remained rather timid in dealing with Trudeau and came late to the struggle with France and Quebec.[24] Though he writes a competent summary of events in his memoirs, he seems at the time to have left that struggle largely to his under-secretary.[25]

On 29 October 1968 Cadieux took the opportunity of a long meeting with Trudeau to say that he could not continue as under-secretary of state unless he was kept informed clearly and directly from the prime minister himself, rather than through all these intermediaries. Cadieux said that he felt like a cook working in the cellar to a series of contradictory orders shouted down to him by various people passing by.[26] Trudeau took this concern in good part and asked for advice on how to improve matters, adding that it was no use hoping to keep in touch by written memoranda, as he already had more of these than he could manage. The most practical solution seemed to be to keep in touch by telephone and to meet from time to time.

Pierre Trudeau also made the department anxious in other ways. He had a tendency to organize consultations with university professors, such as Ivan Head and James Eayrs, and to put matters of foreign policy before various groups of the general public. He did this, he told Cadieux, with the intention of bringing about a fundamental change in Canadian foreign policy. He thought that the department applied the Official Secrets Act in such a way as to give advising professors the feeling that some things were being kept from them. Cadieux did not think this was a serious problem; worse, he thought, when Trudeau went abroad he was sometimes more interested in having fun than in meeting foreign statesmen and playing a part in international affairs. Indeed, at the Commonwealth Conference in January 1969 Cadieux observed with some anxiety that Trudeau was attending social events and having breakfasts with lady friends even before he had read the files concerning the subjects of the conference. This tells us something about Cadieux, of course, but in his eyes the issues ought to have engaged Trudeau more seriously.

Cadieux worried too about the prime minister's inclination to discuss some matters with foreign leaders without keeping the department fully informed. Cadieux was shocked to discover in April 1969 that Trudeau had talked more candidly with Couve de Murville and U.S. President Richard Nixon about withdrawing Canadian forces from NATO than with Sharp and Cadieux himself.[27] Finally, not long before he was sent as Canadian ambassador to Washington, Cadieux concluded that Pierre Trudeau was not much interested in foreign policy and intended to concentrate on internal affairs. In particular, Gaullist aggression was being met by patient withdrawal rather than by the counter-attacks that Cadieux had been planning. It is true that much was hoped for when de Gaulle resigned on 28 April 1969, after being defeated in a referendum the previous day. By the time it had become clear that the aggressive Gaullist policies were still in force under his successors, Cadieux had gone to Washington and left the direction of the department to a successor.

BEHIND THE SCENES

Emerging Policy

Cadieux had faced Gaullist aggression almost alone in the years 1967–70 and done his best to fight back. The strain and frustration had been exhausting. Unwilling to trust Paul Martin and not entirely happy with his successor, Mitchell Sharp, who believed in leaving matters to his under-secretary, Cadieux discussed his problems most often with his wife. "He would sit me down at the table at any time of day or night and explain his ideas," Mme Cadieux recalls. During one crucial meeting he told Prime Minister Trudeau that he would occasionally lie awake most of the night worrying some problem and then suddenly shout out "Eurêka!," to the exasperation of his sleeping wife. The only senior member of the department whom he respected enough to consult about knotty problems was Norman Robertson. When Robertson died in May 1968, Cadieux wrote to his widow in letters of 17 May and 24 October, "As you know, during all these years Norman has been wonderfully kind and generous to me. After my father, there is no one to whom I am more indebted. Above all, Norman was a shining example of the virtues that we wish to practice in our profession. He was wise, he was not self-seeking. And yet when he had to be, in defence of principles, he was firm and fearless."[28] "I realize now that I am on my own. Yet almost every day I ask myself: 'How would Norman have reacted'? And just to do this helps very much."[29]

These were not merely comforting platitudes. Some of Cadieux's memos and his own widow confirm that Norman Robertson was indeed his hero and mentor. To clear and record his thoughts almost on a daily basis, however, Cadieux sent intimate letters to his old friend Paul Tremblay, Canadian ambassador to Belgium, and wrote his personal journal, sometimes three or four times a day, in the form of private memoranda.

These memos, on which the present chapter is largely based, offer glimpses of the three-part policy that Cadieux and his colleagues worked out for Canada to cope with Gaullist France and nationalist Quebec – maintain relations with France, participate in *la francophonie*, and develop ways to oppose Gaullist France. First and foremost, he endeavoured to avoid an open breakdown of diplomatic relations with France. This was because he foresaw that a suspension of Franco–Canadian relations would give Quebec good grounds for claiming to represent all French Canadians, perhaps Canada as well, in Paris and thus give Paris an excuse to recognize Quebec openly as sovereign and independent. He wrote to Tremblay on 19 September 1967, "Obviously, the French are behaving like pigs but if we recall the ambassadors we shall put Quebec in a situation where it will have an official and exclusive monopoly of relations with France."[30] Six months later he was explaining the same idea to Tremblay again, "The danger is that de Gaulle may withdraw his ambassador, that [Premier] Johnson may maintain that Ottawa has never been sincere in its desire to develop relations with France and that he, Johnson, Ottawa having no diplomatic relations with Paris, was well placed to represent French Canadians in the world of la francophonie."

In March 1973 Cadieux told a former French ambassador to Canada that if he could live through the events of July 1967 again he would recommend to Prime Minister Pearson to arrest de Gaulle and hold him in prison until he apologized and that such a breach of international etiquette would have been no worse than de Gaulle's speech in Montréal on 24 July.[31] Reflecting on this point again eighteen months later, in September 1974, he still thought that it would have been a good step to arrest de Gaulle but concluded that it might have been strategically too risky.[32] The essential point, as he saw things in 1967–68, was to defend Canada's juridical position. "On this," he wrote, "Jules [Léger, Canadian ambassador in Paris] does not see things as we do. What is certain is that if we neither say nor do anything, later when de Gaulle has gone, they will say that we have tacitly consented to the status that Quebec seems to be establishing, at least in relations with certain French-speaking states."[33]

Second, Cadieux did his best to encourage vigorous Canadian participation in *la francophonie*. By cultivating strong cultural relations with the French-speaking countries Canada might hope to engage Quebec together with other provinces, particularly New Brunswick, Ontario, and Manitoba, in Canadian policy abroad and thereby weaken bilateral links between Quebec and Paris. It was to this end that Ottawa began to offer more aid and stronger diplomatic links with French-speaking countries in Africa. Cadieux's hope was to open diplomatic posts in as many of those countries as possible. During 1968 and 1969 he records his department's struggle with the Treasury Board, and particularly Simon Reisman and Sylvain Cloutier, to obtain more funds for these purposes.

Cadieux engaged in a third activity which was to think of new ways for opposing Gaullist France and perhaps weakening its aggression towards Canada. In February 1968, he decided to bring de Gaulle's political opponents to Canada, regretted failing to invite Mitterrand who had recently visited the United States, and promptly asked the department's cultural service to get in touch with Jean-Jacques Servan-Schreiber, a prominent neswpaper editor, and with J.R. Tournoux, author of *La Tragédie du Général*. Tournoux arrived a week later, spoke critically about de Gaulle and Gaullism on the CBC, and was entertained at a lunch on 27 February. Cadieux also looked into the possibility of opening Canadian consulates in Guadeloupe, Martinique, and Alsace, "if the population there is sufficiently hostile to de Gaulle."[34]

He wondered whether French rights to the islands of Saint-Pierre and Miquelon might be challenged on the grounds that their original cession was for use as fishing bases, whereas France was now employing them for military and commercial purposes. In view of de Gaulle's offensive comments about Jews during the press conference of 27 November 1967, Cadieux thought it might be possible to stir up the Israelis against him in some way. And in view of the French decision to withdraw from NATO's command structure, some hostile response might be planned in conjunction with the German and British governments. "Of course," he wrote to Tremblay on 19 February 1968, "we have no illusions about the immediate yield of these measures. Neither the English nor the Americans nor the Germans have found the secret of controlling 'mon Général'. I see scarcely any possibility for us to succeed where they have failed."

At the lunch for J.R. Tournoux, the person sitting at Cadieux's left, a socialist deputy from Rouen named Tony Larue, told him that the Gaullist police routinely bugged his telephone and those of all members of the National Assembly.[35] Cadieux replied that he and his colleagues, when in Paris, supposed that their phones were tapped;

thirty years later, Mme Cadieux now tells me that in the 1960s a *femme de ménage* in Paris advised her to avoid the telephone at their hotel and to use a pay phone in the street.[36]

With such things in mind Cadieux planned to tell the Mackenzie Commission of Inquiry on National Security, when he appeared before it near the end of February 1968, that it was time Canada had a more effective counter-intelligence service. "The French do not hesitate to use microphones and listening devices in Paris hotel rooms. In my opinion, we ought to be better informed about what foreign agents, official and unofficial, are doing in Canada. *Le Canard Enchaîné* was writing openly last summer that France had been sending *barbouzes* to Canada loaded with money, who must have engaged in unsavoury work [qui ont dû se livrer à des besognes pas très catholiques]."[37]

Cadieux asked Pearson during an interview on 11 March 1968 whether Canada should be intercepting the telegraph messages and telephone conversations of the French embassy. Pearson agreed that it should be and promised to raise the matter discreetly with the solicitor general, Lawrence Pennell, and the minister of justice, Pierre Trudeau.[38] The other members of the cabinet, Paul Martin in particular, were not to be consulted. Unfortunately, Pearson's agreement on this occasion was exceptional and probably led nowhere. He was not as strong or decisive as Marcel Cadieux and was already thinking of his retirement.

Responding to the Gaullists

From time to time during the late 1960s Cadieux returned to the problem of coping with the underhanded activities of the French consulate at Quebec City. "It is clear," he reflected on 6 September 1968, "that France, in using its Consulate at Quebec as an unofficial embassy for political operations, is violating the Convention of Vienna." He knew that de Gaulle was totally indifferent to the legality or morality of this activity and that "provincial agents such as the Morins, the Patrys, the Cholettes, and other birds of the same plumage are only too pleased to conspire with the French against Ottawa." None of them would be likely to provide evidence of what the consulate was up to, and evidence was what the federal government needed in order to take up the matter with the French ambassador. Cadieux regretted that Canada had no service for espionnage or counter-espionnage that could gather such evidence. Canada is passably well equipped for dealing with the dangers of Communism, he thought, but not for defending itself against Quebec separatism and French efforts to encourage it. Still, this cannot be the first time a country has faced foreign interference: with this thought in mind, Cadieux asked Max Yalden and other colleagues in the department to give the problem serious study.

Ever watchful of French manoeuvres, and well-informed by people on both sides of the Atlantic, Cadieux was quick to see how the Gaullist government's hostility was taking on various disguises. On 8 and 9 February 1967 he told the French ambassador and his counsellor of "our surprise at being faced with a *fait accompli* by the French government's decision to grant its patronage to a company [une société] organized by Monsieur Bousquet for the purpose of stimulating the affairs of the francophone movement."[39] Still interested in that development seven months later, he wrote to Tremblay in Brussels on 19 September, "We have come to much the same conclusions as the Belgians on the subject of *la francophonie*. The French, by devious means, are using that machine to manipulate the other French-speaking countries. In our case, their famous 'private' associations which in reality are directed by the Gaullist party, are seeking to put Quebec in Canada's place in all circumstances ... The next offensive in this field will result in the creation of a meeting of Ministers of Education at which no doubt Quebec will represent Canada." Raymond Bousquet, French ambassador in Ottawa from 1962, had indeed been working to this end, along with other members of the French Quebec mafia. In spring 1964 he and Xavier Deniau had visited Paul Gérin-Lajoie, a prominent Quebec official, who recorded how they conspired at his house in Dorion, Quebec.[40]

Among the private or semi-private Gaullist agencies that Cadieux had in mind was the *Association de solidarité francophone* founded in November 1966 partly at the instigation of Raymond Bousquet, who was made president in January 1967. Bousquet intended it to be an umbrella or central agency for all the other burgeoning agencies in *la francophonie*. It soon had headquarters at 3 avenue Franklin Roosevelt, Paris 8ᵉ. A few months later, a Gaullist initiative led to the establishment of the *Association internationale des parlementaires de langue française* (AIPLF), founded on 18 May 1967 in Luxemburg, where it brought together representatives from twenty-seven national parliaments and six regional legislative assemblies. Its headquarters were soon fixed in Paris at 235 blvd Saint-Germain. When this body met again for three days in September 1968 at Versailles, its secretary-general was none other than Xavier Deniau, doing his best to encourage the representatives of Quebec to act independently in this context.[41]

Already in February 1968, Cadieux had asked Arthur Blanchette, the department's director of francophone affairs, to make a study of "the uses France is making of *la francophonie*."[42] Thus was the department kept abreast of the Gaullist mafia's many disguises, such as the *Association France–Québec* founded in 1969 (and a very large organization today). A glance at the list of its founders told Cadieux all he needed to know: it included Xavier Deniau, J.M. Domenach, Bernard Dorin, Martial de la Fournière, Pierre-Louis Mallen, and Philippe Rossillon. The membership of other less sinister Gaullists, such as Michel Bruguière, F.X. de Périer, and Auguste Viatte did nothing to reduce the menace of their more aggressive countrymen in Cadieux's mind. That the French government was ready to assist these various agencies became evident when the *Haut comité pour la défense et l'expansion de la langue française* was created by presidential decree on 31 March 1966, with twelve to eighteen members under the chairmanship of the French prime minister. They were to advise the government and suggest practical ways of promoting French in the world. It was as the *rapporteur général* of it that Philippe Rossillon worked among French-speaking communities in various parts of Canada in those years.

Taking another tack in facing the French menace, Cadieux decided to inform the public and spent one and a half hours on 12 March 1968 briefing Peter Newman about de Gaulle's cunning use of *la francophonie*, particularly of the small African members. He wanted Newman to bring out some articles that the French government would not like, to explain "why certain French-speaking countries such as Belgium and Switzerland, as well as Canada, should avoid [French] movements that remind one of the Cominform and of the Nazi Bund of sinister memory."[43] Ivan Head, then temporarily employed in the Department of Justice, was encouraged to publish "a very good article" supporting the federal point of view in the *Montreal Star* on the following Saturday. Yet another such article, written by George Szablowski and printed in *Le Devoir* in mid-March 1968, was sent off to Tremblay in Brussels. In the hope that publications such as the *American Journal of International Law* might expose de Gaulle's objectionable policies, Cadieux asked Max Yalden to write a White Paper (Livre blanc) on the limits of provincial authority in a federal state to deal with foreign affairs. This paper might also be useful, he reported to Tremblay, to a "société de propagande fédérale" recently founded in Montréal to publish replies to René Lévesque's book, *Option Québec*, and to the writings of André Patry and Jacques Brossard.[44]

Ministers' Responses

The foregoing steps and the thoughts behind them show that Cadieux was deeply angry with the Gaullist government and ready to fight back. He saw what it was up to and what it was trying to achieve. Unfortunately, he was surrounded by people in authority who knew less than he did, refused to believe most of what he told them, and took only a passing interest in the problems he raised. Until the end of November 1967 they tended to regard him as a wild extremist and even laughed at his views and proposals. They seldom did what he thought necessary even when they began to see that his judgment had been sound. On hearing that the federal cabinet had applauded him for his foresight in dealing with General de Gaulle, he commented that this did nothing to change the situation. "In other words," he wrote on 29 November 1967, "I am handsome, I smell good, I am intelligent, but no one listens to me."[45] He disagreed with Jules Léger, our ambassador in Paris, who feared de Gaulle's wrath and wanted to "walk on tiptoe" in order not to provoke him. Cadieux disagreed, too, with the cabinet and even despised it for its weakness and confusion. "We passed the morning," he wrote to Tremblay on 2 May 1968, "explaining to a divided, ignorant and frightened group of Ministers that for the last three years the federal wet hen has been losing all of its feathers, one by one, so that its behind is beginning to be embarrassingly visible. You see how it is. The Ministers want to fight on condition that they suffer no blows. They want a tough statement but one that will not provoke anyone. In short, we are to turn left and right at the same time, to do something and nothing."[46]

Certain individuals in the cabinet were particularly trying. Some of them were accusing Cadieux and External Affairs of being anti-French fanatics, inflexible and destructive of peaceful diplomatic relations. Troublesome in a different way were "idiots like Jean-Luc Pepin" who were prepared to give France technical information from Canadian nuclear laboratories without any consideration of how the French might use it. "I had to wage a war to the death for more than a week," Cadieux wrote to Tremblay on 16 May 1968, "to bring the government round against the advice of that sombre imbecile Pepin, and to send a telegram to [Lorne] Gray, now in Paris, to tell him not to commit himself to delivering our information to the French before 25 June."[47]

Even worse than these, in Cadieux's view, was Maurice Sauvé, the federal minister of forestry and rural development, whom he suspected of surreptitiously keeping Quebec and Paris informed. "With Sauvé in the cabinet," he wrote to Tremblay, "what is more infuriating is that Quebec like France must know exactly why we do not react in the circumstances."[48] He suspected Sauvé of revealing in 1967 and early 1968 that the government was paralysed by internal divisions, by uncertainty about the succession to Lester Pearson, and by reluctance to break off diplomatic relations with France because that might strengthen French bilateral relations with Quebec. Cadieux was not alone in his suspicions of Sauvé and could agree even with Paul Martin on that point.[49] Judy LaMarsh and Tom Kent, too, were sure that Sauvé was leaking information to Claude Morin and others in Quebec and France.[50] "It seems to us," Cadieux wrote to Tremblay on 16 May 1968 (without clarifying his royal "us"), "that this Government is stuffed with imbeciles (farci d'imbéciles) and that it is a miracle if each time [there is a crisis] we succeed in doing something."[51]

CONCLUSION

In retrospect, it seems clear that in Canadian policy towards France Cadieux's harsh words might be repeated today. We are living even now with the consequences of the federal government's failings in those years. And Cadieux foresaw these consequences with profound exasperation. As the senior civil servant in the Department of External Affairs he was well placed to keep abreast of French interference through the 1960s and tried not to take it lying down. But decisions in matters of foreign policy were made by his political masters, who were free to ignore his advice for their own reasons. All too often, in Cadieux's view, their reasons were founded on short-term political objectives, such as winning the next election, or on personal failings – ignorance, laziness, vanity, sometimes even disloyalty. The indifference of the Canadian public was another factor, based partly in turn upon the shortcomings of journalists and radio analysts.

By 1970, when he was posted to Washington, it was time for him to turn away from what was becoming an oppressive burden of anxiety, put his mind to other things, and leave the problems of France and Quebec to someone else. And we must now look at how these problems affected Cadieux's successors.

Prime Ministers versus Presidents

In this chapter we see how the Gaullists and an imperial French presidency have baffled a series of Canadian prime ministers for three decades. In retrospect, the strangest thing in the struggle over Quebec is that the government in Ottawa in effect defined it as mainly a diplomatic matter and left it to the Department of External Affairs, which sought variously to channel contacts between France and Quebec through Ottawa, to limit Quebec's presence on the world stage, and to involve Canada in la francophonie but could do little to restrict the influence of France on Quebec's government, which continued to evolve. So anxious was the embassy in Paris to avoid antagonizing de Gaulle that it tried to stop RCMP agents from supplying Ottawa with newspaper cuttings about French efforts to assist the separatist movement.[1] And the minister for external affairs in the late 1960s, Paul Martin, merely fretted and tried to carry on business as usual. In his memoirs, he expresses anxiety over French behaviour from 1963, rising to anger in 1967–68, but tells us that he did nothing and could do nothing. His account of Canadian foreign policy in these years is filled with hesitation and weakness: "Unless we wished to show discourtesy to France ... we were hamstrung," and many other such lines.[2] Even so, his memoirs, written in retrospect, show his policy towards France in a falsely favourable light. In reality, he appears woefully inadequate in Marcel Cadieux's personal journal, as do most ministers since.[3] The situation has remained virtually unchanged for thirty years, as we see in this chapter. We look first at Canadian prime ministers and French presidents in terms of their unequal resources of power in diplomatic struggles; second, at the ongoing evolution of relations between France and Quebec; and third, at Canada's handling of Gaullist aggression during the last thirty years.

CANADA AND FRANCE

Canadian Prime Ministers

Prime Minister Lester Pearson admitted again and again to "a feeling of despair and angry frustration" in dealing with Gaullist France but responded with virtually nothing but words and recoiled again and again from taking action.[4] He proved incapable even of holding to a firm policy of resistance, as we saw in chapter 7. Any vigorous step, such as arresting Frenchmen who came to Canada with the intention of promoting Quebec's independence, never seems to have entered government minds. Indeed, such a suggestion even now would be met in Ottawa with alarm or incredulous laughter. To put the matter in crude terms, de Gaulle found himself opposed by words from the Canadian ambassador and his colleagues most of the time, words from the secretary of state for external affairs occasionally, but never anything but words and these only very rarely from the prime minister. To say that the government hid behind the Department of External Affairs may be going too far – but not much.

The first time the prime minister spoke out against the Gaullist attack on Canada was in September 1968. Until then the federal government even ignored or turned aside questions asked in the House of Commons by people such as W.B. Nesbitt, who could see that there was something wrong.[5] True, in July 1967 Lester Pearson had pronounced de Gaulle's "Vive le Québec libre" speech unacceptable, but in the mildest and most moderate way, and had then made it plain that he regarded the matter as closed. The views of his cabinet colleagues, such as Arthur Laing, who wanted to break off relations with France, were set aside as being wildly right-wing and unreasonable.[6] On 10 September 1968, however, the *Globe & Mail* (p. 1) reported that de Gaulle had said, in a press conference dealing mainly with Biafra, that he considered federal states to be faulty because they stifled the aspirations of nations within them. He denounced Canada along with Cyprus, Malaysia, Nigeria, and Rhodesia – all formed by Britain, be it noted. As usual, it did not seem to occur to him that unitary states such as France might be stifling the aspirations of Basques, Bretons, Catalans, and others. Two days later, Prime Minister Trudeau denounced French interference in Canada in an angry speech that was heralded with large headlines in the Canadian press. The occasion for this outburst was the report of a five-day visit of a French agent to a French-speaking group in Manitoba a few weeks earlier. On 14 September 1968 the press carried details drawn from an RCMP investigation of that agent, but it quoted Trudeau incorrectly as having accused him of being a "secret agent".[7] During a television appearance on 18 September, Trudeau did accuse General de Gaulle of "trying to destroy Canadian unity."[8]

The person whose activities so provoked Trudeau was Philippe Rossillon (1931–1997), whom the RCMP knew to have been visiting Canada on various errands since 1963, and probably earlier. They also knew that he had been in contact with Quebec separatists and with members of the *Front de Libération du Québec* (FLQ). Claude Morin admitted to having met him in 1963.[9] It turned out, however, that Rossillon had gone to Manitoba in August 1968 at the invitation of the French-Canadian Cultural Society of Red River, whose members, reported variously as seventeen, thirty-five, forty, or fifty in number, had met him in Paris during a visit in the summer. They were ordinary French-speaking residents of Manitoba interested in their heritage. One of their members, a pharmacist in the village of Saint-Pierre, some fifty kilometres south of Winnipeg, protested that he and his society were loyal federalists. Rossillon's visit was "secret" only in the sense that it was private rather than official, and he had not notified either the Canadian government or the French ambassador, Pierre Siraud. Rossillon's hosts, however, had told Ottawa of his visit, and in response the Department of the Secretary of State had sent out its director of exchanges and travel, René Préfontaine. As these details emerged, the French authorities and some people in Canada began to scoff at Trudeau's handling of the affair. The *Globe and Mail* reported on 16 September that Jean Lesage was in agreement with Trudeau, but it also published a page-long article by Claude Ryan, translated from *Le Devoir*, and repeating the old refrain about the need for cultural contacts with France. Trudeau was beginning to be visibly embarrassed.

Trudeau seems to gone off half-cocked in this affair, just as Pearson had done in July 1967, and he soon felt obliged to drop the issue in what amounted almost to a retreat.[10] He was baffled, for one thing, by the ambiguity of French cultural contacts that seemed legitimate enough in themselves but could reasonably be suspected of concealing political indoctrination, encouragement for separatists, or worse. Preventing such results without crushing the contacts called for a ruthlessness and determination that no Canadian prime minister has ever had or wanted to have. It is not clear whether the full range of Rossillon's activities was understood. He was in fact canvassing French-speaking communities in New Brunswick as well as Manitoba, looking for ways to initiate or strengthen their ties with France.[11] It could be argued, as indeed the French Quebec mafia did argue, that all this effort was purely linguistic and cultural. In any event, a Canadian prime minister's exposing Rossillon and denouncing his contacts in Canada was a little like his denouncing a diplomat at a Soviet embassy suspected of espionnage: that is, it removed the individual but left the rest of the damaging apparatus still in place. As in Pearson's response to the events of 24 July 1967, the Gaullists were protected by a smoke-screen of ambiguity and, on the whole, got the better of Trudeau.

Part of the problem was the government's anxiety to manage domestic public opinion as well as French interference. Cabinet ministers and their officials in Ottawa have a habit of dealing with sensitive Anglo–French issues like parents trying to conceal embarrassing subjects from the children, signalling mysteriously across the dinner table, speaking in soothing half-truths, changing the subject at awkward moments, pretending lofty indifference. After all, Pearson and Trudeau knew – or ought to have known – that these troubles were not new. De Gaulle and his government had been insulting Canada and encouraging Quebec's independence movement throughout the early 1960s as we saw above in chapter 3 and as may be seen in the memoirs of Paul Martin and of Lester Pearson and in Marcel Cadieux's personal journal.[12] How could Pearson and Trudeau not know that the French ambassador, François Leduc, had been making contact with the French-speaking community in Manitoba even before Rossillon did so; that de Gaulle had already made several insulting diplomatic gestures; that his government had been cultivating Quebec in outrageous ways?

One of their concerns in facing this hostility was to avoid doing anything that might provoke "the children" – that is, the English-speaking public – lest they rise up in indignation, and the French-speaking public in Quebec, already partly aroused by separatist extremists. How strong the official desire was to reassure investors we can only guess at. In retrospect it seems clear that the government muddled along by concealing as much as possible and making indignant speeches about what could not be concealed. The purpose of such speeches was to give an impression that Canada was being firmly defended, with its problems in good hands. For it was clear throughout that de Gaulle and his government were impervious to criticism, unmoved by anything said in Ottawa or at the embassy in Paris.

The French Presidency

One of the problems was that the prime minister of an English-speaking country is not equipped to face a president of the French Fifth Republic. Quite apart from any differences in personal ability or preparedness, there is not what an informed observer might describe as a level playing field. The constitution of the Fifth Republic, drawn up by

Charles de Gaulle and his friends, adopted on 4 October 1958 for his own purposes, and strengthened in 1962, gives the head of state almost unlimited powers. These have been concealed by the relatively moderate use made of them by de Gaulle and his successors, but they are there nevertheless, as students of the Fifth Republic never fail to remark. The president is in office for seven years, nearly twice as long as a typical Canadian prime minister. He chooses his prime minister and all the other ministers, much as the American president does, and he is not reponsible to the National Assembly in any way whatever. Moreover, he is master of the National Assembly, as de Gaulle made clear on many occasions – for instance, in a note of 10 July 1962 concerning its intention to refuse funds for French nuclear weapons: "If the National Assembly were to censure the government, particularly on a question of this kind, and given that it would be an act of opposition against the head of State who, as everyone knows, believes atomic power to be necessary, this would immediately result in the dissolution of the Assembly."[13]

Such a threat bears out the history and text of the constitution, a careful reading of which leads to the conclusion that the president may take any powers and make any arrangements he deems useful for his purposes.[14] The constitution allows him, for example, to dismiss the prime minister for his own reasons, and President Pompidou dismissed Chaban-Delmas in July 1972, not because he had lost the confidence of the National Assembly – Chaban's government had recently won a massive vote of confidence – but because Pompidou wished to get rid of him. The president is, to put it bluntly, a constitutional dictator in all but name.[15] As in other dictatorships, in France various secret services operate with only minimum presidential supervision and achieve the objectives of the state by means that no healthy democracy would allow. They are permitted in France for what Cardinal Richelieu in the 1630s called "raison d'État."

The most obviously dictatorial feature of the constitution is article 16, which permits the head of state to assume emergency powers whenever he thinks there is an emergency. General de Gaulle did assume emergency powers from 23 April to 30 September 1961, when he thought France threatened with civil war. Less obvious is the revolutionary past that allowed de Gaulle to face the elected National Assembly in 1962 and dominate it. Two traditions made this possible. First, the republican principle of popular sovereignty in France makes a majority vote of the people more fundamental even than the constitution itself. After all, it was just such a vote that gave the constitution validity in the first place. Second, until 1969 the sovereign people looked with such favour on General de Gaulle that he could win a mandate whenever he asked for it – even one to overpower the elected National Assembly. Thus supported, in 1962 he changed the constitution to have the president, too, chosen by popular vote rather than by an electoral college, as before. As a result, the president as well as the National Assembly represents the popular will.

In a second expression of the same authoritarian right, de Gaulle cowed the National Assembly by holding a referendum on 28 October 1962, on the constitutional changes he wanted, in which the public supported him with 13 million votes out of 21 million. Then, to get a less troublesome assembly, he dissolved it and waged his own political campaign in November 1962 to ensure election of a working majority of Gaullists. It is this extraordinary series of events that permits us to declare that the French president holds the powers of a constitutional dictator. It may be objected that in making these arrangements de Gaulle had the popular will behind him. The trouble with this objection is that earlier dictators in France, and in other countries too, have won popular mandates by similar processes of referendum or plebiscite: Napoleon I, Napoleon III, Benito Mussolini in Italy, Adolf Hitler in Germany, and others.

To be fair, we must admit that when a referendum went against de Gaulle early in 1969 he resigned and retired from political life. But he chose to do this, it was not mandatory and hardly reduced the powers of the presidency. To exercise these extraordinary powers, de Gaulle had soon built up a presidential staff, in and near the Élysée, of about one hundred, together with subordinate personnel. President René Coty had employed no more than a dozen, Vincent Auriol even fewer, and the presidents of the Third Republic typically fewer than half a dozen.[16]

The French public put up with de Gaulle as a constitutional dictator for three principal reasons. First, he offered a practical alternative to the paralysis and confusion of the Fourth Republic (1946–58) and before it the Third Republic (1875–1940), both remembered most clearly for their failings. Second, his independence as leader of the Free French during the Second World War, and his patriotism as the only postwar alternative to a communist government, won him a wide measure of public trust and fitted him to "rescue" France from the Fourth Republic, which was deadlocked in 1958 over Algeria. And third, the French were used to his kind of government because he was only the latest of a series of such leaders. There is a long national tradition of this type of paternal government.

The president of the Fifth Republic would be out of place in the history of any English-speaking country, but he is a familiar enough figure in the constitutional history of France. Several régimes have been built and dominated by a father-figure, sufficiently respected among the public to win political support whenever necessary. The Vichy régime of Maréchal Philippe Pétain is not, perhaps, a fair example, because he was propped up by the German forces of occupation, though he was more widely supported in France than people now care to remember. The role of Georges Clémenceau late in the First World War and afterward is not a good example, either, because he had what were essentially wartime emergency powers. A better example is the Emperor Napoleon III, nephew of the great Napoleon I, who ruled France from 1851 to 1870 in a dictatorial manner, exiling or imprisoning political opponents, employing a secret police force, setting policies in every field, and pursuing an extraordinarily aggressive foreign policy. In short, Napoleon III ruled France much as Charles de Gaulle did in the years 1958 to 1969. There were differences, of course, but the similarities are striking.

Two Clashing Traditions

The Canadian prime ministers facing de Gaulle and his successors have had no comparable national experience to guide them. No general or admiral has ever imposed himself in Ottawa in a coup d'état with the consent of an admiring public, rewritten the constitution to give himself total authority, arranged to dissolve Parliament whenever it got in his way, ruled the country from 24 Sussex Drive with selected friends and followers, built up the armed forces, and dazzled the Canadian public with an aggressive foreign policy intended to make Canada a GREAT POWER by bullying other countries. Nowhere in Canadian history is there an example of authoritarian government; such essential features of Canadian democracy as the annual budget, parliamentary representation, and civil control of the army were inherited from England. To understand them, and not to take them for granted, Canadians would have to study British history, but in general they do not.

No Canadian government has faced foreign aggression independently. Prime Minister John A. Macdonald never had to face Napoleon III, and if he had Great Britain would have done it for him, much as it faced the German Kaiser for Robert Borden in 1914, Hitler and Mussolini for W.L. Mackenzie King in 1940, and Stalin for St Laurent. When Napoleon III sent a naval expedition to Quebec in 1855, the British government warned him against going any further, as we see below in chapter 15. In the conflicts of the twentieth century, Canadians have played a valiant part, but their prime ministers have been followers, never leaders, in those events.

With no direct recent experience of aggression, internal or external,

Canada expects its prime ministers to be peace-mongers. Lester Pearson had to pretend that his strategy for a military response to an armed uprising in Quebec (explained below in chapter 10) was intended for conflict resolution abroad, lest it damage his image as the winner of a Nobel Peace Prize. Much of the history of Canadian foreign policy is a story of peace-making, peace-keeping, foreign aid, and campaigns for disarmament. As a result, federal ministers have had great difficulty in understanding the issues in the conflict with Gaullist France; the prevailing tendency has been to deny the very existence of this cold war or to pretend that it is really something else. Nobody in Ottawa holds an office suitable for fighting it. Canadian foreign policy has been a profoundly collective affair, in which no minister of the crown has held the powers of a de Gaulle or a Napoleon III. Seldom politically secure, ministers have spent much time and effort winning votes and trying to please the public. To make France over in Canada's image, it would be necessary to bring back the constitution of the Third Republic, in which the president had mainly ceremonial duties and the prime minister was politically dependent on a majority vote in the National Assembly – all quite different from the Fifth Republic.

A Byzantine Response

Faced as it was with a Quebec response to French overtures, the Canadian government decided that its objective must be to persuade France and Quebec to conduct their relations through Ottawa, or at least with the knowledge and consent of the federal government. Franco–Quebec cooperation was to take place within the purview of the government of Canada. As long as diplomatic and constitutional protocol was observed, what happened between France and Quebec need not be examined very closely. In any event, de Gaulle soon discovered that the government's limited objectives were intended not really to stop him but to avoid nasty conflicts and to save face. Federal officials were concerned primarily to maintain diplomatic procedures, to conduct business as usual, and not to "over-react." They fell back on what Jean Chapdelaine, one of the principals in the affair, laughingly calls "the byzantinism of Ottawa." When, for example, the governments of France and Quebec drew up an agreement to cooperate, it was not to be called "an accord, no: it shall be an 'entente', crowned by an exchange of notes between the ambassador of France and the Canadian minister for External Affairs."[17]

Following in de Gaulle's footsteps, a series of French civil servants and political figures deliberately snubbed Ottawa in the late 1960s by travelling only to Quebec. The first was the minister of education, Alain Peyrefitte, in September 1967, followed closely by the minister of youth and sport, François Misoffe. When the government raised objections with the French authorities, the reply was that education was a provincial matter in the Canadian constitution and that there was no federal minister of education. This argument had already been advanced by Quebec's government as it prepared to sign an entente with France on 27 February 1965; and again on 22 April, by Paul Gérin-Lajoie, in a speech to a university audience from Belgium, France, and Switzerland.[18]

It was insultingly repeated at Quebec City in October 1969 by an official French visitor, Jean de Lipkowski, who had also refused even to make a courtesy visit to Ottawa. In a press conference on 15 October Prime Minister Trudeau was outspoken in criticizing Lipkowski for interfering in Canadian affairs. Even more interesting in retrospect, however, Pierre Laporte denounced Lipkowski on 22 October in a vigorous, patriotic speech.[19] What followed these criticisms? Leaders of the FLQ concluded, for this and other reasons, that "Pierre Laporte was the person responsible for all of our troubles," and they murdered him scarcely a year later.[20] The Quai d'Orsay's editors used the FLQ's word in referring to his murder as an "execution"![21] In any event, the French government paid no attention whatever to the objection that it was interfering in Canada's internal affairs by interpreting its constitution; and Marcel Masse, as Quebec's shadow foreign minister, went on defending Quebec's "right" to negotiate as a sovereign power, repeating the arguments he had put forward in a speech in Paris to the *Association de la presse diplomatique* early in January 1970.[22] Exchanges of this kind occurred again and again, with little if any modification in France's insulting practices. These practices were deliberately insulting, as Bernard Dorin tells us, and intended to encourage Quebec to ignore and treat the federal government in a like manner.[23]

In March 1968, Jean-Daniel Jurgenson, director of the American division at the Quai d'Orsay, together with Jean Basdevant, director general of cultural relations, visited the Acadians at Moncton, New Brunswick, again without bothering to pay even a courtesy visit to Ottawa. This sort of thing went on sporadically for the next quarter-century, in spite of anything the Canadian government said, because it did nothing to back up its objections. In 1970 Philippe Malaud, secretary of state for the French civil service, visited Quebec to open the new *École nationale d'administration*. When Mme Christian Scrivener, French *Secrétaire d'État d'économie et des finances*, flew to Quebec for a meeting of the *Association Québec–France* on 16 October 1976, she said that was her twenty-fourth visit.[24] Two decades later, in September 1995, Philippe Séguin, a senior official, could still visit Quebec at Jacques Parizeau's invitation, without even making a courtesy call to Ottawa, in order to assure the province of French support in winning its independence from Canada in case of a "yes" vote in the forthcoming referendum. Canada's ambassador in Paris, Benoît Bouchard, described Séguin at that time as "a loose cannon," which caused some indignation, but the Canadian government took no practical steps in prevention or retaliation.[25] By July 1997, when Séguin appeared as President Chirac's representative at the unveiling of a statue of de Gaulle in Quebec City, the federal government was entirely cowed and merely tried to pretend that it was normal for official French visitors to ignore Ottawa in their visits to Quebec.

FRANCE AND QUEBEC

Quebec on the World Stage

Closely related to the question of official French visitors was another: whether Quebec might act alone in international relations or whether these were to be reserved for the federal government, as stipulated in section 91 of the British North America Act, 1867. The French government set out deliberately to establish Quebec as an independent, sovereign state by inviting it to send representatives to conferences from which Ottawa was, if possible, to be excluded. Instead of treating this provocation with the firmness it deserved, the federal government engaged in a series of undignified diplomatic manoeuvres to outwit the French and upstage the Québécois. The conferences were about education as a field for Franco–Quebec cooperation and la francophonie. The governments of France and Quebec conspired – this is the right word – to have invitations sent to Quebec but not to Ottawa, or at least to make sure that a Quebec delegation would negotiate independently and be seen to do so. Members of the French Quebec mafia, notably Yvan Bourges and Bernard Dorin from the Quai d'Orsay, and Philippe Rossillon, were dispatched on occasion to Gabon, Niger, and Zaïre to put pressure on the African hosts of francophone conferences.[26] The federal government did its best to obtain invitations that recognized it as the sovereign power in Canada and to prevent Quebec from receiving separate invitations or from sending independent delegations.

These manoeuvres are described in detail by a Canadian diplomat who took part in them, Eldon ("Pat") Black, as well as by Dale Thomson in a historical study.[27] A good short account appears in a book by J.L. Granatstein and Robert Bothwell.[28] Even briefer, though well worth reading, is the summary in Mitchell Sharp's memoirs.[29] But these volumes, excellent though they are, should be read in conjunction with accounts published in France and Quebec, which put a different slant on events, as may be imagined.

Dorin tells with smug satisfaction how the French Quebec mafia managed to have Quebec flags flying everywhere at a conference in Paris in spring 1967 and no Canadian flag at all.[30] The Quebec delegation succeeded in sitting alone under its own flag, for all the world as an independent power. Our government took no firm steps against the French, but, being less cowed by a little African state such as Gabon, it kept our ambassador out of Libreville from 19 February 1968 and suspended relations with that country until 7 October 1969. "In fact," Lester Pearson candidly admits in his memoirs, "we were more angry with France than with Gabon, which would never have attempted this ploy on its own initiative."[31] Why then were diplomatic relations not suspended with France? Probably, as Marcel Cadieux reported, because Paris might then have been able to cement even firmer relations with Quebec City.

This phase of the cold war with France went on through a series of francophone conferences. The principal ones were held at Libreville in February 1968; in Paris in April 1968; at Kinshasa (Zaïre) in January 1969; at Niamey (Niger) in February 1969; in Paris again in December 1969; at Niamey again in March 1970; and in Paris a third time in June 1970. At some of these gatherings the Canadian government contrived to incorporate the Quebec delegation in a much larger federal one, which included representatives of the French-speaking communities in Manitoba, New Brunswick, and Ontario. But Ottawa took no resolute action against Paris.

It was the president of Niger, Hamani Diori, who reprimanded three French officials, Mathieu Defosses, Bernard Dorin, and Philippe Rossillon, on 18 February 1969 at a conference in Niamey "for prompting Quebec to assert sovereignty in international affairs over the issue of the delegation listing and the flag displays."[32] Unfortunately, Diori had no firm loyalty or commitment to Canada: while visiting Quebec in September that year he let himself be persuaded by the Quebec authorities to return directly to Niger, a painful snub for the federal government, avoided only by inducing him at the last minute to continue on to Winnipeg.[33]

The story of the diplomatic duel between Ottawa and Paris as told by Eldon Black shows that the Canadian government had no sensible appreciation of the political objectives underlying the cultural exchanges between France and Quebec. Ottawa limited its own efforts to enforcing its constitutional right to represent Canada abroad and to preventing Quebec from behaving as an independent, sovereign power. This was all very well, but what effect was French political propaganda having on the separatist movement in Quebec? Black understands from years of unpleasant personal experience how hard the struggle against the French government was during the late 1960s and the early 1970s. Surely no one knows this sector of the Franco–Canadian diplomatic scene better than he. In some respects, however, his account places him and his colleagues among that part of the Canadian public that continued to see Franco–Quebec relations as purely cultural, linguistic, or ethnic and which interpreted the aspirations of Quebec separatists as only expressions of cultural and linguistic anxiety.

The effects of French influence on the political orientation of the Quebec public seems to have escaped these observers altogether. Did Black not notice that the hundreds of Quebec students who went over to study in France were, or quickly became, separatists? It is a matter of record that some four hundred of them greeted the electoral victory of the Parti québécois on 15 November 1976 with wild delight; "one looked in vain for a Liberal supporter."[34] The influence of French university life on Quebec young people then was likely to be in a separatist direction, but Black, like many others, seems not to have noticed the political aspect of the struggle. For him there were only the diplomatic and security aspects. Beyond his department's campaign to defend the federal management of Franco–Quebec relations there were only the policing efforts to prevent violence of the FLQ variety and the federal government's policy of trying to satisfy Quebec in matters of language and culture.

Canada, Quebec and la Francophonie

The Canadian government turned to the business of satisfying the desires of the French-speaking populations at home. The most obvious step was the Royal Commission on Bilingualism and Biculturalism (1963–69), which travelled across the country and produced several volumes of a detailed report with many recommendations. The result was an ambitious federal policy of making Canada bilingual or tolerable, at least, for people in either official language. The federal civil and military services, mainly English-speaking, began to recruit bilingual French Canadians in ever greater numbers. The higher ranks of the armed forces were soon opened to French-Canadians as never before.[35] Bilingual schools sprang up; large numbers of children attended classes, or entire schools, of "French immersion," though some of these children seem to have acquired a good grasp of neither language. Government policies led to a kind of competition with Quebec in relations with France: federal exchange agreements to match Quebec's exchange agreements, and Canadian participation in French-language activities to match Quebec's. In particular, the Canadian government began to take an interest in *la francophonie*.

Stirred by Quebec's involvement in *la francophonie*, Ottawa endeavoured to recover the leadership of Canadian participation by bringing in representation from New Brunswick, Ontario, and Manitoba. Paul Martin declared that he had "always held strongly to the belief that Canada's foreign relations ... should express the bilingual and bicultural character of our country," and he went on to speak about growing relations with France and the French-speaking world. At Marcel Cadieux's suggestion, External Affairs had approved a plan in December 1963 for academic and cultural exchanges with Belgium, France, and Switzerland.[36] Canadian universities and the Canada Council were to take part. In the course of 1965, a framework for a general cultural agreement with France was worked out, with a million dollars budgeted for this purpose.

Spurred on by the knowledge that France and Quebec were making separate agreements of their own, such as one signed in November 1965, the Canadian government went on to allocate substantial sums for aid to French-speaking Africa – nearly $20 million in the period 1961–66 and twice that sum in the late 1960s.[37] Towards the end of 1967 the minister of justice, Pierre Trudeau, was dispatched on a good-will mission to a half-dozen francophone countries in Africa: Cameroon, Ivory Coast, Niger, Senegal, Togo, and Tunisia. He was able to speak to their governments as a federalist French Canadian; to see for himself what possibilities there might be for a Canadian presence in Africa instead of merely a Quebec presence; and to measure the palpable hostility of the French government to the intrusion of what it regarded as an "Anglo-Saxon" country. Prime Minister John Diefenbaker had sent the Canadian ambassador in Paris, Pierre Dupuy, on a tour of ten of Africa's French-speaking countries as early as autumn 1960 and was beginning to act on his report before any threat from Gaullist aggression was perceived.[38] But aid offerings proved useful in strengthening the government's hand in the diplomatic struggle within *la francophonie*.

In January 1966 External Affairs established a new Cultural Affairs Division. Diplomatic services had not normally concerned themselves with cultural affairs, and this new division was an implicit acknowledgment that *la francophonie* had political implications, essentially as an expression of French cultural imperialism. A journalist gave a hint of this when, on 20 March 1970, twenty-one countries signed a convention at Niamey, Niger, creating an *Agence de coopération culturel et technique des pays francophone* (ACCT). "In a political sense," he wrote, "[the creation of an agency for cooperation] is really a creative myth such as Sorel understood it: men and institutions, at the crossroads of feeling and action, putting into effect a natural and conscious solidarity created by the community of culture."[39] Nevertheless, under Brian Mulroney's government Canadian efforts redoubled, so that by September 1987, when the second francophone summit met in Quebec City, Canada was contributing 32 per cent of ACCT's budget, and Quebec another 3 per cent.[40] ACCT, later renamed the *Agence de la francophonie*, represented forty-seven countries by 1997 and had 205 paid employees, 102 of them at its headquarters in Paris, paid out of a budget of 500 million francs, two-thirds of it from France.[41]

The Canadian government's interest in la francophonie in the 1970s was matched by a similar interest on the part of certain sectors of the Canadian public, notably in the universities, always ready to launch into new endeavours. Among the intelligentsia there was an immediate outburst of sympathy for French Canada and for things French and little reflection on the political implications. People in the Canadian Institute of International Affairs, for example, were willing to study such subjects as "Canada's role in a French commonwealth," apparently unaware of the Gaullist ambitions that are the main subject of this book. One such study, published in the October 1967 number of the institute's journal, *Behind the Headlines*, rejoiced that already one-third of all Canadian personnel sent abroad in programs of foreign aid had been assigned to the French-speaking world, mostly in Africa.[42] Canadians were invited to join in a reorientation to extend their activities beyond the English-speaking world into the world of the other founding people. At international gatherings two groups of French Canadians were to be seen, one from Ottawa, the other from Quebec. While the former were acting out of a desire to satisfy Quebec's aspirations, the latter were already marching towards what their PQ government, and even many Liberals, regarded as an inevitable political independence. At a dinner in 1981 to celebrate the twentieth anniversary of the *Délégation générale du Québec* in Paris, Canadian Senator Maurice Riel overheard Louise Beaudoin, the *Déléguée générale*, "teasing her minister by begging him to tell the assembled company there and then the date when the independence of Quebec was to be proclaimed."[43] So much for the purity of Franco–Quebec cultural relations!

French Influence in Quebec

Those relations were vigorously cultivated by the *Office Franco–Québécois pour la jeunesse*. Its supervisory body, the *Conseil d'administration de l'office franco–québécois pour la jeunesse* (OFQJ), met in

Paris on 17–18 April 1969 under the joint chairmanship of Joseph Comiti and Claude Morin. They decided to arrange for four thousand young *cadres* to be exchanged between their two countries, twice as many as the previous year.[44] Early in 1977 a journalist reported that each year about thirteen hundred young Québécois had been able to spend time in France under the auspices of the OFQJ, and as many French young people had come to Quebec. These exchanges wax and wane.[45] During the 1970s a great many Quebec students went to study in France, but the numbers dropped off in the 1990s. Students began to move in the other direction. In the academic year 1996–97, nearly twenty-three hundred French students registered at Quebec universities for a variety of reasons, mainly to do with closer and more kindly supervision – a difference that will be appreciated by any Canadian who has studied at a French university.[46]

To staff its swelling civil service, the Quebec government founded an *École nationale d'administration* in 1970 on the French model. Its purposes were much like those of the French ENA founded by Michel Debré in 1945 (and reformed by Couve de Murville beginning in 1968) in order to attract and educate people with scientific, economic, and technical interests, as well as the traditional "well-rounded" intellectuals, with a view to renewing the higher ranks of officialdom with another generation of Gaullists as the first generation retired, mainly during the 1970s.[47] The government of Quebec had sent officials for training at the French ENA and intended to model its own on it; it invited Philippe Malaud, French secretary of state for administrative reform, to inaugurate it during his visit on 23–28 September 1970.[48] In addition, it also hoped to train career civil servants as reliable Quebec nationalists and separatists.[49] From the beginning it was unmistakably devoted to the cause of Quebec's independence, as may be inferred from a list of its faculty, which has included such separatist zealots as Louise Beaudoin, François Cloutier, and Claude Morin. In this and other ways, Quebec's ENA has been preparing a generation of officials fitted to lead the province in its bid for international standing as an independent state, rather different from most of their counterparts, accustomed to lives in provincial capitals.

THE ONGOING BATTLES

The Late 1960s

Neither Prime Minister Pearson nor even Prime Minister Trudeau ever seems to have taken steps to halt the processes of indoctrination sketched above. Claude Morin wondered in 1972 "why, apart from a

few verbal outbursts, Ottawa has always limited itself to relatively dis-
creet interference when it was often extremely irritated at the turn
France–Quebec affairs were taking."[50] Various arrangements between
the French and Quebec governments have continued with no apparent
regard for Ottawa's objections. The *Commission permanente de
coopération franco-québécoise* held its tenth meeting from 30 November to 4 December 1970 in Paris under the chairmanship of Pierre
Laurent, then director-general of cultural, scientific, and technical relations at the Quai d'Orsay, and was duly attended by a Quebec delegation headed by Yves Michaud.[51] A quarter-century later, in 1996, it
held its fifty-fourth meeting, again in Paris.

One explanation for the federal government's reluctance to oppose
France in the years before 1972, according to Claude Morin, is that it
had always believed that de Gaulle alone was the cause of the
trouble.[52] Certainly the embassy in Paris held this view.[53] Once de
Gaulle was out of the way, then "France herself would be urging
Quebec to step back into the provincial ranks. This is not now sure, by
any means," Morin concluded in 1972, ominously but correctly.[54] The
diplomatic struggle continued. In 1973 *Le Devoir* assured its readers
that the new French minister of foreign affairs, Michel Jobert, was as
ready to focus attention on Quebec as de Gaulle had been.[55] Jobert was
as acerbic and undiplomatic as de Gaulle himself.

Nevertheless, when the Parti Québécois won the provincial election
of 1976 and René Lévesque took office as premier, Prime Minister
Trudeau took up the issue of Quebec separatism once again, had a
report prepared for the cabinet meeting of 13 January 1977, and considered what steps to take. His ministers held various opinions on the
issue, with only Warren Allmand from Montreal arguing in favour of
a firm stand.[56] Nothing practical of any kind came out of this meeting.
On the activities of the French Quebec mafia I have found no sign of
government knowledge or concern. Since May 1995, when another
Gaullist, Jacques Chirac, was elected president of France, the French
government has stood ready, as it assured Jacques Parizeau that year,
to assist the Quebec government in its struggle for independence. Its
declared policy of "non-ingérance, mais non-indifférence" must be
interpreted as the usual hypocritical Gaullist denial, like that which
accompanied the *Rainbow Warrior* affair.

Part of the explanation for the Canadian government's hesitant
policy is an almost continual French campaign to reassure it. For
example, during the 1960s Couve de Murville played a role somewhat
like that of the kindly, reassuring interrogator in a team trying to get
information from a victim being tortured at the hands of his partner,
the tough, cruel interrogator. French foreign minister from 1958 to

1968 and prime minister for a year after that, Couve tried to reassure the Canadian government again and again after one of de Gaulle's attacks. Evidently his job was to soften resistance by offering comfort to the people in Ottawa and suggesting that things were not so bad as they seemed.[57] In October 1963 Paul Martin, with a naïve faith in his "friendship" with Couve, found him "understanding and anxious to help when I explained that Canada genuinely wished to improve its official contacts with his country."[58]

In an interview with de Gaulle himself, Paul Martin was reassured in mid-June 1967 that the forthcoming presidential visit would be pleasant and trouble-free.[59] Martin talked – or rather listened – to de Gaulle in Paris for thirty-five minutes, during which the general expressed regrets for the Vimy incident and put it down to a misunderstanding. As Marcel Cadieux summarized the event in a memo of 27 February 1967, "Général de Gaulle has finally shown what he is up to (montré de quel bois il se chauffe). On Saturday afternoon, [Hervé] Alphand [at the Quai d'Orsay] had M. [Jules] Léger [Canadian ambassador] come to his office and told him that the General prefers that Prince Philip should not be present at the ceremonies organised at Vimy Ridge on 9 April next. He thinks that even if the Prince is the honorary Commander of a Canadian regiment, his presence at Vimy will spoil the French Canadian character of the ceremony that the General especially wishes to emphasize." Martin and de Gaulle discussed the UN, the Russians, the Israelis, the Near East, and Vietnam, but not *la francophonie*. De Gaulle talked nearly all the time and mostly about Vietnam. He looked older, thinner and tired but was very friendly, Martin reported to Prime Minister Pearson. "Il était très amical." Martin said he would be welcome in Quebec, at Ottawa, and also at Toronto. De Gaulle said that he had a pleasant memory of a visit to Toronto four or six years previously. Whatever he thought of his Toronto call, in 1960 de Gaulle had trounced his ambassador in Canada for including that city on his official round of visits.[60] Nevertheless, Martin's encounter with de Gaulle had the intended anaesthetic effect. "The General was reassuring on the subject of his [forthcoming] voyage to Canada."[61]

Thus reassured, Martin and Pearson raised no serious objection, as we saw above in chapter 4, to de Gaulle's reaching Quebec City by sea and then travelling to Montreal before going on to Ottawa. A month later, after de Gaulle's disastrous visit, Martin thought that he and his "friend," Couve de Murville, would settle things. "Couve urged us to do nothing precipitate; time would heal the wounds that his president had opened," writes Martin in his memoirs.[62] Again more than a year later, at Quebec City on the afternoon of 30 September 1968 Couve assured Pierre Trudeau "that France did not believe in separatism; she

considered that this policy was folly; she had no interest in the disintegration of Canada."[63] Couve used this interview to try to reassure
Trudeau and seems to have succeeded.

Meanwhile, Marcel Cadieux, under-secretary of state for external
affairs, had a deeper understanding of what was happening and
remained properly sceptical about Couve's "friendship."[64] Meeting
Couve's bleak and hostile successor in Washington some years later,
Cadieux reflected that Couve, "especially if he foresaw unpleasantness
between us, would have been gentle and deployed all his charms upon
his Canadian colleagues in order to disconcert them or weaken
them."[65] Posted in Brussels later as Canadian ambassador to the European Community, Cadieux again observed him in action. "As will be
seen, M. Couve de Murville remains faithful to his Gaullist convictions
and outlook," he wrote home to Ottawa, reporting on a lecture that
Couve had given in Antwerp.[66]

Cadieux's efforts to oppose French interference during the late 1960s
were undermined by many of his compatriots who were being taken in
by French reassurances. Another example occurred in September 1967,
when the French minister of education, Alain Peyrefitte, created con-
sternation by visiting Quebec while ignoring Ottawa. Just before
boarding his return plane for Paris, he telephoned from Montreal to
Mme Pauline Vanier, distinguished widow of the late governor general.
In a secret letter to Cadieux, which she told him she had typed herself
in order that not even her staff should know of it, she recounted how
Peyrefitte had had a long phone conversation with her. He had been
affable and gracious and had hoped he had not damaged relations
between France and Canada. He had sent her a big bunch of flowers.
She was charmed. "I tell you all this," she wrote to Cadieux, "because
it proves that after all he is not too much under the influence of 'the
big boss.'"[67]

Yet another example of the Gaullist propensity to smile at the Canadian government while stabbing it in the back took place in 1970. The
secretary of state for external effairs, Mitchell Sharp, on an unofficial
visit to Paris, "was pleased and grateful when the French foreign minister, Maurice Schumann, greeted me on my arrival at the airport and
gave me lunch at the Quai d'Orsay. Following lunch, he invited me to
his office to see an inkwell that had once been used by Talleyrand ...
While I was looking at this historic piece, he said that his real purpose
was to tell me privately that President Pompidou was determined to
have better relations with Canada. And relations did continue to
improve. My next official visit to France was to attend de Gaulle's
memorial service in Notre-Dame on 12 November 1970."[68] Friendly
personal attention by Gaullist ministers – so nice and so kind – had an

anaesthetic effect on Sharp. For these were the people, Pompidou and Schumann, whose government in these very years was lending vigorous support to Quebec's efforts to establish an independent diplomatic life at international conferences.

Diplomats at the French embassy in Ottawa have also played a part in the reassurance campaign. They did so in the 1960s and have done so ever since. As early as February 1967, for instance, Marcel Cadieux had long conversations with the ambassador and the counsellor about Franco–Canadian relations. "Carraud, the Counsellor, kept telling me all evening that our anxieties are exaggerated, that France does not want to interfere in our affairs, that we must not make mountains out of the General's whims [lubies] and that it is better to let the storm pass."[69] Almost exactly thirty years later, on 5 February 1998, I heard the French ambassador Loïc Hennekinne repeatedly try to reassure a small audience at Carleton University that France has never had, and has not now, any intention of interfering in Canadian affairs. When I asked his opinion of activities such as those of Bernard Dorin, Jean de Lipkowski, Alain Peyrefitte, and Philippe Rossillon, he made a joke of them by comparing them with a Canadian newspaper columnist who had expressed wild, francophobic feelings. Some in the audience realized that the words of a mere journalist are not to be seriously compared with diplomats and officials like Rossillon, recently given a hero's funeral in Paris, and Dorin, honoured by his government with the rank of *ambassadeur de France*, or with ministers of state such as Peyrefitte. But there can be no doubt that official French disinformation on the subject of the Paris–Ottawa–Quebec triangle has tended to undermine the resolve of those in Canada who might otherwise have fought back.

Mulroney's Conservatives

Such French efforts have had an appreciable effect not only on Liberal governments. Looking back now, we can see that the Conservatives of Brian Mulroney, elected in 1984, coped no better with France and Quebec than had their predecessors. Mulroney's compromise with the government of Quebec, announced on 8 November that year, proved to be only a short-term measure. According to the entente they had signed the previous day, Quebec was to be free to take part in francophone summits (*Sommets francophones*) as an "interested observer" when matters of world-wide political or economic importance were being discussed but was to be freer still in discussions of cooperation and development.[70] A delegation from Quebec was to be one of the forty-one groups to attend the first conference of heads of francophone states and governments in February 1986. As announced in a front-page article in *Le Devoir*, this agreement seemed to be only the next step in Quebec's emancipation as an independent power.[71]

Certainly the PQ government regarded it as such; Louise Beaudoin, described in *Le Devoir* as "la Ministre des Relations extérieures," publicly rejoiced. And well she might, as the agreement had been worked out and negotiated largely by a Quebec separatist, Lucien Bouchard, friend and adviser to Mulroney, who sent him to Paris as ambassador immediately after the Conservative victory in 1985.[72] The agreement of 7 November 1985 was still deemed to be in force at the francophone summit meeting of November 1997 in Hanoi. Because of it, Jean Chrétien and Lucien Bouchard quarrelled only intermittently during most of that meeting.[73]

Bouchard in his memoirs puts the Mulroney government's policy towards France in the best possible light but cannot dispel the impression that Mulroney was behaving as a naïve idealist in basing it on his admiration for France and his desire to reconcile Quebec with the rest of Canada. Mulroney hoped it might be effective in the wake of the separatists' defeat in the referendum of 1980 and in the conflict over the repatriation of the Canadian constitution in 1982. However, Bouchard, even as Canadian ambassador in France, never swerved in his commitment to a separate, sovereign Quebec. Neither did Marcel Masse or Gilles Loiselle, two other Quebec nationalists who served under Mulroney. Did the prime minister imagine that they might be persuaded to become loyal Canadians? Or did he not care? There were precedents for allowing a Quebec separatist to represent Canada abroad, it is true, such as the appointment of Jean-Marc Léger as secretary-general of the *Agence de coopération culturelle et technique* in 1968. In retrospect, however, any ordinary English-speaking Canadian might be excused for concluding that the new policy of reconciliation was nothing more than a way of winning political support in Quebec. So it must have seemed to Preston Manning when he argued during the election campaign in May 1997 that federal political leaders from Quebec were too often tempted to compromise with the Parti Québécois in order to gain votes in their province.

Whatever Mulroney may have intended, the francophone summits that his agreement allowed Quebec to attend became diplomatic battlegrounds not much different from earlier conferences. The first was held in Paris from 17 to 19 February 1986. François Mitterrand's friendly visit in May 1987 notwithstanding, Quebec and Ottawa went on wrangling over the arrangements in much the same atmosphere of suspicion and hostility as before.[74] Anyone familiar with French history might have predicted such a result by reflecting on the absence of compromise in the French diplomatic tradition. To concede a point is not likely to draw a French authority to concede a point in return; the typical French response has been to draw the conclusion that an opponent is weakening and so may be induced to concede even more if pushed even harder. For one reason or another the government of Canada never saw fit to oppose Gaullist France except on the sale of Canadian uranium, as related below in chapter 13.

The Present

The triangular diplomatic struggle in Paris among the Canadian embassy, the *Délégation générale*, and the French government still goes on today. Personnel and issues change: Michel Lucier, an ex-priest and friend of Lucien Bouchard, was appointed *Délégué général* from 1 June 1997; a new Canadian ambassador, Jacques Roy, was named not long before; and the French National Assembly was dissolved pending an election on 25 May and 1 June. But the wrangling has continued on the same petty level that still seems to concern diplomats but rarely comes to public attention. In 1996, for instance, Quebec was invited to send representation to a beer festival at Strasbourg in April 1997, but funds were lacking when the time came, and so Canada went alone instead, seeing in this an opportunity to win a diplomatic advantage. Also in April and doubtless also as an economy, the Quebec film festival at Blois was cancelled just as the Canadian government was opening an expensive new cultural centre in Paris at 5 rue de Constantine. Meanwhile, the Canadian ambassador has been trying, ineffectually it seems, to persuade the French government to reverse its decision to ban asbestos and asbestos products from France, these being Canadian exports.[75] As another example of the same petty politics, a struggle took place in the first half of 1997 over the status of David Levine, the Quebec government's "delegate for multilateral affairs" in New York. Ottawa refused to issue the necessary credentials and diplomatic visas for him to deal with the United Nations and other international agencies unless he were given a title that did not create the impression that he represented the Canadian government in New York. Near the end of June, Quebec backed down, but it is hard to see how Ottawa imagines that it can defend its authority, much less its dignity, by such ineffectual methods.[76]

Jacques Parizeau has been counting on French support, particularly in his plan to manipulate the international community of nations in such a way as to obtain swift recognition of an independent Quebec. The problem as he saw it during his years as premier was to overcome American opposition. Accordingly, he worked out a plan with his high-ranking friends in Paris to have the French government give Quebec full recognition as soon as its independence had been declared. The governments of many French-speaking countries might reasonably be counted on to follow suit, and in Parizeau's opinion the United States would thereby feel impelled to do the same, possibly even to take the lead. He explained this plan on various occasions – for example, in an interview with *Le Devoir* published on 6 July 1993, prompted by Parizeau's meeting with twelve representatives of the European Union in Aylmer, Quebec, on 8 June.

As *Le Devoir* put it, "The sovereigntist leader has a trump card in his hand, the famous French 'lever' which would consist of playing France (deemed by M. Parizeau more sympathetic towards recognition) against the United States ... [In Parizeau's own words], 'The Americans do not want to be second. Quebec entering the concert of nations supported by France, with the u.s. pulling back, would not be, shall we say, very clever.'"[77] In view of this and other such remarks from Parizeau over the years, it was somewhat naïve of the Canadian public to be surprised by Michel Vastel's analysis of Parizeau's book, *Pour un Québec souverain*, in *Le Soleil* of Quebec City on 7 May 1997.[78] Out of touch, as usual, with the Quebec press, the public had not yet grasped Parizeau's strategy of using French patronage in this way and doing so, on French advice, by a declaration of independence from Canada immediately after obtaining a sovereigntist majority in the referendum of 30 October 1995.

What, for example, did the federal government do about Lucien Bouchard's visit to Paris that was planned for autumn 1997? In the few days ending 8 July 1997, arrangements for this visit were made in Paris by Sylvain Simard, "le ministre des Relations internationales du Québec," who passed an hour in what is described as an "entretien chaleureux" with the new French minister for foreign affairs, Hubert Védrine.[79] He also had appointments with other cabinet ministers, including half an hour with the prime minister, Lionel Jospin. In accordance with these arrangements, Premier Bouchard, Simard, Louise Beaudoin, and Bernard Landry were in Paris from 28 September to 2 October in conference with Chirac, Jospin, Philippe Séguin, and others.

CONCLUSION

The history of Franco–Quebec relations these past thirty years teaches us what these meetings are for: to conspire once again for the separation of Quebec from Canada. Indeed, the separatist organ *Le Devoir* is not shy about discussing the revival and reinforcement of the separatist/sovereigntist campaign, and its Paris correspondent assures us that Jospin is a friend of the PQ.[80] He knows "how to handle the subtle dialectic of the 'non-ingérence' and of the 'non-indifférence' that takes the place of a Quebec policy for France."[81] Prime Minister Jean Chrétien and his government continued to endure insult and contempt, apparently feeling powerless to intervene and trying to pretend that such activity is of no importance. The Canadian ambassador, Jacques Roy, was denied even the courtesy of an invitation to a reception for Bouchard held at the *Délégation générale du Québec* on 29 September 1997, a gratuitous insult typical of Gaullist, and now of Quebec separatist, behaviour.[82]

The history of the last three decades also teaches us that the Canadian government will again do nothing, not even wring its hands now. It appears indeed to have washed its hands of what has come to be called "the unity issue". Members of the Canadian public have been writing more and more frequent letters of protest at the ineffectual policy of the Canadian government: in the *Financial Post*, the *Ottawa Citizen*, the *Globe and Mail* and even in the *European!*[83] The federal election of June 1997 is now behind us, and the public has once again left matters in the hands of a government for which the separation of Quebec has become merely a political matter, to be left only to the consciences of residents in what is still the province of Quebec. Is the government silenced, are its hands tied, by a desire to do nothing, to avoid conflict at any cost, to turn the other cheek, all in order to reassure investors? Is the government paralysed by its large membership of politicians and servants, civil and military, from Quebec, of whom an unknown number have ambiguous feelings about the separatist campaign? Or is it half-converted to the cause of Quebec sovereignty? The Canadian tax-payer might well assume the latter upon discovering that, for example, the federal government helped to pay for such anti-Canadian propaganda as Jacques Parizeau's *Pour un Québec souverain* (1997), Claude Morin's *Les choses comme elles étaient: une autobiographie politique* (1994), Gaston Cholette's *Au service du Québec: souvenirs* (1994), and Robert Pichette's *L'Acadie par bonheur retrouvée: De Gaulle et l'Acadie* (1994). The title page of each one acknowledges financial help from the Canada Council.

Troubled Police Forces

De Gaulle's visit to Quebec in July 1967 confirmed, if confirmation was needed, that France ought to be watched for its evident intention to support the Quebec separatist movements, particularly the Parti Québécois (PQ). By the time Pierre Elliott Trudeau succeeded Lester Pearson as prime minister of Canada in April 1968, the visit and subsequent steps had begun to have some effect in Ottawa. An important question, never satisfactorily answered, is what use the Canadian government made of its police forces in response to the French government's aggression. In the five sections of this chapter I look at the activities of the RCMP, revelations about its work, the October crisis of 1970, the policy vacuum created by the government's ambivalence about Gaullist aggression, and the emergence of the Canadian Security Intelligence Service (CSIS). Police, we should note, cannot take the initiative in a democracy such as Canada and, apart from submitting reports, can only wait for orders from the government.

THE RCMP'S ACTIVITIES

In the late 1960s Pierre Trudeau seems to have been concerned primarily with opposing the separatists and inclined to see Gaullist hostilities in that political context. It is doubtful whether he saw them as manifestations of imperial intent. After all, French interference was recent, unexpected, and the work of an ageing statesman and his followers, and it had to be set against an old Franco–Canadian friendship that had apparently grown during the two world wars. With memories of Canada's efforts to defend France in 1914–18 and to free it in 1944, few if any Canadians then understood the twisted, chauvinist vision of the Gaullists. Not many do even today. An elderly French statesman, Georges Bidault, declared at the time that de Gaulle's encouragement for Quebec separatists was intended to damage the integrity of Canada, and he thought that it represented revenge for Canada's refusal to sell France uranium in the 1950s and early 1960s. So also thinks a Canadian diplomat, Max Yalden, present at some of the negotiations over uranium sales to France.[1] Another bitter French memory was of the leading part Lester Pearson and Canada had played in the international campaign to stop the Anglo–French attack on Egypt over the Suez Canal in 1956.[2] But knowledge of Gaullist hostility had no effect on the government. The political struggle that Trudeau wanted to wage was directed against the Quebec separatists.

Trudeau seemed to doubt, John Starnes recalls, whether there was much hostile French activity and refused to allow the RCMP to undertake thorough surveillance of the French embassy.[3] This omission is puzzling because the French ambassador in the troubled years 1965–68, François Leduc, behaved in a hostile and reprehensible fashion that caused the secretary of state for external affairs and his under-secretary a great deal of anxiety. Paul Martin persisted in thinking that Leduc might only have been obeying orders, but a colleague of Leduc's assured Cadieux that "he was a Gaullist fanatic and that he entered into the President's game without hesitation: in his [the colleague's] opinion if he had been honest he ought to have resigned."[4] At least two other French ambassadors to Canada, one earlier and the other later, are named by Bernard Dorin as having been willing to encourage the Quebec separatists: Raymond Bousquet (1962–65) and Pierre Maillard (1979–81).[5] Furthermore, the French consul general at Quebec City in the years 1967–72, Pierre de Menthon, recalls that "everyone, whether at the embassy or at the consulate general in Montreal, assisted [the consulate general in Quebec City] as best they could in the [aggressive] enterprise desired by the president of the republic."[6]

It was no secret that the French embassy in Ottawa was behaving like the agency of an enemy power, much as Soviet diplomats did; the Cadieuxs were copiously informed of this by Hamilton Southam's second wife, who had been married to a French diplomat. "The personnel at the embassy smile at us willingly," Marcel Cadieux concluded, "but in reality, behind our backs, all these people seek to subvert the French Canadian milieu as much as they can, to attach them to France, to discourage them from seeing their future in federal Canadian terms."[7] When a new ambassador, Pierre Siraud, arrived in August 1968, Cadieux was keen to tell him "that we are not disposed to accept an arrangement whereby we have an official ambassador in Ottawa, who calmly treats with us in matters concerning English Canada, and an unofficial ambassador at Quebec who deals with the Quebec government behind our backs and takes care, in short, of questions that interest French Canadians."[8] And an official at External Affairs told Peter Worthington of the *Toronto Telegram*, "We are getting a bit sick of these so-called French trade commissioners and commercial people coming to Canada and then disappearing into Quebec."[9]

The RCMP was undoubtedly keeping track of all this activity, but neither Lester Pearson nor Pierre Trudeau seems to have grasped all the implications of the RCMP reports they were given.[10] Pearson's response to de Gaulle's "Vive le Québec libre!" speech and Trudeau's outburst in the House of Commons in September 1968, against the activities of Philippe Rossillon in Manitoba and the Maritimes, appear to have been only that – angry words – not parts of a well-considered policy. Trudeau needed time, as any new prime minister would, to gain control of his many responsibilities. One of the things missing was a full realization of Gaullist intentions and the policy behind them. Whatever the cabinet knew, its policy was apparently to keep the public in the dark. In September 1968 Marcel Cadieux only wished the full truth could be revealed about Rossillon, "evidently an employee of [Jacques] Foccart, belonging to the espionnage service." As things were, Canadian journalists could see that the government was angry about French activities but did not really know why.[11]

A year later Trudeau and his government were taking French intervention more seriously. This was after they had learned about the activities of Jean de Lipkowski, the French diplomat – unable to keep his mouth shut, according to Canadians acquainted with him – who ignored Ottawa, travelled directly to Quebec City in October 1969, and there criticized the Canadian government and constitution. The Security Intelligence Branch (SIB) of the RCMP had used electronic surveillance to pick up Lipkowski's conversations during his visit.[12] There was still no policy for dealing firmly with such cases, and he returned home unscathed, even victorious, as did other aggressive Gaullist visitors. The Trudeau government remained more interested in the Quebec hosts than in the French guests.

But having had nearly two years to gather information about the separatist movement, the government wanted to know whether that group was drawing funds from abroad. This was one of three questions then raised, the other two being whether there were FLQ members in the PQ and whether any separatists were in positions of trust and responsibility within the federal government. With these questions in mind, Trudeau drew up a memorandum on 17 December 1969 and arranged a cabinet committee meeting to discuss it in two days' time. His memo was entitled "Current Threats to National Order and on Quebec Separatism."[13] (The crisis of October 1970 and the victory of the PQ in Quebec on 15 November 1976 had not yet taken place.) But Trudeau had already convinced his colleagues that the question of national unity was of primary importance.

Six ministers and thirteen senior civil servants attended the meeting on 19 December, the purpose of which was to arrive at a concerted policy to deal with the troubles then looming. As a result of that gathering, the government asked the SIB to discover what it could about support for the PQ in France, Algeria, and Belgium and about FLQ membership, if any, in the PQ. The question about separatists in the federal government seems also to have preoccupied the SIB, though this was not explicitly stated and there is some disagreement about whether anything was done about it.[14] Already the SIB had begun to gather information about movements of French visitors in Canada and of people such as Jean-Guy Cardinal and Marcel Masse, who travelled frequently between Quebec and France. The Communications Branch of the National Research Council (CBNRC), which later became the Communications Security Establishment (CSE) under the Department of National Defence, had meanwhile resumed intercepting French radio and other signals, as it had done during the Second World War. Thus, from August 1967, possibly a little earlier, and through the 1970s, Ottawa inquired diligently into French machinations in support of separatist movements.[15] John Starnes, appointed on 1 October 1969 to direct the SIB, took over his new duties on 1 January 1970 and set himself to gathering information. Roughly speaking, the government's instructions were to regard the separatists with the same care and suspicion as the Communists had been until then.

Later that year, before a firm security policy had been formulated, FLQ terrorism reached a climax in the "October crisis," which lent new urgency to the problem of separatism. It remains unclear whether Gaullist elements had a hand in the crisis. Certainly there were Frenchmen active in the separatist cause at the time: François Dorlot, Paul Gros d'Aillon, Jacques Lucques, Pierre-Louis Mallen, and Philippe Rossillon, for example. Lucques and a younger Frenchman, Richard Bros, were active in the terrorist FLQ groups, and late in 1970 Bros, who had evidently sought refuge in England after the October crisis, "was found dead in a London jail cell, hanging by his shirt."[16] Lucques had already been arrested on 18 August 1962 in Ville Mont-Royal for painting red "Québec libre" slogans and again on 12 April 1963 as one of the secret founders of the *Comité de libération nationale*. He was also leader of the *Front républicain pour l'indépendance* (FRI), was editor of the incendiary underground journal, *Québec libre*, and had founded a publishing house called *Éditions Chénier*, which published books such as *Peuple de la nuit* (1966) by Joseph Costisella, a professor of literature.[17] But no details have yet been made public about French government agents working secretly with the FLQ. In any event, accounts of the October crisis are invariably based on an assumption that Trudeau appears to have made: that French activity on behalf of the Quebec separatists was only a small part of the independence or sovereignty movement and did not need to be treated separately.

Whatever Trudeau thought, Canadians have had a tendency, in this as in other subjects, to focus on Canadian activities and to regard transatlantic intervention as quite secondary. Marcel Cadieux seems to have been the only high-ranking civil servant with a serious and informed interest in French interference. Few studies of Trudeau and his régime have dwelled on the subject for more than a line or two, except for reporting on de Gaulle's visit in July 1967.[18] Two otherwise outstanding books – one on the RCMP intelligence service and the other on Canada's place in Western secret service networks between 1945 and 1985 – had little to say about the French intelligence system or Gaullist intervention in Quebec.[19] Whatever Canadian intelligence services were reporting, Ottawa was not concerned much about French intervention except in its diplomatic aspect, which, not being secret, is comparatively well understood. A confidential cabinet memorandum of 12 January 1977, soon after the first PQ victory, shows that even then the federal government did not take French interference seriously.[20] When more information is released from government files, it may turn out that French visitors sympathetic to the separatists were under proper surveillance. As far as I can discover, however, the PQ's fund-raising in France, beginning in 1969 and described by Marc Lavallée, who played a part in it, was not detected by Canadian intelligence services.[21] It remained merely a rumour.

Shortly after 1 January 1970, when John Starnes took up his duties at the SIB, he turned to investigating foreign interference in Canada. Almost immediately he asked Joseph Ferraris to set up G Branch, with headquarters in Ottawa and a liaison officer in Paris. Until then, liaison with France had been conducted through an officer posted in London who was scarcely qualified, as he did not even speak French. This reflects a general defect in the SIB at the time – a shortage of bilingual officers. The first liaison officer sent to Paris, John Walsh, soon fell ill and had to be recalled. In 1972 Inspector Joseph Ferraris went over to replace him, and there he undertook the European side of a campaign known as Operation Ham. This endeavour, initiated by Maurice Goguen, an experienced SIB officer, became known to the public later for its dubious and colourful activities in Quebec, much aired by the Keable and McDonald commissions, but Ferraris and his colleagues spent the four years 1972–76 in Paris trying to discover what support the FLQ and the PQ had in France.

G Branch carried on with surveillance of the Gaullist threat until 1973. From 1973 to 1976 this work was in the hands of the newer Foreign Interference Unit in Counter-Intelligence Branch. It was in these years that the RCMP gradually came to use every means at its disposal in the struggle. G Branch gathered information from various sources not yet made public and from informers such as Claude Morin, who reports that its agents questioned him about some thirty suspects, "most of them Frenchmen, some Québécois and a handful of people from other countries."[22] Prominent among them was Philippe Rossillon, who on one of his many visits, it discovered, was carrying a briefcase with some $250,000, presumably for use in his collaboration with nationalists in New Brunswick and Quebec. Rossillon and Xavier Deniau were both present in Quebec about the time of the momentous election on 15 November 1976. Indeed, René Lévesque said he had had an interview with Deniau soon after the vote.[23] These visits were brought to public notice by a broadcast in Montreal on CTV's, W5, possibly as a result of leaks from the RCMP, which certainly found them more sinister than French or Quebec officials would admit to. The findings of the Foreign Interference Unit were, in any case, incorporated in reports for the prime minister.

Though Trudeau did not attach much significance to French encouragement for the separatists, he did give permission for surveillance of the consulate general in Quebec.[24] There were good reasons for this decision. The political activities of the consulate were vastly increased, beginning in 1967, on instructions from the Quai d'Orsay and de Gaulle himself, as Consul General Pierre de Menthon tells us in detail. The staff increased more than ten-fold and new offices were rented, new functions undertaken, and fresh contacts made. With stealth and caution – "ne rien brusquer" Couve de Murville urged – the consulate applied itself to strengthening relations with the Quebec government and pressing Franco–Quebec cooperative ventures. In continual contact with the deputy minister for intergovernmental affairs, Claude Morin, the consul general "took advantage of even the least occasion to advance step by step and make a move forward (poser un jalon)."[25]

The consul general writes, "The movement was underway and the General seemed to admit that it would undoubtedly result in 'independence in one form or another, this not necessarily excluding confederation.' For us it is desirable that the French Canadians have the benefit of independence."[26] In de Menthon's opinion, successes were achieved in two fields of activity: gradual recognition of Quebec sovereignty in international affairs, particularly in French-speaking collaboration;

and freedom for officials to travel between Paris and Quebec City without bothering to take account of Ottawa. As usual, of course, the political activities of the French Quebec mafia were concealed by a mantle of cultural and linguistic exchanges to which no one could sensibly object.

These activities did not go unobserved. With the tacit approval of the federal authorities, who did not inquire closely but left operations to the RCMP, police agents were soon engaged in a series of manoeuvres that were illegal but deemed necessary. Listening by electronic "bugs," recording telephone conversations, copying or stealing records, rough or threatening interrogations, even burglary – all these methods were used from time to time. It is not clear why the RCMP thought this thuggery would pass unchallenged, but no doubt one reason is that other police forces around the world seemed to do pretty much whatever they wished. International practices in this field may have been thought suitable for the Canadian force. In France, for instance, brutality and invasion of privacy were common practice, seldom questioned.[27] Whatever their reasoning, RCMP officers managed to steal a list of the members of the PQ on the night of 8–9 January 1973. They did so under John Starnes's orders.

CLOSE SCRUTINY OF THE RCMP

Little by little, however, these activities came to light. One event that brought out some of them was the trial in 1976 of an ex-RCMP agent, Robert Samson, suspected of planting a bomb in a Montreal garden.[28] Goaded by the court about this, Samson blurted out that he had done worse things for the RCMP, and the court persuaded him to talk about what these were. Journalists again – such as John Sawatsky in the *Vancouver Sun* on 7 December 1976 – took up these revelations. Then two RCMP agents who had been dismissed in 1973, Don McCleery and Gilles Brunet, came forward with information about other such deeds. Superior officers in the RCMP tried to pass off all these revelations as unimportant and, for instance, on 17 June 1977 granted unconditional liberty to three senior officers, Cobb, Cormier, and Coutellier, even though they had pleaded guilty to charges brought against them. There was considerable public outcry; the public was not to know until many years later that Brunet was in fact a spy working for the KGB and doing his best to sow confusion.[29] In 1977 the Quebec government was induced to establish an inquiry, the Keable Commission. Its revelations began to reach up into the senior ranks of the federal government, which in turn, on 6 July 1977, set up the McDonald Commission to investigate, apparently to keep the revelations under its own control.

Between them, these two commissions brought out much more of the illegal activities of the RCMP during the 1970s and even earlier. In the process, other authorities were induced to make confessions or revelations: on 28 October 1977, for instance, the solicitor general of Canada, Francis Fox, admitted that the RCMP had conducted "Operation Ham" against the PQ, and on 16 November he talked about the "Featherbed File," which the RCMP had assembled from undercover studies of the private lives of many leading Québécois.[30] Only a week earlier, Radio-Canada showed that private mail had been opened systematically for several decades – a process that came to be called "Operation Cathedral." The McDonald Report was submitted on 26 January 1981, and the Keable Report, on 6 March. The intervening four years of hearings had shown without a doubt that the RCMP was guilty of illegal behaviour over the previous twenty years, probably longer. However, a great deal was already known about its doings in Quebec even before these reports appeared. As early as 1978 Louis Fournier and five friends were able to publish a study based on a twenty-five page list of police activities they had compiled.[31]

Journalists continued to search for new information. From time to time, some incident or other aroused fresh curiosity about the RCMP's doings in those years. One of the major ones was the discovery by a CBC journalist, Norman Lester, that one of the leading figures in the PQ, Claude Morin, had been recruited as an informer for the RCMP in 1969 by Raymond Parent. Morin's original assignment was to observe communist and other left-wing activity, but as the RCMP moved on to surveillance of the Quebec separatists it questioned him about them too. Another RCMP officer, Léo Fontaine, had interviews with Morin during the early 1970s. When this was eventually discovered and announced on the radio on 7 May 1992, the public in Quebec was shocked and angry.[32] Many hostile articles appeared in the French- language press. Morin was widely denounced and much shaken by this public response. Presumably to clear his name, certainly to explain his relations with these RCMP officers from his own point of view, Morin discussed them at length two years later in his memoirs, *Les choses comme elles étaient: une autobiographie politique*.[33]

Thus a great deal of information about the security operations of the RCMP accumulated over the years. What particularly exercised the Canadian public was the illegal operations. For example, on 6 October 1972 RCMP agents had broken into the offices of the *Agence de presse libre du Québec* at 3459 rue Saint-Hubert in Montreal and stolen a quantity of documents. One of their purposes in so doing was to have a list of the members of the *Mouvement pour la défense des prisonniers politiques du Québec*, which shared premises with the *Agence de*

presse libre.[34] "Bugs" had been placed in the rooms of certain PQ
leaders, such as Louise Beaudoin and René Lévesque.[35] Suspects had
sometimes suffered brutal treatment at police hands. There had evidently been a lawless disregard for justice and civil rights.

It also became general knowledge that the federal government was
trying to play down this exposure of the RCMP and to excuse it on the
grounds of national security. In spring 1978 the Keable Commission
tried for three months to gain access to RCMP documents, but Ottawa
argued that it had no right to do so.[36] On 31 October 1978 the
Supreme Court of Canada formally prevented the commission from
making a full inquiry into the activities of the RCMP and ordered it to
confine its investigation to the doings of suspected individuals. Naturally the public viewed this as an official effort to conceal police misdeeds. As more and more evidence emerged, the political opposition
used it to good effect in Parliament, and the federal government was
more and more discredited.[37] At the same time, a counter-current of
public support for the RCMP, deeply rooted in the public mind, encouraged the government to hope it could survive this trouble.

The public also observed that the government seemed to be refusing
to take responsibility for RCMP misdeeds. One of the big issues pursued
by journalists was whether or not Ottawa had ordered or authorized
the RCMP to commit the illegals acts. In the absence of definite proof,
it was difficult to know, but journalists in Quebec inferred from the
accumulated evidence, incomplete though it was, that Trudeau's government was guilty but unwilling to take responsibility for deeds done
in its name. Pierre Cloutier, for example, concluded in *La Presse* of
Montreal: "All of these brute facts lead me to believe that the McDonald Commission, faced with an unprecedented scandal, chose to keep
the secret and to say nothing, using routine procedure to bury the
explosive testimony of Mr. Starnes in the darkness of the shadows."[38]
Others, too, came to this conclusion. Archie Barr, an officer in the SIB,
alleged that the government had known perfectly well about RCMP
covert activities and was just pretending ignorance to protect itself
from public censure.[39]

While the RCMP was attacked by a part of the Canadian public for
its thuggery, it suffered criticism in federal government circles for a different reason. Some politicians and officials had long thought that it
was unsuitable for secret service work; others accused it of being inef-
ficient, even incompetent. Stories circulated about uneducated consta-
bles with primitive political ideas investigating trade unions and even
university professors, such as the "Waffle" Group of the New Democratic party, for holding the sort of left-wing views denounced by
Senator Joseph McCarthy in the United States.[40] Marcel Cadieux

reproached the force for giving him no useful information whatever during the six years he was under-secretary of state at External Affairs. "We had to fight off the assaults of France while deprived of the means that a modern intelligence service could have given us."[41] These opinions came out gradually; the RCMP had friends as well as critics, and defended itself with skill and determination.

THE OCTOBER CRISIS

The October crisis brought this conflict out into the open in 1970. By using the War Measures Act, calling out the army, and thus by-passing the RCMP, the government seemed to show that it had lost confidence in the police forces. Certain cabinet members, such as Jean Marchand, were openly sceptical of the RCMP's abilities. The accessible records of the October crisis do not warrant a single, steady view of what was done, much less what ought to have been done, and dealing with the hurly-burly of a crisis is of course harder than meting out criticism in retrospect. However, at least two contradictory opinions are widely held in Ottawa: one, that the government was justified in calling out the army and imposing the War Measures Act; and the other, that the police forces ought to have been left to deal with the crisis in their own way.

Trudeau and Pelletier would like us to believe that they turned to the army because the SIB of the RCMP gave them too little information.[42] Lester Pearson, the previous prime minister, seems to have shared their views.[43] Mitchell Sharp, then secretary of state for external affairs, hardly notices the issue of the RCMP's role.[44] Some observers believed that a cabinet committee appointed by Trudeau on 7 May 1970 had already decided to impose the War Measures Act in case of trouble.[45] If so, it may have been because of the army's anxiety to prevent FLQ terrorists from seizing atomic weapons near Val d'Or, Quebec.[46] Certainly an emergency meeting of higher officials on 22 October 1970 decided, in the absence of any RCMP representation, to establish a task force that might draw up analytical reports of a type that the RCMP seemed incapable of producing. This decision was taken by R. Gordon Robertson of the Privy Council Office (PCO), Marc Lalonde of the Prime Minister's Office (PMO), Donald Wall of the Security Panel, Lieutenant-General Michael Dare of the Canadian Army, a certain William Little, and Deputy Solicitor-General Ernest Côté. As a result, a task force in the PCO began to analyse the files of the SIB independently of the RCMP.[47] This procedure, like the use of the army to deal with the October crisis, seemed to show a loss of confidence in the RCMP.

The RCMP was, and is, defended by John Starnes, director general of the SIB from 1970 to 1973, who believes that it did its job well: "Information was consistently provided to the federal government in written and oral briefs."[48] The work of the PCO task force was fine but unnecessary. If RCMP agents were thin on the ground in Quebec, this was not only because it then had too few bilingual officers but also because Quebec had its own provincial police – the Sûreté du Québec (SQ) – with which the RCMP collaborated. If some federal authorities were ill-prepared for the October crisis, this was because they had no practical idea of what to do with the information they received.[49] That Trudeau and General Allard's Mobile Command were prepared, as we see below in chapter 10, did not reflect badly on the RCMP.

However that may be, it was only at the urgent request of authorities in Quebec City and Montreal that Ottawa agreed to impose the War Measures Act at all. Their request, Gordon Robertson (then secretary to the cabinet) recalls, began with a telephone call from Julien Chouinard, secretary to the Quebec provincial cabinet, who told him that the SQ, busy looking for British Trade Commissioner James Cross's kidnappers, needed to be able to arrest more suspects and hold them longer than was legally possible except under the War Measures Act.[50] It was thus that in mid-October the mayor of Montreal, the premier and the minister of justice in Quebec, Trudeau, and their advisers, all in touch with one another by telephone, took matters into their own hands. It may be, as one retired RCMP agent believes, that Mayor Jean Drapeau was hoping to pass the expensive police operations of the time on to the federal government in order to save money! But the essential point is that the War Measures Act was imposed in response to pressing appeals from authorities in Quebec.

The federal government was divided in its response. A sign of its confusion is that cabinet ministers offered a variety of explanatory statements. The minister of justice, John Turner, spoke to the House of Commons about a huge conspiracy to subvert democratic government in Canada. The minister of defence, Donald MacDonald, talked about a carefully planned "revolutionary timetable." And Jean Marchand, minister of regional economic expansion, thought there were three thousand armed FLQ terrorists who had "infiltrated all the vital places of the province of Quebec, all the key posts where important decisions are taken."[51] There was much talk of an impending coup d'état. On 30 October Trudeau said he thought an attempt had been made to form a "provisional government" in Quebec.

Furthermore, there seem to have been two, possibly even three, crisis centres in Ottawa: a Strategic Operations Centre answerable to the prime minister, was headed by Jim Davey, Marc Lalonde and his parliamentary secretary Jean-Pierre Goyer; one at the Château Laurier

Hotel (as explained in chapter 10 below), which may not be the same as the afore-mentioned; and another in the Department of External Affairs, directed by Claude Roquet, who played a notable part in the release of James Cross but who subsequently fell under the spell of a leading Quebec separatist, Louise Beaudoin, and so became an employee of the PQ government of Quebec![52] Joseph Ferraris, an officer in the SIB, alleges that the War Measures Act and its consequences interrupted police work and held up the rescue of James Cross by three weeks.[53]

POLICY VACUUM

When the use of the RCMP and its undercover activities were exposed by the McDonald and Keable commissions, and in the writings of journalists such as Richard Cléroux, Gilles Paquin, and John Sawatsky, there was an outcry in English-speaking Canada as well as Quebec by people for whom abuses of police powers seemed more dangerous than French influences. The two commissions set the tone for public debate by exposing and denouncing the RCMP and the government that seemed to have authorized its illegal practices. The RCMP was widely denounced, and the purpose of its activities was forgotten or passed over as trivial. The obvious efforts of the federal government to avoid taking responsibility for the SIB added to the confusion. Public opinion was thereby drawn to focus on what, in the context of this study, was essentially a school of red herring. I do not mean that the illegal activities of the RCMP were anything but reprehensible, or that the federal government ought not to have been called to account for them. What I mean is that the dangers of Quebec separatism and of French encouragement were obscured in the hue and cry. In their efforts to embarrass the government and the RCMP over illegal police activities, the public overlooked the political dangers of French intervention, which had been aired in the press occasionally since September 1968.

Take, for example, a leading article on the subject by Michael Mandel in the March 1982 number of the *Canadian Forum*.[54] Nowhere does Mandel show recognition or concern for what the federal government had been trying to achieve. Not one word does he spare for the need to monitor separatist and French efforts to indoctrinate the population of Quebec. His careful and detailed journalistic summary of legal objections to the behaviour of the government and the RCMP is admirable in itself, but it is one-sided and shows total ignorance or disregard for the government's efforts to inform itself about the FLQ and its French friends. As a result of widespread public criticism of this kind, these efforts faltered, as the government endeavoured to recover its footing. This result was, of course, as much the fault of the government as of its critics. The net effect, however, was that official opposition to separatism and to French support for separatism was restricted to little more than the diplomatic manoeuvres of the Department of External Affairs. Security forces within Canada were all but emasculated in this field.

What seems to have been forgotten is that the RCMP had been combating a movement dangerous to Canadian unity and ought therefore to have been encouraged to go on with its task in some more acceptable way. After all, in most countries such police behaviour, illegal or not, would have been regarded as more or less excusable for reasons of national security. Even in Canada a large part of the public could have been relied on to take this view of things. Many of the police witnesses who appeared before courts and commissions (writes Cléroux) spoke as though they were waging a war. In their view, the struggle against the FLQ and the PQ, not yet established as a democratic party, warranted such nasty methods as seemed necessary. Looking back on events from the late 1990s it is difficult not to conclude that they had a point in dealing with opponents such as the hostile elements in the Soviet Union and the French Fifth Republic. As we see below in chapter 10, Canadian officers with a knowledge of revolutionary warfare were expecting an uprising of what they thought was an armed political party. Even if we say nothing of the KGB, of which the evils have been sufficiently exposed, the French Quebec mafia has never been disciplined or brought to order in France, almost no matter what it has done. After an initial round of criticism in the French press, de Gaulle's outrageous speech in Montreal on 24 July 1967 received official and public support in France. Nothing like the Canadian public's assault on the RCMP and the government responsible for it could occur in France. National security, "raison d'État," and French prestige abroad have been sufficient reasons in France for such acts as blowing up the *Rainbow Warrior*, insulting the Canadian government, and launching a series of official and semi-official campaigns to encourage and assist the separatist movement in Quebec.

The Trudeau government seems to have been preoccupied with its own political quandary. Whatever the reasons for Trudeau's focus on the Quebec separatists, it exposed his government to charges of fighting a political battle under a false banner of national security, and some Quebec observers have indeed levelled that charge.[55] The RCMP, for its part, "adopted a completely non-partisan stance," as John Starnes later assured the McDonald Commission.[56] But in hindsight it looks very much as though a safer and clearer case could have been made by waging the struggle against French interference, even on the basis of what was then known about it, rather than against separatism.[57] Certainly the anti-separatist campaign that Trudeau proposed was hampered by divisions within his cabinet. John Turner, then minister of justice, was anxious about the political dangers of being seen to use federal forces for settling political problems in Quebec.[58] Gérard Pelletier thought that as long as it was not illegal to believe in separatism then a distinction had to be drawn between the violent FLQ (then active) and the peaceful political movement for a separate Quebec. The most hawkish minister in support of Trudeau was Leo Cadieux, at National Defence, who favoured using the army as it was used in October 1970. Outside cabinet, Marcel Cadieux (no relation of Leo's), was also a hawk, as we saw in chapter 7. Leonard Higgitt, who was in charge of the RCMP, wanted only clear purposes and clear orders.

One fateful step of the federal government was to decide that peaceful, "democratic" political activity in favour of Quebec's independence was legitimate, whether French or Québécois, and that only violence or conspiracy to bring about violence need be firmly dealt with. This policy, which many saw as inevitable, emerged slowly, almost absentmindedly, during the struggle to limit the activities of the RCMP and was enshrined in the act that set up the new civil Canadian Security and Intelligence Service (CSIS) in 1984.[59] No such policy is evident in the report of the Royal Commission on Security, submitted on 23 September 1968 by its chairman, M.W. Mackenzie, which first recommended establishment of a civil Canadian security agency separate from the RCMP.[60] The result of the reforming process thus begun was that no federal authority undertook to oppose French collaboration with the PQ and other influence in Quebec. The French consulate general, as Pierre de Menthon tells us, was left to do almost anything it wished in support of the separatist movements.[61] Separatist leaders were free to conspire with their French friends on both sides of the Atlantic and to arrange for seminars, scholarships, publications, exchanges, classes, and so on that might promote their separatist ideology.

The practical effect of these developments is that for at least thirty years the powerful, one-sided campaign to convert the Quebec public to the separatist ideology has been nobody else's official business. Canadian diplomats resisted Quebec independence in the international sphere, and Canadian policemen watched for the criminal activities of the FLQ and its foreign friends. Neither of these authorities thought it necessary to oppose foreign interference in Quebec politics. On the whole, this is still their opinion. In 1997 I questioned several members of both the diplomatic and the police services who were in responsible positions during the 1960s and 1970s. Almost none of them thought

French support for separatism mattered. Indeed, some of them hardly understood what I was talking about. "What do you want to do, declare war?," one of them shouted at me sarcastically. Others refused to believe that French-speaking Canadians would be influenced from France. The typical diplomatic view was that French activity was part of the normal intellectual process in the world of *la francophonie*. Security officers in the RCMP, which had been entrusted with national security matters until 1984, had spent their time in Canada and France tracking the FLQ and its contacts abroad. Their assurance to me – "The French had very little influence in Quebec" – meant that there was little evidence of French people or money being used in the violent projects of the FLQ or the funding of the PQ. Any political effects of French indoctrination seem to have been overlooked by federal authorities.

One of the troubles that dogged the SIB of the RCMP was uncertainty about exactly what it was trying to combat. Many agents much of the time seem to have thought, like the Trudeau government, that the Quebec separatist movements were the enemy. But this attitude took them into the dangerous waters that overwhelmed the SIB. It became apparent that a political opponent, such as the PQ was to the Liberal party, is not the same as a foreign enemy of the country. Certainly liberal principles militated against official denunciation of the PQ. And if the PQ was not an enemy, how could its French friends be seen as enemies? Somehow the treason, sedition, or political subversion of conspiring to break up Canada did not seem reprehensible unless it were violent or broke some specific law.

Surveillance of the French consulate general in Quebec produced no proof of criminal violence or conspiracy, only evidence of active separatist sympathies.[62] Unfortunately for Canada those very sympathies, applied in the promotion of French separatist doctrine, were reinforcing the Quebec separatist movement. But the peaceful promotion of French revolutionary theory to build up support for independence was not illegal and was, in any event, hardly understood in Ottawa. Somehow, the PQ interpretation of this process came to prevail in Canadian public opinion: that preparing the Quebec public for the process of "liberation" was merely a normal part of the democratic process. A part of the public, indignant over the behaviour of its principal police force, was pressing for justice and democratic control of police behaviour. The PQ, Richard Cléroux, Louis Fournier and his colleagues, Pierre Godin, and others write as though it were scandalous for the federal government and the RCMP to watch and oppose the separatist movement. "It did not seem to matter to them," writes Cléroux, "that the PQ had been a recognized political party with the legitimate objective of taking Quebec out of Canada by legal means."[63] How, one wonders, did that objective come to be legitimate? And yet in spite of Cléroux's words, it had mattered to the RCMP: the commissioners had raised objections when Lester Pearson's "special committee" of the Security Panel had urged it in a meeting of 29 September 1967 to spy on the Parti Québécois.[64]

For many citizens, such scruples and the idea that the PQ's program was legitimate, as long as it was peaceful, would seem right and normal, but others would be readier to accept another interpretation. When did it become acceptable and legal (they might say) for a party of people to work for the division of the country? Is that sort of work not what is meant by such terms as "sedition," "subversion," and "treason"? When did the PQ come to be regarded as a legitimate, democratic movement? The question is important, because that was when the French Quebec mafia's activities also became respectable and no longer preventable. As allies or patrons of the separatists, the French could scarcely be kept out once the PQ had been tolerated as merely a democratic political party. The federal government – at what point? – seems to have lost the moral advantage and allowed itself to be shamed into inactivity.

EMERGENCE OF CSIS

The demise of the SIB has not improved matters. For its own reasons, the Trudeau government took advantage of the RCMP's unpopularity to take national security out of its hands. The first step in the process was to concede that the RCMP had behaved so badly that it could no longer be trusted with the management of security in Canada. Trudeau agreed with those who wanted to establish a central agency to assist in coordinating a security policy. After holding the McDonald Report for some seven months, until 25 August 1981, the government put forward a plan for a new civil security agency to replace the SIB. Passed into law in 1983, this plan was revised and developed by a committee chaired by Michael Pitfield. It was adopted on 21 June 1984, right at the end of Trudeau's years, not long before the Conservatives won the election of 4 September 1984. On 16 July 1984 the old SIB was quietly converted, in effect, to the new Canadian Security Intelligence Service (CSIS).[65] CSIS hired the security officers from the old RCMP, who moved to a building on Wellington Street, opposite the National Archives, and carried on. This not being ideal accommodation, in due course they moved again into a larger building at 1941 Ogilvie Road in the Gloucester suburbs east of Ottawa, where they still are.

Meanwhile an older intelligence agency, the Communications Security Establishment (CSE) under the Department of National Defence,

long busy with listening to foreign radio signals, carried on as before
in the Sir Leonard Tilley Building and in several buildings on Heron
Road.[66] However, the CSE began to make special efforts to break into
communications between Quebec and France after the election of the
PQ government on 15 November 1976. An officer of the CSE, Mike
Frost, employed from 1972 to 1990, alleges that the Trudeau government then "wanted to know everything that was said and done
between Quebec and France."[67] One of the first steps was to establish
a special section called "French Problem." Then the governments of
Norway, and possibly of other Scandinavian governments, were asked
whether they could intercept French communications, as they had been
doing Soviet ones for many years, and selling Canada their findings.
Frost declares that the Norwegian services did so and were particularly
successful in recording telex messages.[68] In addition, the CSE's secret
"Pilgrim" project, of which he was a working member, did its best to
monitor French communications from various parts of the world,
notably at Rabat on the Atlantic coast of Morocco.[69]

Unlike the RCMP, the CSE and CSIS are not police forces and have
neither the mandate nor the means to take action against a national
enemy. Their business is surveillance. They have presumably continued
to watch the PQ's connections with France, but watching the PQ and its
friends in the French Quebec mafia is not going to prevent it from split-
ting the country. Merely keeping track of such political threats brings
to mind the child's story of Teddy Robinson, the teddy bear asked to
watch bread toasting on the breakfast table: he watched it turn brown
and then black. When the toast burst into flames, Teddy was still faithfully watching it. Is the purpose of the intelligence agencies merely to
watch in order to keep the cabinet well informed about the breakup of
the country? One might assume so, because the government appears to
have done almost nothing to impede the efforts of the PQ and its
friends in France.

By the time CSIS had been formed in 1984, the Trudeau era was
almost ended. Brian Mulroney's government, which won the election
of 1984, took a wholly different tack in dealing with the separatists
and their French patrons: reconciliation, compromise, a fresh beginning were hopes of the Mulroney approach. But it did not have the
desired effect, and the new beginnings soon bogged down in the fanatical determination of the PQ to take advantage of every opportunity,
including those offered gratuitously by Mulroney, to push on with its
policy of separation/sovereignty. None of Mulroney's separatist ministers – Gilles Loiselle, Marcel Masse, or Lucien Bouchard, soon to be
ambassador in Paris – changed their minds or modified their separatist
inclinations.

A Military Response

The Gaullist cold war with Canada attracted the attention of certain Canadian army officers – and the prime ministers they served – who were facing the terrorists of the *Front de libération du Québec* (FLQ) from 1963. The story of their efforts to deal with the threats they saw remains obscure but can be sketched in its main lines on the basis of Major-General Dan Loomis's recollections and research as well as those of John Ross Matheson.[1] The FLQ was, of course, a domestic movement, but it had foreign connections that may be glimpsed in the records and testimony of the time. Not only did it have members from France, Algeria, and Belgium, but it was evidently linked in some way with simultaneous terrorist activities in other parts of the world. In the peculiar circumstances of the 1960s the FLQ had a place in a pattern of fanatical enthusiasms that can be traced partly to France, with its revolutionary tradition, and even to Charles de Gaulle and his followers.

To understand how this could be, it is essential to realize that the FLQ was an armed political party similar to the Irish Republican Army (IRA), the Algerian *Front de la libération nationale* (FLN), and similar movements of the time; that is, it had a military wing and a political wing, according to the revolutionary precepts explained below. François Schirm, a former soldier in the French Foreign Legion, had founded the principal armed part of the FLQ, the *Armée républicaine du Québec* (ARQ), in 1964.[2] While its forces engaged in violent acts during the following years, its colleagues in the political wing of the FLQ used methods that included the recruiting of foreign fund-raising sympathizers and other kinds of support abroad. Though neither unified nor coordinated, the groups or cells of the FLQ followed the IRA and FLN models, which had not been notably coherent, either. The warfare of liberation in the 1960s did not depend, even in theory, on unified organization. Many people, including university faculty and military men with no knowledge of revolutionary warfare, are inclined to misinterpret this subject, as much of the writing about the October crisis shows.

This chapter looks first at the general context – postwar insurrections and revolutionary theory. Next it considers the response to Quebec's situation orchestrated by Lester Pearson which led to creation of mobile command under General Allard. Finally it re-examines the October crisis and offers some conclusions.

CONTEXT

Postwar Insurrection

Military observers alert to the dangers of grass-roots violence and armed insurrection had much to think about during the 1960s. The subject is as old as recorded time, but there was something particularly alarming about the terrorist activities that broke out in various parts of the world soon after the end of the Second World War. For one thing, the governments of the Soviet Union, the People's Republic of China, and some of their satellite countries were fomenting revolution wherever they could, for their own ideological reasons. For another, insurrection was being formulated in theoretical and practical manuals that encouraged angry people to sow terror and confusion in the name of whatever cause they chose to adopt or to invent. And France with its revolutionary tradition – memories of 1789–94, 1830, 1848, and 1871 – attracted revolutionaries. After all, it had offered a home to most of the nationalist, socialist, and communist revolutionaries of the nineteenth century. There was every reason to anticipate that it would likewise offer shelter and encouragement to insurgents from Quebec, and it did indeed do this, as we saw above.

Popular insurrection was in the air, especially in student and labouring circles, when I first arrived in Paris in September 1953. Trade unions belonging to the huge *Confédération générale du travail* (CGT) were obedient to the Communist party, as was one of the two systems of youth hostels, the *Confédération nationale des auberges de jeunesse.* Communist organizations like these identified themselves by the false comradeship of an immediate *tutoiement* (use of the familiar "tu" rather than the the formal "vous" in address) followed by an assumption that whoever came to them was also ready for a "people's revolution" or a politically motivated general strike. There was intense activity at the Communist party headquarters, where editorials were written for *L'Humanité*, the inflammatory communist daily that formed opinion in the growing left wing of the French public. Heads popped up in the windows as I steadied my antique folding Zeiss camera to take a photograph of the building under its huge sign, "Parti Communist Français." They seemed excessively self-conscious, even though Communists had, after all, played a leading part in the wartime resistance movements against the Nazi German occupation and regarded the Fourth Republic as merely a temporary obstacle to their own inevitable triumph.

The French Communist party of the early 1950s was winning more than 20 per cent of the popular vote in the national elections. Communists were preponderant in certain government departments, such as the Ministry for National Education. As a student of French history at the Sorbonne, I was quickly informed that a prominent member of the party was a historian, Albert Soboul (1914–92), who was preparing to publish a thesis on the terrorists of 1792–94, and his teacher holding the chair of the French Revolution, a socialist named Georges Lefebvre (1874–1959), was famous for his doctoral thesis on peasants in the *Département du Nord* during the revolution.[3] Two of Lefebvre's foreign admirers, George Rude and Kåre Tønnesson, both communist friends of Soboul, took me under their wing. With their guidance, I soon purchased Lefebvre's *Révolution française*, a masterful Marxist interpretation generally accepted by professional historians, French and foreign, in those years.[4] I was reminded that Stanley Ryerson, a prominent Communist historian in Canada, had studied in Paris during the 1930s.

It seemed the most natural thing in Paris then to buy and read, as I did, *Technique du coup d'état* by a well-known Italian journalist and writer, Curzio Malaparte (1898–1957), who set out to show the methods by which revolutionaries had subverted and then overthrown governments in France in 1799, Russia in 1917, Poland in 1920, and Italy in 1922.[5] In the first edition of the book, published in 1931, for which Mussolini's government imprisoned him for five years, Malaparte had concluded with a chapter correctly predicting that Adolf Hitler would soon overthrow the Weimar Republic in Germany. Malaparte's purpose, as he explained in the 1948 edition of the book, had been to arouse liberal democratic governments to the dangers of such coups d'état, and he lamented that so few had proved able to defend themselves. Liberal democrats were too often victims of their own tolerant, benevolent weaknesses.

Another student of the coup d'état, its uses, and its prevention was Charles de Gaulle. Indeed, Curzio Malaparte relates how he and de Gaulle watched events in the streets of Warsaw from the same window of the Hotel Bristol while an uprising overthrew the Polish government in August 1920.[6] De Gaulle was then thirty years old, serving as a *com-*

mandant attached to General Henrys, head of the French Military Mission to Poland. An attentive student of history and the events of his time, de Gaulle knew how Leon Trotsky (1879–1940) had directed the overthrow of the tsarist government in 1917 by training terrorists to infiltrate the armed forces, the police, trade unions, and student groups and then to take control of the Russian nerve centres – railway and telegraph stations, army and police headquarters, town halls, and trade unions – pretending all the while to be acting in the name of "the people". Thanks to this knowledge and to Winston Churchill's support, de Gaulle was ready for the Communists, backed by the Soviet Union under Stalin, as they set out to take command of France at the liberation in 1944. The triumphant march of French regiments along the Champs Élysées on 26 August was a soldier's solution to the problem of Communist subversion and insurrection. The patriotic national pride that went with that march served as an ideological antidote to the Communist propaganda that might otherwise have undermined resistance to a Communist takeover. Needless to relate, de Gaulle was also ready for the uprisings of the summer of 1961 and those of May 1968 that might have overcome a less prepared leader. Similar uprisings had overthrown French governments, as he well knew, in July 1789, August 1792, July 1794, November 1799, 1814, 1815, July 1830, February 1848, September 1870, and (in a sense) June 1940.

The patriotic ideology that de Gaulle used to win public support for his régime in 1944 and again in 1958 turned against him, and against France, in the colonies overseas. No one understood the nationalist uprising in Indochina and Algeria better than he did. By 1962 the Chinese-inspired national liberation movement in Vietnam and the *Front de la libération nationale* (FLN) in Algiers had deprived France of colonies it had fought hard to keep. These losses came as profound shocks. At the end of my first year in Paris I witnessed the national anger and dismay that swept through France when Dien Bien Phu in Vietnam fell to communist forces on 7 May 1954. I happened to be in Paris again in the summer of 1962 when similar anguish seized public opinion as the government was negotiating the independence of Algeria. The effect of these defeats on de Gaulle and the Gaullists, however, was to convert their own French nationalism into that species of imperialism that has been attempting to subvert the Québécois, the Acadians, the Walloons, and the people of the Swiss Jura ever since. Their old empire lost, Gaullists took to developing another by encouraging the nationalism of French-speaking peoples in Quebec and elsewhere by precept, by indoctrination, by cultural exchange programs, and by financial assistance.

Only one part of the Gaullist imperial enterprise concerns us in this chapter: support and encouragement for creation of a republic in Quebec by popular insurrection. This endeavour is impossible to document at present in its entirety, and people disposed to reject anything short of documentary proof may pour scorn on such a hypothesis. Fortunately the Canadian prime ministers of the 1960s and the military officers they recruited took the threat seriously. Not that they saw it as a purely French threat; on the contrary, it seemed to them to be a Quebec revolutionary movement with French and other foreign support. They thought of the element from France, including the political leaders discussed in the press, such as Philippe Rossillon and Xavier Deniau, and also the two or three thousand young conscripts, the *coopérants*, doing duty as teachers and assistants in various businesses and offices, only as parts of a gathering of foreigners sympathetic to the separatist movement, including people from Algeria, Cuba, the Soviet Union, and other countries in Latin America. The undercover revolutionaries from France, such as Jacques Lucques and others discussed above in chapter 3, do not appear to have been identified as French by authorities in Ottawa.

THEORY AND PRACTICE OF REVOLUTION

The few observers in Ottawa who thought about these dangers were aware, however, of the revolutionary writings, particularly the manuals on revolutionary warfare, published in the 1960s and earlier. Probably the fundamental work in this field had been done in the 1930s by Mao Tse-Tung (1893–1976).[7] Studying the methods and theory of Leon Trotsky during the Russian Revolution, Mao saw that they were intended for the purposes of sudden, short-term insurrectionary movements. His own contribution was to apply the ideas of the great German strategist Karl von Clausewitz (1780–1831) to the Marxist methods and so to provide a kind of recipe for protracted revolutionary warfare, which became the basis for future wars of national liberation.[8] Mao Tse-Tung's works, promoted by his practical successes in China and elsewhere in Asia, were soon accessible in translation and became the inspiration for further manuals of a similar kind. Prominent among them were the writings of a Spanish-American revolutionary, Ernesto ("Che") Guevara (1928–67) that were read by a few responsible authorities in Canada as well as by would-be revolutionaries. Guevara's *Guerilla Warfare* (1960), followed by his "Guerrilla Warfare: A Method" (1963) and "Message to the Tricontinental" (1967), were recipes for the overthrow of governments.[9] His principal targets were the military dictatorships in Latin America, where his advice and example proved to be particularly successful, and Fidel Castro based his triumphant campaigns in Cuba on similar methods.

Revolutionaries in other countries quickly adapted the ideas of Mao and Che Guevara for other circumstances. In 1961 an Algerian revolutionary, Frantz Fanon (1925–61), published in Paris *Les damnés de la terre*, which was widely read by Quebec intellectuals and soon translated as *The Wretched of the Earth*. In France, Regis Debray (b. 1940), one of the heroes of the May 1968 uprising in Paris, had already published his reflections on the campaign he had fought in Bolivia with Guevara under the title *Revolution in the Revolution?*[10] In Canada, Pierre Vallières drew on Che Guevara in some of his incendiary writings, and there was much talk of him in the Montreal revolutionary journal, *Québec Libre* (1963–5). Vallières also paid close attention to the writings of a Guatemalan, Jean José Arévalo, which appeared in the early 1960s.[11] Another guerrilla leader, George Grivas, with a reputation resulting from his determined resistance to British rule in Cyprus during the 1950s, wrote memoirs that were translated in 1964.[12] In 1969 there appeared yet another influential manual, Carlos Marighella's *Mini-Manual for Urban Guerrillas*.[13]

These writings gave rise to even more studies of them by observers of various kinds. For instance, in 1961 an American brigadier general, Samuel B. Griffith, published a full translation of Mao's writings, with commentaries.[14] Through the 1960s military officers and others, particularly in the United States, published their own studies of a branch of warfare that was coming to be known as insurgency and counter-insurgency, or "low-intensity warfare."[15]

Students of the subject also worked through the records of some famous examples of insurgency and counter-insurgency campaigns. T.E. Lawrence (1888–1935) published two famous accounts of how, under his leadership, Arabs fought successfully against their Turkish overlords during the First World War.[16] General W.J. Slim (1891–1970) had led a successful campaign against Japanese forces in Burma during the later stages of the Second World War, which was refined by the British for use against the Communist terrorists in Malaya after the war.[17] The FLN in Algeria waged a winning campaign against French forces and achieved national independence in 1962.[18] In practical terms, Canadian peacekeeping forces also learned a good deal about guerrilla methods in the 1950s and 1960s while on missions in Kashmir, Palestine, Gaza, Sinai, the Congo, and Lebanon.[19] Then, in May 1968, students in and near Paris, some of them self-styled Trotskyists and Maoists, carried out a near-revolution under the leadership of people such as the German-Jewish student, Daniel Cohn-Bendit.[20]

The year 1968 was indeed a remarkable one for observers of insurrection and counter-insurgency.[21] Students and Black activitists in many parts of the United States rose up during that year, and I witnessed one such event at Cornell University that was featured in *Time* magazine and had surprising effects on the faculty and administration. The Department of History, for instance, felt that some sort of revolution of authority was required in response to the trouble, proposed to admit students to departmental committees, and seemed to be generally rattled. A kind of revolutionary committee was formed by a group of young faculty and postgraduate students. Meanwhile, a posse of armed forces in the nearby town of Ithaca was poised to provoke a shoot-out with the students. In some personal turmoil and feeling very much like a Canadian alien, I quit the department and returned to Canada with indelible memories of the atmosphere of hysteria that I had left behind. This experience was trivial, of course, by comparison with the Russian invasion of Czechoslovakia in August that year, which soon provoked a popular insurrection of a more serious kind.

What students of guerrilla warfare learned from all this, but particularly the military campaigns and insurrectionary manuals, was that it was possible for a relatively small group of determined leaders to topple a government by sustained low-level revolutionary warfare. Provided they had a cause to which they were committed, whether nationalist, Communist, or what might be called romantic/liberation, a few leaders could provoke the armed forces of a country to take violent measures that might then arouse a revolutionary sympathy among the population in general. In the case of Quebec, for example, nationalism was sufficiently strong that in certain circumstances it might quickly raise large crowds in support of separatist leaders, or so a few students of protracted revolutionary warfare in Ottawa believed. This was what a small high-ranking group set out to prepare for, anticipating a war for national liberation in the St Lawrence Valley.

OTTAWA'S RESPONSE

A War of Liberation in Quebec?

The leader in Ottawa's preparations for dealing with modern insurrection, according to General Loomis, was Prime Minister Lester Pearson. Whatever his failings in the politics and diplomacy of dealing with Gaullist aggression, Pearson showed far-sighted imagination and firm resolve in stimulating military preparedness. His own experience in the army, overseas and subsequently as a historian and diplomat with the League of Nations, had led him to appreciate the dangers of subversion and insurrection of the kind that was being practised in various parts of the world. When FLQ violence broke out in 1963 he was quick to see that something ought to be done, and done soon, to prepare for a revolutionary situation that police forces might not be able to cope with, particularly if they happened to be infiltrated by Quebec terrorists.

He seems to have been attentive to the advice of certain army officers from Quebec, perhaps Jacques Dextrase and also Gilles Turcot, once General Allard's second-in-command in the Royal 22nd Regiment. As one of his parliamentary assistants recalls, Pearson gave a lecture on "Keeping the Peace" at Carleton University on 7 May 1964, which showed that he already had in mind the preparations soon to be carried out secretly in the Canadian forces.[22] So complete was the compartmental separation of the planning groups and the secrecy surrounding their preparations that there is no known list of those who were privy to what was going on. Indeed, many people continue to deny that any such operations were afoot, on the grounds that they would have known if there were.

It was not long before Pearson called on General Jean Victor Allard (1913–1996), the senior serving French-Canadian officer, who, as he knew, was a keen student of revolutionary warfare in all its forms. In mid-June 1965 he appointed Allard to head what was to be called a Mobile Command. Allard discusses this phase of his career in his memoirs without making reference to the anti-FLQ objectives, partly because he did not wish to embarrass his descendants with a record of his work in that field and partly, of course, because he was expected to keep the campaign secret.[23] He was a soldier with experience commanding the 22nd Regiment during the Second World War and the Canadian Brigade during the Korean War. General (later Governor General) Georges Vanier thought him "a splendid fellow ... full of courage and initiative."[24] Not all of Allard's initiatives were well received by the government – he once suggested interposing Canadian troops between the Arab and Israeli forces in the 1960s – but he was capable, imaginative, and well versed in insurgency warfare. As head of the secret anti-FLQ planning group, Allard was answerable to Prime Minister Pearson and, from April 1968, to his successor, Pierre Trudeau.

But Trudeau may already have been in the secret earlier, as one of two parliamentary assistants to Prime Minister Pearson, the other being John Ross Matheson. It appears that Matheson was entrusted with liaison concerning the military side of the preparations, and Trudeau looked after the political and social side – what General Loomis calls "the hearts and minds." Matheson stresses, however, that neither Pearson nor Allard told him what was afoot. He knew what the Mobile Command was for only because, as an experienced military officer (badly wounded in the Second World War), he knew that CF-5 aircraft would be useful for nothing else but service within Canada; he interpreted Lester Pearson's lecture on peacekeeping at Carleton University on 7 May 1964 as directed at Quebec, and he saw other such signs.[25]

In Pearson's small, impromptu group of close advisers were Léo Cadieux, minister of national defence; Jean Lesage, a close friend of Pearson's and premier of Quebec until June 1966; and possibly others with responsibilities in Quebec, such as Jean Drapeau, mayor of Montreal, and Lucien Saulnier, chairman of the Greater Montreal Municipal Council. There may have been others, but most cabinet ministers who might have been expected to join this group, including Paul Hellyer, were not in it. Nor was General Loomis, but, being attached as a subordinate to General Allard, he could see what was going on, and Allard trusted him. Loomis understood what was happening because he had studied the British campaign against the Communists in Malaya, Fidel Castro's campaign in Cuba, the Algerian war of national liberation from French authority in North Africa, the equivalent campaigns against the French imperial régime in Indochina, and others. He, like Allard, had also studied the revolutionary literature from the works of Mao to those postwar revolutionaries who had expanded Mao's concepts to deadly "wars of national liberation."

For obvious political reasons, members of Pearson's small "kitchen cabinet" (to borrow another of Loomis's terms) were expected to keep their activities absolutely secret. There being every reason to withhold knowledge of the campaign from the FLQ, the preparations were made as an exercise in learning from the above-mentioned counter-insurgency campaigns and scrupulously avoided any reference to the situation in Quebec. This was believable in the context of the new two-part policy of peacemaking and peacekeeping adopted by the Canadian government, and it was hardly noticed, in any case, because of the political upheaval caused by the prime minister's policy of integrating the three armed forces into a single one under the authority of his minister of national defence, Paul Hellyer.

However, it being evident that the House of Commons ought to have at least some knowledge of this policy, Canada being a parliamentary democracy, Allard, with Loomis's assistance, prepared a memorandum that Allard used to brief the eleven-member Parliamentary Defence Committee of the House of Commons on 21 June 1966.[26] For this, they spent a long morning at the military base in Saint-Hubert near Montreal. They cast the vocabulary, examples, and diagrams in their briefing all in terms of various foreign counter-insurgency campaigns and made no mention of Quebec. However, one member of this committee, John Matheson, had no doubt about the real purpose of the Mobile Command, and it seems probable that other MPs guessed what was happening. Still more of them would certainly have tumbled to it in retrospect after the campaign had been launched against the FLQ in Montreal, more than four years later, in mid-October 1970.

Allard's group did not inform police forces, except for the anti-terrorist police squad of the Montreal force. That group they trusted, possibly because Premier Jean Lesage and other civil authories belonged to Prime Minister Pearson's secret planning group and because of their concern for collaboration with the Mobile Command.[27] The other police forces were thought to have been compromised. The Quebec provincial police seemed to have been infiltrated by the FLQ or its sympathizers; the RCMP was in close touch with the U.S. Federal Bureau of Investigation (FBI), and Pearson had no wish to let the Americans in on this matter. Members of the kitchen cabinet under him wanted to direct things themselves. General Loomis says that the U.S. authorities were nettled by their exclusion in and after October 1970. They had made their own preparations for insurgency in Quebec and were taken by surprise by decisive and successful action by the Canadian government and Canadian forces.

In addition to the secrecy so evidently essential, a certain discretion was required to avoid misunderstanding of General Allard's campaign as it was being prepared during the 1960s. People who had not studied insurgency warfare were scarcely able to grasp the point of it. Many soldiers were opposed to adapting military forces for what looked to them like police work. After all, the Canadian army, like others at the time, had been trained for warfare against equivalent military forces such as those of Nazi Germany, Fascist Italy, and the Soviet Union. "Low-level" warfare against insurgent populations was as yet unfamiliar to most. Loomis relates that at one time Allard asked him to brief his vice-chief of defence, General "Freddy" Sharp, about it all, and Sharp, puzzled by the project, remained highly sceptical. Allard was amused at this. It is perhaps significant that most of the "kitchen cabinet" were French-speaking people familiar with the Battle for Algiers, other recent French experience in Asia and Africa, and also with the insurgency and counter-insurgency that has been such an important element in French history. One has only to think of the military campaigns waged against the insurgents in Paris during June 1848, April and May 1871, and August 1944 – events that have no recent equivalent in the history of any English-speaking country. To understand them required a good knowledge of French politics and history, not something acquired by every officer and politician in Canada.

The Mobile Command

The military side of the preparations consisted of setting up a Mobile Command that could deploy and direct the armed forces rapidly in the event of an emergency operation at home or abroad. It was one of the new commands established by the Central Integration Planning Group, which had as its principal task, under the Minister of Defence, Paul Hellyer, to implement the government's decision to unify the airforce, army, and navy into a single force. Part of the plan, too, was to renounce the use of nuclear weapons in accordance with the Pearson government's decision, and this naturally caused anxiety among military officers who knew that, whatever the ethical and political merits of this decision, it would render the Canadian forces vulnerable and inferior in "high-intensity war." The Liberal government's apparent pacifist inclinations were trying for officers and others concerned with serious matters of defence. The prospect of low-intensity operations did little to restore morale, as there was clearly no need for nuclear and other "high-intensity war" weapons in pacifying revolutionary organizations.

In his memoirs, General Allard, put in charge of the Mobile Command from mid-June 1965, was careful to make no mention of the FLQ or Montreal as targets: references to possible fields of operations are all to the Middle East, Cyprus, central Europe, and the Northwest Territories.[28] This was in accordance with the essential secrecy of the Mobile Command's main purposes, to which only a few of the people around him were privy. He established headquarters at Saint-Hubert, near Montreal, which were officially opened on 19 October 1965. To assist him, he soon had two officers whom he liked and respected and to whom he attributes much of the Mobile Command's success, though neither was permitted to know its secret purposes. These were his chief organizer, Major Ramsay Withers, whom he had known for eleven years, a future chief of the Defence Staff; and Major-General Roger Rowley, the capable commander of the First Canadian Division. One of the latter's merits was that he had been studying the various kinds of warfare that the Mobile Command might be expected to meet, including the guerrilla operations with which Allard himself was familiar.[29]

The three officers reckoned that they would need about thirty-seven thousand fighting men, in addition to administrative staff at bases and headquarters. The government was at first unwilling to provide for so many soldiers and likewise reluctant to pay for the equipment that such an airborne regiment might need. Another set of difficulties arose in arranging to integrate units stationed in Germany, Cyprus, and widely separated parts of Canada. Allard managed to overcome these difficulties well before October 1970. Meanwhile, an insurrection in the classic manner had long been anticipated. On 18 October 1967, three months after de Gaulle's infamous visit to Canada, Paul Martin ordered an inquiry into allegations that radio broadcasts from Cuba were inciting Québécois to revolt.[30] In November so-called *États généraux*, redolent of French revolutions since 1789, were held in Montreal, and the next month the legislative assembly was converted into an "*Assemblée Nationale*," another French revolutionary institution, with effect from 31 December 1967. The revolutionary significance of this seems to have been entirely lost on ordinary observers from the English-speaking press. The FLQ grew in confidence during the next two years, all the more during the troubled year 1968 with its many insurrections around the world, particularly the May uprisings in Paris. It seemed reasonable at that time to anticipate similar violence from the university campuses in Montreal.[31] The FLQ had the sympathy of the great majority of writers, university professors, and other intellectuals in Quebec and a fair amount of vocal support in France. Seventeen professors were among the fifty-eight intellectuals who, in October 1966, had signed a public letter of sympathy with the FLQ terrorists Pierre Vallières and Charles Gagnon, viewing them as political prisoners.[32]

THE OCTOBER CRISIS

When James Cross was kidnapped on 5 October 1970, Liberal Premier Robert Bourassa was out of the country, and Pierre Laporte, the minister of labour, was deputy premier and acting premier. That is at least one reason why he too was kidnapped five days later. It was as a result of Laporte's disappearance and an escalating level of demonstrations sweeping through Montreal that the *États généraux*, with Claude Ryan much in evidence, concluded on 14 October that there was no government and so began to discuss the possibility of setting up a provisional one that might seek international recognition for a sovereign Quebec.[33] On the evening of the following day, Pierre Vallières (out of prison by then) addressed a huge student rally in eastern Montreal, urging his audience to rise up and fight for the liberation of Quebec.[34] Early next morning, 16 October, the prime minister invoked the War Measures Act, which made the political wing of the FLQ illegal, and the following day Pierre Laporte was murdered.

It was not this murder and the kidnappings leading up to it, however, that preoccupied General Allard's Mobile Command. The army was preparing to deal with an uprising anticipated on Carlos Marighella's principles, with the populace in Montreal siding with the revolutionaries, who would be provoking the army and the police to use force and then winning further sympathetic support by posing as oppressed and bullied. The army had its own considerable intelligence service in touch with the Montreal anti-terrorist squad. Also, as part of Lester Pearson's two-part strategy, the Liberal members of Parliament in Quebec and their riding associations had been gathering, collating, storing, and disseminating information about the political activists supporting the FLQ throughout the province.[35] One of the government's main purposes was to thwart foreign allies of the FLQ and prevent them from mustering to form a defensive force as allies of a sovereign Quebec. Another was to effect a rapid deployment of troops in order to forestall the insurgency plan the FLQ called "Opération Libération."[36] Part of this plan was to undermine public confidence in the civil order, as *Le Devoir* explained on 19 October: "Urban terrorism directly threatens the citizen who in the street, at his work, and at home is everywhere in danger of violent death. He has the depressing feeling of being a target, isolated and without defences. The fact that the public authorities and the police are incapable of guaranteeing his security increases his confusion."[37]

At the same time, elements in the population disposed to support an insurrection were certain to take courage. Therefore, if military units could be deployed in force to show the flag in Quebec with pipes and drums playing and weapons in full view, they could reassure the public and also discourage any insurrectionary feelings. This was what, in the event, did occur. Without knowing the underlying theory, Police Commissioner Jean-François Duchaîne in Montreal nevertheless understood that these military operations were intended to intimidate.[38]

Pierre Trudeau was prime minister by then and throughly versed in the purposes of the mobile command. And to direct the entire military exercise General Allard was brought back to Ottawa from New York, where he happened to have been sent, after his retirement from the army, as a representative of the Quebec government. Contrary to what he says in his memoirs about living in Quebec, ready to defend himself from the FLQ with a commando chain (!!), he was undoubtedly busy at command headquarters in Ottawa.[39] The chief of the Defence Staff at the time, General Frederick Sharp, was kept out of the way at a Canadian intelligence-watching station in Bermuda, and the vice chief, Lieutenant General Michael Dare, commanded the troops during the criticil period in October 1970. An ad hoc "war room" was set up in the

Château Laurier Hotel in Ottawa, where Allard and civil officials met. It was laid out like a convention room, with a bar and much coming and going, but in the back was an operations centre, where the planning and day-to-day business went on. It was, of course, quite separate from the crisis centre in the East Block run by Claude Roquet of External Affairs.

General Loomis says that as Canadian intelligence services had broken the Vichy French signal codes during the Second World War, they had a good idea of what the French forces were up to since then. He believes there were troops of the French Foreign Legion stationed at Saint-Pierre and Miquelon that may have been intended to respond to a call for international support for the provisional government of an independent Quebec. Also in Canadian waters was a Soviet fishing fleet that was known to be manned by a brigade of Russian marines, probably also ready to join in the impending "liberation" of Quebec. Thus it may well be that the Canadian move to extend the off-shore limit to 200 miles at this time was part of the counter-insurgency strategy and not merely fortuitous.[40] A Canadian naval detachment in the St Lawrence, which had been under the command of Commodore Jette in the mid-1960s, was probably still active. For air support, CF-5 fighter aircraft, suitable for duty in that kind of low-intensity warfare, were ready at Saint-Hubert, Quebec, and at other air bases covering the Ottawa and St Lawrence valleys.[41]

When the FLQ struck in October 1970, the forces were mobilized and deployed, with admirable efficiency, earlier than invocation of the War Measures Act (WMA) and under the terms of the National Defence Act. What the WMA did was to assist the civil authorities by countering the FLQ's political wing and declaring it to be involved in an unlawful association. There were strict rules and conditions for implementing the WMA. And they were part of the two operations, code-named "Essay" for the one centred in Montreal and "Ginger" for the other in Ottawa. As these operations were put into effect, troops acting in aid of the civil powers as peace officers, or assisting the RCMP and other police forces, moved into Quebec from as early as 12 October under the Commander Mobile Command near Montreal. Among other movements, Loomis and the First Royal Canadian Regiment were coincidentally flown back from Cyprus and deployed in western Quebec to defend electrical and other vital installations, particularly in the vicinity of Hull.[42] Loomis was acting under the orders of Brigadier General Radley-Waters, who commanded the forces in the National Capital Region from his headquarters in Ottawa. The result was that the FLQ suffered a tactical, even a strategic, defeat.

General Loomis readily admits that the police forces acting under the

Criminal Code would no doubt have picked up the kidnappers of Cross and Laporte without this military show of force. But the political-insurgency process, code-named "Libération" by the FLQ, might have been launched successfully in the meantime. The WMA was necessary to provide the police with powers for dealing with the political wing of the FLQ. And it was the police, not the army, after all, who drew up the lists of suspects for the arrests that were made. How certain and real was the danger of insurrection is one of the main unresolved questions in the whole affair. Of course, many observers, particularly well-meaning liberals and left-wingers, think that the apprehended insurrection and the military steps to forestall it were all nonsense. Some well-informed ones, however, such as Gérard Pelletier, knew the political forces in sympathy with the FLQ were substantial and the danger correspondingly great.[43] As things turned out, the government under the leadership of Pierre Trudeau did act decisively in 1970, following the strategy and concepts laid out by Lester Pearson after his election and the beginning of the FLQ bombing campaign in 1963.

Accordingly, what the government, backed by the police and army, was ready to prevent was a situation in Quebec in which a provisional government would be proclaimed, would attract groups of international sympathizers, would plant the flag of an independent Quebec, and would present a revolutionary face at the border with Ontario so that nothing short of an invasion would stop it. The population might well, it seemed, join the revolutionaries in defence against the counter-revolutionary "outsiders" from Ontario, and world opinion might soon come out in defence of the new independent "people's" Quebec. Already the FLQ had a successful example, rhetoric, and some practical training and assistance from the FLN in Algeria. As a result of their preparations, Allard and his army command group were able to march the troops through Montreal "with pipes and drums playing and bayonets fixed" to establish their presence as being in command and ready for insurgency. The population saw them as saviours and not as foreign "reactionary" invaders.

Nipped in the Bud

How much French support was to be expected for a war of national liberation, to be waged by the FLQ and its political wing, remains unclear. General Loomis suspects, as we saw above, that the French government had transferred troops of the Foreign Legion to Saint-Pierre and Miquelon, with the intention of involving them, should the opportunity arise.[44] He believes certain Quebec leaders were in touch with these French authorities and that there were some three thousand *coopérants* in Quebec also more or less ready to assist in the process of engaging the civil population in support of the insurgents once the *États généraux* had declared Quebec an independent state and sought international recognition. It was reasonable at the time to believe that these forces were intended to form parts of an international coalition that was to include Algerians, Cubans, and Soviets, as well as French. The beauty of the insurgency plan was that, based on the Algerian, Indo-Chinese, Malayan, and other models, it did not need organized armies to launch it. Insurgency could feed on social and/or political discontents such as those already aroused in Quebec. Charles de Gaulle had heightened these discontents during and after his visit in July 1967.

In any event, the government's actions to deploy the army under the National Defence Act and to counter the FLQ's political wing by the War Measures Act stopped an anticipated war of national liberation abruptly almost before it began. By the end of 1971 the FLQ had concluded that violence would not succeed in Canada, and, as a consequence, the armed struggle for national liberation gave way to the constitutional struggle for sovereignty, waged with all the intensity and tactics of the armed conflict, but without violence. Thus began a new phase in the struggle for Quebec against the separatists and their French friends. A fundamental change was signalled by, for example, Pierre Vallières's admission in a meeting with Pierre Trudeau that he himself intended to engage henceforth in peaceful political agitation rather than revolutionary violence.[45]

It must be stressed, in conclusion, that the second phase of Lester Pearson's two-part strategy was the peacemaking designed to win the hearts and minds of the public in Quebec by removing causes of discontent, social, economic, and political. Many different activities contributed to this peacemaking phase. Perhaps the very first event to turn the public against the FLQ was its cold-blooded murder of Pierre Laporte, but much more sustained were the alternatives to armed struggle put forward by the federal government. Various programs for political and civic improvement were put into effect during the next few years. Regional development initiated by Jean Marchand, repatriation of the constitution following several conferences, and youth groups such as the Company of Young Canadians, which Lester Pearson had saved from dissolution in 1967, are examples.[46] Among the symbolic changes were the new Canadian flag, shorn of all British and French historic symbols and inaugurated on 15 February 1965, and the new Order of Canada, both of these enthusiastically promoted by John Ross Matheson.[47] One way or another, the separatists in Quebec were gradually pacified and won away from the insurrectionary methods to which they had become accustomed by October

1970. Ten years later, in 1980, the public voted against the separatist proposals put forward in the referendum of the Parti Québécois. How permanent were the successes of Pearson's two-part strategy remains to be seen, but they helped to keep Canada together for a generation, perhaps longer. Now, however, with the separatists of the PQ entrenched in Quebec, firm measures may be needed to get them out as they gradually turn themselves into an ethnic dictatorship.

PART THREE

Imperial Dreams

Quebec in a World-Wide
Cultural Empire

Quebec is tied to France by a tissue of direct relationships, as we saw in chapter 8, but it also has a set of indirect links in the multilateral system called *la francophonie*. I cast this chapter in terms of four stages in the evolution of that system and Quebec's links with it. First, a world-wide union of French-speaking countries and minorities emerged in French Africa in the 1960s as a surrogate for the former French empire there. Second, Charles de Gaulle saw Quebec as a lost part of France that needed to be "liberated" from Canada and drawn back into the French-speaking world. Third, for the government of Quebec, *la francophonie* has offered a way of playing a part in international affairs independently of Canada. The scope of affairs has been limited, of course, by Quebec's constitutional position as a Canadian province and by the very nature of the organization, but using Gaullist models with French encouragement, Quebec has acted more and more as a sovereign power and been so treated by at least some of its partners in this body. Fourth, its activities in this organization may soon lead, by a short step, to a place in the community of sovereign nations, or such is the vision of the separatist Parti Québécois that governs the province at present. Though the character of *la francophonie* is ambiguous, like so much French activity in relation to Quebec, it has clearly been evolving as a political grouping.

THE FRENCH, AFRICA, AND LA FRANCOPHONIE

Ambiguity marked the very beginning of *la francophonie*. French sources tell the story of how African leaders took the founding initiative in the 1960s, and it is only by probing more deeply into those years that the historian comes to see underlying French initiatives. One of the earliest accounts was compiled in June 1970 by P.J. Franceschini, a journalist writing in *Le Monde*.[1] According to him, President Léopold Senghor of Senegal published reflections about the French language, "a marvellous tool found in the ruins of the colonial régime," in a special number of the journal *L'Esprit* in November 1962. After preliminary conversations, Senghor and President Habib Bourguiba of Tunisia met at Tunis in May 1966 to discuss a project for a French-speaking community, and the next month the *Organisation commune africaine et malgache* (OCAM), meeting at Tananarive in Madagascar, charged President Hamani Diori of Niger to present a project to the French government. Diori discussed these ideas with General de Gaulle in January 1967, only six months before de Gaulle's visit to Quebec in July. In spite of some objections by African leaders such as President Sekou Touré of Guinea, plans proceeded from step to step until March 1970, when the second conference at Niamey in Niger approved creation of an *Agence de coopération culturelle et technique des pays francophones* (ACCT). The representatives of twenty-one governments, including those of Canada and Quebec, signed the founding convention on 21 March and accepted Jean-Marc Léger of Quebec as the *secrétaire général*. It was at this point that Franceschini wrote his brief history of the movement.

He did not fail to sketch the struggle, discussed above in chapter 8 over the status of Quebec that took place at the Niamey conference or to allude to "certains militants francophones" from France who were "ardents partisans de l'indépendance du Québec." What is missing is any explanation of the position of the founding African statesmen in an informal French commonwealth of erstwhile colonies, a position that profoundly affected their role in *la francophonie*. Ostensibly independent since 1960, soon after de Gaulle came to power in the Fifth Republic, the French-speaking African countries were still controlled by Paris. Under the rubrics *francophonie*, "foreign aid," "cooperation," and the need to defend its own nationals, France has dominated its former colonies in order to maintain influence, to play a leading part in the world, and to obtain uranium, petroleum, and other valuable products. In de Gaulle's view, this was necessary for France to retain its great power status, and it was he who devised and implemented what can be described only as an imperial policy. He taught French people "that domination and cooperation are only different forms of the same national ambition," Alfred Grosser observed as early as 1965.[2] His successors have simply continued his policy in Africa, just as they have carried it on in Canada and elsewhere. Most of them have talked of reforming it, but none has made any substantial changes. As one specialist puts it, "Paris has never ceased to think of its African policy as merely an instrument in the service of its policy of power."[3]

A former Canadian diplomat, on reading the above paragraph, sent the following comment: "As I was accredited to Liberia [as ambassador], I remember conversations with the French ambassador in which he implied that he had a mission to develop close ties with his host government. I am almost sure the then president of France paid a one-day visit to Monrovia and that the president of Liberia was invited to pay a state visit to Paris. The Liberians were thrilled: this was the first time any metropolitan power had paid this kind of attention to them. Politically they were orphans. They were also invited as observers to the Franco–African summit. As Liberia has been in a state of anarchy for years I don't think the French have got much out of it, but at least they have it in mind as part of their 'empire'."[4]

The French have kept in place an economic and military commonwealth or empire in Africa for forty years or more.[5] From 1948 on, France had maintained a monetary zone – a *Communauté financière africaine* (CFA) – based on its artificial support for the value of the CFA *franc* throughout its former African colonies. As these won political independence in 1960 or soon afterward, the French government contrived to maintain influence in them by making offers that the new national leaders could hardly refuse: to form, train, and arm their forces; to provide technical advisers; to supply needed goods and to take African products in exchange; and generally to patronize and protect the new governments. From the French point of view, this policy was successful. Thirteen states accepted such patronage in 1960, and by 1996 there were twenty-three of them.[6]

Although the governments of these states joined the international French-speaking movement, and have indeed formed a majority of its members, the principal basis of French patronage has been military. Its French African monetary zone, based on the CFA *franc*, was less successful than its military zone. The CFA was mutually beneficial for a few years but was losing its value long before it was ended on 11 January 1994, for the CFA *franc*, too long propped up artificially, then had to be devalued by 50 per cent.[7] Meanwhile, most of the French-speaking African countries have been buying their weaponry from France – 100 per cent of it, in Chad, Centrafrique, and Sénégal.

In addition, France has maintained large forces in Africa, varying from a total of 60,000 in the early 1960s to some 10,000 early in 1997. These have intervened in the affairs of one country or another on more than thirty occasions, usually according to military agreements.[8] "Military involvement is perhaps the most distinctive part of the French relationship with Africa," writes Ieuan Griffiths.[9] As late as June 1997, another five hundred French soldiers, making a total of 1,250, were being sent to Brazzaville, Republic of Congo, apparently to pacify the

warring supporters of the new ruling group headed by Pascal Lissouba
and those of the former military ruler, Denis Sassou N'Guesso.[10] What
all this means in political terms is that France has been propping up
military dictators in most of French-speaking Africa, including tyrants
such as Jean-Bédel Bokassa in the Central African Republic (Centrafrique), long a special friend of Valéry Giscard d'Estaing, and President Mobutu Sese Seko in Zaire, who was at last driven out by rebel
forces in May 1997.[11] The principal benefit for France has been in
prestige, or what Louis XIV used to call "la gloire," but there has also
been some benefit in trade. Much of France's supply of uranium, for
example, has come from Niger and Gabon.[12] The French petroleum
giant, Elf, has been taking one-fifth of its oil from Gabon, thanks to
astute Gaullist directors, such as André Tarallo, a Corsican who
wielded influence in several French-speaking African countries through
the 1970s and 1980s.[13]

In Africa, as elsewhere, there are signs now that resistance to French
domination is increasing. English and American influence has had
some effect in Rwanda with a return of exiled Tutsi leaders, and this is
not the only setback for France.[14] There were plans in Paris late in July
1997 to begin closing French military bases in Centrafrique.[15] Troubles
have grown since one of the great French controllers or managers of
post-colonial Africa, Jacques Foccart (1913–1997), died early in 1997.
A faithful Gaullist from 1940, he became a legend in his own lifetime
as one of the powers behind the presidential throne. For almost forty
years, from about 1960, under de Gaulle and most of his successors
Foccart had an office in the Élysée Palace as a presidential adviser and
manager for African affairs. He was on familiar terms with most
French-speaking African leaders, dispensed the enormous power and
patronage of his government among them, and quietly led a variable
team of French officials who exercised more influence in Africa than
any of the other old colonial powers. It is widely believed, though officially denied, that Foccart directed a secret, informal intelligence and
police service that was occasionally used in a villainous manner to
achieve French purposes.[16] On Foccart's activities there have been
many journalistic investigations, all manner of revelations in personal
memoirs, and several books, including a thousand-page interview with
Foccart himself, shortly before his death.[17] Using all the available
sources, Douglas Porch and François-Xavier Verschave have written
scholarly summaries that expose the ruthless imperial thuggery of de
Gaulle and Foccart.[18]

As this French post-colonial empire in Africa shows, *la francophonie*
has a characteristic ambiguity in that its linguistic and cultural charac-

ter has been too often tinged with economic, political, and even military elements. The African leaders who are deemed to have founded *la francophonie* had their place in an informal French empire and in that sense were scarcely free agents. In the Canadian Department of External Affairs, Marcel Cadieux was well aware of this, at least in January 1974 when he discussed French Africa with a Belgian priest representing the Vatican in Washington, DC. "Like us," Cadieux wrote to his friend Paul Tremblay, "he believes that the French have abused the situation. These countries have only the appearance of independence. It is France that has been pulling the strings and in practice reserving monopolies everywhere."[19] Power and influence seemed to lurk behind all the talk of a common language and culture.

This situation seemed all the more menacing because postwar France had been doing its best to maintain its colonies and to build up an arsenal of weapons. France has indeed been one of the principal suppliers of sophisticated weaponry to countries around the world, not only in Africa. On this side of the Atlantic, the old colony of Saint-Pierre and Miquelon has been developed as a naval base. It was part of de Gaulle's unspoken message to Quebec in 1967 that he was arriving in military uniform on a warship and stopping at Saint-Pierre. Thirty years later, when Jacques Parizeau journeyed to Paris before the referendum of 1995 to seek French support, Jacques Chirac and other French authorities assured him that if he won a "yes" vote they would immediately come to his side to lend him support. After Chirac was elected president in May 1995 there was even talk of having him flown immediately to Quebec City to play a big brother's part in breaking the federal bonds and declaring Quebec independent. Some experienced diplomats, such as Max Yalden, see nothing threatening in all this, but it would be as well to keep a careful watch.

FACTORING IN QUEBEC

It is the development of a French-speaking commonwealth – a kind of empire – that holds our attention in this chapter. Quebec has been drawn into an organization that was promoted, if not founded, by former French colonies in Africa, which France was continuing to patronize and even, in some measure, to control. It was perhaps natural that the Quebec lobby in France should see Quebec in the same light as these colonies. A good number of the lobby's officials had experience in the erstwhile colonies of French-speaking Africa in one way or another. And ex-imperial civil servants interested in Quebec were to be expected, in view of the decolonizing process of the 1950s, especially the long struggle with Algeria that de Gaulle brought to an end by granting independence in 1962. About a million French people had then moved to France from Algeria, and some of the colonial administrators were beginning to turn to other overseas tasks. Some of them took an interest in the older colony of Quebec, as de Gaulle thought of it. Other observers, too, began to bracket Quebec with French-speaking African countries: the University of Vermont invited the Canadian ambassador in Washington, Marcel Cadieux, to a ceremony on 13 June 1971 in which President Senghor of Sénégal was to receive an honorary degree, and where a "Colloquium on African and Canadian Literature of French Expression" was to follow.[20]

Badly shocked by the loss of their African colonies, de Gaulle and his followers seem to have thought that the twentieth-century forces of nationalism, which had done such damage to the French empire, might also be made to work in its favour. This idea has two elements: first, it links Quebec and Acadia, as ex-colonies of France, with the French-speaking parts of Africa, and second, it assumes that they need to be "liberated" from Canada. In the Gaullist view, Quebec and Acadia are long-neglected colonies, parts of the French nation that have been colonized by Anglo-Americans for two centuries but have miraculously preserved their language and culture. To the end of his presidency he persisted in seeing Quebec as one of the French colonies, essentially no different from those in Africa. In his new year's message to his people on the evening of 31 December 1968 he mentioned the liberation of Québécois and Biafrans in the same breath. France had become strong and stable enough, he said, to assist "the French people of Canada in the free conduct of their own national life; or to recognize valiant Biafra's right to dispose of itself."[21] The peoples of ex-colonies are all naturally fitted, he thought, to play active parts in the French-speaking movement of our time. Biafra, part of an ex-British colony, had an anomalous place in this scheme of things which we examine below in chapter 13. Gaullists continue to think in these terms: in January 1980 a member of the French National Assembly, Pierre Bas, drew the attention of the foreign minister to "the 300,000 Acadians in the Atlantic regions of Canada [who] constitute a stateless people [un peuple sans État] whose personality has been forged by their painful history and isolation."[22] The flag adopted a century ago by the Acadians seems to be a symbol of nationalism – except to those who describe it as "the flag of Acadia, that is to say the French *tricolore* flag," with obvious imperial symbolism.[23]

De Gaulle and his followers set out to draw Quebec and Acadia into what was becoming a French cultural empire. As Robert Gildea observes, "The Canadian axis was fundamental for the emergence of Francophonie as a serious force in the world."[24] The nationalist politicians in Quebec and Acadia thus found themselves fraternizing with African leaders who were cultivating an international French-speaking league that offered them various advantages. A new system of imperial power has been gradually worked out and put into effect. It takes the form of a cultural and linguistic zone in which France patronizes, develops, and exploits "backward" countries, all the while indoctrinating them with an ideology familiar to students of French history. By any common measure Belgium and Canada are not, of course, backward countries, but the Gaullist vision is of their French-speaking minorities as downtrodden, politically backward peoples ready for the same patronage as is being meted out to former African colonies.

A Franco-African summit conference drew the French-speaking heads of state together in Paris on a number of occasions, notably on 13 November 1973 under President Pompidou's chairmanship. It is this zone that is commonly referred to as *la francophonie*, the lands wherein French is the sole, or at least an important, medium of communication – lands all reached since 20 January 1975 by an international radio network, *Radio-France internationale*. Since 3 January 1998 a French-language television network, TV5 USA, has been broadcasting over large parts of North America twenty-four hours a day; its funds come 50 per cent from France, 30 per cent from Canada and Quebec combined, and 10 per cent each from Belgium and Switzerland.[25] More and more highly organized, *la francophonie* is a zone wherein France does not always dominate but offers assistance, imposes itself in various ways, and lays ambiguous but ominous claims of a patronizing kind.

Linking Quebec and Acadia with the rest of the ex-colonies of France is only the first part of the Gaullist imperial idea. The second part is the doctrine that they are to be liberated from Canada, as African countries have (allegedly) been freed from France. In one of de Gaulle's notorious speeches in Quebec in July 1967 he said that he was reminded of France at the liberation in 1944. Since that visit his idea of "liberation" has become part of the separatist ideology, formulated usually in one of those grand rhetorical phrases about the natural right of people "to dispose of themselves." Until de Gaulle's proclamations on this point, it had been widely accepted, even in some French-Canadian circles, that Quebec had been liberated from France in the middle of the eighteenth century by British arms. Canadian historians imbued with a ready sympathy for Quebec tend to balk at this idea now, but it was certainly the view of generations of Québécois in the past, who shared Sir Wilfrid Laurier's idea that it was Britain that had given Quebec liberty. In Laurier's words, "We are faithful to [France] the great nation that gave us life; we are faithful to [Great Britain] the great nation that gave us liberty."[26] In a lecture on political liberty delivered on 26 June 1877, he explained at length how British institutions left French Canadians free and equal. "The French," he added, "have had the name of liberty, but they have not yet had liberty itself."[27]

Others in Quebec shared the same ideas both before and after Laurier's time. A large political element that followed Louis-Hippolyte Lafontaine during the 1840s and 1850s believed that Quebec was best governed within the British Empire, wherein the parliamentary system offered French Canadians the greatest possible freedom and protection. Two British governors in particular, Sir Charles Bagot and Lord Elgin, had succeeded in winning a section of French-Canadian public opinion to a policy of loyalty to the empire as the best political environment possible in the circumstances.[28] Even Louis-Joseph Papineau, until he became a revolutionary and then fled abroad, was an enthusiastic admirer of British political institutions and in 1820 described the French government of his time as "arbitrary and oppressive".[29] Much later, his grandson Henri Bourassa, another leading politician, thought the British Empire offered liberty, decentralization, and a respect for minorities that was not to be hoped for under any other authority.[30] Bourassa developed these ideas in many speeches and essays, some of which compared France unfavourably. For instance, on one occasion he wrote, "The compensation for the troubles and misfortunes of the English conquest was that it rid us of French rule ... Bondage for bondage, it is better to be a colony of England than of any other imperial nation ... The British régime awakened constructive energies in us and an instinct for political action, which the French régime would never have done, for under it everything depended upon the king's pleasure."[31] These ideas persisted in some Quebec circles; loyalty to the crown was expressed as recently as April 1963 by Premier Jean Lesage.[32]

Unlike de Gaulle's rhetorical phrases, those of Bourassa, Lafontaine, Laurier, and Papineau were full of historic meaning. The liberty Britain gave Quebec by the Quebec Act, 1774, as they knew, was much the same as that which the French Revolution of 1789 gave to France a quarter-century later. That is, it consisted of elected representative government, the rule of law, a relatively humane and fair system of criminal justice, civil control of the army, religious freedom and toleration, freedom of the press, freedom of the citizen from arbitrary arrest and arbitrary confiscations of property, and freedom from arbitrary taxation. Canada and France had very few, if any, of these liberties and securities under the Bourbon monarchy. It was to obtain them that the French nation rose up in 1789 and proceeded to draw up its first constitution in 1791. But Britain had given Canada some of these liberties more than twenty years earlier. Québécois knew this at the time. Of course none of these liberties was complete, pure, or perfect. Of course there were still political battles to be fought and won, as there are even today, but so there were in Britain and in every other country. The rebellion of 1837 in French Canada, the struggle for colonial self-government in English Canada, and the struggle over the Reform Bill of 1832 in England, not to mention the long struggle against slavery and the slave trade – none of these justify Gaullist claims that Quebec was oppressed in the British Empire after the Conquest, oppressed still in Confederation after 1867, and needs now to be liberated.

Charles de Gaulle and his followers never had any respect for what statesmen in Quebec meant in saying that Britain had given Quebec freedom and so liberated it from Bourbon France. With their imperial, authoritarian, chauvinist views, they did not even understand classical nineteenth-century liberalism. De Gaulle shared with twentieth-century dictators and with the Bonaparte emperors a contempt for parliamentary politics as being nothing but a corrupt struggle of private interests. His passionate, ethnic patriotism, with its imperial overtones, has aroused sympathetic echoes in some Quebec circles. Claude Morin, long one of the intellectual leaders of the separatist movement, believed that Quebec's emergence as an independent presence on the international stage owed a great deal to de Gaulle, so much indeed that the debt to him for that was even greater than for the encouragement that he afforded by his "Vive le Québec libre!" speech.[33] Absorbed in his theories, Morin does not seem to have noticed how ruthlessly the Gaullist government was manipulating Quebec in its world-wide chess game against the United States. To be fair to Morin, it must be admitted that the Canadian government was also largely blind to this aspect of Gaullist policy and tended to swallow the rhetoric and propaganda about France's ancient cultural ties with "the French of Canada." Cultivating French-speaking peoples throughout the world has led to a triumph of Gaullist strategy and mystification, permitting the French government to manipulate governments in Africa, the Mediterranean, Asia, and elsewhere, as well as Quebec. France has been a pioneer in wielding what some theorists, such as Joseph Nye at Harvard University, have begun to see as a new way of "achieving the international coercion necessary to maintain global dominance."[34]

"LIBERATING" WALLONIA, LOUISIANA AND THE SWISS JURA

To grasp the full scope of the Gaullist imperial campaign it is worthwhile pausing to investigate other parts of it, beginning with the efforts

to stir up the French-speaking Belgians, or Walloons. The evidence is
fragmentary but startling to me as it was to Marcel Cadieux when he
gathered it. Among the memoranda that make up Cadieux's confidential journal is one written on 15 March 1973 during his time as Canadian ambassador to the United States. It reads, in part:

I lunched [today] with [Francis] Lacoste, the former Ambassador of France to
Canada (1955–1960). After leaving Ottawa, he went to take up a post in
Belgium. France under de Gaulle undertook a major effort to annex Wallonia.
Agents, money, were sent over the border to shake the allegiance of Liège. The
Belgians were alarmed. They finally had proof of this French intervention and
called in the Ambassador to ask him for explanations. The latter, Lacoste,
made a report to Paris and asked for explanations. He received the reply that
he ought to have made a denial and given his word that France was doing
nothing reprehensible. Lacoste replied that before giving his word he wanted
assurances. He was recalled.

In short, the policy of De Gaulle with respect to Belgium was the same as the
one he adopted in the case of Canada. He wanted to arrange that the loss of
Algeria would be compensated and his reign would not be characterized as a
period in which the French presence in the world was diminished. He was
hoping to make up [the losses] by putting his hand on Quebec and Wallonia.[35]

This report raises the question of Gaullist provocation in Belgian Wallonia.

The position of French-speaking Belgians is not unlike that of Acadians as well as Québécois, and it is instructive to compare the two.
There are differences, of course, but the similarities are not without
interest for us. The Walloons have a history more complicated than
that of the Québécois and Acadians, but with a similar outcome. They
were parts of the French empire for long periods but ultimately taken
from France when coalitions of neighbouring countries made determined efforts to resist French imperial expansion. After Napoleon's
demise in 1815 the Congress of Vienna pushed the northern French
frontiers back more or less to where they had been in 1789 and created
a buffer state as a defence against France. This included Belgium but
was called the Kingdom of the Netherlands and was ruled by the Dutch
house of Orange.

The Kingdom of the Netherlands was somewhat artificial, combin-
ing as it did two peoples who had been enemies since the sixteenth
century, one Roman Catholic and the other largely Calvinist. It was
hardly surprising that in 1831 the Belgians revolted against their union
with the Dutch in order to form their own kingdom. The issues that

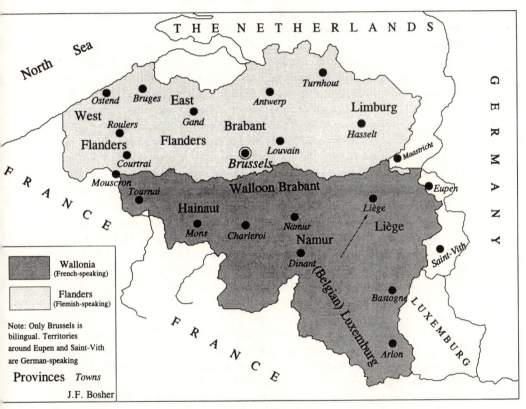

THE NETHERLANDS

North Sea

GERMANY

West Flanders
Ostend
Bruges
Roulers
Courtrai
Mouscron
Tournai

East Flanders
Gand

Brabant
Antwerp
Turnhout
Louvain

Brussels

Limburg
Hasselt
Maastricht

Eupen

FRANCE

Hainaut
Mons
Charleroi

Walloon Brabant

Namur
Dinant

Liège
Liège

Saint-Vith

(Belgian) Luxemburg
Bastogne
Arlon

LUXEMBURG

FRANCE

Wallonia
(French-speaking)

Flanders
(Flemish-speaking)

Note: Only Brussels is
bilingual. Territories
around Eupen and Saint-Vith
are German-speaking

Provinces *Towns*

J.F. Bosher

Map 3   Belgium

divided them at that time, however, were not linguistic or cultural; it did not seem to matter then that Belgium had both Dutch-speaking Flemings and French-speaking Walloons. In the twentieth century, however, cultural and linguistic issues have gradually brought the two groups into conflicts within Belgium that are similar to those in Canada. And as in Canada, the French-speaking part of the country has been falling behind economically and demographically. The Walloons are becoming more and more resentful of the vigorous and prosperous Flemings, with their increasing political preponderance.[36]

As the Flemings press their cause and advance in Belgium, some groups of Walloons have begun to think of breaking away from Belgium in order to become part of France. Right after the Second World War, on 20 October 1945, a huge Walloon congress held at Liège voted in favour of joining France, and this action was what inspired de Gaulle to concentrate on that city when trying to attract the Walloons. But then, in a second, more thoughtful vote, Liège was nearly unanimous in supporting the principle of independence within a Belgian federal constitution.[37] This arrangement has seemed more feasible since a linguistic boundary was drawn by a law of 8 November 1962, which made Flemish the official language in Flanders and part of Brabant, and French the official language in the territories now labelled *Wallonie*. The only remaining bilingual part of Belgium is Brussels, the capital. This separation between Flemings and Walloons was, in a sense, confirmed by a constitutional revision of 14 July 1993 that converted Belgium from a single unitary kingdom into a federal kingdom. By constitutionally defining the country as a federation of the two cultural groups, this revision gave them legally separate identities and began to open the way, at least in some citizens' minds, to separation.

Many Walloons have the same French view of their identity as Québécois have: that is, they tend to stress their differences from the Flemings. And some feel that they are not only a separate nation, but also a part of the French nation by virtue of their linguistic, cultural, and historical ties. People such as these can be stirred by writings on this theme such as *Belgique Requiem* by René Swennen, a book first published in 1980 but now being reissued in a second edition. Walloon separatists use the term "rattachisme" to stress their hope of rejoining France, and the issue they raise is as contentious in Belgium as Quebec separatism is in Canada. The Paris journal *Le Point* was speaking to this sector when it reported the state of the Belgian conflict in February 1997 under the title, "Belgique: Wallonie, la tentation française".[38] How far the Fifth Republic is in fact tempted to interfere in the Walloon part of Belgium is shrouded in characteristic ambiguity, but from the sixteenth century to the nineteenth France did have its eyes on what was then a group of Habsburg provinces in the Netherlands. Indeed, Belgium was created a neutral buffer kingdom in 1839, by an international conference, explicitly as a barrier against French expansion. This is easily forgotten because the neutrality of Belgium was, in the event, violated not by France but by Germany in 1914 and 1940. However, under Charles de Gaulle the Fifth Republic took up the old French ambitions in a new form.

In his official statements, de Gaulle pretended to take the view that France could do nothing about the Walloons unless they collectively broke out of Belgium and approached his government. "Of course," ran the gist of his argument, "if one day a political authority representative of Wallonia came officially to France, that day we would respond favorably, with full hearts, to a request that had every appearance of legitimacy."[39] As Lacoste told Cadieux in 1973, de Gaulle made strenuous efforts during the 1960s to bring that about by underhanded means. Gaullists, including Philippe Rossillon, were delighted to contemplate pushing the national frontiers northward to encompass Wallonia as of old.[40] The RCMP knew then that he and others in the French Quebec mafia had joined a movement in 1958 called *Patrie et Progrès*, which intended to work towards French recovery of the French-speaking populations of Canada and Belgium.

That was at a time when France was desperately fighting to keep Algeria, but the loss of that colony did nothing to reduce the imperialism of a sector of French public opinion. Marcel Cadieux had seen the patronizing way in which the French government had treated French-speaking Belgians after the Second World War. In October 1966 he again witnessed that typical Gaullist attitude in Couve de Murville's dismissal of Brussels as "rather provincial. Speaking in the grand manner of times past, [Couve] even added that the city had no great newspapers and that it would be difficult to send 'persons of quality' there."[41] When they heard of these statements, Belgian diplomats were furious. Some Walloon observers were anxious lest de Gaulle interfere in Belgium as he was doing in Canada.[42]

In summer 1964 Rossillon and Pierre Gravel of the International Committee for the Independence of Quebec, based in Paris, had attended meetings of a Walloon movement in Brussels, where they saw hundreds of Walloons shouting "Vive le Québec libre!"[43] A delegation had then delivered a petition to the Canadian embassy there calling for the independence of Quebec. According to reports in 1968, Rossillon and Gravel were still in touch with Belgium, and French funds were aiding the secessionist *Parti wallon* in Belgian elections.[44] Indeed, Rossillon himself tells us that when he was banned from Canada for five years in 1968 he turned to what he calls "the francophone lobby" in Wallonia as well as in other lands with French-speakers – Haïti, Mauritius, Niger, and Seychelles.[45]

Whether the international cultural activities of *la francophonie* have been encouraging the political movement of the Walloons since the 1960s and 1970s is not clear, but it seems probable. As André Patry and Claude Morin tell the story of Quebec-Walloon relations, in which they both played roles, Quebec began by dealing with Brussels but soon developed a policy of escaping from the Canadian federal embrace and of dealing, at the same time, with Wallonia rather than Belgium.[46] Gaston Cholette, director of cooperation in the Quebec ministry of youth, conferred with the Belgian consul general in Montreal as early as November 1963 and in the following May went to Brussels to talk to the Belgian government about cultural exchanges.[47] A plan was slowly devised between them but came to nothing at that stage. Canada endeavoured for many years to confine Quebec's relations with the Walloons within the terms of a Canada-Belgium cultural accord signed in 1967. The Quebec government dragged its feet on this, and told its Belgian contacts that it would not work within a Canadian–Belgian agreement (*accord-cadre*).[48] All through May 1967, Cadieux and his department struggled to prevent such alarming developments as a visit of the Belgian crown prince to Quebec without federal officials in attendance.[49]

The Walloons for their part were not free to conduct their own cultural relations abroad until 1982, when constitutional changes separated the Walloons from the Flemings. It was in 1982 that a *Centre d'études canadiennes* was established at the Free University of Brussels.[50] Since that year Quebec missions have gone to visit the Walloons each year, many of them to establish common terminology for scientific and technical fields.[51] In November 1996 a party of about forty Walloons, under the leadership of Robert Collignon, the "Ministre-président de la Région wallonne de Belgique," paid a four-day visit to Quebec for the purpose of increasing technological cooperation. Collignon conferred with Premier Bouchard, three other ministers, and several businessmen.[52] The purpose of this and other such visits was industrial and technological, but it would be difficult to imagine a PQ government confining the discussions to non-political subjects.

The Quebec government, following the French example, has formed a relationship with the government of another territory of French-speaking people bordering on France. This is the Swiss canton of the Jura, near the French border, which is somewhat smaller that Wallonia. It has a largely rural population more on the scale of Acadia than of

Quebec. Its six French-speaking districts have a population of only 126,094 and feel a need to defend themselves culturally and linguistically against their vigorous German-speaking Swiss neighbours.[53] The Jura has been nevertheless more independent than Wallonia and has long called itself a republic as well as a canton within the Swiss confederation.

On 9–10 June 1978 it welcomed delegations from Quebec, Acadia, and Belgium at a French-speaking conference.[54] On 1 July 1983, at its tiny capital city of Porrentruy, a town of scarcely 26,000 people living beneath a medieval castle, René Lévesque and Jacques-Yvan Morin, together with two representatives of the Jura, signed an "*Entente gouvernementale* between Quebec and the Republic and Canton of the Jura, desirous of tightening the close and amicable links that unite them and of creating new ones."[55] Exchanges of officials, other visitors and information have followed. The contracting parties treat one another as independent for many purposes, and this relationship is therefore quite different from the dozens of arrangements that Quebec has made with governments of American states and with countries that have small minorities of French-speaking citizens.

At the very time Rossillon was involved with Acadian nationalists he was also befriending a champion of French-speaking Louisiana, James Domengeaux. "This was the beginning of a fruitful association," Robert Pichette tells us, "for Rossillon and Domengeaux worked out a whole French strategy for Louisiana, that ended by including Belgium and some Acadians from the Maritimes."[56] Among other things, Domengeaux founded the *Conseil pour le développement du français en Louisiane* (CODOFIL), which celebrated its twenty-fifth anniversary in 1993, shortly after his death.[57] Rossillon used to visit Louisiana twice a year and was able to found a journal there, *La Gazette de la Louisiane*.

In April 1973 Domengeaux invited the Canadian ambassador in Washington, Marcel Cadieux, to attend a meeting at Thibodaux in Louisiana. Cadieux obliged but quickly realized that the occasion had been arranged to lend respectable support to CODOFIL. He also saw the Gaullist initiative in the background, all the more because he was followed about by a group directed by Philippe Rossillon's secretary and claiming to represent the ORTF. "I couldn't help saying to her, 'that damned Rossillon turns up everywhere'" which, says Cadieux, sent her off for a whispered conversation with her companions.[58] He went on to reflect later that here was evidence of French interference in the United States.

Although there could be no hope of arousing an independence movement, it was clear that the French initiative there was similar to that in Quebec. In setting up cultural centres and holding international conferences, the Gaullists were doing just what the Nazis and Soviets had done, and for similarly underhanded purposes. This was Cadieux's reflection; he added: "The dreams of empire and domination inspired by Gaullism and the narrowest French nationalism are thus manifested in these clandestine and tortuous enterprises of Rossillon, Foccart and Company."[59]

Domengeaux and his friends, who had never heard of Foccart (Cadieux discovered) and were oblivious of Rossillon's real motives, set out to revive the French language among Louisiana's Cajuns (or Acadians), and by 1977 French was being taught in Louisiana by no less than two hundred and fifty-seven *coopérants* or other foreign teachers, of whom one hundred and sixteen were French, ninety-six Belgian, forty Québécois and four Swiss.[60] Domengeaux led parties from Louisiana on visits to Paris and Brussels, where they were welcomed and encouraged in their task of promoting the French language.[61]

CONCLUSION

Rossillon continued to take an interest in the Walloons and the Jurassiens as well as the Cajuns of Louisiana. So much is clear in the journal *Les Amitiés acadiennes*, published by the association of which he was president for some twenty years. He was still presiding over it after he had retired from his civil service posts and, indeed, almost until he died on 6 September 1997. Several of his articles over the years made comparisons of the Acadians and the Belgian Walloons, under titles such as "Belgique et Acadie" (July 1977, 1–3), "Illusions constitutionelles et réalités politiques" (April 1979, 4–5), "La crise politique belge" (spring 1988, 3), and "L'évolution de la question belge," (winter 1991, 3).[62] And the Acadians themselves have made connections with Walloons in Belgium and French-speaking Swiss groups in the Jura region. Acadians belong to an organization of these and other francophone groups in or near Switzerland that was formed in Geneva in 1971. From the Gaullist point of view, efforts to stimulate separatist movements among Acadians, Jurassians, Québécois, and Walloons were all parts of the same imperial endeavour. De Gaulle envisaged a new French cultural and economic empire based on language, history, and misty feelings of cultural affinity. Who could tell what its limits would be?

The Bureaucratic Habit

During the past three decades Quebec has begun to adopt a system of organization and methods that is an age-old part of French civilization. This is a bureaucratic habit visible throughout the history of France, but especially in the political consequences of the French Revolution.[1] Not all French observers are aware of this habit as being peculiar to France, because they tend to imagine that other countries are similarly organized; but residence abroad enlightens a few. Foreigners who live in France for a period of years are puzzled, to say the least. "The price of State worship, as in France," a journalist comments in the *New Yorker*, "is that real things and events get displaced into a paper universe – the State is possible only because everything has been neatly removed from life and put into a filing cabinet." An observant British journalist adds, "France is run by an élite political body [of people who] believe that the French method of central administration through bureaucracy is superior to all others forms of government. Government by experts is their basic tenet."[2]

But officials facing the public are rarely "experts." As a student at the Sorbonne in 1953–54, I carried eight identity cards in return for twenty-seven passport photos required by bureaucrats around Paris; days passed as I waited in endless queues trying to satisfy the Préfecture de Police, which insisted on having approval from the Sorbonne, which in turn wanted police certification before granting approval.

In this chapter I explain the French example – constitutions, defence of the language, francisation, and bureaucratization – and its influence on Quebec, with its proliferating bureaux, its "language police," and its regimented cultural activities, centrally directed. Exploring that bureaucratic universe takes us once more into *la francophonie*, where we meet again some of the French Quebec mafia working in state-funded agencies created to bring about Quebec's independence.

CONSTITUTION AND RE-CONSTITUTION

The bureaucratic habit is rooted in the French written constitution. And one of the first steps of an independent Quebec would be to follow the French example by electing an assembly to draft a constitution, clause by clause. In a speech to a thousand cheering Quebec sovereigntists gathered on 23 May 1998 at Saint-Laurent, north of Montreal, Jacques Parizeau proposed a constitutional committee to begin the process.[3] Quebec is thus likely to follow the example of France, where the first constitution was drawn up in Paris during the first two years of the revolution by committees of an assembly that had come together to offer advice to their sovereign king. In taking the momentous decision to have a constitution, they were acting on the revolutionary principle that they represented the nation in a single assembly rather than the clergy, nobles, and townsmen in three separate estates. The document they adopted on 3 September 1791 named the king to the position of chief executive in a government of three separate powers – executive, legislative, and judicial – divided, as in the American constitution adopted a few years earlier.

The French constitutional history that began in 1789 does not, however, give Quebec an example of a permanent national structure like that of the United States, which has remained in place since the American revolution more than two centuries ago. What the French revolution set in motion was a constitutional process in which France adopted fifteen constitutions one after the other in less than two centuries. These are listed in Table 12.1. As this list suggests, the permanent feature of the process is the revolutionary step of securing the nation's approval for a new constitution to replace the one that has just been scrapped, usually in a political crisis. If an independent Quebec were to follow the French example, the result might be a similar series of revolutions, seemingly without end.

A large though unknown part of the Quebec public is already imbued with French revolutionary ideas. When, thirty-five years ago, the separatist *Rassemblement pour l'Indépendance Nationale* (RIN) met on 13 September 1963 to turn itself into a political party, its congress sang the terrorist song *Ça ira*. When on 23–26 November 1967 radical nationalists held a meeting of what they called the Estates General (États généraux) in the Place des Arts, Montreal, they were re-enacting the opening stage of the French Revolution. In December the provincial legislature formally renamed itself the National Assembly (Assemblée nationale) and has been so called ever since; but this is a French republican name that carries with it two centuries of revolutionary history. To describe Jacques Parizeau's budget of 1973 as "le

Table 12.1
French written constitutions

Date	Régime	Rulers or situation
3 Sept. 1791	Constitutional monarchy	Destroyed on 10 Aug. 1792
24 June 1793	First republic	Committee of Public Safety
22 Aug. 1795	Directory (directoire)	Cabinet council of five men
25 Dec. 1799	Consulate (consulat)	After Napoleon's coup d'état
2–4 Aug. 1802	Consulate (consulat)	Napoleon named consul for life
18 May 1804	Empire	Napoleon named emperor
4 June 1814	Restoration monarchy	LouisXVIII, a Bourbon, ruling
22 April 1815	Napoleon's hundred days	After escape from Elba
14 Aug. 1830	July monarchy	Louis-Philippe, an Orléans, ruling
4 Nov. 1848	Second republic	Louis-Napoleon named president
14 Jan. 1852	Second empire	Louis-Napoleon named Napoleon III
25 Feb. 1875	Third republic	Modified in 1879, 1884, and 1926
10 July 1940	L'état français of Vichy	Maréchal Philippe Pétain presiding
10 April 1946	Fourth republic	Parliamentary régime
4 Oct. 1958	Fifth republic	Presidential régime of de Gaulle and successors

Source: Jacques Godechot, ed., Les constitutions de la France depuis 1789 (Paris: Garnier-Flammarion, 1970).

budget de l'An I" was to identify it with the events of 1792–93.[4] An I (Year I) was the first year of the revolutionary calendar that began with the republic on 22 September 1792, and a reference to it could not have been intended to evoke the dawn of the Christian era, as some have thought.[5] The imagery and nomenclature of revolutionary France are used in Quebec to signify militant liberation, but it would be well to remember that the revolutionary and Napoleonic forces that "liberated" continental Europe were in fact conquering them no less than were the Soviet forces that "liberated" Hungary, Czechoslovakia, Poland, and the Baltic countries. The civil equivalent to the French conquering armies was the all-powerful central government that was beginning to rule supreme.

As long as Quebec follows the French constitutional example, it will struggle to establish complete central authority and will have the greatest difficulty in accommodating the claims of Aboriginal peoples, the city of Montreal, the federal government, corporate groups, and private citizens. This difficulty is inherent in the French-type constitution's opposition to federalism. The sovereignty of the nation remains unique and indivisible. For the sake of preserving national unity, which ranks with liberty, equality, and fraternity, no municipal, provincial, or regional authority has been tolerated unless it has remained subservient to the central government. Paris fought a civil war against the *fédérés* of certain outlying provinces in 1792–94 and succeeded in crushing the heresy of *fédéralisme*.[6] Later challenges to the state met similar uncompromising hostility.

A political crisis in France severe enough to bring down a régime and its constitution may sometimes alter the functioning of the government but is likely to leave the administrative machinery intact. Even the French Revolution in its most violent and destructive phase hardly changed the personnel that had been in place since the reign of Louis XVI.[7] In spite of its constitutional instability – or perhaps because of it – France is ruled by a powerful set of administrative bureaux relatively larger than those of other Western countries. One quarter of the working population in France is employed by the state, compared to 17.8 per cent in Italy, 15.7 per cent in Germany, and 14.4 per cent in the United Kingdom.[8] French bureaucracy is centralized because its authority stems from a single constitution sanctioned by the sovereign nation, and its tentacles reach out over the entire country into banking, business, education, manufacturing, transport, and other activities.

A typical French constitution, which imposes this centralized bureaucracy, begins with a declaration of the citizen's rights and freedoms. These are fine, abstract statements of intent and have grown from the seventeen clauses of the one that prefaced the constitution of 1791 to approximately thirty adopted on 27 October 1946 and renewed on 4 October 1958.[9] But declarations of rights on paper seem powerless to curb the bureaucracy, which continues to regulate, tax, harass, arrest, imprison, and impose paperwork to a degree that Canadians would consider abusive. A French-type constitution in Quebec would almost certainly impose the same heavy hand of day-to-day administration.

The basis of the system, as we saw above, is the written constitution sanctioned by the nation in a popular referendum. In order to draw up and sanction its constitution the nation must be a separate, independent, sovereign people, not bound by any authority outside itself and, in de Gaulle's phrase, "free to dispose of itself." But Quebec is still bound by the Canadian confederation, which is intolerable in French constitutional terms because it prevents the people from constituting itself ("se constituer") as a nation in an elected constituent assembly. French-educated and francophile citizens in the province were hoping to begin the process when, in November 1967, they held their Estates-General assembly in Montreal. The next stage of the original French constitutional process has not yet been reached, but Quebec has in the meantime gone some way in adopting other features of the centralized, bureaucratic state.

The PQ government seems to have caught the bureaucratic mentality merely by shifting its attention from the rest of Canada to France and *la francophonie*. As a journalist with *La Presse* of Montréal remarked, "French Red Tape Lives on in Quebec."[10] Pierre Arbour relates from direct experience how bureaucratic controls in business and industry have been abusive.[11] The provincial system of taxation is a more expensive burden than in other provinces.[12] Life in Quebec is beset with the requirements of an authoritarian, French-style government that imposes more and more paperwork, regulations, and even rules for speaking and writing. The conclusion seems inescapable that French influence tends to carry the bureaucratic habit to other French-speaking parts of the world, as may be seen from *la francophonie*'s baffling tangle of *agences, associations, bureaux, centres, comités, commissariats, conférences, conseils, délégations, fédérations, instituts, offices, services* and *sociétés*.[13] All modern societies are bureaucratic to some extent, but to live in France is to discover a measure of central authority more oppressive than in any other Western country. Quebec seems to be following this example.

Some French Canadians are aware of the danger. As early as 1967, Gérard Tougas expressed horror at "the incredible administrative methods left by France to its former colonies." He went on to reconstruct the intellectual steps "by which the French thought up the diabolical complications of their political management ... the numerous constitutions adopted ... the passion engendered by the discussion of each constitution and the learned, abstract commentaries that accompany them ... which have always astonished the Anglo-Saxons." and the oppressive bureaucratic methods that are invariably set up to implement them. "What," he asks in alarm, "is the state of mind of the African formed by the French administration and imbued with its methods?"[14] The question is pertinent because the republics of Gabon and Niger, for example, came into existence with constitutions of 19 February and 12 March 1959, respectively, modelled on the many French constitutions of the past two centuries: they even acknowledged "the Declaration of the rights of man and the citizen of 1789."[15]

LA DÉFENSE DE LA LANGUE

France has set another example for Quebec by increasing old bureaucratic efforts to protect its language. Laws imposing the use of French throughout the kingdom, even where Breton, Catalan, Basque, Provençal and local dialects of French were common, began in the sixteenth century, and the Académie française acted as a guardian of the language from 1637. For the next three centuries the government was content to leave its defence to academies and journalists, but since 1972 it has been intervening more and more. In that year, a decree appointed commissions to find French equivalents for foreign words that were creeping in and to standardize technical, scientific, medical, commercial, and other terms. This decree was sanctioned by President Georges Pompidou, who had taught French before going into politics. All government employees were expected to learn and use the official terms being thus established. Between January 1973 and March 1974 the government issued at least forty-nine regulations and circulars concerning the new terminology.

Meanwhile, similar commissions were busy settling problems of terminology among Quebec, Belgium, and other French-speaking parts of the world. For the most part, an English–American vocabulary that was being adopted the world over – at least fifteen hundred expressions – was now to be more and more discouraged by law and replaced with a French vocabulary devised by the official commissions. I well remember the list of words a French friend in business, who otherwise knew no English, had adopted during and after the 1960s: "marketing," "brain-storming," "le job," "take-off," "time-table," "leader," and others now being officially discouraged.

The Pompidou terminology commissions proved to be only a beginning. In December 1975 the National Assembly passed the "loi Bas-Lauriol," named after two of its members, forbidding the use of foreign (i.e., English) words in publicity, on the television, or on the radio whenever there were alternative French words.[16] This law was subsequently reinforced with various circulars but proved well-nigh impossible to enforce. Approaching the subject from another direction therefore, the government set up a *Conseil supérieur de la langue française* in October 1989, and in June 1992 it pushed through a constitutional amendment declaring fatuously that "the language of the Republic is French." These efforts rose to a climax with the notorious "loi Toubon," adopted on 4 August 1994, reinforced by various decrees, regulations, and circulars in 1995 and 1996, all laying down rules for the strict use of French in the written communications of business and official enterprises, in conferences and learned meetings, in teaching, and in public announcements and advertisements.

As might have been expected, there were widespread objections to these regulations. Scientists said they could not do their work without using English, the universal language of science. Journalists made fun of what many saw as a futile maginot line of linguistic defence. Others protested against such bureaucratic oppression. But Jacques Toubon and his many supporters, voluble as ever, defended the new laws as republican, democratic and founded on the historic efforts of earlier

French authorities. The result was a compromise, for the French senate and constitutional court both reduced the force and application of the Toubon law. Its defenders have not given up, however. In 1997 the *Commission générale de terminologie et de néologie* in the Ministry of Culture issued instructions for replacing the term "E-mail" with the abbreviation "Mél," which is to be used like "Tél," the official abbreviation for "Téléphone."[17] All this must give cause for thought in the English-speaking circles of Canada wherein all is voluntary, all is an amiable chaos, and an inverted snobbery of indifference prevails.

Since the 1960s Quebec has made a series of official efforts to join in the language disciplines launched in the development of *la francophonie*. Quebec City was encouraged to do so in October 1967, a few weeks after de Gaulle's visit in July, when the second international conference on the French language (*biennale de la langue française*) met at Montreal.[18] Seven years later, after much political agitation, the Quebec National Assembly adopted Bill 22 declaring French to be the only official language of the province. In 1977 Quebec adopted a "Charter of the French Language," revised in 1983, that was to reinforce the unilingual policy and guide the work of the *Régie* (or *Office*) *de la langue française* throughout the province. A set of Franco–Quebec agreements – *les accords Bourassa–Chirac* – laid down that the work was essentially to persuade organizations, public and private, to improve the French used in the workplace and to make use of specialists in various fields of vocabulary.

The unilingual policy in Quebec has given rise to a growing system of persuasion, leading occasionally to compulsion. A *Commission de protection de la langue française* was set up in 1977 to implement the French–language charter adopted with Bill 101 in Quebec, abolished by the Liberal government of Robert Bourassa in 1993 and revived by the Quebec minister of culture, Louise Beaudoin, in 1996. From 2 September 1997 this commission was directed by Odette Lapalme, daughter of a former premier, George-Émile Lapalme.[19] Its officials, popularly called "language police," have been persecuting English-speaking people more and more. The story of a shop being harassed for selling an English-speaking parrot may be apocryphal, but it conveys the atmosphere of Quebec's bureaucratic efforts to discourage the use of English.[20]

ATTACK IS THE BEST DEFENCE

"From 1975 to 1979," writes the historian of Quebec's linguistic relations, "missions of francisation were carried out on a grand scale."[21] Officials in Quebec City joined in the international campaigns of *la francophonie* with a will. In this, too, they were following the French example. Paris promoted French abroad much earlier and on a greater scale than it did at home. Some of its agencies have given employment and a convenient cover for the members of the Quebec lobby or mafia. There are private organizations among them, but most are state run. They have multiplied during the past forty years on a scale that has led to the publication of directories listing their names, purposes, and leading members.[22] The directories and most of the agencies they list are funded by France, though other countries in *la francophonie* sometimes contribute.

One of the mafia's contributions to Quebec independence and to French influence in general has been devotion to the politics of *la francophonie*. Work in this field entails not only organizing meetings, resolutions, and agreements of delegates from French-speaking countries but also insisting that French be used as much as possible by international organizations. For instance, during the critical years 1966–73 Philippe Rossillon was chairman (*rapporteur général*), later a rank-and-file member, of the *Haut comité pour la défense et l'expansion de la langue française* created by presidential decree on 31 March 1966 and attached to the office of the French prime minister. On 9 February 1984, it was replaced by a *Commissariat général de la langue française* and a *Comité consultatif de la langue française*, both set up to advise the prime minister. Then, on 2 May 1986 the prime minister's role in this field was increased by the establishment of a *Secrétariat d'État chargé de la francophonie*.[23] Three years later, on 2 June 1989 a *Conseil supérieur de la langue française* was established with nineteen to twenty-five members named for four years, and also a *Délégation générale de la langue française*, both attached to the prime minister's office. Xavier Deniau has been particularly active as chairman of the official *Comité de la francophonie* and of another body it recommended to the government, the *Comité interministériel pour les affaires francophones*, established by presidential decree of 17 May 1974. Pierre-Louis Mallen was entrusted with the task of "enforcing respect for the French language" at the Olympic Games. Objections were raised to the American use of English on the internet because it reached into France.

In this field of international "francisation," some members of the mafia, notably Pierre Maillard, Pierre Messmer, and Gilbert Pérol, have been active in what are ostensibly non-governmental organizations, though most are funded by the state in one way or another. Two examples are the *Association pour la défense du français et du patrimoine linguistique européen* and the *Institut Charles-de-Gaulle*.[24] In the course of a long diplomatic career, Maillard served as president of the former (1983 and 1988) and a member of the latter (1983). Some members have given lectures. For example, on 16 September 1968 Jean de Lipkowski, then *secrétaire d'État* in the Department of Foreign Affairs, spoke at Cannes to the international congress of Richelieu Clubs.[25] About eight hundred Quebec or other French-Canadian businessmen had travelled to France for that congress, and six of their leaders were invited to lunch with de Gaulle at the Élysée Palace.[26] In Canada, the Richelieu Clubs encourage Quebec nationalism and are sometimes regarded as successors to the *Ordre de Jacques Cartier.*

Xavier Deniau has been chairman of the *Association francophone d'amitié et de liaison* (AFAL), founded in 1974 with headquarters in Paris. In 1997 it was publishing a quarterly review called *Liaisons* and claiming to have one hundred and twenty members. He and Bernard Dorin have both been active in the *Association France–Québec*, a growing body of French people with a mission to help Quebec "to liberate itself" from Canada, and Dorin prides himself on being a *Membre-fondateur* of it. He accompanied de Gaulle on his visit to Quebec in July 1967 and then served as adviser to Alain Peyrefitte, the minister of education, who came over the following September to arrange cooperative ventures in education and cultural exchanges. As we saw in chapter 5, Philippe Rossillon presided for twenty years over a non-governmental body called *Amitiés acadiennes*, similar to the *Association France–Québec*, which publishes a small quarterly journal. He was also listed as the "Administrateur" of a Paris *Institut de recherche sur l'avenir du français*, which publishes a linguistic atlas of the world.[27]

Their generation is not, of course, the first to make serious efforts to promote French culture and language abroad. Governments in Paris have had a policy of "cultural imperialism" since the Middle Ages, and strident claims for the primacy of French have been heard since the sixteenth century.[28] The *Alliance française*, founded in 1883 by a group of intellectuals under the chairmanship of Paul Cambon, has been teaching French and otherwise encouraging French culture in Canadian cities and all over the world. In the early 1960s, soon after the Fifth Republic began, the *Alliance française* had eleven hundred committees and affiliated groups maintaining a total of nearly six hundred libraries, more than one hundred film clubs, and hundreds of language schools, all scattered through a hundred countries. It had then a growing membership of about 25,000. By 1980 there were some twelve hundred management committees throughout the world and about 290,000 pupils learning French in its classes. By 1997 more than 350,000 pupils were attending language courses at one thousand and fifty-six Alliance centres in one hundred and thirty-four countries.

Another 224,000 students were enrolled at four hundred and fourteen French schools abroad – not run by the Alliance française – two-thirds of them under the aegis of an *Agence pour l'enseignement du français à l'étranger*.[29]

For ten years beginning in 1977 a lawyer, professor and Liberal politician, William Graham, became president of the *Alliance française* in Toronto, in accordance with its normal practice of securing the patronage of a distinguished local francophile personage. By 1986 there were fourteen branches in Canada, with a total membership of sixteen hundred and seventy and some thirty-three hundred pupils in French-language classes. Eight teachers from France were employed in this system. The Winnipeg branch had established a kindergarten (*jardin d'enfant*) offering French immersion to children aged three to six years.[30] Branches in most Canadian cities served as centres for a variety of francophone townspeople – some of French or other French-speaking extraction, others retired teachers, professor, or diplomats – to gather for social purposes and to hear lectures or concerts.

More and more French books have been exported, but already in 1961 French publishers sent out 13,000 tons of books, about half to Belgium, Switzerland, and other part of western Europe, 6 per cent to Latin America, 2 per cent to Asia, and most of the rest to Africa. This was in an old tradition, it is true. For some years before the Second World War, France had exported on average some twenty-four million books a year.[31] By 1971 the French government itself was sending out, each year, 450,000 volumes worth nine million francs for use in French libraries abroad.[32] Exports to Canada have grown large only during the Fifth Republic in the process described in this book, mostly owing to the efforts in Paris. The cultural and technical division of the Ministry for Foreign Affairs began to promote language and culture around the world between the two world wars, especially under the energetic leadership of one Jean Marx. It resumed this work after the liberation of 1944 and was soon organizing courses of study in French in various countries, awarding some seven hundred scholarships to foreign teachers of French for brief visits to France, and nearly as many scholarships for a full year of study. I enjoyed the first of many years in France, a year of study at the Sorbonne in 1953–54, on one of these, for which I remain duly grateful.

The promotion of French language and culture abroad has some-times been listed under the rubric of "foreign aid." On close inspection, a great deal of French foreign aid turns out to have been in the form of cultural promotion, such as the dispatching of forty thousand teachers and technical assistants who, in some years, formed half of all those sent out by the developed nations.[33] Such facts qualify the claim that France has been exceptionally generous to the poorer parts of the world: foreign aid in 1963 amounted to 1.33 per cent of the gross national product (GNP); by 1971 it had declined, as in most countries, but still reached 0.63 per cent of GNP. Whatever the nature of French aid, it kept the Quai d'Orsay so busy that in 1974 a new division for cultural matters was created. By 1997 there were no less than one hundred and sixty institutes or centres of French culture in the world costing French tax-payers some six hundred and twenty-five million francs a year. Of these centres, one hundred and thirty were directed and half financed from the Quai d'Orsay. The rest were in Africa and consequently directed and financed by the *secrétariat d'État à la coopération*.[34]

Special cultural projects were launched, such as the long-drawn-out celebrations, at Chicago, Oxford, and elsewhere abroad, of the French Revolution's second centenary beginning in 1989. About the same time, President François Mitterrand started a project for an enormous new *Bibliothèque nationale de France*, now almost completed on the left bank of the Seine at Tolbiac in the Paris suburbs. It is intended not only for scholars but also for the general public and for "the diffusion of French on the planet" by every possible means.[35] Its catalogue was accessible in 1997 at http://www.bnf.fr on the internet. It has to be admitted that no other language has been defended and promoted with such official tenacity.

Special efforts were made in the 1960s to work out and implement what became known as a "cultural common market" for the francophone countries in general as well as between France and Quebec. This term referred to a proposal to facilitate the exchange of books, journals, and personnel and of radio/television programs using a satellite. The project for a cultural common market was discussed at several levels. In particular, the *Association internationale des parlementaires de langue française* took up the project with its secretary general, Xavier Deniau, during its three-day meeting at Versailles in September 1968.[36] A project for a francophone satellite was examined with a view to simultaneous transatlantic broadcasts of television and radio programs, but time differences and other technical problems eventually discouraged planners. This project was dropped, but cultural cooperation expanded enormously in other directions: funds set aside for it grew rapidly from five million francs in 1967 to twenty-six million in 1969 and thirty-five million in 1971. This was in addition to sixty-five million being spent on French teachers, libraries, and exchanges to promote the language abroad.[37]

POLITICS AND BUREAUCRACY IN LA FRANCOPHONIE

Francophonie is usually discussed as though it were merely the cultural fraternizing of French-speaking peoples. It is based, however, on the ideology of nationalism, and the theory behind this ideology bears repeating because it is alien to the English-speaking nations and easily misunderstood. It defines a nation as a people with a common language, culture, and history and declares it to have a right and duty to exist as a separate state. Its independence and sovereignty are fundamental to its existence. And in France there is only puzzled contempt for a country such as Canada that pretends to be "multicultural". Multiculturalism makes no sense whatever to an average educated Frenchman, heir to the French political tradition; it contradicts his deepest national beliefs and he simply rejects it. Most Gaullist statesmen, diplomats, and politicians are missionaries for an aggressive nationalism of the kind the PQ has adopted in Quebec.

The ideology of national sovereignty in this French revolutionary sense led to a kind of imperialism. It was on this theory that the armies of the first French republic made war on the kings and princes of Europe in order to "liberate" the nations that were said to be held in subjection. Yet liberation by French forces was an act of patronizing superiority that implied wide use of French. The French language served as "a political weapon" from April 1792, when French armies invaded German-speaking and Dutch-speaking lands.[38] From then until Napoleon's defeat in 1814–15, written constitutions of a French type, expressing the principles of national sovereignty, were imposed on the conquered peoples and revised according to constitutional changes in France. Sympathetic groups in every country responded to the French ideological message, somewhat as groups of Communists responded to the Soviet Union's message in the twentieth century. While ruling, patronizing, and reorganizing these countries, however, French authorities also exploited them, taking goods, money, horses and even art treasures back home.

In the informal French empire of the twentieth century, the erstwhile colonies, and any other French-speaking countries that wish to join, are patronized and dominated, but not in the old Bourbon or Bonapartist way. In the Gaullist universe of the late twentieth century, French armies have been used occasionally, but the common language and culture have become the principal vehicles for French leadership. Recognizably French constitutions, expressing national sovereignty and other abstract ideas, have been imposed on member states. When French African colonies were granted independence they adopted French-type constitutions that were imposed on them much as the triumphant French authorities handed out constitutions to conquered countries from 1792 to 1814.

La francophonie is based on something more than a common language. With French goes a particular civilization, only partly recognized and acknowledged. The ruling authorities in Paris, Quebec, and all the old colonial capitals are continually assuring one another that la francophonie is not merely literary: it embraces the economic, technological, and scientific fields of our time. The member countries have become fields for French investment and the implanting of French institutions. Paris expects them to accept French leadership and to glory in the common culture, history, art, science, public works, and business enterprise. In this way Gaullist France has been groping towards formation of a cultural and economic empire based on more than the use of the French language. It was with economic collaboration in mind that Premier Bouchard and a large party of cabinet ministers and businessmen made an official visit to France from 28 September to 3 October 1997. This much is widely recognized, but other aspects of this empire are silently and unconsciously assumed by most members.

Recent francophone summit meetings have been developing political policies. Between 19 and 21 May 1997 about fifty countries had representatives at a conference of French-speaking cabinet ministers in Montreal. From 12 to 16 November that year, the heads of French-speaking countries met in Hanoi for their seventh summit meeting.[39] A Vietnamese resident in Montreal argued publicly that it would be futile to hold such a conference in Hanoi because the Communist government there had virtually eliminated use of French and had adopted English as its prevailing foreign language.[40] However, confronting an apparently lost cause is nothing new for the francophone movement. And it was also meeting to elect a secretary general of the Communauté des pays francophones; "then la francophonie may become a strong political reality," Jacques Chirac had predicted during the previous July, "an actor playing a full part in international relations. It will bring to them the values that inspire us." Chirac was speaking to the mayors of eighty-five French-speaking cities of the world, including Montreal, Quebec City, and several African capitals, meeting in Brussels at the Association internationale des maires francophones (AIMF).[41]

La francophonie took a political turn at Hanoi in mid-November 1997, as Chirac suggested it might. This occurred while the forty-eight associated governments laid out a program for the next two years, after which they planned to meet again at Moncton, New Brunswick. As usual, the long-term political intentions or hopes were not spelled out but began to unfold in some opening steps. A secretary-general was appointed, who turned out to be Boutros Boutros-Ghali, the Egyptian statesman who had presided over the United Nations until his renewed candidature had been opposed by the United States. The effect was to give the francophone summits an executive, for two years at least, and to entrust it to a figure rejected by the United States. Was this merely one more act of French opposition to American leadership in the world? Boutros-Ghali denied any feelings of hostility to the United States, as required by the unspoken rules of ambiguity observed by francophone authorities.

His appointment had yet another political aspect: he represented a country that was in no way French-speaking, and he spoke mainly English at his own press conferences. It began to appear that *la francophonie* was now open to membership by countries in which hardly anyone speaks French, and several applied to join: Poland, Roumania, Moldavia, and Bulgaria. The reasons for their adherence were far from clear. There were indications that the first policy to be pursued by this new political being might be a defence of human rights, arguably consistent with the established values of French culture that are said to accompany use of its language.

A concern for human rights did credit to Jacques Chirac and Jean Chrétien, who suggested this new political direction of the francophone summit. Observers wondered, however, where it would lead, particularly as the African governments at the summit would have preferred to confine francophone policies to more familiar cultural and economic spheres. Economic and financial aid to Third World countries was their concern. Naturally, they would also have preferred to see one of their own appointed to the new post of secretary–general. But Boutros-Ghali was able to announce at Addis-Ababa that his organization would be collaborating with the Organization of African Unity (*Organisation de l'Unité Africaine*), at least in economic and cultural matters.[42]

These changes in the character of the francophone community provoked criticism, and not only from observers outside the French-speaking community. A columnist in the Brussels journal *Le Soir* was scathing about the new political orientation, which had resulted, in her view, from undue pressure by Jacques Chirac. "Why, in the name of what – if it isn't political ambition, the desire to carry weight in world affairs – go on building up a family [of nations] that is no longer francophone except in name and is nothing but a juxtoposition of diverse interests?"[43] Such criticism is so evidently well founded that it must occur to other observers. But there is no shortage of people ready to put the leaders of the francophone movement in the best possible light, and journals such as *Le Devoir* (Montréal) and *France–Amérique*, supported in New York by *Le Figaro* (Paris), will always be glad to print what they write.

The new secretariat general of the francophone summit takes its place amid two sets of institutions that have grown up in the service of *la francophonie*: one to serve the French-speaking union, mainly in Paris, and the other distributed among the members, such as Quebec, or abroad in its foreign service. A whole universe of bureaux dealing with *la francophonie* turns slowly round and round in Paris, and the *Association de solidarité francophone* was established in November 1966 as an umbrella for all the others. Paris became the centre for international French-speaking associations of sociologists (1958), universities (1961), parliamentarians (May 1967), lawyers and jurists (1968), historians and geographers (1969), and mayors (1979). The central *Agence de coopération culturelle et technique* (ACCT), founded at Niamey, Niger, as we saw in chapter 8, by a treaty that twenty-one states signed on 21 March 1970 grew by 1997 to a membership of forty-two states and two participating governments – Quebec and New Brunswick. At its headquarters in Paris its secretary general, assisted by four directors general, supervises eight regional bureaux. Its budget is contributed mainly by France (46 per cent), Canada, including Quebec and New Brunswick (35 per cent), and the Belgian *Communauté française* (12 per cent).[44]

Since the francophone summit meeting of 1991 – the *Sommet de Chaillot* – ACCT has been the principal agency implementing summit decisions and providing a secretariat for *francophonie* in general. The *Sommets* met in Paris in 1986, Quebec in 1987, Dakar again in 1989, Chaillot in 1991, Mauritius in 1993, Cotonou (Benin) in 1995, and Hanoi in 1997, and plans have been made to gather in 1999 at Moncton, New Brunswick. These *Sommets* crown the growing galaxy of agencies that make up *la francophonie*, and new ones may be added at any time. For example, shortly before Bastille day in July 1992, some two hundred and fifty "intellectuals," French and foreign, made an urgent appeal to the president of the republic and his government for the "the defence of the French language," and the result was a new association called *Avenir de la langue française*, with an office in Paris.[45] The bureacratic instinct springs eternal in France.

As a proud member of *la francophonie*, Quebec has tried to keep up with its partners, most of which are governments of sovereign states. When the *Délégation générale du Québec* was established in Paris, it was not long before it had an officer appointed to maintain liaison with the central agencies for *la francophonie*. The *Délégation* eventually came to include a special immigration service directed by Roger

Thériault, and cultural services as well.[46] A library and cultural centre
were added in the rue du Bac, and a number of offices dealing with cultural and immigration matters: a *Centre de coopération inter-universi-
taire franco–québécoise*, established in 1984; a *Centre québécois de
coopérations industrielles*; an *Office Franco–Québécois pour la
jeunesse*; not to mention the various non-governmental bodies such as
Amitiés acadiennes and the *Association France–Québec* boasting sixty
regional associations with a total membership of over five thousand
members and a journal, *France–Québec*, which had published a
hundred issues by 1996 when it was renamed *France–Québec Magazine*.[47] French-speaking civil servants at all levels were appointed to
represent Quebec for the business of *la francophonie* in Paris, the latest
of whom is Michel Lucier, recently promoted to the post of *Délégué
général* du Québec in Paris.[48]

At Quebec city, another group of agencies works for *la francophonie*. Among these is an *Office de la langue française*, established in
1961 at Quebec in the Ministry of Cultural Affairs, to promote the
defence, improvement, and diffusion of French, in collaboration with
other agencies at home and abroad; *Québec dans le monde*, founded
1983 in Quebec, which claims three hundred members (of which one
hundred and twenty-five are other organizations); an *Association
Québec–France*, founded in 1971 and not to be confused with its
opposite number, the *Association France–Québec*. *Québec-France*
publishes a quarterly bulletin and claims to have thirty-two hundred
members in twenty-two regional branches. A corresponding group of
foreign francophone governments has offices in Quebec City or occasionally Montreal: a *Délégation Wallonie–Bruxelles au Québec*, an
Agence Québec Wallonie–Bruxelles pour la jeunesse, founded in 1984,
and of course a *Consulat général de France à Québec*. On 20 March
1998, celebrated as the *journée internationale de la francophonie*, the
Quebec government established a *Maison de la francophonie* in the
provincial capital at 150 boulevard René-Lévesque. There ten associations have set up their files.[49]

By 1990 the total staffs of the agencies posted abroad by the government of Quebec were more numerous than all of the other provincial foreign agents put together (see Table 12.2). To coordinate all this
activity, the government of Daniel Johnson established in 1967 what it
called the *Ministère des affaires intergouvernementales* (MAI), intended
particularly to direct all its growing agencies abroad. The MAI is really
a ministry for foreign affairs in waiting. Indeed by the 1980s it had
come to be called the *Ministère des relations étrangères* and had
expanded into offices in the place George, Quebec City, and begun to
carry out some of the tasks of a foreign ministry, especially in France.

Table 12.2
Provincial Representation Abroad in 1990

Province	Staff	Posts
British Columbia	53	9
Alberta	60	6
Saskatchewan	11	5
Manitoba	4	4
Ontario	163	19
Quebec	405*	27
Nova Scotia	13	5
New Brunswick	2	2†
Newfoundland	1	1‡

Source: Mel Hines, *Canadian Foreign Policy Handbook* (Montreal: Jewel Editions, 1996), 59–61.
*Including 88 in Paris.
†Both in the United States.
‡Hong Kong.

On 11 February 1980, a few days before a federal election and a few months before the first Quebec referendum on sovereignty, the minister's *directeur de cabinet*, Louise Beaudoin, joined in a debate in Paris to celebrate the appearance of a book explaining the separatist campaign: *Dossier Québec*, edited by Claude Glayman and Jean Sarrazin (Paris: Stock, 1979). She took the opportunity to denounce Pierre Elliott Trudeau for "his dull and boring speeches" and assured the assembled company, which included the editor-in-chief of *Le Monde*, André Fontaine, that the separatists would win the forthcoming referendum. In any event, she added, they would continue their separatist campaign because it was certain that Quebec would become a sovereign state in ten or twenty years.[50] She was acting as a senior member of Quebec's informal "Ministry for Foreign Affairs" and a senior civil servant in the growing bureaucracy of her province.

The Aggressive Fifth Republic

In dealing with the French Quebec mafia it is essential to understand the aggressive character of the Fifth Republic in which its members enjoy their high offices, political authority, and long careers. Three subjects may help to show how Gaullist France has been behaving and what one may expect in dealings with it: the *Rainbow Warrior* affair and the *force de frappe*; French uranium purchases in Canada and Africa; and French interference in Africa, with examples from Guinea, Biafra, and Rwanda. Such observations may lead the reader to a conclusion reached as early as October 1969, well before the *Rainbow Warrior* incident, by Marcel Cadieux, under-secretary of state (deputy minister) in Canada's Department of External Affairs. He remarked sadly but lucidly, in his intimate diary, on the basis of first-hand knowledge and experience, "It is well established for whoever knows the activities of the Gaullists that the latter never trouble themselves much over legality and protocol. On the contrary they act with brutality and their methods, not what one might think at first, are more like those of veritable gangsters than of civilized European statesmen."[1]

THE *RAINBOW WARRIOR* AND THE FORCE DE FRAPPE[2]

In July 1985, French secret service agents planted two limpet bombs on the bottom of a ship called *Rainbow Warrior* that was moored peacefully in the harbour at Auckland, New Zealand. These bombs exploded on 10 July, sank the ship, and killed a photographer, Fernando Pereira, who was aboard. He was there working with the environmental agency Greenpeace, to which *Rainbow Warrior* belonged. The ship was in New Zealand on a mission to do what it could to observe and hamper French nuclear testing on an island in the Pacific Ocean, in French Polynesia not far from Tahiti. In mid-July 1985 nobody knew who had blown up the ship, as the French government had intended this act of sabotage to be secret and solemnly denied any knowledge of it.

President François Mitterrand set up an inquiry under Bernard Tricot, which exonerated France in a report on 19 September – "Tricot lave plus blanc!," as French wags said when the report was discovered to be just a whitewashing.[3] How false the report was emerged when the New Zealand police carried out an investigation; after a few weeks they were able to establish not only that French agents had done the deed, but that they had acted under orders from their government. French authorities impeded investigations at home as best they could. But the New Zealand public assisted in the investigation to a degree that drew the wonder of French commentators, who had never before witnessed such an exhibition of "sens civic."

It became clear that high officials such as Charles Hernu, French minister of defence, and Admiral Pierre Lacoste, head of the *Direction général de la sécurité extérieure* (DGSE) secret police, had deliberately set out to destroy the *Rainbow Warrior*. This was admitted at last in a television appearance on 22 September by Prime Minister Laurent Fabius and a new minister of defence, Paul Quilès, who replaced Hernu. Much vital evidence was gradually discovered by French journalists, who alone within France seemed willing to challenge their government. In particular, *Le Monde* published a damning account of the government's guilt on 19 September. It soon emerged that two teams of DGSE agents had spied out the ship, befriended its crew, and generally prepared the way for a pair of expert divers from the French army, Captain Jean-Luc Kyster and Adjutant Jean Camasse, both trained at a base near Aspretto, Corsica, who flew in, did the dirty deed, and flew out again undetected.

When this official skulduggery was discovered, the French government was not in the least repentant. In response to New Zealand's vigorous protests it became abusive and even threatened to impede the sale of New Zealand butter and other products in Europe – a frightening prospect for a small country that depended on its sales of these products abroad. President Mitterrand flew out to the Mururoa Atoll in September 1985 expressly to declare that the nuclear testing would go on as planned. All that happened was that Hernu and Lacoste were obliged to resign. But six months later Hernu was decorated with the Légion d'honneur. The guilty secret service agents were punished little if at all and widely regarded as heroes in France. An officer of the DGSE teams, Alain Mafart, was promoted to colonel a few years later.[4] A female agent who had helped to prepare the attack, Dominique Prieur, wrote a book about it.[5]

It would be hard to avoid the conclusion that France behaved, as it has so often in the past, as an international bully, totally unconcerned about world opinion, much less about the morality of its actions. One of the reasons for its complacency is that it knows it has the support of the great majority of French people. Most French citizens like their government to throw its weight around, just as the public of two centuries ago was pleased when Napoleon conquered most of Europe. This is a fault of the French nation, at least in great majority, not merely of one government. The incident of the *Rainbow Warrior* makes sense only in the context of French policies over the centuries. But why, in detail, did the government act as it did?

French nuclear testing in the South Pacific resulted from General de Gaulle's decision to maintain an independent nuclear deterrent. In 1961 and 1962, soon after he took office, de Gaulle tried to create an integrated European foreign and defence policy that would be independent of the United States and – no one doubted – dominated by France. This policy was developed in what were called the Fouchet Plans. There was no illusion in Paris that Europe would be secure without u.s. armed forces, but de Gaulle thought that he and not the American president ought to lead Europe. When his partners in the European Economic Community rejected and opposed his plans, de Gaulle took France out of the NATO command structure in 1966 and began developing an independent nuclear striking force, *la force de frappe.*

At first, the Sahara Desert had offered a site for French nuclear testing, and bombs had been exploded there in 1960–63. However, after Algeria had won its independence in 1962, it objected to such tests, and so the French government chose another part of its overseas empire for nuclear testing: an island in the South Pacific. When other countries objected – especially Australia and New Zealand, of course – de Gaulle replied in his usual haughty terms. He said that this was purely a French matter, to which no one else had any right to object. His government then went on to say that any country that opposed French nuclear testing there would be regarded as an enemy.[6]

The first program of tests on the Mururoa Atoll began on 2 July 1966 with a 25 – 30 kilotonne atmospheric explosion. There followed another forty explosions, culminating on 15 September 1974, when Australia and New Zealand won their case before the World Court at The Hague. To meet that court's decision against France, Paris began a series of underground explosions at nearby Fangataufa Island on 5 June 1975. Ten years later it was still testing bombs, but once more on the Mururoa Atoll, where it set off a great blast on 9 May 1985.

It was then that Greenpeace undertook to make one of its peaceful protests against these atomic tests. Greenpeace was encouraged in doing so by a growing body of world opinion against nuclear testing as being environmentally damaging. Canada, like several other countries, had protested from time to time, such as on 10 May 1972, against these tests. A yacht from Vancouver, the *Vega*, had sailed in protest during that summer; it had been rammed by a French naval vessel on 1 August, and the Canadian skipper, David McTaggart, a millionaire from Vancouver, had been badly hurt.[7] Greenpeace was also encouraged by the Treaty of Rarotonga (in the Cook Islands), signed in August 1985 by most of the Pacific countries. This treaty declared a South Pacific Nuclear Free Zone, aimed mainly at France. It is against this background that the *Rainbow Warrior* affair may best be seen as an act of international terrorism.

The events of 1985–86 were, as it turned out, only the beginning. In July 1995, ten years after the incident, the government of Jacques Chirac, a strong Gaullist who succeeded François Mitterrand, began to make preparations for another series of nuclear tests on Mururoa Atoll. Greenpeace promptly sent out another ship, *Rainbow Warrior II*. This vessel got as far as the waters around the atoll when, suddenly on Sunday, 9 July, she was rammed by a French naval vessel carrying about one hundred and fifty commandos. These men boarded her, smashed windows and doors, and used tear gas to overpower the crew. They then seized the crew, interrogated them, put them back on the ship, and dragged her out into international waters. This French aggression was promptly denounced by New Zealand, Australia, Germany, the United States, Italy, Canada (rather meekly, as usual), and eventually Japan.

In response, the French prime minister, Alain Juppé, "shrugged off the criticism, saying that the assault was justified to ensure respect for the law."[8] Protest demonstrations were organized in several countries: about one hundred demonstrators gathered outside the French consulate in Toronto; similar protests were made wherever there are French authorities in Canada. Among the demonstrators in England was Marelle Pereira, daughter of the photographer who was killed in the French attack on the *Rainbow Warrior* in July 1985. Meanwhile, the French went on exploding atomic bombs in Mururoa – eight of them – until late in 1995, as if nothing had happened, totally indifferent to world-wide protests.

Two characteristics of these French nuclear experiments made them particularly objectionable and open to challenge of the kind that Greenpeace undertook. First, the dangers to the indigenous populations in both the Sahara and the Pacific were unknown and apparently of little concern to French authorities, as recent revelations have shown.[9] Great radioactive clouds bore down on the Sahara and on Pacific Islands such as Mangareva, Pukarua, Reao, and Tureia. All expressions of concern for the safety of the populations affected were silenced by French authorities. Second, this authoritarian silencing was only part of the total censorship imposed on news of these experiments as being vital parts of the sacred *force de frappe*. A coordinated secret police service, composed of agents from the *Service de documentation extérieure et de contre-espionnage* (SDECE) – predecessor of the DGSE – the *Direction de la surveillance du territoire* (DST), and the *Direction centrale des renseignements généraux* (DCRG), was established at Papeete in French Polynesia about 1964 but disguised as a "Bureau d'Études." Its business was to protect the nuclear experiments from any opposition or any exposure by journalists and to prevent publication of any information that might alert or warn the indigenous populations about what was happening. In addition, the records of the military agency in charge of nuclear experiments, the *Direction des centres d'expérimentations nucléaires*, found their way into the military archives in the Château de Vincennes, Paris, but soon after a historian began to study them the minister of defence, Alain Richard, had them closed. Since 1 December 1997 they have been inaccessible.

FRENCH URANIUM PURCHASES:
CANADA AND AFRICA

Ever since Charles de Gaulle founded the Fifth Republic, it has been pursuing a policy of nuclear development, both civil and military, that has required large quantities of uranium. De Gaulle was intent on keeping up with the British in nuclear weapons and defeating American efforts to prevent him from doing so under the terms of the U.S. non-proliferation policy. One of his reasons for doing this was that French scientists had gone far in nuclear research before the war, notably in the use of heavy water, and from 1940 to 1944 had been working in Britain and at Montreal with British and Canadian scientists.[10] Consequently, it did not take France long to catch up in nuclear science. Writing in 1984, just before the *Rainbow Warrior* affair, one specialist declared, "France has the largest present commitment to nuclear power outside the United States. ... And the dividing line between [French] military and civilian uranium activities is ambiguous."[11]

More than twenty-five years earlier, before the first French atomic bomb had been exploded in February 1960, de Gaulle's government had already begun to make strenuous efforts to procure uranium from Canada because deposits in Ontario and Saskatchewan were extensive, accessible, and not threatened by political instability, as some of the African deposits were. However, negotiations for sales to France broke down in 1957 over disagreements about prices and the Canadian requirement that inspectors should ensure that the uranium was being used for peaceful purposes.[12] In January that year Lorne Gray, an official with Atomic Energy of Canada Ltd, told Bertrand Goldschmidt, head of the French *Commissariat à l'énergie atomique*, that Canada intended to impose a limit of two hundred tons on uranium exports to all countries except Great Britain and the United States.

Here was another exhibition of the kind of "Anglo-Saxon" collaboration that infuriated de Gaulle, and he took control of the French government in the crisis of the following year. He was incensed again in 1959 when Howard Green, secretary of state for external affairs in John Diefenbaker's government, supported an Afro–Asian resolution in the United Nations denouncing France for its testing of nuclear bombs in the Sahara.[13] When de Gaulle visited Canada two years later, Diefenbaker made Canada's opposition to his nuclear policy quite clear, and the visit was not a happy one.[14] Newspapers in Canada made a feature of this quarrel over nuclear policy. In 1964 and 1965 another French effort to secure Canadian uranium failed because of the inspection requirements that Prime Minister Pearson explained to the House of Commons on 3 and 19 June 1965. The government would not ratify a contract that Denison Mines had concluded with France to sell $700 million worth of uranium.[15]

On 30 September 1968 the minister for external affairs, Mitchell Sharp, agreed to sell $1.5 million worth of plutonium to France during the next three years. This was reported the next day with recollections of the abortive negotiations in 1965–67 for a much larger sale of uranium over a period of twenty-five years.[16] Ottawa was continuing to insist on a system of inspection to ensure that uranium sold would be used only for peaceful purposes, and the French government would not agree to this condition.[17] The plutonium sold was for use in nuclear reactors and was too little, and in any case inappropriate, for nuclear weapons. A French company, Mokta (Canada) Ltd, continued exploring for uranium in northern Saskatchewan, but de Gaulle was furious.[18] Here began much of the Gaullist hostility to Canada.

Angry but not defeated, de Gaulle fell back on supplies that were being developed in France and, even more, in two former French colonies in Africa, Niger and Gabon. These countries had won their independence from France in 1960, but de Gaulle had contrived to retain a useful relationship with them by supporting their one-party, dictatorial governments and offering material aid. To nurture its African "domaine réservé" de Gaulle made official visits to former colonial capitals in August 1958, July and December 1959, and August 1966; and his successor Georges Pompidou did the same in February 1971.[19]

In these circumstances Paris had no difficulty in controlling exploitation of uranium deposits there. Between 1947 and the early 1970s, French prospectors in Gabon discovered five such deposits. Production and sales were managed by the *Compagnie des mines d'uranium de Franceville* (COMUF), made up of a consortium of French companies, with Gabon's government retaining an interest of no more than one-quarter. The French *Compagnie générale des matières nucléaires* (COGEMA) held nearly one-fifth of COMUF's shares and during the 1980s was buying 60 per cent of the total production. But production was declining then, having reached a peak in 1977; world uranium markets began to shrink thereafter.

Meanwhile, after many years of exploration in Niger and some small preliminary discoveries, at some time during 1966 the French atomic energy authority found a large deposit of uranium at a remote location called Arlit, some 850 kilometres northeast of Niamey.[20] Production began in July 1971, and already the French press was confidently predicting yields so abundant that France, which patronized Niger in the same manner as it did Gabon, would soon become a uranium exporter.[21] An all-weather road was built to Arlit in 1980, and by that time another deposit at Akouta had also begun producing. President Hamani Diori's successor, Seyni Kountche, managed to secure a one-third share of uranium sales, but from 1971 France took about three-quarters of Niger's entire uranium production.[22] This was the largest source of French external supplies. From 1980 to 1989, South Africa and Namibia sold uranium to France, and it appears that from 1981 to 1992 a modest quantity was obtained from the United States and Canada.

The Canadian supplies were produced by a consortium of four French companies working at Cluff Lake in northern Saskatchewan under the name of Motka, and then Amok, which was yielding some fifteen hundred metric tonnes of uranium a year by 1982. The French-government enterprise called COGEMA undertook to buy 80% of its production, but the quantities actually shipped were reduced by Canada's Atomic Energy Control Board, which regulates sales according to an act of Parliament passed in July 1972. Sales to France faded out altogether after 1992.[23] COGEMA is still working uranium deposits in northern Saskatchewan. To fulfill its nuclear ambitions, France has not hesitated to seek uranium wherever it may be found, and in 1996 this was in Russia.[24]

Here then is another side – the supply side – of France's nuclear policy that also entails explosions in Pacific islands and an obstinate refusal to join with other countries in united defensive strategies that might in some way hamper the independent *force de frappe* on which Gaullist France has always prided itself.

France has continued to maintain its independent position, unwilling to enter any international or multinational military organization unless it feels that it can dominate it. This attitude is consistent with French policy on the manufacture and sale of fighter planes, guided missiles, and other weaponry. A loyal Gaullist, Marcel Dassault (born Marcel Bloch), built up the postwar French aircraft industry with the assistance of a wartime German engineer, Herman Oestrich, and had a leading jet fighter, the Mirage III, ready for the French air force and for sales abroad a few years before de Gaulle returned to power in 1958.[25] From 1951 Dassault represented the Oise department in the National Assembly and put his wealth, influence, and aircraft industry at de Gaulle's disposal. The *force de frappe* of the 1960s and 1970s, which de Gaulle used so ruthlessly in his foreign policy, owed much to Dassault. But it is important to stress, as specialists do, that this militant policy has emanated from the government, specifically the Élysée Palace, not from the arms industry, powerful though it is. "De Gaulle wanted to equip France," one writes, "with an armaments industry that would allow the country to free itself from its dependence on the United States."[26]

In a typically French fashion, he set up a mixed public and private authority, the *Délégation générale pour l'armement*, which has continued to carry out this militant Gaullist policy. By 1978 France had built four nuclear submarines to match the four British Polaris submarines; in 1980 it launched a fifth, and in May 1985, a sixth.[27] From 1983 on, three French atomic submarines were on constant patrol and were supplemented by land-based intercontinental missiles, set up on the Plâteau d'Albion – a total force greater than the atomic forces of Great Britain. For the historical reasons sketched in this book, there was no cooperation whatever between Britain and France in this field. And during the Strategic Arms Limitation Talks – SALT I and II – both nations specified that their nuclear forces should not be counted in with the U.S. forces. France maintained its forces even when the Berlin wall came down and the Cold War ended. Specialists observe that "France was the only major power to increase its defence expenditure for 1990."[28]

The full extent of Gaullist preparations for war has not yet been revealed, as may be seen from new information that emerges from time to time. A good example is a huge testing range for poisonous gases and other chemical weapons maintained secretly by the French gov-

ernment from 1962 to 1978.[29] It was an enormous patch of the desert
in Algeria near Morocco called B2–Namous, which de Gaulle insisted
on keeping when negotiating the independence of Algeria at the Evian
conference in 1961. By a secret clause in the independence treaty, the
French Ministry of National Defence was allowed to continue using
B2–Namous and four nuclear testing ranges, Colomb–Béchar, Ham-
maguir, In–Ekker, and Reggane, for five years. At the expiry of this first
agreement, the four ranges were closed in 1968, but at de Gaulle's
insistence B2–Namous was retained for another five years. This agreement was signed on 27 May 1967 by the French ambassador at
Algiers, Pierre de Leusse, and a representative of the Algerian president, Houari Boumediene, with the understanding that it would be
kept strictly secret. When it came up for renewal in May 1972, the
Algerians exacted a large loan in exchange, as well as a share in the
chemical weaponry being developed, and President Giscard d'Estaing
accepted these terms. The French finally abandoned B2–Namous in
1978 but continued their chemical warfare experiments at two places
in France – Bouchet and Mourmelon (Marne) – until 1987. These
secret arrangements were recently admitted by de Gaulle's minister of
national defence, Pierre Messmer, in an interview with a journalist.[30] It
goes without saying that the French government had repeatedly denied
their existence.

Consistent with their warlike preparations, French governments
have resisted efforts at international disarmament ever since the Second
World War, and with particular firmness under the Fifth Republic. In
March 1962 de Gaulle's government refused to occupy its seat at the
Geneva disarmament conference. This "empty chair" policy, which
continued long after de Gaulle's demise, was one of the methods that
France used to undermine what it regarded as the unfair intention of
the great powers to monopolize nuclear weaponry.[31] France likewise
boycotted the nuclear non-proliferation treaty in 1968 and most other
international disarmament agreements until 1978, when Giscard d'Estaing's government put forward a set of proposals that tended to bring
France into line with most other countries. But this gradual accommodation also owed something to widespread recognition that French
objections to earlier disarmament proposals had some merit.[32]

One of the pressures on the French to enter into some collective,
international agreement – some sort of military collaboration – is the
increasing cost, in recent years, of sophisticated modern weapons.
France has been able to pay for them by two methods: by cutting back
its conventional forces more and more and by selling arms abroad.
France has for many years been one of the leading manufacturers and
suppliers of sophisticated weaponry to most of the unstable, troubled

parts of the earth. South Africa acquired French submarines and Mirage fighter planes, probably in exchange for uranium from mines in Namibia. France went on selling arms to Iraq until 1977; and Saddam Hussein's air force is equipped with French aircraft. His missiles, too, are French, at least in part.[33] During 1982, Argentina was using French missiles and fighters in its invasion of the Falkland Islands and the subsequent war with Britain. Only a year or so ago the French sold fighter aircraft to Taiwan (much to the fury of the Chinese). How long they can go on selling sophisticated weaponry round the world is not clear, but certainly no moral or humanitarian considerations will persuade them not to.

While the rest of the Western countries have been eager to respond to the collapse of Russian imperial strategy, the French government has been very wary of reducing its armed forces. France did not want to sign the Intermediate Nuclear Forces Treaty for a reduction of forces, in Washington in December 1987, and Jacques Chirac was among those who tried to obstruct its adoption. The French public was then in agreement over that.[34] Socialist governments have carried on these military policies and maintained the national commitment to the *force de frappe*. Since 1995 Jacques Chirac has revived and reinforced the *force de frappe*.

A show of military force is inherent in Gaullist policy, as in the imperial French tradition generally. The French Revolution has nearly always been commemorated, paradoxically enough, as a military event, with long parades of armed forces and events revolving around the Arc de Triomphe, with its lists of French victories and fighting heroes carved in stone.[35] Such national celebrations continue to this day: for more than an hour on 14 July 1997, President Jacques Chirac and senior members of his government watched a parade of four thousand soldiers, twenty-seven of the latest model of Leclerc tanks, and other military equipment, while warplanes flew overhead, leaving trails of red, white, and blue smoke.[36] Not so belligerent as the First Republic, which declared war on a growing list of enemies in 1792–93, the Fifth Republic glories in its military readiness, undeterred by memories of the sobering defeat of the Third Republic, which thought it was ready to resist the German armies in 1940, or of extensive French collaboration with the Nazi occupiers under Vichy.

From the time of de Gaulle's leadership, France has been almost a rogue state, not the most threatening or troublesome in the world, but by no means one of the world's good citizens. In particular, it has steadily sought to undermine the Canadian–American policy of non-proliferation, invariably pursuing its own narrow defence interests above all else.[37] It has maintained a policy of military independence, sometimes refusing to collaborate with international military and judicial authorities. Early in 1998 French journalists began to compile evidence of a range of scandalous French military interventions, particularly in Bosnia and Rwanda, combined with truculent resistance to recognizing international courts of justice.[38] Authorities in Paris boycotted the international tribunal set up at Arusha, Tanzania, to try those who massacred the Tutsi population of Rwanda in 1994.[39] Since April 1996 the French government has been obstructing the formation of a permanent international criminal court intended to try crimes against humanity such as the Pol Pot régime's massacre of two million Cambodians – a permanent version of those set up to deal with Nazi atrocities and with the massacres in Rwanda and the former Yugoslavia.[40]

GAULLIST VIOLENCE IN AFRICA

The example of Guinea

In chapter 11 we saw how France organized a post-colonial association of French-speaking African countries in order to keep control over them. President de Gaulle's political and diplomatic activities in Africa were assiduously reported in Le Monde and other papers, but later journalists have discovered a more sinister interference by secret police forces answerable to the Élysée. During the early years of the Fifth Republic most of the work was done by or for the Service de documentation extérieure et de contre-espionnage (SDECE), as the present Direction général de la sécurité extérieure (DGSE) was called before 1981. An African section of about one hundred and fifty agents was organized under Colonel Maurice Robert, who established headquarters in Dakar.[41] They were soon called in to undermine the government of Guinea.

The trouble began on 27 August 1958, soon after de Gaulle returned to power, when he landed at Conakry, the capital of Guinea, for a meeting with the president, Ahmed Sékou Touré (1922–1984). His purpose was to win Touré's support for the Franco–African Community he was planning. Foreseeing the ultimate success of the national independence movements that were already organizing in Africa, de Gaulle wanted to set up a system of post-colonial partnership that might allow France to continue to maintain political control and economic exploitation. He was welcomed enthusiastically on his arrival at Conakry but snubbed and insulted a short time later by President Touré in a harsh speech that amounted to a unilateral declaration of

Guinean independence from French imperial authority. The listening crowd of Africans expressed noisy hostility to France and its president.[42] De Gaulle's response in the years to come and the violent, underhanded methods he resorted to, show what he was capable of and warrant careful study by Canadian authorities.

De Gaulle set out to topple President Touré and to recover French control of Guinea, a policy he and his successors carried on for twenty years. Using the French secret services under the general direction of Jacques Foccart, they engaged in a series of terrorist exercises that began when a referendum called on 28 September 1958 gave popular approval for national independence by a vote of 1,136,324 to 56,901.[43] Touré's régime was a bloody tyranny deserving of no sympathy, but so were those of several other former French colonies. De Gaulle's secret assaults on Guinea were for the purpose of controlling it, not improving it.

The SDECE began by arranging to print and circulate counterfeit money in an effort to undermine the Guinean economy.[44] When Touré made contracts with Soviet and Yugoslav companies, one of the French secret services tried to corrupt or block them. Near the end of 1959 French authorities decided to overthrow Touré by force. Captain Boureau-Mitrecey undertook to conspire with forces of political opposition within the country but in liaison with French agents at Dakar and Abidjan. The scheme failed only because a conscientious Roman Catholic among the troops, unwilling to collaborate in a political murder, consulted a Dominican priest in Dakar, who found a way to pass this information along to the French minister for foreign affairs, Couve de Murville. The ensuing discussion at ministerial level resulted in leaks to the public. Foccart was furious, de Gaulle embarrassed.

In April 1960 French secret services made another attempt to overthrow Touré's régime in collaboration with political opponents in Guinea. It was discovered in time to prevent it, and some of the Guineans in it revealed under torture that weapons were stockpiled over the borders in Sénégal and Ivory Coast. The president of the latter, Houphouët-Boigny, blamed the French high commissioner to his country, Yves Guéna, in an indignant protest. The Guinean government meanwhile arrested a French pharmacist as one of the conspirators and released him only after a noisy public altercation. De Gaulle was again embarrassed but apparently unrepentant.

Yet another scheme was hatched in November 1965. This time the French plotters remained discreetly in the background and only lent their support to a political movement of opposition within the country. Seeing their hand in the affair, Touré denounced Jacques Foccart,

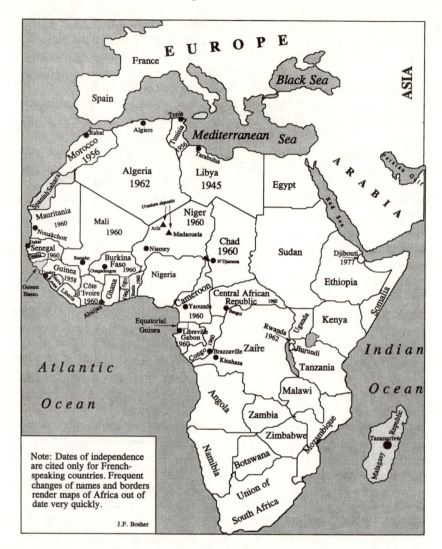

Map 4   Africa: Former French Colonies

expelled all the personnel at the French embassy, and broke off diplomatic relations with France, the better to prevent such intrigues. The French response was to engage the American and German secret services in the same old endeavour to overthrow Touré, and they were not unwilling to assist because of Touré's connections with the Soviet bloc. Plot after plot was attempted, but all failed. The government of Guinea crushed them all with ruthless cruelty and eventually published a col-

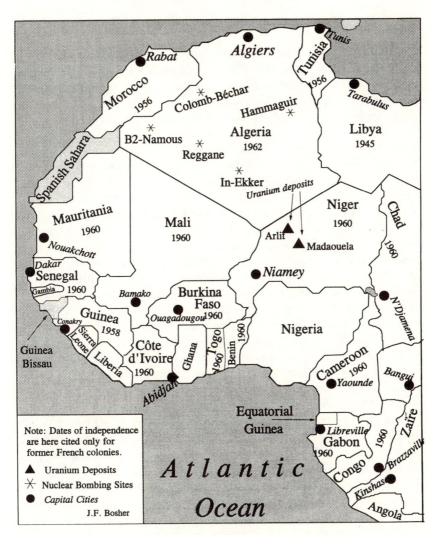

Map 5   West Africa

lection of documents concerning these plots. Among the documents are detailed accounts by people such as Pierre Drablier, a French businessmen, who described how he had been recruited by a French network formed to overthrow Touré's régime. Even if only half of this collection were true, it would still be an interesting case of secret hostility organized by the Fifth Republic.[45] Near the end of his life, Foccart did his best to play down the scale and importance of French interference in Guinea, but that was standard Gaullist disinformation.[46]

Another Example: Secret Support for Biafra

On 30 May 1967 Colonel Emeka Ojukwu, an Oxford-educated Ibo in the Nigerian army, raised a flag of independence in Eastern Nigeria, calling the new country Biafra. A little less than three years later, after about a million Ibos had died by violence or starvation, he had to admit defeat, but until then General de Gaulle supported him openly in some ways, secretly in others. De Gaulle's main reason for encouraging the Biafran revolt was that Nigeria, a former British colony, loomed large near several smaller ex-French colonies, and he thought it would be to the advantage of France if Nigeria disintegrated. It was, after all, only one more of the British post-colonial confederations that aroused his opposition, somewhat like Canada, in his view. He compared Quebec and Biafra more than once in the late 1960s. It has to be added that he was also interested in having direct access to Biafran oil fields.[47] And a typical piece of Gaullist chicanery came into play: the general had not forgiven the Nigerian government for protesting against the third French atomic explosion at Reggane in the Sahara by expelling the French ambassador, Raymond Offroy, in January 1961.[48] As nearly always, it seemed reasonable for him to point out how poor and unfairly treated the Ibos were.

De Gaulle began by inducing various countries, mainly French-speaking ones, to give Biafra diplomatic recognition: Gabon, Haïti, Ivory Coast, Tanzania, and Zambia. Unwilling himself to face the wrath of the rest of Africa and of Britain, he waited and watched for an excuse for France to do the same – just as he watched for an opportunity to recognize a sovereign Quebec. Then he made arrangements with President Félix Houphouët-Boigny to send arms and supplies, brought by sea from France to Gabon, across the border into Biafra. Foccart admits that this operation was intended to remain strictly secret and that he was himself in touch with Biafran authorities.[49] More arms were sent to Biafra through Spanish or Equatorial Guinea, after it became an independent state on 12 October 1968.

De Gaulle's next step was to arrange for a capable French mercenary, Gilbert Bourgeaud, best known under the name Bob Denard, to recruit a force surreptitiously for warfare in collaboration with the Biafran forces. Denard had a long record of postwar service in French colonies, especially Morocco, Algeria, and Indochina. When approached for service in Biafra, he was fighting as a mercenary for Moïse Tchombé who, with French support, was endeavouring to take Katanga province away from Congo (later Zaïre).[50] Denard is a good example of the agents the Gaullist government tended to rely on for conducting underhanded interference abroad, agents who could be abandoned to their fate if circumstances ever warranted. If caught and brought to trial, as Denard was in 1993, he could be discreetly defended by the French government.[51] He was not the only mercenary soldier in the Biafran War. A British corporal retired from the SAS named John Peters was recruiting forces for the Nigerian government.[52] But this was in retaliation for de Gaulle's French interference.

Denard and another agent named Roger Faulques raised mercenary forces in Paris through a "Biafran Historical Research Centre" staffed mainly by Ibos. They had plenty of money supplied by the French government on de Gaulle's authority. The best of the troops they raised, some four thousand men under Rolf Steiner, a former member of the French Foreign Legion, went off from Lisbon singing *The Marseillaise* and fought against Nigerian forces in autumn 1968. They were supplied by agents of the SDECE stationed at Libreville. About the same time, the French government began an airlift of military forces to Biafra scrupulously described as medical assistance and basic foodstuffs.[53]

They began to attract an assortment of international sympathizers ready to help the oppressed Biafran people, exactly the kind of liberation movement Lester Pearson and General Allard anticipated in Quebec about the same time. With a clear view of this parallel, Prime Minister Trudeau firmly refused to recognize Biafra.[54] But by a peculiar irony, the Canadian public took up the cause of "the poor Biafrans" and pressed the government to help them. Various churches were especially anxious to send aid to the rebels. This was the most distressing issue, Mitchell Sharp tells us, in his first year as secretary of state for external affairs. "We had to try to [send aid] in ways that were acceptable to the Nigerian government; otherwise Canada would appear to be supporting the Biafran rebellion."[55] Canada provided transport planes and some supplies, even though Ivan Head, sent over by the prime minister, discovered that most African countries were opposed to the Biafran rebellion and especially resentful of outside interference. With Canadian, Swiss, and other international support, however, the French government felt free to remove some of the secrecy surrounding its covert military operations, and Pierre Messmer, the minister of defence, began to supervise them instead of Jacques Foccart. De Gaulle's presidency was nearing its end when, at a council meeting on 23 April 1969, the general reaffirmed French support for the brave Biafrans' right to "dispose of themselves".

Colonel Ojukwu surrendered less than a year later, and de Gaulle's successor, Georges Pompidou, prudently abandoned the cause. Ojukwu went into exile in French-speaking Ivory Coast and officials of the SDECE expressed regret for the failure of the Biafrans to win their independence. Did they then redouble French efforts to encourage Quebec separatists?

A Recent Example: Support for the Hutu of Rwanda

In 1994 and earlier years the French government was supporting the Hutu against the Tutsi in Rwanda. This was the policy of President Mitterrand directing French foreign policy in the Gaullist tradition; that is, alone with his advisers and without consulting the National Assembly. As far as can be determined, the French government armed the Hutu in the belief that the Tutsi had Anglo–American support.[56] They armed the Hutu even though a cursory review of recent African history shows that Hutu were likely to kill Tutsi if the opportunity arose: they had massacred several thousand in 1959, and another 150,000 had then fled to escape the same fate.[57] In full knowledge of this, the French government shipped quantities of arms to Rwanda until June 1994, notwithstanding official denials, so that the Hutu massacre of some 800,000 Tutsi appears to have been carried out with French weaponry.[58] Furthermore, what touched off the massacre on 7 April 1994 was the destruction of a plane carrying the presidents of Rwanda and Burundi; as it prepared to land at Kigali on 6 April it was shot down by a missile alleged to come from a French stock of Russian missiles. France was said to have seized these missiles from Iraq during the Gulf War.

An international tribunal, firmly opposed by the French government, was eventually established at Arusha in Tanzania to bring charges against the perpetrators of the massacre. A commission in Brussels was soon trying to find out how the massacre began, and from 3 March 1998 a parliamentary commission in Paris, led by Paul Quilès, was investigating the French policy of supporting the Hutu. These investigations came suspiciously late. For nearly four years various witnesses and military and university observers had been urging governments to check out reports of foreign interference in Rwanda.[59]

According to a report in the French weekly *Le Journal du Dimanche*, the United Nations gave General Roméo Dallaire, the Canadian leader of the UN forces, permission to warn the Belgian, French, and U.S. embassies in Kigali about the impending massacre.[60] He sent a fax reporting that the Hutu in the Rwanda government were preparing detailed plans for slaughtering Tutsi. Professor André Guichaoua from Lille University, a consultant with the World Bank, reported evidence of suspiciously close relations between the Hutu and French governments.[61] Edouard Balladur, prime minister in the Mitterrand government who was in command at the time of the massacre, claims that the

French mission code-named Turquoise was the only initiative taken by any of the great powers "to avoid the most dramatic consequences of this genocide."[62] But the Turquoise operation was small and late.

After a nine-month inquiry the Quilès Mission concluded, in its report published on 15 December 1998, that French authorities were not directly implicated in the massacres of April to July, 1994.[63] But the Mission made three damaging admissions: the massacres had been planned a long time in advance, French policy had been blind and confused, and much remained to be discovered about the whole affair. It was not clear how the Mission had disposed of the apparently incriminating testimony of French military officers, such as Admiral Jacques Lanxade, Colonel Bernard Cussac, General Raymond Germanos, and Lieutenant Colonel Grégoire de Saint-Quentin.[64] The Tutsi-led government in Kigali denounced the Quilès report as predictable whitewashing.[65] A senator in Brussels, Alain Destexhe, active in the Belgian equivalent to the Quilès Mission, pointed out several weaknesses in the French inquiry, and those who were following events in Rwanda were left with little doubt that France was supporting and arming the Hutu-led government of Rwanda, which had planned the massacres, on the dubious grounds that the Tutsis enjoyed Anglo-American support.

Inventing a Useful Past

De Gaulle's hostility to English-speaking countries was based mainly on his reading of modern history and his memories of twentieth-century events. Recollections of the Second World War affected his thinking most of all. Shocked by the French defeat in May and June 1940, he kept up his spirits by letting his patriotism dictate heroic myths about what was happening. The news from France that followed him to London was unbearable. He resolved to deny it and to take the salvation and honour of his country upon himself in mystical terms, which he clung to with unshakeable determination. Whatever he said, wrote, and did was part of a private vision, and he imposed it on his followers. The oath of fidelity to himself that he asked them to take – the very essence of Gaullism – implied a commitment to what seemed, to some, like a set of myths with a personal dictatorship likely to follow. Among the fellow-exiles who recorded such suspicions, as we see below, were Henri de Kerillis, a politician, and Robert Mengin, a journalist employed at the French embassy in London.

The present chapter critically explores de Gaulle's (and Gaullist) thinking, first, about the Allies' role in two world wars, and, second, about the Free French he came to lead (after a two-year struggle), their role in France and in the Second World War, and the role of the Resistance. I look, third, at some non-Gaullist assessments of the general during his years in London. Further to explain his attitude to Canada, I go on, fourth, to examine de Gaulle's interpretations of Canadian history, which present France and Quebec as virtually identical peoples, kept apart only by Britain, and portray Britain as a ruthless oppressor of French-speaking North America.

WHO SAVED FRANCE? ALLIED SACRIFICES

The most puzzling aspect of Gaullist hostility is that the English-speaking peoples were the only allies who steadily supported and assisted France in the two major wars of the twentieth century. Buried in French graveyards are hundreds of thousands of Americans, Australians, Canadians, Englishmen, Irishmen, New Zealanders, Scotsmen and Welshmen who fought in the two world wars. Thousands more were crippled for life. In addition, the English-speaking nations spent vast sums to support the war effort. And the American military umbrella in the Cold War with the Soviet Union also protected France for more than forty years.

Germany was the principal enemy of France in three exhausting wars: the Franco–Prussian War and the First and Second World Wars. German armies invaded and occupied all or part of France in 1870–72; 1914–18 and 1940–44. Well over a million Frenchmen were killed by the German enemy in the First World War alone. In the Second World War it was German troops such as those of the Waffen ss Second Armoured Division, not the British or the Americans, who hunted down those who resisted their rule, who committed such atrocities as shooting ninety-nine hostages at Tulle and shooting or burning to death six hundred and forty-two men, women, and children in the village of Oradour-sur-Glâne, south of Limoges, on 10 June 1944.[1] In addition, the German government imposed huge financial reparations on France after the Franco–Prussian War. From that war until 1918, Germany occupied the French provinces of Alsace and Lorraine as if they were parts of Germany. During the Second World War the German government extracted the large sum of four hundred million francs a day from the French authorities. In short, the damage done to France by Germans, in terms of death, destruction, misery, and money, is incalculable. Notwithstanding these facts, known to all students of the history of the past two centuries, General de Gaulle and the Gaullists have persisted in regarding the English-speaking nations as France's principal enemies. Since the Second World War, Gaullist governments have made an alliance and various pacts with (West) Germany, no doubt for good reasons; but they have never ceased to bristle in French relations with Great Britain and the United States. All this is puzzling, to say the least.

The history of French borrowing from the English-speaking countries adds another element to this paradox. Through the intermediary of the British government, France borrowed huge sums from the United States during the First World War. Britain acted as the banker of the Allies and so came to owe the United States about £850 million; but France and the other Allies owed Britain considerably more: £1,300 million plus another £650 million owed by Russia, which had become the Soviet Union. When German war reparations were added to the debt, France and the other continental countries were found to owe Britain a total of £1,450 million. After the war London proposed to the United States to cancel debts all round, but the U.S. government refused. As President Calvin Coolidge said, "They hired the money, didn't they?" and the best settlement the British could get was a debt funded at $4,600 million repayable over sixty-two years and at 3 $^1/_3$ per cent interest.[2] Much of what Britain had borrowed had gone to France, but the French refused to repay it. The result for the British was that their huge investments in the United States, which had built much of American industry since c. 1860, were lost by transfer to the United States in payment for these war debts on which the British could recover very little from France and the other continental allies. Few if any French historians or statesmen ever mention this scandalous episode, much less acknowledge their debt to Great Britain.

After the Second World War, the American government that de Gaulle regarded with such hostility offered France vital aid via the Marshall Plan. From its inception in 1948, this plan was, by any standards, one of the most generous acts of international assistance the world has ever seen, and France was one of its greatest beneficiaries. But two years earlier, in May 1946, the United States had already lent large sums to France under the terms of the Blum–Byrnes agreement. During the 1940s and 1950s, the U.S. government and private American sources lent or gave millions of American dollars to France with virtually no strings attached. True, in providing this money the United States was hoping to prevent the spread of Soviet Communism and Soviet power, but this does nothing to reduce the sheer generosity of its gifts and earlier loans.

What was the Marshall Plan? Its formal name was "The European Recovery Programme," and it was enacted by the U.S. Congress in 1948 more or less as drawn up by the secretary of state, General George Marshall. The plan invited the European countries to estimate what they needed for economic recovery from the war. American aid was to be given in the form of direct grants and loans, but through the Organization for European Economic Cooperation (OEEC), and it was for this that the OEEC was set up. Through it the United States gave Europe about $13.5 billion between 1948 and 1951, in addition to $9.5 billion already given since the war. Of this $13.5 billion, the United Kingdom received $3.176 billion; France $2.706 billion; Italy

$1.474 billion; and West Germany $1.389 billion. These were huge sums, staggeringly large at the time. In the four years of this program, nearly two-thirds of u.s. aid was spent on food, animal feed, fertilizers, and raw materials; 17 per cent on machinery and vehicles; and about 16 per cent on fuel. A large part of the total was spent on trade within western Europe itself.

Then, from 1951 to 1956, the United States went on giving money under the Mutual Security Programme.[3] In addition, American citizens were encouraged to send relief parcels to Europe and did in fact send goods worth a total of about $500 million. As a result, western Europe recovered from the war in much shorter time than it otherwise would have, and the political effects of the postwar poverty and misery – Communist political influence, for example – were very much reduced. Communism thrived on poverty and was stopped in western Europe largely owing to Marshall Plan aid. Ever since that time British governments have expressed their gratitude again and again in all sorts of ways, standing loyally beside the United States, for example, in matters of foreign policy. But France under General de Gaulle and his successors has mistrusted, opposed, obstructed, and insulted the United States at every opportunity. Why?

In the Gaullists' view, whatever the English-speaking peoples have done or given was for France – a sacred cause – and therefore no French citizen, not even de Gaulle himself, need feel any gratitude. This is a quasi-religious view of the matter, which is indeed the usual Gaullist approach. A Christian is not expected to be grateful for other people's offerings at the altar of the church, or for other people's deeds in God's service. Similarly, a Gaullist or other patriotic French citizen may respect the gifts and services of foreigners at the altar of France, for its defence or liberation, but is not likely to feel any gratitude for them. This attitude accounts for a general blindness in France to such things as the irony of publishing, with satisfaction, a review of the damage done to "Canada after de Gaulle" on the same page of a newspaper as a report of Canadian soldiers visiting Dieppe on the twenty-fifth anniversary of the tragic raid that was part of Canada's long effort to liberate France.[4]

Canadians go regularly to France on anniversaries of 9 April 1917 to pay their respects to the thirty-six hundred of their countrymen who died, and the thousands who were wounded, taking Vimy Ridge from the German army after the French army had failed to take it. In recognition of this victory, in 1922 the government of the Third Republic gave Vimy Ridge to Canada in perpetuity. Partly in irritation at this tiny loss of sovereignty and partly as a typically insulting gesture towards Canada, Charles de Gaulle did not attend the fiftieth anniversary of the battle on 9 April 1967 and refused even to send a guard of honour.[5] In a similar way, the Dieppe Raid of August 1942 is remembered in Canada and Great Britain and almost ignored in France. What Gaullists are more inclined to remember is such events as the British retreat at Dunkirk in June 1940 or the Anglo-American bombing raids on French towns during the liberation campaign, such those of 5 January and 14–15 April 1945 on Royan, a town of which Jean de Lipkowski, a prominent member of the French Quebec mafia, was long mayor. Even the more careful and factual French historians customarily lay much of the blame for their own defeat on their British allies and take the immense wartime efforts of Great Britain entirely for granted.[6] Prevailing attitudes in France stand in startling contrast to, for instance, those in Holland and Zeeland. As travelling Canadians soon discover, Dutch people were, and remain, immensely grateful to Canadians for their part in the liberation of their country in 1944. It was typical of the Dutch authorities to organize a public celebration in 1997 to mark the fiftieth anniversary of the Marshall Plan, and typical of the French to ignore it.

DE GAULLE AND THE FREE FRENCH

Gaullist hostility is less easy to explain. One is forced to conclude that the Gaullists have an almost unlimited capacity for self-delusion. This is a familiar phenomenon and not only in France. Like certain other groups of people in other countries, the Gaullists delude themselves in a process of collective affirmation, in which evidence is recognized only if it supports beliefs adopted in advance. Some of their delusions produce the stubborn strength and benefits that a religious faith can offer in the face of adversity and in such cases win the admiration of foreign observers. In the defence of such beliefs French people have sometimes been willing to make great efforts and great sacrifices. Usually in such cases what is at stake is feelings of self-respect and other emotions, the facts of a situation – such as the invasion and occupation of France in 1940 – being almost unbearable. As a painful situation recedes into the past, it becomes maleable, more and more susceptible of interpretation. History lends itself to collective delusions because historical evidence can be selected and adapted. Proof is easily confused with belief, honesty with loyalty. In the case of the Gaullist movement, loyalty to France has generated a set of myths about its erstwhile leader and his activities. There is plenty of contrary evidence, as some French people are aware, but Gaullists are not willing to examine it, much less to subject their myths to it. Most of all, the

Gaullist myths are too useful to sacrifice to truths that have come to
seem alien, even hostile.

De Gaulle's followers believe, for one thing, that he and the Free
French whom he led during the Second World War saved the honour
of France. This does not mean merely that he and his forces fought
against Nazi Germany and Vichy France. It means in Gaullist terms
that Vichy France never existed, which is nonsense or, to put it politely,
a myth. De Gaulle was affirming this notion when, on reaching Paris
in August 1944, he refused to proclaim France a republic on the
grounds that it had never ceased to be one. "No," he said, "the Republic has never ceased to exist. ... Why should I proclaim it?"[7] Though
France had in fact collapsed in the face of German attacks in 1940 and
thrown in its lot with the Nazi invaders, its salvation was, in this sense,
accomplished by de Gaulle and his disciples, over the long term at
least, somewhat in the way that the salvation of the Christian world
was accomplished by Jesus Christ. That is, de Gaulle called upon the
French to believe in him and his doctrine, by an act of faith. And it may
well be that their Catholic past helps French people to subscribe to this
Gaullist myth.

Such belief depends, however, on sublimating a few simple facts that
in no way support the story, except for believers. When the French
army and government collapsed in June 1940, France accepted Pétain
as its leader, he signed an armistice with Adolf Hitler, and the government he headed at Vichy proceeded to collaborate more and more with
Nazi Germany.[8] So did over 90 per cent of the French population. As
Canadian soldiers recall, French troops at Dieppe fired on Allied soldiers during their first disastrous raid on 19 August 1942.[9] Such was
France during the Second World War. The Gaullist version of events is
a series of gilded lies sublimated by the postwar faith of a huge majority of the population. The rest of the world, following a British
example, goes along with this nonsense as a courtesy.

In a study such as the present one, it is regrettable but necessary to
suspend that courtesy in the interests of truth. To continue with the
facts then, when France collapsed, a British general, E.L. Spears, took
some French refugees with him to England in his aircraft on 17 June
1940. One of them, a relatively junior general named Charles de Gaulle,
had no particular qualification to represent his country except that Paul
Reynaud, prime minister of France until the previous day, had recently
named him under-secretary of state for national defence in the hope that
he might be able to help in opposing the triumphant Germans. In
London, Prime Minister Winston Churchill responded to Reynaud's
recommendation and gave de Gaulle rooms in a house at No. 4 Carlton

Gardens, and other support, so that he could try to stir up resistance in France and to rally other French refugees. Churchill arranged for de Gaulle to broadcast to France through the BBC beginning on 18 June 1940. In so doing, Churchill was not intending to recognize de Gaulle, in any sense, as a political leader. De Gaulle's political pretensions were entirely his own. With no official status, no means of any kind, and few friends, de Gaulle could have done nothing whatever by himself, and he says so in his memoirs, though very briefly.[10]

By confining their reading to de Gaulle's memoirs and a few similar writings, Gaullists have been able to sustain a second myth, which is that he and his forces played a substantial part in the war. He and they even seem to regard de Gaulle as one of the Allied leaders, more or less the equal of Churchill, Roosevelt, and Stalin! Scholarly studies and the memoirs of other Frenchmen, not to mention British and foreign observers, show that in fact de Gaulle spent his first two years in London doing battle not with the Germans but with other French refugees, who could not see why he should lead them, and with British authorities too busy to bother with his vanity and delusions.[11] One of de Gaulle's few merits was that he intended to fight on like the British and did not share the pessimistic, defeatist attitude of most French citizens at that time.

But de Gaulle's Free French troops were pathetically few, scarcely seven thousand by mid-August 1940. General Władysław Sikorski's Polish soldiers, as a comparison, came from much farther away, by a treacherously difficult route, in much greater numbers, were almost insanely brave and heroic, and caused much less trouble. Except for the contingents in Africa, the Free French lived for years under British protection and did not fight German forces until June 1942, even later than the Americans. They fought a valiant battle at Bir-Hakeim in North Africa on 10 June 1942 but as usual exaggerate its importance.[12] The five Free French ships that captured and held Saint-Pierre and Miquelon did useful service on the Canadian east coast in 1942–43 but they were few indeed.[13]

Throughout the war one of de Gaulle's principal endeavours was to persuade Anglo–American leaders that Free French forces were bigger and stronger than in fact they were.[14] The colony of French refugees in the United States, including Henri Bonnet, Henri de Kerillis, Alexis Léger (the poet Saint-John Perse), André Maurois, René Mayer, and Jean Monnet, tended to share the opinions of President Franklin Roosevelt, who would have nothing to do with such a pompous and pretentious person as de Gaulle and preferred to deal with others, such as Admiral Jean François Darlan and General Henri Giraud.[15] In France and the French colonies meanwhile, most of the Resistance groups that were able to organize did not regard de Gaulle as their leader.

When the Soviet Union eventually went to war, Joseph Stalin thought de Gaulle of no account and wondered why the British government bothered to take him seriously and to put up with him – he was troublesome, a real nuisance at times, as reliable historical accounts show.[16] Even francophiles such as E.L. Spears and Harold Nicolson came to despise him. Nicolson wrote sadly, "I do not like him ... I should like to admire de Gaulle, but I cannot do so. ... I despair of de Gaulle."[17] Each British observer formed a personal opinion of de Gaulle, and some, such as Sir Alexander Cadogan, thought Churchill sometimes unfairly hostile.[18] But Cadogan's many references taken together show that de Gaulle was nothing short of exasperating. The well-known studies by Larry Collins, Maurice Ferro, and François Kersaudy, for example, are detailed records of how a vain, pretentious, obstructive, paranoid, anglophobic French officer with almost nothing to offer made continual awkward demands and wasted the time and attention of busy national leaders with a war to win.[19] This attitude was reflected in General Spear's well-known lament, "We all have our crosses to bear; mine is the cross of Lorraine."[20]

Churchill and Anthony Eden supported de Gaulle and put up with him for his potential postwar uses in France as an alternative to the Communists – an idea that first General Eisenhower and then President Roosevelt eventually came to share, though not for several years. Until near the end of the war, however, de Gaulle and his small forces played so insignificant a part that had they been absent the Allies would scarcely have noticed. After all, most of the French were in Vichy France collaborating with Nazi Germany. There were brave and capable French men and women among the few who joined the Free French forces, but their collective military significance was small, and their anglophobia sometimes made them a tiresome burden at a critical time.[21]

The detailed diaries kept by, for example Sir Alexander Cadogan, show that French refugees such as Roger Cambon, Charles Corbin, and de Gaulle himself were, if truth be told, obstructive nuisances.[22] De Gaulle and his entourage remained anti-American and suspicious of their British hosts, who were remarkably patient in these circumstances. Unfailingly charitable, people in England led by Lady Soames, Winston Churchill's daughter, campaigned many years later to provide for a statue of Charles de Gaulle, which was ultimately erected in June 1993 outside 4 Carlton Gardens, where Churchill had provided him with offices during the war.[23]

The Free French played only a modest part in the liberation of

France, though one would never guess this from French accounts of the liberation. According to de Gaulle's own account, France, like the city of Paris, had liberated itself. In his 25 August speech at the Hôtel de Ville, General de Gaulle did not mention "our beloved and admirable allies" until near the end.[24] "Paris se libère," de Gaulle boasted in an article published in Canada at the time.[25] Half a century later, on the anniversary of the liberation, this Gaullist myth had become well established. A historian, André Kaspi, bravely tried to expose and discredit it in the anniversary number of Le Monde, but already it was being reaffirmed in the same newspaper by Jacques Chirac, then mayor of Paris, who went on building it up with Gaullist lines such as, "France fought together with the Allies, like an ally and took part in the victory with the same right as our Allies."[26] In a similar way Le Figaro quoted a number of famous French writers to persuade readers that France had liberated itself.[27] Rare and late are admissions such as those of Olivier Guichard, who admitted during the trial of a former Vichy collaborator, Maurice Papon, that France has for too long believed in the story "that the Vichy régime did not exist" and the tale "that the French won the war."[28]

Even scholarly French historians write in such a way as to disguise the insignificant part played by French forces.[29] To read most French studies of the Second World War is to see it as a weird series of side-shows, blown up out of all true proportion. Most French writers glorify every Gaullist move, take the British and American war efforts for granted, and snicker conspiratorially at de Gaulle's antics as he struggled to puff himself up into a wartime leader of an Allied power. Maurice Ferro's more sober and scholarly account is fundamentally similar, concerned mainly to justify his hero's every action and to make sense of his every thought.[30] But, in Brian Crozier's words, "[de Gaulle's] endless wartime clashes with Churchill and Roosevelt, for example – were on a tiny scale and quite marginal to the story of the war."[31]

Focusing on the history of wartime France, any objective student can see that France was liberated by English-speaking forces and, indirectly, by the Soviets. De Gaulle's triumphant march into Paris on 26 August 1944 was staged by the Anglo–American leaders as a way of generating political support for him so that he might keep the Soviet-backed Communist party from taking control. No informed and disinterested student of the period could describe Charles de Gaulle as a hero.[32] He is a hero only to Gaullists and others who have some political or psychological reason to see him as one.

The French résistance was often heroic and became more and more useful to the Allies, but its role has usually been exaggerated in

France.[33] De Gaulle himself tended to disparage it, intent as he was on promoting the glory of his Free French forces. But with characteristic ambiguity he promoted the idea that the French nation had fought back against the German occupying forces. As John Hellman writes, "The construction of the myth of a resisting France that massively confronted the invader was the work of Charles de Gaulle."[34] In French accounts of the *résistance* there has been what looks almost like a national conspiracy to endow it with unsubstantiated numbers and accomplishments. Even the more balanced accounts of scholars such as François Bédarida, who spares ten words more than most French writers for "the allies, whose military power would carry out the Liberation," convey a false impression of the numbers of people in the French résistance and the part it played in the war.[35] In fact, after the war the French government recognized only about 300,000 people as having worked in it and another 100,000 who had died serving it. At best, therefore, there cannot have been more than about 2 per cent of the population in it.[36] Some Resistance movements, such as that of André Girard in Antibes, code named *Carte*, turned out to be largely imaginary when contacted, based on little more than vain hopes that only wasted lives, efforts, and time.[37]

A NON-GAULLIST VIEW

Few French people now see de Gaulle clearly or judge him independently. In the 1940s, however, several people in London were hostile to him and kept their distance, notably Paul Morand and his sixty-three colleagues in the French economic mission in England; Roger Cambon, a diplomat; Admiral Émile Muselier; Louis Héron de Villefosse, also a naval officer; Robert Mengin and André Rabache, both journalists; Denis Saurat, a professor at King's College, London; Émile Delavenay, working for the BBC; Raymond Aron for a time; a number of socialists; the group that published a London French daily called *France*; and of course Communists, Soviet spies and fellow-travellers such as André Labarthe, a scientist already spying for the Soviet Union.[38]

Villefosse, who served under Admiral Muselier, whom he admired, saw de Gaulle's vanity, personal ambition, and authoritarian nature as early as 1940 at their first meeting in London. According to Villefosse, Muselier outranked de Gaulle, had more experience, was more practical, and was twelve years older and altogether a better leader of the Free French forces. He did not play politics as de Gaulle did. He allowed himself to be subordinated to de Gaulle only out of an innate decency and a concern for the common cause. Muselier found de Gaulle exasperating in the 1940s.[39] It was Muselier, not de Gaulle, who founded the Croix de Lorraine, but de Gaulle characteristically took credit for it in later years. Villefosse was one of the few who understood how and why de Gaulle imposed himself on the forces of Free France and then pretended that Free France was his own creation. "In [de Gaulle's] mind the facts are arranged according to his own theories of History, according to the rhetoric of his writings and speeches, with a view to distant goals, slowly matured."[40]

Mengin, another anti-Gaullist from summer 1940 on, has likewise recorded his experiences with de Gaulle and the reasons why he refused to serve under him. Like others, he tells in detail how Winston Churchill soon came to see that he had made a mistake in welcoming and trusting de Gaulle. Another who saw de Gaulle's ambition, vanity, and ruthlessness was Philippe Thyraud de Vosjoli, a French intelligence officer whose account of de Gaulle's career and entourage in those years is clear and intelligent.[41] Yet another who had doubts later was de Gaulle's wartime private secretary, Élisabeth de Miribel. Communist leaders were likewise severely critical of him, such as Fernand Grenier, de Gaulle's air minister, who had good reason to be "sickened by the political manoeuvers of the Gaullist politicians."[42] He could not forget that in 1944 de Gaulle had callously and arrogantly sacrificed a Resistance force of four thousand men on a plateau near Grenoble, who had been counting on his support, and then lied about what he had done.

The wartime staff of the BBC, including several French people who used to meet regularly at Bedford College, have also thrown light on de Gaulle's troublesome conduct. He would have little or nothing to do with them, even though, as Émile Delavenay relates, "the BBC was much better informed than the Free French because it had more numerous and longer established sources."[43] However, de Gaulle and Gaston Palewski, who served him, thought that the French service of the BBC ought to be under their command. Their purposes, according to Delavenay, were political from the beginning; they were already thinking of seizing power in France whenever they could. Another Frenchman active in London and independent of de Gaulle in the early 1940s was Raymond Aron, who worked as editor of a journal called *France Libre*, which was backed by André Labarthe and his wife.[44] Another independent journal called *France*, founded and edited by Pierre Comert, was likewise criticized by de Gaulle.

A more damaging hostility to de Gaulle flourished among the colony of some eighty-five hundred French refugees in the United States who mingled with about 135,000 French people already settled there when the war broke out. These newcomers tended to be suspicious of de Gaulle's claims and his intentions and saw no reason to serve or obey him. Some of them remained more or less attached to Vichy France, as did the U.S. government.[45] Among them were distinguished writers, scientists, politicians, businessmen, actors and public figures: Camille Chautemps, Jean Gabin, Alexis Léger, Jacques Maritain, André Maurois, Jean Monnet, Michèle Morgan, Jules Romain, Robert and Guy de Rothschild, and many more. Not until near the end of the war did some of them come round to support de Gaulle, and with many doubts even then. Several, especially Alexis Léger and Camille Chautemps, had Roosevelt's ear and warned him against de Gaulle.[46]

The most hostile and outspoken of this group, however, was Henri de Kerillis, formerly *député de la Seine* in the Chamber of Deputies, neither a Vichyite nor a Communist, who supported de Gaulle until March 1943 and thereafter denounced him in an American-backed journal, *Pour la Victoire*, as a sinister, ambitious monomaniac. Kerillis's longest explanation for his views, a book written in October 1945, is a passionate warning against de Gaulle that was believable enough at the time, though it subsequently turned out to be unjustified. Unbalanced in some ways, his book is nevertheless worth reading as a record of widely known facts that have since been forgotten. Early in the war, Kerillis knew de Gaulle well.[47] Among the students of our own time who write about de Gaulle as a historical figure, Pierre Viansson-Ponté and André Kaspi are among the few who remain balanced, sceptical, and intelligently detached.[48]

DE GAULLE ON CANADIAN HISTORY

De Gaulle had a sense of history that his supporters never cease to admire. Examined closely, however, it turns out to be a propagandist's grasp of history, ready to distort the events of the past to serve the politics of the present. Brian Crozier concurs with this opinion: "de Gaulle selects the facts and interprets them to his own advantage. It might almost be said that what flatters de Gaulle is history, and the rest, insignificant."[49]

France and Quebec

Concerning Canada, for instance, de Gaulle always talked as though Quebec and Québécois were part of the French nation, France and Quebec linked by deep historical roots and cultural affinities and kept apart only by the British. But this is true only in small measure. For his own political purposes he ignored the hostility that Québécois felt towards France from the French Revolution of 1789 until the mid-nineteenth century, and in some respects until Quebec's Quiet Revolution of the 1960s. He talked as though French Canadians were separated from France after the Conquest of 1759–60 by British oppression, when in fact considerable numbers of them travelled and studied in France, as Claude Galarneau and Pierre Savard relate in detail.[50] French people were allowed to emigrate to Quebec, too; biographical notes on nearly fifteen hundred of them who arrived in the century after 1765 have been compiled by Marcel Fournier.[51] Thus Mallen was distorting history in a typical Gaullist fashion when he wrote: "After the Treaty of Paris (1763) England imposed a veritable cultural blockade around Canada for generations."[52]

Such interruptions of movements between France and Quebec as there were are largely attributable to French aggression in two series of events. First, French intervention to assist the British colonies in North America in their revolution during the 1770s prompted the French Admiral D'Estaing to appeal to French Canadians to rally to the French side in the war. In a proclamation, D'Estaing wrote, "You were born French, and you have not ceased to be so."[53] As Hilda Neatby remarks, "Whatever may have been French policy before 1778, there is no doubt that after that time, France was putting pressure on Canadians to remember their origin."[54] It is significant of Canadian indifference to France at that time that these appeals had no success. Fearful of the new United States of America, which was overwhelmingly Protestant, the people of French Canada remained firmly loyal to their tolerant new British overlords and even helped to repel American invasion forces.

Links between Quebec and France were severed a second time during the quarter-century of the French Revolution and Napoleon's empire. For one thing, France declared war on Great Britain in 1793 and remained more or less permanently at war until defeated in 1814 and again in 1815. For another, the people of Quebec were hostile to the Civil Constitution of the Clergy enacted in 1790 by the revolutionary National Assembly. Thereafter they cut themselves off from the French because of their own strong Roman Catholic hostility to the "godless republic" and even to Napoleon's empire. Napoleon's famous Concordat, which reconciled the French government and the papacy in 1801, was accompanied by a good deal of violence: Napoleon put two popes in prison, and one of them, Pius VI, died there on 29 August 1799, hardly a popular event in Canada at that time or any other.[55] Only in Napoleon III's time (1849–70) did Canadian hostility to France begin to disappear, after the emperor had sent French forces to restore and protect Pope Pius IX on the papal throne in Rome and otherwise favoured the Catholic church.

Even as late as the First World War, however, very few Québécois were willing to fight for France: of some three hundred thousand Canadians serving overseas in 1917 hardly fourteen thousand (4.5 per cent) were French. Among them were some exceptionally brave soldiers, especially in the famous 22*e* *bataillon*, men such as Joseph Keable and Jean Brillant, who won the Victoria Cross; and some such as T.L. Tremblay, who reached the rank of major-general and survived to serve as an inspector-general of the Canadian army during the Second World War.[56] But their total numbers were few indeed. Most Canadian soldiers were of British descent.[57] There was still a prevalent hostility in Quebec to the French republic, child of a godless revolution. "It was only towards the middle of the XXth century," writes Michel Grenon, "on the eve of the *révolution tranquille*, that the apocalytic image of the French revolution gave way to a favorable image."[58] All of this history, which is easy to verify, did not suit de Gaulle's political purposes, and so he simply ignored it.

During the Fifth Republic, de Gaulle steadfastly overlooked French-Canadian support for Pétain's fascist Vichy régime. When in August 1940 Élisabeth de Miribel went to Quebec to win support for the Free French, she found to her horror and despair that an overwhelming majority of French Canadians in Quebec City, and Montreal even more, were Vichyite supporters to the core.[59] Many took the view that the German conquest of France in June 1940 was God's punishment, well merited. In addition, most French Canadians were not interested in fighting to free France from German occupation, or to assist Great Britain and the Empire/Commonwealth, fighting alone against Germany during the first two years of the war. The conscription issue, in which French Canadians overwhelmingly opposed military service even as late as 1944, brought out the insularity of Quebec.[60]

Relatively few French Canadians joined the armed forces (see Table 14.1).[61] The *Régiment de la Chaudière*, the *Royal 22*e* Régiment*, and one or two others were valiant fighting units, but they were so small as to be hardly noticeable among the much more numerous English-speaking Canadian soldiers. There were heroes among them – Major Paul Triquet won the Victoria Cross – but Québécois in the forces came from a province that did not support the Allies, much less the Free French.[62] As Esther Delisle makes clear, Quebec's sympathy for the fascist cause in the Second World War was hastily concealed after the war by a set of generally accepted silences and lies to which Ottawa tacitly subscribed for political reasons. Dozens of French allies of Nazi Germany – members of the vicious *milice*, war criminals who had murdered and tortured people of the *résistance* – went to Quebec after the war and were sheltered and defended there. Even when the truth about their past emerged, as in the noisy case of Jacques Dugé de Bernonville

Table 14.1
Men aged 18–45 in the Canadian armed forces, Second World War

Province	Men aged 18–45	Army	Navy	Air force	Total	Percentage in armed forces
British Columbia	181,000	58,246	11,925	20,805	90,976	50.47
Alberta	178,000	50,844	7,360	19,499	77,703	43.11
Saskatchewan	191,000	52,306	6,472	21,827	80,605	42.38
Manitoba	159,000	48,542	7,782	20,120	76,444	48.12
Ontario	830,000	266,937	40,353	90,519	397,808	47.77
Quebec	699,000	138,269	12,404	24,768	175,441	25.69
New Brunswick	94,000	35,947	2,737	6,453	45,137	48.17
Nova Scotia	123,000	45,020	6,837	7,498	59,355	48.31
Prince Edward Island	19,000	6,333	1,448	1,528	9,309	48.18
Other		6,091	1,156	9,485	16,732	
Total	2,474,000	708,535	98,474	222,501	1,029,510	41.15

Source: C.P. Stacey, *Arms, Men and Governments: The War Policies of Canada, 1939–1945*
(Ottawa: Queen's Printer, 1970), Appendix R, 590

in the years 1946–51, there was no lack of support for them in Quebec.[63]

Most of the help that Canada gave to de Gaulle, the Free French, and the Allied cause came from English-speaking Canadians – the very people whom de Gaulle and the Gaullists have been so fond of attacking and insulting. True, the Canadian government did not give de Gaulle full recognition until 23 October 1943, when it belatedly followed Britain, the Soviet Union, and the United States in recognizing his Provisional Government of France; but that irritating delay was largely a response to Quebec's preference for the Vichy government.[64] Left to themselves, English Canadians would certainly have followed the British in supporting de Gaulle from June 1940. These facts, verifiable in any objective study of the Second World War, have been firmly erased from the Gaullist memory. They are steadfastly ignored on both sides of the Atlantic by most French-speaking people, determined as they are to cling to their own myths.

BRITISH OPPRESSION

There can be no doubt that de Gaulle's invocation of "le Québec libre" was inspired by his home-brewed version of Quebec history – of France abandoning its colony, and of British oppression in Quebec and in Acadia. Gilbert Pérol, who was in a position to know, said, "What is striking in that affair is that the General was truly placing himself in an historical perspective."[65] Let us again sample de Gaulle's history. He says more than once that France governed Canada for two and a half centuries, but there were no French settlements in Canada until 1604 at the very earliest, which allows for only a little more than one and a half centuries until 1763. He says and evidently believes that France "abandoned Canada" at the Conquest and after it.[66]

But the truth is that France was roundly defeated and had no choice but to give it up. To pretend that it "abandoned" Canada is to suppose quite mistakenly that it had room to manoeuvre. In the Seven Years War France virtually collapsed, though in a different way from its collapse in June 1940. Great Britain was entirely master of the situation, and France was in no position to decide whether it should retain Canada or Guadeloupe. Gaullists and others in the French-speaking world prefer to believe, in spite of the evidence to the contrary, that France had abandoned Canada, as René Lévesque said in one of his Paris addresses, when he commented on "the glaring and incomprehensible absence of France" in Quebec in 1759.[67] Glaring indeed, but far from incomprehensible, this absence was the result of bankruptcy and a devastating series of naval defeats.[68] The French government had done its best, and failed, to supply and support Quebec.

Another twisted piece of history, agreed on by French-speaking peoples on both sides of the Atlantic, is that the French Canadians were oppressed for a century after the Conquest. De Gaulle said this more than once, very forcefully at a press conference on 27 November 1967.[69] It is an unhistorical, uncritical view, based on a steady resolve to ignore the historical context. A careful assessment of the Conquest, in the circumstances of European history at that time, does not warrant the Gaullist view. In fact, once the war was over, the British conquerors were relatively benign, and there was little that can fairly be described as oppressive by the standards of that time. The population anticipated confiscations of property, perhaps deportations too, on a large scale and was relieved when these did not take place. From 1774, the population even had political representation. French civil law and the notaries who played such a big part in it were left almost unmolested. The criminal code of Louis XIV (drawn up in 1670) was replaced by British criminal law, but the effect was to remove routine physical torture from the judicial process. In the eighteenth century British magistrates did not torture criminal suspects; French magistrates did. Before the Conquest, at least twenty-nine accused people, including some women, had been tortured in Canada in the normal course of criminal justice to extract confessions from them, and some of them turned out to be innocent![70]

Such oppression as the people of French Canada suffered under British rule bears no comparison with the barbaric events in France during the same centuries, especially in the twenty-five years of the French Revolutionary and Napoleonic régimes, when at least 100,000 men, women, and children were massacred in the Vendée; thousands of clergy were murdered, and more thousands driven to take refuge in England and elsewhere; and several thousand ordinary citizens were shot or guillotined in Paris, Lyon, Marseille, Toulon, and elsewhere.[71] French occupation of conquered European countries between 1793 and 1814 was far more oppressive than anything that occurred in Canada: the conquered peoples were heavily taxed and otherwise forced to support French armies. On more than one occasion Napoleon or another general punished a rebellious town by turning his army loose upon it with licence to murder, rape, and pillage.

The death toll in nineteenth-century France was also well beyond anything suffered in Canada: hundreds were put to death in the revolutions of 1830, 1848, and particularly in April and May 1871, when the French army shot some twenty thousand in the Paris commune. Political oppression, too, was at times severe, as during the first decade of Napoleon III's Second Empire. Better informed about these events than many people in our time, the great Quebec statesman Sir Wilfrid Laurier took the view, and explained at length, that Quebec had been fortunate to be brought into the British Empire. Studying the Conquest itself in detail, an American historian, A.L. Burt, goes as far as to declare, "Of all the glorious victories that British armies have to their credit, none is more glorious, none is more honorable, than the moral conquest that crowned the military conquest of Canada."[72]

The British conquerors left the Canadian population their Roman Catholic clergy and drove out only the Jesuits. This was remarkably fair and tolerant in that age but appears to be so only in the context of European history. Among the many chapters of European history that need to be revived in Canada are those telling how the Jesuits had already been driven out of Spain and Portugal; how France was already in the process of driving them out at about the same time (1764–65); and how, when Austria proposed to exile them also, Pope Clement XIV decided to suppress the Society of Jesus altogether. British authorities did not persecute French Canadians as Catholics, even though French authorities everywhere had long been persecuting their own and other Protestants. Many Protestant families in France had been broken up by force, the men chained to row as slaves in the galleys, the women and children imprisoned in convents.[73] A considerable number of the British troops who occupied Canada at the Conquest were French Huguenot refugees, as indeed was the commander-in-chief of the

British army, General Wolfe's superior, Jean-Louis Ligonier. As a young man he had escaped from Castres, in Languedoc, to England.[74] The very terms *résistance* and *réfugié* derive from Huguenots resisting and escaping from Bourbon France, which was widely and justly regarded as oppressive in the seventeenth and eighteenth centuries.[75] The French thought so themselves, indeed, when they rose in the revolution of 1789–94. In view of all that, only a Gaullist or an ignorant or biased person can be critical of the British treatment of Catholics in Canada. It is a matter of record that the first British governors, Murray and Carleton, were decidedly sympathetic to the conquered population, even benevolent.

As for the deportation of the Acadians, this was an act of military oppression in a situation of "cold war" between the War of the Austrian Succession (1743–48) and the Seven Years War (1756–63). It was a tactical expedient, harsh but judged necessary at the time, as a specialist, Naomi Griffiths, concludes.[76] Her deep sympathy for the Acadian population must be shared by everyone, but so must her interest in establishing a true version of their history. The Acadian past has become a historical minefield. The commonly published Acadian view of the expulsion, as conveyed in, for example, the quarterly French journal *Les Amitiés acadiennes*, is grossly one-sided and fits easily into the Gaullist myths about the past.

On 5 January 1990 a lawyer of Acadian origin, Warren Perrin, who was also president of the *Conseil pour le Développement du Français en Louisiane*, made a formal request to the British government for official recognition that the expulsion of the Acadians 235 years earlier had been a denial of their rights and "a criminal act." Perrin was even ready to take his case to law. In expectation of a British apology, a monument was to be put up in Louisiana. In the event, the British government gently but sensibly side-stepped this issue.[77] Its view was that the world would dissolve in chaos if each generation in every country were required to apologize for acts of their ancestors done in entirely different circumstances and according to entirely different standards.

Closely examined, Governor Charles Lawrence's problems turn out to have been military, and so was the solution that he and his government found. Acadians, Abenaki, and Micmac had long joined in the guerrilla warfare that had become almost normal between the French and English settlements.[78] Members of the clergy in Acadia, notably abbé Jean-Louis Le Loutre, were organizing resistance to British rule in the country and likewise inciting Native peoples.[79] Besides, the French authorities had set an example by planning to deport Protestant populations whenever they could. In 1686 Louis XIV had planned to expel all the Protestant inhabitants from the colony of New York if he succeeded in conquering it.[80] Ten years later French forces had in fact deported several hundred English settlers from Newfoundland.[81] Also, the persecution of the Huguenot Protestants in the French empire was much worse than the exiling of the Acadians. There was no moral difference between the British and the French in the matter of deportations, but only the practical difference that in Canada French policy failed, whereas British policy succeeded. However, present-day political uses of Acadian feelings are only to be expected from Gaullists, whose history is handmaid to their politics.

Gaullism and the
French Imperial Tradition

Charles de Gaulle was hostile to the English-speaking peoples – long the bane of France's imperial dreams – on historical grounds. At the same time, that hostility affected his reading of history; as we saw in chapter 14, he adopted versions of the Second World War and of Canada's past that suited his beliefs. What needs to be added to the story is that his beliefs were widely shared in France, familiar to most people in Quebec, and part of an imperial tradition that helps to explain his career and his policy towards Canada. Our inquiry into that tradition takes us back, in this chapter, through centuries of efforts by statesmen, armies, and navies to establish French leadership in the world. The history of those efforts and of their frustration by Britain is woven inextricably into the French imperial tradition in which de Gaulle has a place.

It was by frequent references to that tradition and by winning a place in it during the Second World War that de Gaulle gained the political support of a majority of French voters and, in a different way, the devotion of the French Quebec mafia. Even his name, suggesting as it does an antique spelling of ancient Gaule, touches the French imagination, though the name refers to a goad, or a fishing or vineyard pole called a "gaule," and some think it derives from the Flemish "waulle" meaning "wall."[1] This chapter illustrates the French imperial tradition with brief accounts of three events that are at once parts of the collective French memory and episodes in the history of Canada. The earliest is France's defeat by Great Britain in what is often called the "Second Hundred Years War"; the second is the expedition of the sailing vessel *La Capricieuse* to Quebec in 1855; and the last is the glorifying of de Gaulle during and after his lifetime.

THE SECOND HUNDRED YEARS WAR

Familiar though this story will be to some readers, it bears repeating, with stresses on certain parts that are the sources of so much anti-English feeling. Hostility to *les Anglo-Saxons* can often be traced to biased exerpts from the history of this long struggle. The Second Hundred Years War consisted, in fact, of seven wars between 1689 and 1815, but all can be seen as parts of a single conflict because, except for the last of them, they left France and England – Great Britain from 1707 – each still hoping to master the other.[2] The underlying competition went on in spite of changes in wartime alliances and in the issues being fought over. In this analysis the issues count for more than the alliances.

Among the causes of the first two wars in the series, religious conflict counted for more than is customarily admitted and left a residue of bad feeling after dying down in the eighteenth century. As an *Anglais* in France, I have been reproached more than once with having planted Protestants in Catholic Ireland, where the armies of Louis XIV tried to get a foothold during the Nine Years War (1689–97). My reply was that regiments of Huguenot French refugees fought for England in the Irish battles of the 1690s, but this was received with indignation and disbelief, though there is no lack of evidence for it.[3] France had been hoping to catholicize the British Isles, where a Catholic protégé of Louis XIV, King James II, shared that hope from his crowning in 1685, the year in which Louis XIV outlawed the Huguenots, until 1688, when he fled to France as Dutch William III invaded England with five hundred ships under the banner, "The Liberty of England and the Protestant Religion."[4] Early in the War of Spanish Succession (1702–13) British forces captured the French bishop of New France on his way to Quebec and held him prisoner near London for five years.[5] A flicker of religious conflict survived even in the revolutionary and Napoleonic wars, as thousands of exiled French clergy – Roman Catholics this time – took refuge in England.[6] Some of them found their way to Canada where they reinforced hostility to France.

An Anglo–French dynastic struggle entered into most of the seven wars, and those of the Spanish Succession and the Austrian Succession (1744–48) found the two antagonists on opposite sides. In the Nine Years War (1689–97), sometimes called the War of the English Succession, Louis XIV tried to dislodge his leading enemy, William III, from the English throne, and the next war found him refusing to recognize William's successor, Queen Anne, on the grounds that she was a Protestant wearing the crown that historically belonged to a Catholic successor of James II. That was a side-show in the struggle over the grandson whom Louis XIV had hustled over the Pyrenees to seize the Spanish throne in 1701, but Louis's successors did their best to help the Jacobite pretenders to overthrow George I and II.[7]

The American Revolution gave France an opportunity to deprive George III of his American colonies, and French arms played a major part in the War of American Independence.[8] The Franco–American alliance is still celebrated each year in both countries. In 1793, it was the execution of Louis XVI on 21 January that provoked Britain to withdraw its ambassador to France as the first step in a struggle that was to last, on and off, for twenty-two years. The bitterest French memory of all is that when Napoleon was at last defeated in 1815, Britain imprisoned him on the remote Atlantic island of St Helena until he died in 1821. Only with Lord Palmerston's permission were his remains brought back to France in 1840, ferried slowly up the Seine in a black barge with a cross at the bow, and installed in a tomb like a shrine in Les Invalides in Paris, which has remained the centre of a Bonapartist cult to this day.

Trade and empire may have weighed more than dynasty and religion in the seven decisions to go to war between 1689 and 1815. French ships under a Canadian commander, Le Moyne d'Iberville, captured Newfoundland and drove out the fleets of the Hudson's Bay Company in the 1690s. The memory of d'Iberville's warship, *Pélican*, which defeated three British ships in Hudson Bay in September 1697 has been kept bright by the construction in the 1980s at Malbaie, Quebec, of a full-sized replica.[9] By 1710, however, British forces had recaptured Newfoundland and Hudson Bay, never again to give them up except to the Dominion of Canada. Efforts to capture Quebec City failed in that period. Pierre-Louis Mallen tells how he and Martial de la Fournière discovered and cherished a medal struck by Louis XIV to celebrate Admiral Walker's vain effort to take Quebec in 1690. They were particularly pleased because the medal bore the ominous inscription, "Kebeka liberata."[10] At the Treaty of Utrecht (1713), however, Acadia became part of the British Empire along with Newfoundland and Hudson Bay.

France promptly founded the naval base of Louisbourg on Cape Breton Island, but British and British-American forces captured it twice, in 1745 and 1758. A French armada dispatched to Acadia in 1746 under the duc d'Enville dispersed and disintegrated in a manner so appalling that the French government hushed it up; it left the merest trace in history until a Canadian, James Pritchard, told the full story of the disaster in 1995.[11] The French lost bases in India in 1757, Quebec City in 1759, and the whole of Canada in the Treaty of Paris (1763). They sought revenge by sending forces to assist the American rebels during the 1770s in their war of independence from Britain. But France gained almost nothing for its efforts, except the empty satisfaction of helping to humiliate an old enemy. The expectation of direct trade with the United States in tobacco and other products was disappointed, and the French state tobacco monopoly had to continue purchasing from English and Scottish firms.[12] Few of the colonies lost in earlier wars were recovered. The British retained Canada, Acadia, India, some of the principal West Indian islands, Gibraltar, and naval supremacy in general.

Trade and empire were at stake in the wars of the French Revolution and Napoleon; the struggle was long and hard-fought, but by 1815 France had been badly worsted. Napoleon's Continental System ultimately failed to manage the trade of Europe to his advantage. A British naval blockade caused havoc, and other fleets seized French overseas colonies. As a result of the British decision in 1807 to put an end to the slave trade, a naval squadron off the west coast of Africa interfered with French slave ships until the Second French Republic stopped the trade in 1848.[13] Meanwhile, it was only with British permission that French forces crossed the Mediterranean to begin the conquest of North Africa in the 1830s. The list of humiliations in the seventeenth, eighteenth, and nineteenth centuries is very long. Among them are the failures of all the French armadas that were prepared to cross the English Channel for the invasion of the British Isles – in 1689, 1691, 1692, 1696, 1708, 1744, 1759, and many times between 1776 and 1805.[14]

France appears at first sight to be a victim, but comparisons of the two warring countries do not show it in a favourable light. Britain was far from vindictive and seldom took full advantage of its victories; never, for example, not even in 1813–15, did British forces occupy France, strip it of portable wealth, abuse the population, and settle down as imperial overlords, which is what French forces did in the European countries they occupied between 1794 and 1813.[15] Louis XVIII arrived in the van of a British army in 1814 and restored the Bourbon monarchy with London's blessing. French humiliation lay in an enforced subordination that was to continue. More recently, British forces drove out General Marchand at Fashoda on the upper Nile River in December 1898. An even fresher memory is of the sinking of the French fleet at Mers-el-Kébir, near Algiers, on 3 July 1940, to prevent it from falling into German hands. De Gaulle had the good sense to see the desperate need for the sinking, but the Vichy French government in a fury bombed Gibraltar in retaliation.[16] To sum up, the decline of France that began in the reign of Louis XIV was owing above all to Great Britain, the only European power that French forces could not conquer, devastate, or dominate, and the power that again and again organized successful anti-French coalitions. Herein lies much of the hostility to *les Anglo-Saxons* in the French imperial tradition.

THE VISIT OF *LA CAPRICIEUSE*

When in 1967, about two centuries after the British Conquest, General de Gaulle decided to travel to Quebec in a warship, he was doing more or less what Napoleon III had done a century earlier. The emperor did not come out personally, it is true, but he sent a representative in a warship, *La Capricieuse*, with messages and gifts intended to remind the people of French Canada of their French heritage. The story of this voyage is worth telling for its uncanny resemblance to de Gaulle's a century later. Though de Gaulle was not formally an emperor, his policy towards Canada was remarkably imperial, and *Le Colbert*'s symbolic mission was much like that of *La Capricieuse*.

Napoleon III began to take an interest in French Canadians when they responded to his efforts to favour the Roman Catholic church. After 1849, when he sent an army to support the pope against revolutionary forces in Italy, and took other steps to please Catholics, French Canadians became less hostile to post-revolutionary France. Early in 1855, a group of enthusiastic Québécois set up a much-admired Canadian pavilion, or kiosk, at the famous Paris exhibition of that year (*Exposition universelle de Paris*).

Prompted by this event and perhaps other gestures from Quebec, Napoleon III's government decided to send out a warship on a visit. This voyage had a friendly face, as its ostensible motives were commercial and diplomatic, to open up trade and friendship, but in retrospect it became clear that Napoleon III had deeper motives. Like de Gaulle a century later, he was probing to find out how far the people of French Canada might be stirred up to remember their French origins and welcome French initiatives. He seems to have been hoping to exploit Quebec for whatever influence and glory his empire might be able to make of it. In summer 1855 he sent a three-masted sailing vessel – a corvette – across the Atlantic to Quebec.

To put this venture in true perspective, it is well to remember that it was only one of Napoleon III's initiatives abroad. For example, when French forces took Saigon in 1859 as a first step in conquering Cambodia, they did so ostensibly to protect Catholic missionaries, or so the emperor said.[17] For another example, he dreamed of building a Latin Catholic state in the Americas under French protection. In collaboration with other governments, in 1861 he dispatched a large French force across the Atlantic which soon captured Mexico City and put an

Austrian archduke, Maximilian, on the throne of what was intended to be a Catholic empire. When his allies withdrew, he continued the project alone. French Catholics were persuaded to regard this as a Catholic crusade. Unfortunately for Napoleon, Mexicans gathered, resisted, brought in the United States, eventually defeated Maximilian (1867), and shot him, along with several thousand French soldiers. What these and other such incidents show is that it would be naïve to regard the expedition of *La Capricieuse* as an innocent diplomatic initiative.

La Capricieuse, under Captain Paul-Henri de Belvèze with a crew of two hundred and forty men, arrived at Saint-Pierre and Miquelon on 18 June 1855 and reached Quebec City on 13 July . Belvèze had two sets of instructions – one public and the other private. The public ones were to represent France in presenting various books and pictures as gifts to the *Institut Canadien* at Quebec City and to try to interest Canadian authorities in trade and friendly relations with France. The private instructions were to report "on the political, moral, religious, and military situation" in Canada.[18] There was by then a French vice-consul at Quebec, and he had known of the ship's arrival a month in advance. As a result, an official welcome had been arranged at Quebec by the mayor, the town council, and notable citizens. The governor of Lower Canada also sent a party to join in this welcome. *La Capricieuse* stayed about one month, during which Belvèze toured both Lower and Upper Canada, made about fifty speeches, and was welcomed and fêted everywhere he went (mainly by steamboat), including Toronto.

The visit of *La Capricieuse* has at least three aspects: an official one, a public one, and a secret one. The official aspect is clear enough. British and Canadian officials, both English and French, made Belvèze welcome as best they could in public speeches and toasts to Anglo–French friendship. The French imperial standard (not the *tricolore*) was flown everywhere together with the Union Jack. Friendly responses greeted Belvèze's urging that steps be taken to encourage trade between Canada and France. One such response, for example, was the generous welcome of the mayor of Quebec City, Joseph Morrin, a medical doctor born in Scotland, educated in Britain, a loyal British subject, and a strong Presbyterian. He made a speech that included lines such as, "In setting foot on this welcoming land of Canada, you are still walking on land that is entirely French, in spite of long years of separation. ... Le Canada c'est la France. ... France ... *fille aînée de l'Église*. ... etc."[19] The mayors of Toronto (on 9 August), Ottawa, Kingston, and many other places gave the visitors equally warm welcomes. All this was normal diplomatic courtesy.

But the visit took on quite a different aspect for French Canadians.

They came crowding in from far and near, waxing more and more enthusiastic, until there was an emotional atmosphere that amounted to a kind of hysteria. In Montreal, Belvèze made a speech on the *champ de mars* – the parade square – to a crowd estimated at about ten thousand people. "All to the accompaniment of saluting cannons, fireworks etc.," Belvèze wrote to a friend later. "If I did not die of indigestion, I was likely to die of vanity."[20] On 15 August, which was the Feast of the Assumption and also the anniversary of Napoleon I's birthday, Belvèze laid the first stone of a professional school. And the speeches on both sides became more eloquent, and ever more French and nationalistic. "Three things constitute a nationality," Belvèze said on one occasion, "customs, language and religion."[21]

The original understanding had been that his visit was not political, and yet a political undertone crept into the proceedings more and more. Stories with political symbolism began to circulate: for instance, about an old man who asked that a French officer should visit him in hospital. When an officer consented to do so, the old man gazed at him for a long time and said, "Oh, to have seen eyes that have seen France."[22] As they became aware of the gathering subtext, Canadian and British officials became more and more anxious about what was really happening.

This introduces the third aspect of the visit. For some Québécois and some French people the expedition seems to have been an early event in what they hoped might be a revival of French influence in Canada. Was the emotional nationalism that Belvèze aroused French Canadian or French imperial? Nobody was quite sure. A Quebec poet, Octave Crémazie, wrote poems expressing and arousing these unspecified emotions, the most famous one being about an imaginary French soldier from Montcalm's army, *Le Vieux Soldat Canadien*, dreaming about the French returning to take command of Canada, welcomed and glorious. It ends with lines urging French Canadians to keep fresh their memories of France. However, Crémazie changed his mind later when he went to live in France (to escape his creditors after the bankruptcy of his bookshop) and found that his ancestral homeland did not suit him at all. But in the 1850s his poems were in tune with French imperial propaganda. In 1857, a certain J.G. Barthe published a book in Paris, *Le Canada reconquis par la France*, with a preface suggesting that the British government should cede Quebec to France.[23]

The imperial undertone of Belvèze's visit had a mixed reception. Liberal statesmen in Quebec tended to feel that Canadians gave their allegiance to England but that their hearts were French, as Wilfrid Laurier put it a little later.[24] But how Québécois might respond to a French fraternal appeal was uncertain. And was there a political significance to the tumultuous, emotional welcome that they gave to *La Capricieuse*? Knowing Napoleon III's ambitions, we must at the very least be wary of assuming the visit to have been a purely innocent enterprise. Surely it was no more innocent than was de Gaulle's mischievous visit in 1967.

Governor General Sir Edmund Walker Head sized up the expedition as quietly aggressive, sinister, and altogether objectionable. He wrote a dispatch complaining about it to London. The British government then protested to Paris, which, to save face, played down the whole affair and disgraced Belvèze, and that put an end to the matter, on that occasion at least.

In a second initiative, Napoleon III responded to appeals on behalf of the Acadians. A French historian acquainted with their story made two visits to the Acadian communities, began to correspond with many people there, and published two much-read books about them.[25] At his suggestion, one of his new-found Acadian friends, abbé Georges-Antoine Belcourt, wrote to the emperor, who granted sums of money to pay for two projects: French books for a library in Quebec City, and the migration and settlement of French-speaking people from Prince Edward Island to the new parish of Saint-Paul de Kent in New Brunswick. This patronage is interpreted by Acadian observers as purely cultural, but it was not welcomed by the authorities in Canada, who saw it – not without reason for those familiar with the history of the Second Empire – as an imperial gesture that might turn out to have political implications.[26]

GLORIFYING CHARLES DE GAULLE

In the life of the Fifth Republic, now nearly forty years old, Europe has witnessed an immense effort in France to glorify its founder and first president, Charles de Gaulle. The first steps were taken much earlier by the man himself, who wrote and spoke of "de Gaulle" by name, in the third person, as the saviour of France. "De Gaulle's history lesson," writes a French historian, "was intended to drive home several fundamental truths. First, the French owed their salvation and redemption to 'de Gaulle', a double of whom the author speaks in the third person. ... To read him, you might think that the man of June Eighteenth [date of his first wartime speech on the BBC] had fought a solitary battle."[27] In the eleven years of his presidency, 1958–69, he and his followers imposed him on the nation as if he had been a king or an emperor, and this campaign of glorification continued after his death in 1970.

The magnificent place de l'Étoile was renamed place de Gaulle, and on the Arc de Triomphe at its centre a bronze engraving of de Gaulle's first radio appeal on the BBC was unveiled on 19 June 1990. Cities all over France have renamed countless avenues and squares after him. The class of 1970–72 at the *École nationale d'administration* (ENA) adopted his name for its *promotion*. An *Institut Charles-de-Gaulle* was founded in Paris in 1971 and has held many meetings and published many books, all to the glory of its namesake. In November 1990 "a massive apotheosis" occurred at the UNESCO headquarters to celebrate the one hundredth anniversary of his birth and the twentieth anniversary of his death.[28] The legend of de Gaulle grew to such proportions that truth was buried under its weight.

A glance at the appropriate shelves of any large library shows an enormous outpouring of books about him, his government, and his followers. Even his writing is venerated: de Gaulle was "powerful by the Word (puissant par le Verbe)," Pierre de Menthon writes with reverence.[29] "His sentence," declares Maurice Druon of the Académie française, "has the sumptuous cadence of Corneille, of Bossuet, of Montesquieu, of Chateaubriand. But on looking more closely at his work, one may discern methods of composition in it, turns of narrative that bring to mind especially the *Mémoires* of Tacitus and even more of Caesar."[30] A few books about de Gaulle are critical or scornful, but the cumulative effect is to glorify him to the point that he must appear to the untutored as a truly great man. In Quebec, where little but the province's own history is taught in schools, many observers have expressed the view, since de Gaulle's visit in 1967, that he was perhaps the most distinguished statesman of his age; and this assessment would not shock some people even in English-speaking Canada. In other words, the propaganda by de Gaulle's followers and admirers has had a considerable effect on the thinking of French-speaking people. Any true or reasonable measure of the man has been lost to view except to those with an exceptional knowledge of history.

De Gaulle's disciples carry on a tireless campaign to glorify their leader. Since the end of the Second World War, a party of them has met each year on 18 June outside No. 4 Carlton Gardens, within sight of St James' Park in London, to celebrate their master's first appeal over the BBC. In 1993, on 23 June, a bronze statue of him was set up there and inaugurated by Queen Elizabeth the Queen Mother in an official ceremony with a good number of Gaullists present, including Jacques Chirac and Philippe Séguin.[31] Some 2.65 metres high, this statue shows de Gaulle aged forty-nine, as he was when he arrived in June 1940, and is marked with words from him inscribed on a slab of grey marble: "To all of the French. France has lost a battle. But France has not lost the war. (A tous les Français. La France a perdu une bataille. Mais la

France n'a pas perdu la guerre.)" It thereby repeats yet again one of the general's melifluous lies on which Gaullism is based. France had in fact lost the war, and it was rescued and freed by the English-speaking peoples. But by repeating the master's mantra of denial over and over, fanatical Gaullists have created a principle that ignores truth and takes its place in the ideology of French nationalism.

The campaign to glorify de Gaulle has succeeded nowhere more than in Canada. A bridge from the north end of Montreal Island to the mainland has been named after him. More spectacular, a large bronze statue of him was unveiled in Quebec City during a ceremony on 23 July 1997 to commemorate his visit thirty years earlier. Some forty-five French officials – politicians and others – attended. First among them was Philippe Séguin, leader of the Gaullist opposition in the French National Assembly and a prominent member of the French Quebec mafia, representing President Chirac and sent over at the expense of the French government. His speech on this occasion, extensively reported in *Le Devoir*, was redolent of de Gaulle's own rhetoric, studded with vague references to History and to themes calculated to stir the hearts of French Canadians. Speaking of de Gaulle's visit to Quebec in July 1967, Séguin said: "History, once again, de Gaulle had succeeded in creating it. And once again, as always, as he had done on 18 June, as he had done in Africa, and notably in Algeria, as he had done at Phnom-Penh, he had done it by betting on men. Magnificent, yes: for from that day, many things, many men also, began to change, which a great number of men and women of Quebec, including you yourself, Monsieur the deputy-premier [Bernard Landry], you your-selves, ladies and gentlemen, but also the men and women from France, gathered around Pierre Messmer, have come to witness today."[32] On and on he went, quoting Nietzsche, Goethe, Jean-Marc Léger, de Gaulle, and himself in a peroration that seemed to suggest that the Plains of Abraham were now no longer a symbol of defeat but only the site of this new bronze monument, which "recalls forever the most beautiful clear message of General de Gaulle to all the peoples of the universe."

The other official visitor from France on this occasion was Pierre Messmer, an old wartime companion of de Gaulle and later his prime minister and minister for war, now eighty-one years old, present at the invitation of the Quebec government. In the scrupulous and charitable opinions of some Canadian diplomats, such as Eldon Black, Messmer ought not to be listed with the mafia members – "We always had good relations with the ministry for war," Black assured me.[33] But the presence of other "mafia" members on Messmer's staff and his words in

Quebec on 23–24 July 1997 suggest that so faithful a Gaullist retainer must have been a supporter of Quebec independence, albeit in a quiet and dignified style and without the ugly anglophobia of Dorin, Mallen, or Séguin.

Interviewed by *Le Soleil*, the Quebec City daily, Messmer defended de Gaulle's "Vive le Québec libre!" speech, whose federalist critics, he said, opposed it only with worthless arguments. "With the passage of time, one can see that this shock-formula was the expression of an undeniable principle: the right of a people to dispose of itself."[34] He went on to say that if de Gaulle had not expressly opposed erection of statues to himself there might now be ten thousand of them in France, whereas in fact there are statues only in foreign countries: one in London and the one now being unveiled in Quebec City. Messmer, like the rest of the Gaullists, seems impervious to the irony of their leader's statue being tolerated in English-speaking countries to which he owed so much and to which he gave only ingratitude and insults. All that counts for Gaullists is the glorification of their hero.

In addition to the two official French guests, Séguin and Messmer, at least forty-three other French people attended the unveiling in Quebec. The consul general there was one of them. But most came from France at their own expense and intended to go on to tour around the province. Most were members of the *Amis de l'Institut Charles-de-Gaulle*, including leading members of the French Quebec mafia, in particular Philippe Rossillon and Bernard Dorin. The latter made a speech in the garden of the city hall on the morning of 24 July. He assured his audience that de Gaulle's "Vive le Québec libre!" speech had been carefully planned: the notorious phrase "was not an improvised cry."[35]

The French contingent was large, vocal, and contemptuous of the federalists who tried to interrupt the proceedings, but Quebec's PQ government had organized and promoted the event. It commissioned the statue for some $135,000 from the artist Fabien Pagé of Donnacona and chose the site, which is on the edge of the Plains of Abraham, the Plains themselves being federal ground, not at the disposal of the Quebec government.[36] Premier Bouchard was absent in California, presumably visiting his wife's family there, but the vice-premier, Bernard Landry, and the mayor, Jean-Paul L'Allier acted as official hosts, and Jacques Parizeau, a former premier, was also present. *Le Devoir* on that day published a long article on Franco-Quebec relations by Jean-Marc Léger, now splendidly presented as "Ancien diplomate québécois et consultant international."[37] In another long article, Jean Chartier recounted the history of the efforts of France's Quebec mafia to assist the separatist movement – this from the PQ's point of view.[38]

A few unfavourable printed comments surfaced. For example, Charles Halary, a sociology professor at the Université du Quebec à Montreal, regarded the event as a piece of inappropriate mysticism by a Gaullist old guard who would have done better to celebrate their hero in France.[39] William Johnson, as staunchly federalist as ever, published a brief account of the anti-Canadian Gaullist conspiracy.[40] And Liberal leader Daniel Johnson *fils*, son of the man who was premier when de Gaulle came in July 1967, refused to attend the ceremony.[41]

Indifferent to all opposition, most of the PQ leaders and their French visitors moved on the next day to celebrate the thirtieth anniversary of de Gaulle's "Vive le Québec libre!" speech of 24 July at the city hall in Montreal. A taped recording of that address played over the loudspeakers, and public figures added words of their own. The head of the *Société Saint-Jean Baptiste* of Montreal, Guy Bouthillier, said that de Gaulle had helped the Quebec people "by refusing to accept defeat" and showing that "defeats are not definitive and victories are always possible for those who are determined to succeed."[42] Other speakers included Pierre Messmer; Jacques Parizeau, who declared that the sovereigntists would win the next referendum; and an official of the French Communist party, Francis Wurtz, who talked about Quebec's identity. Also present were Marcel Masse, a provincial cabinet minister and sometime federal minister, and Raymond Villeneuve, a former terrorist of the FLQ, who had been in jail when he heard de Gaulle's speech in 1967.

The resulting apotheosis of de Gaulle must remind any student of French history of similar efforts to glorify the Bonaparte emperors and the Bourbons. Louis XIV was systematically glorified by his followers and large sections of his public. A cult of the Sun King lent him a mystical aspect and exaggerated his deeds.[43] This long campaign also had its effect on opinion throughout Europe and much of the world. In the 1680s an official campaign began to sponsor the building of a *place Royale* in as many French cities as possible. One was built at Quebec City, along with a statue of the king.[44] Napoleon is similarly glorified in ways that have little to do with recognizing him as one of the great generals of all time. The monuments to him, and some of the literature, express a cult raising him to the rank of an immortal, who, like Joan of Arc, personified the soul of France. "Sire," Victor Hugo began a poem celebrating the transporting of Napoleon's remains to Paris in 1840, "vous revenez dans votre capital."[45] With similar reverence has Charles de Gaulle been glorified by his faithful followers and a part of the public on both sides of the Atlantic.

– 16 –

On se Souvient

For thirty-five years the ruling élite in France has tended to look harshly on Canada. From the time Charles de Gaulle assumed the leadership of his country in the coup d'état of May 1958 that gave rise to his Fifth Republic, as we saw in chapter 2, Canada was in his sights as one of the English-speaking countries that seemed to stand in the way of French prestige. His sweeping vision of history's unfolding resembled the Soviet Communist vision in its scope and in the rigid, fanatical certainty with which he acted on it. Across the historical chessboard that he saw in the 1950s and 1960s *les Anglo-Saxons* had been closing in on France in a game that he himself was playing. He had marked them long before as his most serious opponents. Having set up the Fifth Republic so that he alone was moving the pieces on the French side, de Gaulle saw Canada as part – a small part – of the opposition. It was a pawn on the Anglo–American side of the board. He wanted its uranium for his atomic power plants and his bombs, the first of which exploded in the Sahara Desert on 13 February 1960; then it occurred to him that on the opposing side were French-speaking Canadians who might be turned to his advantage.

Gaullist encouragement for Quebec separatists is hard to assess, but we have neglected it for too long. Canadian authorities have been slow to understand the Fifth Republic. They have been too long under the spell of the Third and Fourth. During the Fourth Republic, which was overthrown in 1958, ambassadors such as Francisque Gay were sent to Ottawa with instructions to refrain from political interference and to assist in the peaceful accommodation of the two principal ethnic groups in Canada.[1] Gay travelled extensively and had a benevolent attitude towards the English-speaking part of Canada, which he rightly thought to be friendly towards France and French culture. His approach was much like that of André Siegfried, who wrote of Canada before and after the First World War with respect, affection, and no desire to promote the French at the expense of the English.[2] It is this benevolent republican view of the Canadian confederation that is remembered in some circles in Canada even today. The many English-speaking Canadians who join the Alliance française or make efforts to learn French usually have such an attitude. The alliances of two world wars are what they take to be the norm in Franco–Canadian relations. There have been many Canadian soldiers just like my uncle Norman Simister, an English immigrant who spent years in France during the First World War, married a French-speaking Belgian, and became an invincible francophile with a fluency in the language and a stock of French songs and poems that entered into the lore of my family.

Looking eastward from Ottawa, Canadian authorities see Quebec looming large on the horizon; France is only part of the vague beyond. In the blackening clouds of hostility gathering in the east it has been difficult to distinguish the French from the Québécois. Plainly, French indoctrination is by no means the only source of independence theory in Quebec. Without French interference Quebec would still have a strong movement in favour of sovereignty. Only by careful study can an English-speaking Canadian discern the theory, example, and direct influence of France that have been encouraging the Quebec and Acadian nationalist movements and lending them a confidence and strength they would not otherwise have. Whole books about Quebec separatist politics are written with little or no reference to France. Many Québécois and Acadians say that they detest the French for their arrogance, especially their gratuitous, patronizing criticism of Canadian French dialects. Yet, as the chapters above tell, a vital part of the separatist movement has been drawing inspiration and comfort from the Gaullist Fifth Republic. Educated Québécois make this very point over and over again. They and some activists in France, whom we have come to call "the French Quebec mafia" or "the Quebec lobby in France," believe that a generation or two of vigorous indoctrination may induce the province's population to support the separatist/ sovereigntist objectives of the Parti Québécois.

These chapters do not lead to a precise policy towards Quebec or even towards Gaullist France. It is not for historians to tell legislators, justices, and civil servants what to do next. But if historical study seldom, if ever, solves practical problems, it may sometimes throw a different light on them. This volume challenges the Gaullists' and Quebec separatists' view of the last three or four centuries, including these past thirty years, and so exposes the myths by which they live. Of course the revisions offered here are not the only ones possible and may themselves be open to further revision, but the important point is that investigation is certain to discredit some of the historical assumptions on which Gaullists and Quebec separatists base their policies. The myths and dogmas by which they live will not survive a confrontation with historical evidence. The honest pursuit of truth may gradually set them free. If they are determined to remember – *Je me souviens*, in Quebec's well-known motto – at least their backward gaze, and ours, might be brought to focus on more facts and fewer old archetypal fables. Some historians in France are already making that effort, but during the 1995 referendum campaign, as John Ralston Saul observes, "The federalist leaders didn't even deal with the most basic contradictions in the PQ's historical argument."[3] Discovering and facing what happened in the past would put us all on a different footing. Then we might be able to say, without giving way to Gaullist/separatist ideology, "Moi aussi, je me souviens."

Notes

CHAPTER ONE

1 "Le timbre de la discorde: l'intention de la France de commémorer le 'Vive le Québec libre!' du général de Gaulle suscite un tollé au Canada anglois," *Le Devoir*, 1 March 1997, A6; Jacques Aubry, "France Set to Scrap De Gaulle Stamp," *Ottawa Citizen*, 11 June 1997, A1–A2.

2 Le Devoir (Montréal), "Le timbre de la discorde,"Saturday 1 March 1997, A6.

3 Pierre-Louis Mallen, *Êtes-vous dépendantiste?* (Montreal: Éditions de la Presse, 1979).

4 *Les Amitiés acadiennes*, no. 24 (2ᵉ trimestre 1983), 16. Also on this committee were Martial de la Fournière (a diplomat), Pierre Lefranc (president of the Institut Charles-de-Gaulle), Pierre Maillard (former ambassador in Ottawa), two of the latest French consuls from Halifax and Moncton, and Maurice Schumann.

5 "Des Français pour la souveraineté du Québec," *Le Devoir*, 26 Jan. 1995, A9. Among the others were Michel Fichet, former president of the Association Paris-Québécois; Gilbert Pérol, ambassadeur de France; and several members of the French Academy.

6 Gérard Pelletier, *La crise d'octobre* (Montreal: Éditions du jour, 1971), 225.

7 Toronto *Globe and Mail*, 17 Sept. 1968, 3.

CHAPTER TWO

1 Thierry Wolton, *L'histoire interdite* (Paris: Lattès, 1998), 101–4.

2 Paul Gérin-Lajoie, "De Gaulle et le Québec," *Espoir*, no. 86 (Sept. 1992), 104–6; De Gaulle, *Discours et messages, avec le renouveau, 1958–1962* (Paris: Plon, 1970), 185.

3 Sidney Pollard, *Peaceful Conquest: The Industrialization of Europe, 1760–1970* (Oxford: Oxford University Press, 1981); W.O. Henderson, *Britain and Industrial Europe, 1750–1870* (Liverpool: Liverpool University Press, 1954); Alan S. Milward and S.B. Saul, *The Economic Development of Continental Europe, 1780–1870* (London: Allen and Unwin, 1973); Félix Ponteil, *L'éveil des nationalités et le mouvement libéral, 1815–1848* (Paris: Presses Universitaires de France, 1960), 688–9.

4 François Crouzet, *De la supériorité de l'Angleterre sur la France: l'économique et l'imaginaire XVIIᵉ–XXᵉ siècle* (Paris: Perrin, 1985), 452.

5 Ernest Labrousse et al., eds., *Histoire économique et sociale de la France*, 3 vols., (Paris: Presses Universitaires de France, 1970), II, 237–49, 304, 321; Harold T. Parker, *The Bureau of Commerce in 1781 and Its Policies with Respect to French Industry* (Durham, NC: Carolina Academic Press, 1989), 67–8, 109–13, 133–5; 152–5; Parker, *An Administrative Bureau during the Old Régime* (Newark: University of Delaware Press, 1993), 64, 79–81, 87, 96; André Rémond, *John Holker: manufacturier et grand fonctionnaire en France au XVIIIᵉ siècle, 1719–1786* (Paris: Marcel Rivière, 1946).

6 Henderson, *Britain and Industrial Europe*, 10–101, 211–18.

7 J.F. Bosher, "French Administration and Public Finance in their European Setting," *The New Cambridge Modern History*, 12 vols. (Cambridge: Cambridge University Press, 1965), VIII, 575, 584, 586; Bosher, *The French Revolution* (New York: W.W. Norton, 1987), 54–6, 96; Bosher, *French Finances, 1770–1795: From Business to Bureaucracy* (Cambridge: Cambridge University Press, 1970), 22–4, 42, 209, 303; P.G.M. Dickson, *The Financial Revolution in England* (London: Macmillan, 1967).

8 See below, chap. 12.

9 *Encyclopédie méthodique, partie finance*, 3 vols. (Paris: Pankoucke, 1784), I, 145–6.

10 Pierre Chaunu, "Preface," in François Crouzet, *De la supériorité de l'Angleterre sur la France: l'économique et l'imaginaire XVIIᵉ–XXᵉ siècle* (Paris: Perrin, 1985), iv.

11 Douglas Johnson, "De Gaulle and France's Role in the World," in Hugh Gough and John Horne, eds., *De Gaulle and Twentieth-Century France* (London: Edward Arnold, 1994), 91–2; Jean Lacouture, *De Gaulle*, 3 vols. (Paris: Seuil, 1984–6), III, chap. 13; John Newhouse, *De Gaulle and the Anglo-Saxons* (New York: Viking Press, 1970), 241, 265, 267, 293, 299; David S. Yost, "France," in F.O. Hampson et al., eds., *The Allies and Arms Control* (Baltimore, Md.: Johns Hopkins University Press, 1992), 162–88.

12 Richard Simeon and Ian Robinson, *State, Society and the Development of Canadian Federalism* (Toronto: University of Toronto Press, 1990),

178–9; Dale C. Thomson, *Jean Lesage and the Quiet Revolution* (Toronto: Macmillan, 1984), 83–5.

13 Yves Bélanger, *Québec Inc.: l'entreprise québécoise à la croisée des chemins* (Montreal: Hurtubise, 1998), 109.

14 *La Presse*, 20 April 1960, 1; 21 April 1960, 53; *Le Devoir*, 21 April 1960, 3.

15 Pierre Arbour, *Québec Inc. et la tentation du dirigisme* (Montreal: L'Étincelle, 1993).

16 Marc Levine, *La reconquête de Montréal* (Montréal: VLB, 1997); Paul-André Linteau, *Histoire de Montréal depuis la confédération* (Montreal: Boréal, 1992).

17 Lionel Bellavance, *Les partis indépendantistes québécois de 1960–73* (Montreal: Les anciens canadiens, 1973), 11.

18 Ibid., 12.

19 Gaston Cholette, *Au service du Québec: souvenirs* (Silléry, Que.: Septentrion, 1994), 34.

20 Robert Pichette, *L'Acadie par bonheur retrouvé: De Gaulle et l'Acadie* (Moncton: Éditions d'Acadie, 1994), 113–15; Diane Francis, *Fighting for Canada* (Toronto: Key Porter, 1996), 169ff.

21 G. Raymond Laliberté, *Une société secrète: l'Ordre de Jacques Cartier* (Montreal: Hurtubise, 1983), 63.

22 Pichette, *L'Acadie*, 113; André D'Allemagne, *Le R.I.N. de 1960 à 1963: Étude d'un groupe de pression au Québec* (Montreal: Étincelle, 1974), 17–18.

23 The most thorough and scholarly study is Laliberté, *Une société secrète*; two entertaining personal accounts by members who left the Order are Roger Cyr, *La Patente* (Montreal: Éditions du Jour, 1964), and a shorter work, Michel Gratton, *French Canadians: An Outsider's Inside Look at Quebec* (Toronto: Key Porter, 1992), chap. 2, "La Patente."

24 Simeon and Ian Robinson, *State*, 137–40, 178–80; Thomson, *Jean Lesage*, 18–20.

25 The Tremblay Commission's report was *The Royal Commission of Inquiry on Constitutional Problems*, 5 vols., (Quebec City: Queen's Printer, 1956).

26 Michael Behiels, *Prelude to Quebec's Quiet Revolution: Liberalism versus Neo-Nationalism*, 1945–1960 (Montreal: McGill-Queen's University Press, 1985), 206–11.

27 Ibid., 34–6.

28 Paul-André Linteau et al., *Histoire du Québec contemporain*, new ed., 2 vols. (Montreal: Boréal, 1989), II, 421–32.

29 Thomson, *Jean Lesage*; Robert Chodos and Nick Auf der Maur, eds., *Quebec: A Chronicle, 1968–1972* (Toronto: Lewis & Samuel, 1972).

30 *Le Devoir*, 21 April 1960, 7.

31 Conrad Black, *Duplessis* (Toronto: McClelland and Stewart, 1977), 490–1.

32 Ibid., 493–6.

33 Thomson, *Jean Lesage*, 312, 412ff.

34 Interview with Charles Lussier, 24 July 1997.

35 Arthur E. Blanchette, ed., *Canadian Foreign Policy, 1955–1965: Selected Speeches and Documents* (Toronto: McClelland and Stewart, 1977), 384–7.

36 "'Je me souviens!', c'est la devise de la province de Québec. En la voyant en votre personne, la France vous en dit autant." Charles de Gaulle, *Discours et messages; avec le renouveau, 1958–1962* (Paris: Plon, 1970), 353–4.

37 *Le Monde hebdomadaire*, no. 675 (21–27 Sept. 1961), 6; no. 677 (5–11 Oct. 1961), 6; Thomson, *Jean Lesage*, 410–16.

38 Brian McKenna and Susan Purcell, *Drapeau* (Toronto: Clark Irwin, 1980), 139–40.

39 Ibid., 140–1.

40 Ibid., 147–9.

41 W.G. Andrews, *Presidential Government in Gaullist France* (Albany, NY: Suny Press, 1982), 201–10; Robert Gildea, *France since 1945* (Oxford: Oxford University Press, 1997), 104–6; Maurice Larkin, *France since the Popular Front: Government and People, 1936–1986* (Oxford: Oxford University Press, 1988), 197; James F. McMillan, *Twentieth-Century France: Politics and Society, 1898–1991*, 2nd ed., (London: Edward Arnold, 1992), 174.

42 Behiels, *Prelude*, 12.

43 Ibid., 11–14; Jean-Claude Robert, *Du Canada français au Québec libre: histoire d'un mouvement indépendantiste* (Saint- Laurent, Que.: Flammarion, 1975), 215; Paul-André Linteau et al., *Histoire du Québec contemporain, tome II: le Québec depuis 1930*, new ed. (Montreal: Boréal, 1989), chap. 37, "L'omniprésence de la ville"; Chodos and Auf der Maur, eds., *Quebec*.

44 *La Presse*, 12 Oct. 1963, 3.

45 Arbour, *Québec Inc.*, 112 and passim.

46 William D. Coleman, *The Independence Movement in Quebec, 1945–1980* (Toronto: University of Toronto Press, 1984), 12; Bélanger, *Québec Inc.*,110–41.

47 Bélanger, *Québec Inc.*, 113; Arbour, *Québec Inc.*, 92–5.

48 Bélanger, *Québec Inc.*, 125.

49 Coleman, *The Independence Movement*, 121–3; Wayne Skene, *Delusions of Power: Vanity, Folly and the Uncertain Future of Canada's Hydro Giants* (Vancouver: Douglas and McIntyre, 1997), 102ff.

50 Arbour, *Québec Inc.*, 21–2.

51 Jean-Pierre Teinturier, "La coopération France-Québec," *Commerce*, 70 (1968), 44–8.

52 Robert, *Du Canada français*, 237.

53 Arbour, *Québec Inc.*, 114–5.

54 Bélanger, *Québec Inc.*, chap. 7; Miqué, *La Presse*, 27 Nov. 1998, B3.

CHAPTER THREE

1 Thierry Wolton, *Le KGB en France* (Paris: Grasset, 1986); Christopher Andrew and Oleg Gordievsky, *KGB: The Inside Story of its Foreign Operations from Lenin to Gorbachev* (New York: Harper Collins, 1990), 405, 444–5; P.L. Thyraud de Vosjoli, *Lamia* (Boston: Little, Brown & Co., 1970), 315–17, 244–5.

2 Jérôme Dupuis and Jean-Marie Pontaut, "Charles Hernu était un agent de l'Est," *L'Express* (Paris), 31 Oct. 1996, 26–32.

3 Douglas Porch, *The French Secret Services: A History of French Intelligence from the Dreyfus Affair to the Gulf War* (New York: Farrar, Straus and Giroux, 1995), 410–12, 416, 474; Richard Cléroux, *Pleins feux sur les services secrets canadiens: révélations sur l'espionnage au pays* (Montreal: Éditions de l'homme, 1993), 219, 228–32.

4 For the story of Gaullist activity among the Acadians, see below, chap. 5.

5 Gérard Beaulieu, ed., *L'Evangéline, 1887–1982: entre l'élite et le peuple* (Moncton: Éditions d'Acadie, 1997), 131, 351ff.

6 Interview with Max Yalden, 22 Jan. 1998.

7 Pierre-Louis Mallen, *Vivre le Québec libre* (Paris: Plon, 1978, and Montréal: Presses de la Cité, 1978); *Êtes-vous dépendantiste?* (Montreal: Éditions de la Presse, 1979); and "La dette de Louis XV," *Les cahiers d'histoire du Québec au XXᵉ siècle* (Centre de recherche Lionel–Groulx), no. 7 (spring 1997), 39–58.

8 Philippe Thyraud de Vosjoli, *Lamia, l'anti-barbouze* (Montreal: Les Éditions de l'homme, 1972), 423. On this author, whose brother Jacques Thyraud was a lawyer, a senator, and the mayor of their home town of Romorantin, see Roger Faligot and Pascal Krop, *La Piscine: Les Services Secret français depuis 1944* (Paris: Seuil, 1985), 277–81.

9 Peter Worthington, "Former de Gaulle Man Claims: French Agents Active in Que.," Toronto *Telegram*, 12 Sept. 1968, 1, 2, 4, and "Spy Scene Holds Little Comfort for the West," 19 Sept. 1968, 7.

10 Claude Morin, *Les choses comme elles étaient: une autobiographie politique* (Montreal: Boréal, 1994), 204.

11 P.L. Thyraud de Vosjoli, *Lamia, l'anti-barbouze* (1970), rev. and trans (Montreal: Les Éditions de l'homme, 1972), 7–16. Criticized by some as unreliable, *Lamia* seems sober, sensible, and convincing, as Douglas Porch thinks, though its story may be exaggerated here and there; see

Porch, *The French Secret Services*,186–7, 270–2, 372, 401, 409–10, 412, 416, 437.

12 J.L. Granatstein and David Stafford, *Spy Wars: Espionage and Canada from Gouzenko to Glasnost* (Toronto: Key Porter, 1990), 201–10; Dale Thomson, *Vive le Québec libre* (Toronto: Deneau Publishers, 1988), 159.

13 Patrice Chairoff, *Dossier B ... Comme Barbouzes* (Paris: Éditions Alain Moreau, 1975), 94–5.

14 "[Philippe] Rossillon a été mis en contact avec un militant du FLQ nommé Gille Pruneau, qu'il aurait aidé à se réfugier en Algérie." Louis Fournier, *FLQ: histoire d'un mouvement clandestin* (Montreal: Québec/Amérique, 1982), 52–3.

15 Rossillon was reported to have contacted, among others, Marcel Chaput, Réginald Chartrand, François Dorlot, Jean Drouin, Jacques Lucques, and Jacques Poisson. Michel Roy, "Le dossier (?) Rossillon," *Le Devoir*, 14 Sept. 1968, 1 and 6.

16 Worthington, "Former de Gaulle Man Claims," 1, 2, and 4.

17 Faligot and Krop, *La Piscine*, 302–5; Fournier, *FLQ*, 184ff, 235.

18 Thierry Wolton, *Le KGB en France* (Paris: Grasset, 1986); Andrew and Gordievsky, *KGB*, 405, 444–5. Soviet defectors in 1954 reported that they "found intelligence work particularly easy in France," and the full extent of their penetration of French governing circles has yet to appear. Francis Temperville was tried in October 1997 for spying for the Soviet Union on the French *Commissariat à l'énergie atomique* in 1987 and was sentenced to nine years in prison (*France-Amérique*, 1–7 Nov. 1997, 8; and 8–14 Nov. 1997, 5.)

19 Richard Cléroux, *Services secrets canadiens: révélations sur l'espionnage au pays* (Montreal: Éditions de l'homme, 1993), chap. 5, "L'affaire Claude Morin," 228ff.

20 For example, Pierre de Menthon, "Les activitiés du consulat général de France à Québec, 1967–1972," *Études gaulliennes*, 7 (1979), 89–94; Pierre de Menthon, *Je témoigne: Québec 1967, Chili 1973* (Paris: Cerf, 1979).

21 Eldon Black, *Direct Intervention: Canada–France Relations, 1967–1974* (Ottawa: Carleton University Press, 1996), 116; Faligot and Krop, *La Piscine,* 302–5.

22 National Archives of Canada (NAC), MG 31 E31 (henceforth Cadieux Papers), vol. 13, file 13–2, secret memo, 20 Nov. 1970 (12 pp.), 11.

23 Ibid., file 13–5, confidential memo of 10 Sept. 1974, 2–3.

24 Dan G. Loomis, *The Somalia Affair: Reflections on Peacemaking and Peacekeeping* (Ottawa: DGL Publications, 1996), 23.

25 For the story of the *Rainbow Warrior*, see below, chap. 13.

26 Vincent Jauvert, "Quand la France testait des armes chimiques en Algérie," *Le Nouvel Observateur*, 23–29 Oct. 1997, 4–10.

27 Chairoff, *Dossier B*, 94–5; Bernard Dorin, "Un combat de quarante ans pour la cause du Québec," *Les cahiers d'histoire du Québec au XX*^e *siècle* (Centre de recherche Lionel–Groulx), no. 7 (spring 1997), 24–38; Philippe Rossillon, "Coopération France–Acadie," in *Études gaulliennes* 7, no. 27–8 (Sept–Dec. 1979), 137–46; Granatstein and Stafford, *Spy Wars*, 201–10; Nicolas Fournier and Edmond Legrand, *E ... comme espionnage* (Paris: Alain Moreau, 1978); Pierre de Menthon, "Les activités du consulat général de France à Québec, 1967–1972," *Études gaulliennes*, 7, (1979), 89–94; Claude Morin, *Les choses comme elles étaient: une autobiographie politique* (Montreal: Boréal, 1994), 199ff, 325ff.

28 Jean-François Lisée, *Dans l'oeil de l'aigle: Washington face au Québec* (Montreal: Boréal, 1990), 40ff. and chaps. 2–4.

29 NAC, Cadieux Papers, memo, 8 Dec. 1966 (3 pp.)

30 RCMP security brief 117–93–037 obtained at the Solicitor General's offices, 340 Laurier Ave., Ottawa; John Bryden, *Best-Kept Secret: Canadian Secret Intelligence in the Second World War* (Toronto: Lester Publishing, 1993), 23–4, 42, 125, 174, 193, 198–223, 239–41, 254, 315–19; Michael Frost, *Moi, Mike Frost, espion canadian: activités ultrasecrètes à l'étranger et au pays* (Toronto: Éditions de l'homme, 1994), 96, 142–3, 150–3, 238–42; testimony of Joseph Ferraris to the McDonald Commission, 14958–61, D.C. McDonald et al., *Commission of Inquiry Concerning Certain Activities of the RCMP* (Ottawa: Queen's Printer, 1981).   .

31 See Georges Suffert, in *Le Point*, 21 June 1976; *Libération* (Paris) 21 June 1976, 20 May 1977; *Economist Foreign Report* (London), 16 Nov. 1977; *Sunday Times* (London), 20 Nov. 1977; *Times* (London), 5 May 1978; *Daily Telegraph* (London), 5 May 1978; Gilles Perrault, *Un homme à part* [Henri Curiel] (Paris: Barrault, 1984); Gilles Perrault, "Henri Curiel, citoyen du tiers-monde," *Le Monde Diplomatique* (April 1998), 24–5; Claire Sterling, *The Terror Network: The Secret War of International Terrorism* (New York: Reader's Digest, 1981), chap. 3, "The Strange Career of Henri Curiel," 49–69; Gilles Perrault, "Henri Curiel, citoyen du tiers-monde," *Le Monde diplomatique* (April 1998), 24–5.

32 "De Gaulle and a 'Free' Quebec: The Separatists' Noisy Welcome in Every Frenchman's Real Homeland," *Maclean's*, 14 Dec. 1963, 1.

33 *Québec libre*, no. 3 (June–July 1964), 8 (University of Ottawa microfilm, FC2925.9.S37 Q419).

34 Thomson, *Vive le Québec libre!*, 107; Le Devoir, 30 Sept. 1963.

35 *Le Droit*, 5 Oct. 1964, 21; *Citizen*, 5 Oct. 1964, 12; *Debates of the House of Commons, Canada*, session 1965, II, 10 May 1965, 1107, a question by W.B. Nesbitt, member for Oxford.

36 Paul Martin, *A Very Public Life*, vol. II, *So Many Worlds* (Toronto: Deneau, 1985), 574–5.

37 Jean Cathelin and Gabrielle Gray, *Révolution au Canada* (Paris: Presses du Mail, 1963).

38 No such letter is reproduced in de Gaulle's *Lettres, notes et carnets*, 12 unnumbered vols. (Paris: Plon, 1986), where most other such letters are to be found in chronological order. This does not prove that it never existed but does raise the question.

39 Cathelin and Gray, *Révolution au Canada*, 83.

40 Malcolm Reid, *The Shouting Signpainters: A Literary and Political Account of Quebec Revolutionary Nationalism* (Toronto: McClelland and Stewart, 1972), 301–4.

41 André D'Allemagne, *Le R.I.N. de 1960 à 1963: Étude d'un group de pression au Québec* (Montreal: Étincelle, 1974), 64, 70, 74, 121.

42 Cathelin and Gray, *Révolution au Canada*, 82.

43 *Québec libre*, 1, no. 3 (June – July 1964), 8.

44 *Québec libre* (Montreal), 2 no. 3 (Sept. 1965), 12. A photo of Lucques in the April 1965 number (1 no. 11, 5) shows a handsome, clean-cut young man with a small moustache.

45 *Globe and Mail*, 17 Sept. 1968, 2.

46 Pierre Godin, *René Lévesque, héros malgré lui (1960–1976)* (Montreal: Boréal, 1997), passim.

47 "Son gouvernement [celui de Lesage] et celui de Paris règlent entre eux et sans intermédiare le début de l'assistance que la France consacre désormais aux Français du Canada." De Gaulle, *Mémoires d'espoir; le renouveau 1958–1962* (Paris: Plon, 1970), 282.

48 Mallen, *Vivre le Québec libre*, 20.

49 Jean Gargan, "Pour une radio-télévision libre," in *Esprit* (Jan. 1964); see also a special issue of *La Nef*, nouvelle série, cahier no. 8 (Oct.–Dec. 1961).

50 *De Gaulle et Malraux: colloque organisé par l'Institut Charles-de-Gaulle, les 13–15 novembre 1986* (Paris: Plon, 1987), 276, remarks by Dale Thomson.

51 *Le Devoir*, 8 Oct. 1963, 3.

52 Ibid., 16 Oct. 1963, 3.

53 Ibid., 11 and 12 Oct. 1963, 1 both days.

54 Ibid., 10 Oct. 1963, 3; 14 Oct. 1963, 1; 15 Oct. 1963, 1.

55 Ibid., 11 Oct. 1963, 3.

56 "Quoi qu'il en soit, la France est présente au Canada, non seulement par ses représentants, mais aussi parce que de nombreux Canadiens sont de sang français, de langue française, de culture française, d'esprit français. Bref, ils sont français sauf en ce qui concerne le domaine de la souveraineté." *Espoir, revue de l'Institut Charles-de-Gaulle*, no. 20 (Oct. 1977), 8: a statement by Gilbert Pérol.

57 "Il n'est pas question que j'adresse un message au Canada pour célébrer

son 'Centenaire'. ... Nous n'avons à féliciter ... de la création d'un 'État' fondé sur notre défaite d'autrefois et sur l'intégration d'une partie du peuple français dans un ensemble britannique. Au demeurant, cet ensemble est devenu bien précaire." A note that de Gaulle scribbled on 9 December 1966 on a telegram received from the French embassy in Ottawa and quoted in Jean Chapdelaine, "Le général de Gaulle et le Québec," *L'Action nationale* (Quebec), Jan. 1991, 98.

58 Ibid., 96.

59 "D'ailleurs, le Canada français deviendra nécessairement un État et c'est dans cette perspective que nous devons agir"; note to Étienne Burin des Roziers dated 4 Sept. 1963. De Gaulle, *Lettres, notes et carnets* [for 1963], 369–70.

60 Ibid., 388.

61 *Québec libre*, 1 no. 5 (Oct. 1964), 5.

62 Charles King (who was in Martin's party), "French Snub: Martin Rides with Baggage," *Ottawa Citizen*, 7 May 1965, 17; *Debates of the House of Commons, Canada*, session 1965, II, 1107 (10 May 1965), W.B. Nesbitt, member for Oxford.

63 Martin, *A Very Public Life*, II, 584, 589; Robert Speaight, *Vanier: Soldier, Diplomat and Governor General* (Toronto: Collins, 1970), 400.

64 André Patry, *Le Québec dans le monde* (Montreal: Leméac, 1980), 65.

65 Gaston Cholette, *Au service du Québec: souvenirs* (Sillery, Que.: Septentrion, 1994), 104–5.

66 Chapdelaine, "Le Général," 94.

67 W.D. Coleman, *The Independence Movement in Quebec, 1945–1980* (Toronto: University of Toronto, 1984), 143.

CHAPTER FOUR

1 For a good account of developments leading up to de Gaulle's visit in 1967, see Dale Thomson, *Jean Lesage and the Quiet Revolution* (Toronto, Macmillan, 1984), chap. 10.

2 Jean Chapdelaine, "Le général de Gaulle au Québec," *Québec 1967–1987: du général de Gaulle au Lac Meech* (Montreal: Guérin éditeur, 1987), 19–20, citing documents published in the *Quotidien de Paris*, 2 Nov. 1977.

3 He forgot, as any student of de Gaulle might expect, that English-speaking Canadians had not only allowed his forces to capture Saint-Pierre but had actually helped them to do it, this in the face of considerable American opposition. See Douglas G. Anglin, *The St. Pierre and Miquelon Affair of 1941: A Study in Diplomacy in the North Atlantic Quadrangle* (Toronto: University of Toronto Press, 1966).

4 De Gaulle, *Mémoires de Guerre*, III, 216–17 recalled in Robert Pichette,

L'Acadie par bonheur retrouvé: De Gaulle et l'Acadie (Moncton: Éditions d'Acadie, 1994), 67.

5 Captain Hugh Plant's letter to the author, 13 Dec. 1998; but see Jean Victor Allard, *Jean Victor Allard, Mémoires du Général ... , en collaboration avec Serge Bernier* (Boucherville, Que., Éditions de Mortagne, 1985), 299.

6 *De Gaulle au Québec* (Montreal: Editions actualité, 28 Aug. 1967), 26–7.

7 *La Presse* and *Le Devoir*, 25 July 1967, passim.

8 See *Le Devoir*, 3 Jan. 1997, A3; Mike King, "Sovereigntists Honour 30–Year [sic] Anniversary of de Gaulle Speech," *Ottawa Citizen*, 16 July 1997, A3. Dale Thomson cites several versions of how and why it was decided that de Gaulle should reach Quebec by sea; Thomson, *Vive le Québec Libre*, 182ff.

9 These are conveniently brought together, mainly from CBC recordings, in Renée Lescop, *Le pari québécois du général de Gaulle* (Montreal: Boréal Express, 1981), 154–73.

10 One such was the wife of General William Anderson, who was present on the occasion. (The incident was related to me by General Anderson on 30 May 1997).

11 For the letter of 8 Sept. 1967, see Gaston Cholette, *L'action internationale du Québec en matière linguistique: coopération avec la France et la francophonie de 1961 à 1995* (Québec City: Presses de l'Université Laval, 1997), 171.

12 Ibid., 23; Claude Ryan, "Bilan d'une visite," *Le Devoir*, 27 July 1967, 4: "la réaction brutale du Canada anglais, qui fut sans doute la cause première de la dureté du gouvernement fédéral"; Jean Tainturier, "Pourquoi et comment de Gaulle est parti" (critical of the English-Canadian attitude and comments), *Le Devoir*, 28 July 1967, 1; Jean-Marc Léger, "Le vieil antigaullisme de l'Amérique anglo-saxonne," (Critical of the English-Canadian press as being unfairly hostile), *Le Devoir*, 29 July 1967, 4.

13 *Espoir, revue de l'Institut Charles-de-Gaulle*, no. 20 (Oct. 1977), 11–12, remarks by de Saint-Légier.

14 NA, Cadieux Papers, MG31, E31, file 13–4, confidential memo of Marcel Cadieux, 15 March 1973.

15 As Brian Crozier has put it, de Gaulle "must be credited with a kind of genius in the formulation of noncommittal generalities." Crozier, *De Gaulle*, II, 672.

16 Bruce Hutchison, "De Gaulle Ambiguous on Quebec Politics," *Christian Science Monitor*, 26 July 1967, 5.

17 Peter C. Newman, "Head-on Collision Inevitable," *Montreal Star*, 27 July 1967, 9.

18 Paul Martin, *A Very Public Life*, Vol. II, *So Many Worlds* (Toronto: Deneau, 1985), 595, 597.

19 See *Espoir, revue de l'Institut Charles-de-Gaulle*, no. 20 (Oct. 1977).

20 Ibid., 15.

21 Ibid., see remarks by Étienne Burin des Roziers, René de la Sausaye de Saint-Légier, and Gilbert Pérol.

22 *Canadian News Facts* (Toronto, 1967), 62. Prime Minister Pearson assured the House of Commons on 12 April that the French government had been duly informed and consulted beforehand.

23 Xavier Deniau, "Il y a trente ans le voyage du général de Gaulle au Québec," *Revue politique et parlementaire*, 98ᵉ année, no. 983 (1996), 74.

24 Edgar Faure thought so. See J.R. Tournoux, *Le tourment et la fatalité* (Paris: Plon, 1974), 220; Olivier Guichard, *Mon Général* (Paris: Grasset, 1980), 419; Dale Thomson, *Vive le Québec Libre* (Toronto: Deneau, 1988), 238-41.

25 Jean Touchard, *Le gaullisme, 1940-1969* (Paris: Seuil, 1978), 228.

26 Thomson, *Vive le Québec Libre*, 239.

27 Pierre de Menthon, "Les activités du consulat général de France à Québec, 1967-1972," *Études gaulliennes*, 7 (1979), 89; "Promotion au consul de France à Québec," *La Presse*, 16 Sept. 1968, 1-2.

28 Bernard Dorin, "Un combat de quarante ans pour la cause du Québec," *Les cahiers d'histoire du Québec au XXᵉ siècle* (Centre de recherche Lionel-Groulx), no. 7 (spring 1997), 27-8.

29 "On va m'entendre là-bas, ça va faire des vagues," a remark made to Xavier Deniau. Philippe Rossillon, in *Études gaulliennes*, 7, no. 27-8 (Sept.-Dec. 1979), 82).

30 Gaston Cholette, *L'action internationale du Québec en matière linguistique: coopération avec la France et la francophonie de 1961 à 1995* (Quebec City: Presses de l'Université Laval, 1997), 22.

31 Paul Gérin-Lajoie, "De Gaulle et le Québec," *Espoir* (Paris), no. 86 (Sept. 1992), 106.

32 "More Noise from Paris", *Globe and Mail*, 1 Aug. 1967, 5.

33 George Bain, "No More to Be Said," *Globe and Mail*, 26 July 1967, 6, and "De Gaulle versus Canada: A Blow-by-Blow Review," *Globe and Mail*, 29 July 1967, 7.

34 "Provocative and Dishonest", *Ottawa Journal*, 1 Aug. 1967.

35 "De Gaulle Declares War", *Albertan*, 1 Aug. 1967. The editor had read and correctly interpreted the French ministerial statement of July 21 made by Georges Gorce.

36 Charles de Gaulle, *Discours et messages*, Vol. VII, *Vers le terme*, Jan. 1966-Apr. 1969 (Paris: Plon, 1970), 240 note.

37 *De Gaulle au Québec* (1967), 99.

38 Quoted in *Globe and Mail*, 28 July 1967.

39 Donald N. Baker, "Quebec on French Minds," *Queen's Quarterly*, 85 (1978-79), 249.

40 *Le Monde hebdomaire*, no. 979 (20–26 July 1967), 1 and 4.

41 Ibid., no. 982 (10–16 Aug. 1967), 2.

42 Read by Georges Gorse, reported in ibid., no. 980 (27 July –2 Aug. 1967), 3.

43 Ibid., no. 981 (3–9 Aug. 1967), 4.

44 Ibid., no. 982 (10–16 Aug.), 2; no. 983 (17–23 Aug.), 4; no. 984 (24–30 Aug.), 3. Among the special correspondents were André Passeron and Jean-Pierre Tainturier.

45 Defferre was quoted at length in ibid., no. 980 (27 July–2 August 1967), 2; Hector de Galard, "La retraite du Canada," *Nouvel Observateur*, no. 142 (2–6 Aug. 1967), 2.

46 Deniau, "Il y a trente ans," 73–6.

47 Pierre de Menthon, "Les activités du Consulat Général de France à Québec, 1967–1972", *Études gaulliennes*, 7 (1979), 89.

48 Jean Chapdelaine, "Le général de Gaulle au Québec," in *Le Québec 1967–1987, du général de Gaulle au Lac Meech* (Montreal: Guérin, 1987), 16–21.

49 Charles Halary, "L'image du président de Gaulle chez les Français de Montréal," *Espoir* (Paris), no. 86 (Sept. 1992), 60. As for de Gaulle's bitter wartime memories, the comte de Marenches brings his own first-hand knowledge as a witness that de Gaulle "had never forgiven Churchill and Roosevelt for what he considered a supreme betrayal – the invasion of Morocco and Algeria in November 1942 etc." See Count de Marenches and David A. Andelman, *The Fourth World War: Diplomacy and Espionage in the Age of Terrorism* (New York: Morrow, 1992), 54.

50 Baker, "Quebec on French Minds," 250.

51 "Le 'Québec libre' lancé par de Gaulle à l'hôtel de ville de Montréal m'a fait gagner cinq bonnes années," *L'Express* (Paris), 30 Sept.–6 Oct. 1968, 51.

52 "Je leur ai fait gagner dix ans!" Bernard Dorin, "Un combat de quarante ans pour la cause du Québec," *Les cahiers d'histoire du Québec au XXe siècle* (Centre de recherche Lionel–Groulx), no. 7 (spring 1997), 29.

53 François Aquin, "Vive le Québec libre! (1967)," in Andrée Ferretti and Gaston Miron, eds., *Les grands textes indépendantistes: écrits, discours et manifestes Québécois, 1774–1992* (Montreal: l'Hexagone, 1992), 369–72.

54 René Lévesque, *Attendez que je me rappelle ...* (Montréal: Québec/ Amérique, 1986), 280–2.

55 *De Gaulle au Québec* (1967), 87–137.

56 See, for example, Gilles Bourque, "De Gaulle, politique et stratégie," *Parti pris*, 5 (Sept. 1967), 7–17.

57 Harold King, "Quebec Beats Drum in Paris," *Telegram*, 24 Sept. 1968, 21.

58 John P. Schlegel, SJ, *The Deceptive Ash: Bilingualism and Canadian Policy in Africa, 1957–1971* (Washington, DC: University Press of America, 1978), 245–8.

59 François Aquin, "Pour une politique étrangère du Québec (1968)," in Andrée Ferretti and Gaston Miron, eds., *Les grands textes indépendantistes: écrits, discours et manifestes Québécois, 1774–1992* (Montreal: l'Hexagone, 1992), 373–4.

60 William Johnson, *A Canadian Myth: Quebec, Between Canada and the Illusion of Utopia* (Montreal: Robert Davies, 1994), 148–9.

61 King, "Sovereigntists Honour," A3.

62 Centre de recherche Lionel–Groulx, *De Gaulle et le Québec* (Les cahiers d'histoire du Québec au XXᵉ siècle, Sainte Foy, Que.), no. 7 (spring 1997), 51, 61, 111.

63 "Il faut dire que pour ce qui est des affairs politiques, son frère l'ambassadeur semble avoir hérité de tout le génie de la famille." NA, Cadieux Papers, memo, 26 Dec. 1967 (3 pp.).

64 Robert Pichette, *L'Acadie par bonheur retrouvé: De Gaulle et l'Acadie* (Moncton: Éditions d'Acadie, 1994), 100–1.

65 In a letter dated 7 April 1967, the bishops affirmed the right of Quebec "to existence, to development in all aspects, to civil and political institutions adapted to its genius and its own needs, to that autonomy without which it would not be assured of its existence, its prosperity and its economic and cultural growth." Quoted in Gilles Chaussé, "Révolution française et religion au Québec," in Michel Grenon, ed., *L'image de la révolution française au Québec, 1789–1989* (Montreal: Hurtubise, 1989), 137–8.

66 NA, Cadieux Papers, personal memoranda of 26 Dec. 1967 (3 pp.) and 2 Feb. 1968.

67 Roger Tessier, "Une déclaration inopportune du cardinal Turcotte," *Le Devoir*, 29 Jan. 1998, A7.

68 Stephen Clarkson, "*Vive le Québec libre:* Twenty Years On," *French Politics and Society*, 5, no. 4 (Sept. 1987), 36. John English adopted the same reassuring view in his biography of Lester B. Pearson: *The Worldly Years: The Life of Lester Pearson*, Vol. II, 1949–1972 (Toronto: Knopf, 1992), 345.

69 Keith Henderson, "France Has Been Interfering in Our Affairs for Too Long," *Financial Post*, 9 April 1997, 13; Henderson, "Federal Government Owes Us a National Refendum Act," *Financial Post*, 4 June 1997, 13; Diane Francis, "Canada Still May Face a Grim Secession Crisis in the Next Year or So," *Financial Post*, 3 June 1997, 23; William Johnson, "A Look Back Shows Little Progress Has Been Made in Responding to the Quebec Problem: The Players Change, but the Unity Game Remains the Same," *Financial Post*, 20 June 1997, 11.

70 Marc Lavallée, *Adieu la France, salut l'Amérique* (Montreal: Stanké, 1982), 106ff.

71 Ibid., 115–18.

72 D.C. McDonald, et al., *Commission of Inquiry Concerning Certain Activities of the RCMP* (Ottawa, Queen's Printer, 1981); interview with John Starnes, 18 Aug. 1997.

73 See below, chap. 5.

CHAPTER FIVE

1 Léon Thériault, *La question du pouvoir en Acadie*, 2nd ed. (Moncton: Les Éditions d'Acadie, 1982), 215.

2 Émile Lauvrière, *La tragédie d'un peuple*, 2 vols. (Paris: Librairie Henry Goulet, 1922); a revised edition: *Histoire du peuple acadien de ses origines à nos jours* (Paris, Édition Bossard, 1924).

3 Gaston Cholette, *Au service du Québec: souvenirs* (Silléry, Que.: Septentrion, 1994), 66–9.

4 Ibid., 215–21.

5 De Gaulle, *Discours et messages – Vers le terme – Janvier 1966 – Avril 1969* (Paris: Plon, 1970), 239.

6 *Les Amitiés acadiennes*, no. 10 (Oct. 1979), 3; Robert Pichette, *L'Acadie par bonheur retrouvé: de Gaulle et l'Acadie* (Moncton: Éditions d'Acadie, 1994), 85.

7 Léon Thériault, *La question du pouvoir en Acadie*, 218–19; Pichette, *L'Acadie*, passim.

8 Pichette, *L'Acadie*, 106.

9 "Permettez aux Acadiens de vous dire que votre récent séjour en notre pays nous a déterminés à préserver plus que jamais la culture française dans les régions continuës au Québec, où nous avons survécu." The full text of this letter is quoted, with archival references, in ibid., 107–8.

10 "Nous plaçons en vous tous nos espoirs et vous prions d'agréer les assurances de notre profond respect et notre indéfectible attachement à notre patrie d'origine"; ibid., 109.

11 Philippe Rossillon, "Coopération France-Acadie," in *Études gaulliennes*, 7 no. 27–8 (Sept.–Dec. 1979), 140.

12 Père Anselme Chiasson, o.f.m. cap., "Voyage historique des Acadiens en Europe," *Les Cahiers* (La Société historique acadienne), 2 no. 2, (July 1966), 51.

13 Pichette, *L'Acadie*, 99.

14 For an account of this journey see ibid, 125ff 198.

15 Rossillon, "10e anniversaire des conversations Franco–Acadiennes de Janvier 1968," *Les Amitiés acadiennes*, no. 3 (Nov. 1977), 1; no. 4 (April 1978), 38.

16 Thériault, *La question*, 219; Rossillon, "Coopération France–Acadie," 145.

17 Gérard Beaulieu, ed., *L'Evangéline, 1887–1982: entre l'élite et le peuple* (Moncton: Éditions d'Acadie, 1997), 131.

18 *Acadie Infos*, no. 90 (April–May 1994), 4.

19 *Les Amitiés acadiennes*, no. 4 (April 1978), 34–5, no. 9 (July 1979), 10–11, no 12 (April 1980), 6, no. 15 (Jan. 1981), 4–5, no. 20 (April 1982), 5, no. 25 (3ᵉ trimestre 1983), 7.

20 Gérard-Marc Braud, "Les communautés acadiennes en France," in *Le congrès mondial acadien, l'Acadie en 2004, Actes des conférences et des tables rondes, 16–20 août 1994* (Moncton: Éditions d'Acadie, 1996), 343–50.

21 Thériault, *La question*, 221.

22 See *Le congrès mondial acadien*, 125–32.

23 Beaulieu, ed., *L'Evangéline, 1887–1982*, 317.

24 For analyses and explanations of Acadian society, see the writings of Naomi Griffiths, such as *The Contexts of Acadian History 1686–1784* (Montreal: McGill-Queen's University Press, 1992), and Jean Daigle, ed., *The Acadians of the Maritimes: Thematic Studies* (Moncton: Université de Moncton, 1982).

25 *Acadie Infos*, no. 58 (Dec. 1990), 3.

26 Pichette, *L'Acadie*, 242–3, names the founders, including the editor-in-chief of *Le Figaro* (Yann Clerc) and a number of lawyers, civil servants, business people, professors, and teachers.

27 Auguste Viatte, in *Les Amitiés acadiennes*, no. 6 (Oct. 1978), 5.

28 Among the members were Maillard himself, Pierre-Louis Mallen, Pierre Bas (député in the National Assembly), Martial de la Fournière (ministre plenipotentiare), Pierre Lefranc (president of the Institut Charles-de-Gaulle), and the French consuls posted at Moncton and Halifax. See Philippe Rossillon, "Un comité pour le renforcement des relations franco–acadiennes," *Les Amitiés acadiennes*, no. 24 (2ᵉ trimestre 1983), 16.

29 Interview with Max Yalden, 22 Jan. 1998.

30 Claude Morin, *L'art de l'impossible: la diplomatie québécoise depuis 1960* (Montreal: Boréal, 1987), 136–7.

31 Ibid., 25.

32 NA, Cadieux Papers, memo of 8 Jan. 1968 (5 pp.).

33 Ibid., memo, 15 Jan. 1968 (4 pp.), 3.

34 *La Revue de l'Université de Moncton*, 2 (Sept. 1969), 108–11, and 3 (Sept. 1970), 117–19.

35 See, for example, Rossillon, "Les Acadiens, le Québec et la constitution," *Les Amitiés acadiennes*, no. 18 (Oct. 1981), 3, or Rossillon, "Une tradition s'instaure ... ," ibid., no. 19 (Jan. 1982), 3.

36 *Le Devoir*, 7 Dec. 1985, 1; Hélène Galarneau, "Chronique des relations extérieures du Canada et du Québec," *Études internationales*, 17 (1986), 149–50.

37 Lucien Bouchard, *A visage découvert* (Montreal: Boréal, 1992), 217–18; Pichette, *L'Acadie*, 228.

38 Pichette, *L'Acadie*, 140–1.

39 "Une période de calme appréhension pour les 350,000 Acadiens du Canada," *La Presse*, 17 Nov. 1976, A16.

40 *Les Amitiés acadiennes*, no. 12 (April 1980), 21.

41 For the text of his speech on that occasion, see *Les Amitiés acadiennes*, no. 30 (4e trimestre 1984), 6–7.

42 Jules Richer, "Duceppe heurte des susceptibilités," *Le Soleil*, 4 Oct. 1997, A17; Manon Cornellier, "Duceppe froisse les artistes acadiens," *Le Devoir*, 4 Oct. 1997, A1, A12.

43 Michel Cormier and Achille Michaud, *Richard Hatfield: Power and Disobedience* trans. Daphne Ponder (Fredericton: Goose Lane, 1992), 134.

44 *Acadie Infos*, no. 55 (1990), 2.

45 *Le Devoir*, 18 Feb. 1996, A4, and 21–22 Dec. 1996, A1; *Études internationales*, 28, no. 1 (March 1997), 148.

46 *Acadie Infos*, no. 57 (Nov. 1990), 2.

47 Ibid., no. 58 (Dec. 1990), 3.

48 Sally Ross and Alphonse Deveau, *The Acadians of Nova Scotia, Past and Present* (Halifax: Nimbus, 1992), 190.

49 *Acadie Infos*, no. 59 (Jan. 1991), 1.

50 *Acadie Infos*, no. 65 (July–Aug. 1991), 4.

51 André Maindron, "Quinze ans d'Amitiés acadiennes ou l'Acadie, vue de France," *Revue de l'Université de Moncton*, 27 no. 1 (1994), 287; Philippe Rossillon, "Dernière minute, un ami disparait ...," *Les Amitiés acadiennes*, no. 22 (4e trimestre 1982), 19.

52 Pichette, *L'Acadie*, 245.

53 Réal Pelletier, "L''agent secret français' Philippe Rossillon est mort," *La Presse*, 8 Sept. 1997, A4.

54 Maindron, "Quinze ans," 293–5.

55 Ibid., 296.

56 Rossillon, "Message du président Ph. Rossillon," *Les Amitiés acadiennes*, no. 52 (2e trimestre 1990), 3.

57 "Les relations entre Acadiens et Français se poursuivent à un très haut niveau dans différents domaines dont celui de la politique." Lucien Bertin, "Le général De Gaulle et les Acadiens," *Les Amitiés acadiennes*, no. 54 (4e trimestre 1990), 3.)

58 Rossillon, "Surréalisme," *Les Amitiés acadiennes*, no. 37 (3e trimestre 1986), 3.

59 Pelletier, "L''agent secret français'", A4.

CHAPTER SIX

1 Claude Morin, *Mes premiers ministres: Lesage, Johnson, Bertrand, Bourassa et Lévesque* (Montreal: Boréal, 1991), 274.

2 Dale Thomson, *Vive le Québec libre!* (Toronto: Deneau Publishers, 1988); Eldon Black, *Direct Intervention: Canada–France Relations, 1967–1974* (Ottawa: Carleton University Press, 1996).

3 Jacques Cellard, "Canada: un débat à Paris à l'occasion de la présentation de l'ouvrage *Dossier Québec*," *Le Monde*, 13 Feb. 1980, 6; André Fontaine, "La France et le Québec," *Études internationales*, 12 (1980), 393–402.

4 "Ce n'est pas l'idée de nation qui est rétrograde, c'est l'idée que la nation doive nécessairement être souveraine." Pierre Trudeau, *Le fédéralisme et la société canadienne française* (Montreal: Éditions HMH, 1967), 161.

5 "Des Français pour la souveraineté du Québec," *Le Devoir*, 26 Jan. 1995, A9.

6 Philippe Rossillon has published several articles about the Walloon prospects for independence in *Amitiés acadiennes*; see André Maindron, "Quinze ans d'*Amitiés acadiennes* ou l'Acadie, vue de France," *Revue de l'Université de Moncton*, 27 no. 1 (1994), 281–98.

7 William Johnson, *Anglophobie, Made in Quebec* (Quebec City: Stanké, 1991).

8 *Acadie Infos*, no. 76 (Dec. 1992), 1. Most of them were from the *Société nationale des Acadiens*.

9 Marc Lavallée, *Adieu la France, salut l'Amérique* (Montreal: Stanké, 1982), 106ff.

10 Philippe Rossillon, "Coopération France-Acadie," in *Études gaulliennes*, 7 no. 27–8 (Sept.–Dec. 1979), 144.

11 Ibid., 145–6.

12 Bernard Dorin, "Un combat de quarante ans pour la cause du Québec," *Les cahiers d'histoire du Québec au XXᵉ siècle* (Centre de recherche Lionel–Groulx), no. 7 (spring 1997), 24–38.

13 Pierre-Louis Mallen, *Vivre le Québec libre* (Paris: Plon, 1978), passim; and Mallen, "La dette de Louis XV," *Les cahiers d'histoire du Québec au XXᵉ siècle* (Centre de recherche Lionel–Groulx), no. 7 (spring 1997), 39–58.

14 Pierre de Menthon, "Les activités du consulat général de France à Québec, 1967–1972," *Études gaulliennes*, 7 (1979), 90.

15 Interview with Eldon Black, 15 July 1997.

16 Paul Martin, *A Very Public Life*, Vol. II, *So Many Worlds* (Toronto: Deneau, 1985), 603–4, 581–604 passim; this was also Mme Anita Cadieux's firm opinion; she had often entertained Leduc at home with her husband.

17 NA, Cadieux Papers, telegram from Paris, 24 Sept. 1969.

18 Secret memo from Marcel Cadieux to Prime Minister Pearson, 2 Feb. 1968, with Léger's letter of 25 Jan. 1968 and its enclosure of a dispatch from the French ambassador to the Vatican.

19 Pierre Godin, *René Lévesque, héros malgré lui (1960–1976)* (Montreal: Boréal, 1997), 315.

20 Interview with Charles Lussier, 23 July 1997.

21 Thomson, *Vive le Québec libre*, 303; Dorin, "Un combat," 26–7.

22 Douglas Porch, *The French Secret Services: A History of French Intelligence from the Dreyfus Affair to the Gulf War* (New York: Farrar, Straus and Giroux, 1995), 401, 438–40, 445–6.

23 J.L. Granatstein & David Stafford, *Spy Wars: Espionage and Canada from Gouzenko to Glasnost* (Toronto: Key Porter, 1990), 201.

24 Barre, Bousquet, Charbonnel, de la Chevalerie, Chevènement, Cheysson, Chirac, Deniau, Foccart, de la Fournière, Jurgensen, Lavenir, Maillard, Malaud, Mauroy, Méhaignerie, Pérol, Peyrefitte, Rocard, Rossillon, des Roziers, and de Saint-Légier; Dorin, "Un combat," 26–7, 31, 34–6.

25 Andrew Knapp, *Gaullism since de Gaulle* (Aldershot: Dartmouth Publishing, 1994), 461.

26 Jean-Michel Forges, *L'École nationale d'Administration* (Paris: Plon, 1989), 104–5.

27 Jacques Parizeau, *Pour un Québec souverain* (Montreal: vlb éditeur, 1997), 284.

28 *Le Devoir*, 20 Sept. 1995, A1.

29 Ed Bantey, "Myopic Leadership," Montreal *Gazette*, 27 July 1997, A9.

30 Louis-Bernard Robitaille, "Paris déroulera le tapis rouge pour Bouchard," *La Presse*, 10 Sept. 1997, B1.

31 "France, plus ça change," *Economist*, 344 no. 8,029 (9–15 Aug. 1997), 44–5; Brian Chapman, *The Profession of Government* (London: George Allen and Unwin, 1959), 88–94, 115–24.

32 Guy Thuillier, *L'E.N.A. avant l'E.N.A.* (Paris: Presses universitaires de France, 1983), offers an account of the training of French public officials since the seventeenth century.

33 John Hellman, *The Knight-Monks of Vichy France: Uriage, 1940–45,* 2nd ed. (Montreal: McGill-Queen's University Press, 1997), 233–4.

34 Arnaud Teyssier, "Le Général de Gaulle et la création de l'E.N.A.," *Espoir, revue de la Fondation et de l'Institut Charles-de-Gaulle,* no 103 (July 1995), 31–7.

35 For the ENA and its controversial role in France, see Jean-Michel Gaillard, *L'E.N.A., miroir de l'État de 1945 à nos jours* (Paris: Éditions complexe, 1995); "L'ENA," in *Pouvoirs, revue française d'études constitutionnelles et politiques,* no. 80 (1997); or Jean-Michel Forges, *L'École nationale d'administration* (Paris: Presses universitaires de France, 1989).

36 *Le Monde hébdomadaire*, no. 2525, 29 March 1997, 6; *Economist*, 342 no. 8010, 29 March–4 April 1997, 96; Dale Thomson, *Vive le Québec libre!*, 159; Porch, *The French Secret Services*, 395, 399–400, 438–46, 480–2.

37 See Pierre Viansson-Ponté, *Les Gaullistes: rituel et annuaire* (Paris: Seuil, 1963), and *Who's who in France, dictionnaire biographique* (Paris: Éditions Jacques Lafitte, 1996).

38 Robert Pichette, *L'Acadie par bonheur retrouvé de Gaulle et l'Acadie* (Moncton: Éditions d'Acadie, 1994), 89; *Globe and Mail*, 14 Sept. 1968, 1–2.

39 Thomson, *Vive le Québec libre!*, chap. 13.

40 Alain Peyrefitte, "XXᵉ anniversaire du 'Vive le Québec libre,'" *Québec 1967–1987: du général de Gaulle au Lac Meech* (Montréal: Gérin éditeur, 1987), 13.

41 "J'ai remplacé le prolétariat par la France." See *Le Nouvel Observateur*, 14 Oct. 1968, 8.

42 *Le Devoir*, 16 Oct. 1963, 1.

43 Christopher Malone, "La politique québécoise en matière de relations internationales: changement et continuité 1960–1972," MA thesis, Université d'Ottawa, 1974, 283 note 32; John Hilliker and Donald Barry, *Canada's Department of External Affairs*, Vol. II, *Coming of Age, 1946–1968* (Montreal: McGill-Queen's University Press, 1995), 391–2.

44 *Le Monde hebdomadaire*, no. 1,130 (18–24 June 1970), 6.

45 "Le gaullisme est d'abord un compagnonnage." "Compagnonnage" translates ordinarily as "journeymen's organization," but it also conveys the sense of a brotherhood; Pierre Viansson-Ponté, *Les gaullistes: rituel et annuaire* (Paris: Seuil, 1963), 7; cf. Dominique Venner, *Guide de la politique* (Paris: Balland, 1972), 364, on "Le Gaullisme."

46 *Les Amitiés acadiennes*, no. 19 (Jan. 1982), 19.

47 *Acadie Infos*, no. 120 (Sept. 1997), 1, and *Amitiés acadiennes*, Oct. 1997.

48 *Who's Who in France, dictionnaire biographique* (Paris: Éditions Jacques Lafitte, 1975–6 and 1996–97).

49 Pierre-Louis Mallen, *Vivre le Québec libre* (Paris: Plon, 1978), 11.

50 *Le Devoir*, 25 Jan. 1995, A2, A8.

51 *Acadie Infos*, no. 74 (Oct. 1992), 2.

52 *Ottawa Citizen*, 20 March 1998, A4.

53 Jean Victor Allard, *Mémoires du Général Allard en collaboration avec Serge Bernier* (Boucherville, Que., Éditions de Mortagne, 1985), 451–2.

54 Claude Dulong, *La vie quotidienne à l'Élysée au temps de Charles de Gaulle* (Paris: Hachette, 1974), 206.

55 Pichette, *L'Acadie*, 141ff.

56 Mallen, *Vivre le Québec libre*, 14.

57 Bouchard, Lucien, *A visage découvert* (Montreal: Boréal, 1992), 163.

58 *Études internationales*, 27 (1996), 419.

59 Dale Thomson, *Vive le Québec Libre*, 249.

60 Jean Tainturier, "La visite de M. André Malraux à Montréal a redonné confiance aux Canadiens-Français," *Le Monde hébdomadaire*, no. 783, 17–23 Oct. 1963, 2.

61 André D'Allemagne, *Le R.I.N. de 1960 à 1963: Étude d'un groupe de pression au Québec* (Montreal: Étincelle, 1974), 61.

CHAPTER SEVEN

1 NA, MG31, E31 (Cadieux Papers), vol. 4, personal memo, 29 May 1969 (6 pp.), 1.

2 Ibid., memo, 29 Nov. 1967 (2 pp.). The lengthy account of French interference contained in Paul Martin's memoirs was written in retrospect, many years later, partly to justify himself. It ought to be read in conjunction with Marcel Cadieux's almost daily record, wherein Martin appears largely blind to the French threat and interested mainly in his own political career. Paul Martin, *A Very Public Life*, Vol. II, *So Many Worlds* (Toronto: Deneau, 1985), chap. 18.

3 "... ne peuvent se faire contre la France; nos origines et nos traditions s'y opposent. Il s'agit de savoir s'ils auront lieu sans la France ou avec la France." See John Hilliker and Donald Barry, *Canada's Department of External Affairs*, vol. II, *Coming of Age, 1946–1968* (Montreal: McGill-Queen's University Press, 1995), 393.

4 She says her husband decided not to tell her who his French informant was because when they next met him the expression on her face might give her away.

5 Pierre Godin, *La poudrière linguistique* (Montreal: Boréal, 1990), 188.

6 "Le sous-secrétaire d'Etat aux Affaires extérieures, M. Marcel Cadieux est, de bien des façons, le genre de diplomate le moins diplomate qui soit. Il est reconnus pour son franc parler ... " (*Le Soleil*, 23 Sept. 1965, 8).

7 Cadieux Papers, personal memo, 20 Jan. 1965 (2 pp.), 1.

8 Philippe Malaurie was a professor in the faculté de droit at Poitiers; Pierre Azard was his brother-in-law and lived in Paris. Cadieux's file on this affair, which does not give the analysis he gives elsewhere, is in NA, Cadieux Papers, vol. 6, file 6–13.

9 Cadieux Papers, personal memo, 8 Dec. 1966. Dates cited in this paragraph are those of Cadieux's memoranda.

10 Ibid., personal memo, 19 Dec. 1966 (3 pp.).

11 Ibid., personal memo, 30 Jan. 1967 (Antigua) (5 pp.).

12 Ibid., four-page memorandum to Paul Martin attached to a personal memo dated 28 Nov. 1967.

13 Ibid., personal memo, 25 Oct. 1969 (5 pp.), 3.

14 Interview with J. Gordon Robertson, 18 Feb. 1998.

15 Cadieux Papers, vol. 13, file 13–1, memo of 25 May 1972.

16 Ibid., personal memo, 26 Sept. 1966 (3 pp.), 2.

17 Ibid., personal memo, 17 May 1967 (3 pp.).

18 Ibid., Cadieux to Tremblay, 29 Feb. 1968, 3.

19 "À son avis, il est bien préférable que cette entreprise soit liée à M. Trudeau plutôt qu'à M. Pearson. Il estime que M. Trudeau a l'esprit plus clair que M. Pearson et que ses méthodes de négociation sont plus valables." Ibid., secret memo, 5 June 1968 (4 pp.)

20 Ibid.,, personal memo, 3 March 1965 (3pp.).

21 Mitchell Sharp, *Which Reminds Me ... A Memoir* (Toronto: University of Toronto Press, 1994), 171–3.

22 Interview with J. Gordon Robertson, 18 Feb. 1998.

23 Recollection in ibid.

24 Cadieux Papers, vol. 13, file 13–2, memo of 19 Nov. 1970 (18 pp.), 5–7.

25 Sharp, *Which Reminds Me*, 186–97.

26 Cadieux Papers, personal memo, 30 Oct. 1968 (8 pp.).

27 Ibid., personal memo, 15 April 1969 (1 page).

28 Ibid., Cadieux to Jetty [sic] Robertson, 541 Manor Avenue, Rockcliffe Park, Ottawa, 17 July 1968 (1 p.).

29 Ibid., Cadieux to Jetty Robertson, 24 Oct. 1968.

30 Ibid., Cadieux to Tremblay, 19 Sept. 1967, 5: "Evidemment, les Français se conduisent comme des cochons mais si nous rappelons les Ambassadeurs nous plaçons Québec dans une situation où il a officiellement et exclusivement le monopole des relations avec la France."

31 Ibid., vol. 13, file 13–4, memo of 15 March 1973, reporting a conversation with Francis Lacoste during lunch that day.

32 Ibid., vol. 13, file 13–5, personal memo, 20 Sept. 1974 (1 p.).

33 Ibid., memo of 2 May 1968 (5 pp.), 3.

34 Ibid., memo of 19 Feb. 1968 (9 pp.), 3.

35 Ibid., memo, 27 March 1968 (5 pp.), 4.

36 See *L'Express*, no. 2388 (10–16 April 1997), 24–33.

37 Cadieux Papers, personal memo, 19 Feb. 1968 (9 pp.), 4–5.

38 Ibid., personal memo, 12 March 1968 (4 pp.), 3–4.

39 Ibid., personal memo, 9 Feb. 1967 (4 pp.), 2–3.

40 Paul Gérin-Lajoie, "De Gaulle et le Québec," *Espoir*, no. 86 (Sept. 1992), 104–6.

41 Jean Lacouture, "L'assemblée des parlementaires francophones," *Le Monde hebdomadaire*, no. 1040, 26 Sept.–2 Oct. 1968, 6.

42 Cadieux papers, personal memo, 19 Feb. 1968 (9 pp.), 4.

43 Ibid., personal memos of 19 Feb. 1968 (9 pp.) and 14 March (22 pp.) with a covering letter to Paul Tremblay.

44 Ibid., Cadieux to Tremblay, 22 March 1968. *Option Québec* was pub-

lished in January 1968, four months after *Le Devoir* printed a manifesto that was the heart of it, on 19–21 September 1967. See René Lévesque, *Option Québec* (1968) new ed. (Montreal: Typo, 1997).

45 "Autrement dit, je suis joli, je sens bon, je suis intelligent mais on ne m'écoute pas."

46 Cadieux papers, Cadieux to Paul Tremblay, 2 May 1968 (5 pp.), 2–3.

47 Ibid., vol. 5, file 5–12, Cadieux to Tremblay, 16 May 1968, 2. The date 25 June was marked for a forthcoming federal election.

48 Ibid., Cadieux to Tremblay, 2 May 1968 (5 pp.), 3.

49 Ibid., personal memo, 15 Nov. 1967 (2 pp. + enclosure).

50 John English, *The Worldly Years: The Life of Lester Pearson*, vol. II, *1949–1972* (Toronto: Knopf. 1992), 286.

51 Cadieux Papers, Cadieux to Tremblay, 16 May 1968 (3 pp.).

CHAPTER EIGHT

1 Confidential source.

2 Paul Martin, *A Very Public Life*, vol. II, *So Many Worlds*, (Toronto: Deneau, 1985), 589.

3 See above, chap. 7.

4 Lester B. Pearson, *Mike: The Memoirs of the Right Honourable Lester B. Pearson*, vol. III, *1957–1968*, (Toronto: University of Toronto Press, 1975), 264, 267–9.

5 *Canada, Debates of the House of Commons*, session 1965, II, 1103–7.

6 Martin, *A Very Public Life*, II, 596.

7 *Globe and Mail*, Saturday 14 Sept. 1968, 1 and 2; *Le Monde*, 13 and 15 Sept. 1968, carried reports of the affair by Jean Tainturier, its correspondent in Montreal.

8 *Le Devoir*, 19 Sept. 1968, 9.

9 Claude Morin, *Les choses comme elles étaient: une autobiographie politique* (Montreal: Boréal, 1994), 199ff., 329.

10 *Debates of the House of Commons*, session 1968, I–II, 15, 66–7, 530, 628, 2075.

11 For Rossillon's extensive activities in or with the Acadian communities in New Brunswick, which continued to summer 1997, see above chap. 5.

12 Paul Martin, *A Very Public Life*, II, chap. 18; Pearson, *Mike*, III, chap. 9; NA, MG31, E31, Cadieux Papers.

13 De Gaulle, *Lettres, notes et carnets* [for 1962] (Paris: Plon, 1986), 245.

14 Jacques Godechot, ed., *Les constitutions de la France depuis 1789* (Paris: Garnier-Flammarion, 1970), 411–50.

15 Gildea, too, describes the Fifth Republic as "a republican dictatorship." Robert Gildea, *France since 1945* (Oxford: Oxford University Press, 1997), 45ff; see also W.G. Andrews, *Presidential Government in Gaullist*

France (Albany: SUNY Press, 1982), 127–55, "The de Gaulle Dictatorship"; and Andrew Knapp, *Gaullism since de Gaulle* (Aldershot: Dartmouth Publishing, 1994), 337.

16 Pierre Viansson-Ponté, *Histoire de la république gaullienne* (Paris: Laffont, 1971), 89.

17 "Et quand un accommodement est trouvé sur ce point, on tombe dans le byzantinisme sur les mots: un accord, non: ce sera une 'entente', coiffée par un échange de notes entre l'ambassadeur de France et le ministre canadien des Affaires extérieures." Jean Chapdelaine, "Le général de Gaulle et le Québec," *L'Action nationale* (Quebec), 22 (Jan. 1991), 95–6.

18 Dale Thomson, *Jean Lesage and the Quiet Revolution* (Toronto: Macmillan, 1984), 435; for the texts of the entente and Gérin-Lajoie's speech, see Arthur E. Blanchette, ed., *Canadian Foreign Policy 1955–1965: Selected Speeches and Documents* (Toronto: McClelland and Stewart, 1977), 393–5, 396–400.

19 Jean-Charles Bonenfant, "Les relations extérieures du Québec," *Études internationales*, I (Feb. 1970), 81–2 concerning "l'affaire Lipkowski".

20 C.L.H., "Exclusif: le nègre du Québec," in *L'Express* (Paris), 23–29 Nov. 1970, 81.

21 "Messages de sympathie de MM. Schumann et Chaban-Delmas après l'exécution de M. Laporte: Chr. 17 octobre [1970]," in *La Politique étrangère de la France: textes et documents*, 2ᵉ semestre 1970, 301; and *Revue politique et parlementaire*, 72ᵉ année, no. 815 (Nov. 1970), 106. "Exécution" is the term used by the FLQ. See Pierre Vallières, *L'exécution de Pierre Laporte: les dessous de l'opération essai* (Montreal: Éd. Québec Amérique, 1977).

22 *Études internationales*, I (June 1970), 84.

23 Bernard Dorin, "Un combat de quarante ans pour la cause du Quebec," *Les cahiers d'histoire du Québec au XXe siècle* (Centre de recherche Lionel–Groulx), no. 7 (spring 1997), 24–38.

24 *Le Devoir*, 18 Oct. 1976, 3.

25 Ibid., 9 Sept. 1995, A1

26 John P. Schlegel, SJ, *The Deceptive Ash: Bilingualism and Canadian Policy in Africa, 1957–1971* (Washington, DC: University Press of America, 1978), 463; J.L. Granatstein and Robert Bothwell, *Pirouette: Pierre Trudeau and Canadian Foreign Policy* (Toronto: University of Toronto Press, 1990), 141–4.

27 Eldon Black, *Direct Intervention: Canada–France Relations, 1967–1974* (Ottawa: Carleton University Press, 1996), 203; Dale Thomson, *Vive le Québec Libre!* (Toronto: Deneau, 1988), 329. A general account of these manoeuvres in Africa is given in Granatstein and Bothwell, *Pirouette*, chap. 5.

28 Granatstein and Bothwell, *Pirouette*, chap. 5.

29 Mitchell Sharp, *Which Reminds Me ... A Memoir* (Toronto: University of Toronto Press, 1994), 186–92.

30 Bernard Dorin, "Un combat de quarante ans pour la cause du Québec," *Les cahiers d'histoire du Québec au XXe siècle* (Centre de recherche Lionel–Groulx), no. 7 (spring 1997), 34.

31 Pearson, *Mike*, III, 263.

32 *Canadian News Facts* (Toronto, 1969), 217.

33 NA, Cadieux Papers, secret memo written at New York, 24 Sept. 1969 (4 pp.), 4.

34 Louis-Bernard Robitaille, "Pour les Québécois de Paris, une nuit d'élections historiques," *La Presse*, 17 Nov. 1976, A15.

35 Jean Victor Allard, *Mémoires du Général ... , en collaboration avec Serge Bernier* (Boucherville, Que.: Éditions de Mortagne, 1985), chaps. 11 and 12; J.L. Granatstein, *The Generals: The Canadian Army Senior Commanders in the Second World War* (Toronto, Stoddart, 1993), chap. 9, "The Absence of Francophone Generals."

36 John Hilliker and Donald Barry, *Canada's Department of External Affairs*, vol. II, *Coming of Age, 1946–1968* (Montreal: McGill-Queen's University Press, 1995), 393.

37 Granatstein and Bothwell, *Pirouette*, 141.

38 "M. Dupuy visits French Africa," *External Affairs*, 13 (1961), 94–9; Schlegel, SJ, *The Deceptive Ash*, 225–7, 250–1.

39 "Au sens 'politique', il s'agit plutôt d'un myth créateur tel que l'entendait Sorel: au carrefour de l'affectivité et de l'action, c'est la mise en oeuvre par les institutions et les hommes d'une solidarité naturelle et consciente créée par la communauté de culture." P.J. Franceschini, "La création d'une agence de coopération ... ," *Le Monde hebdomadaire*, 18–24 June 1970, 6.

40 *Univers francophone* (Paris), no. 1, (Sept. 1987), 11. France was contributing 41 per cent, and Belgium 12 per cent.

41 Beaudoin Bollaert, "Le royaume de la francophonie," *France–Amérique*, 15–21 Nov. 1997, 3.

42 Jean Morrison, "Canada's Role in a French Commonwealth," *Behind the Headlines*, 27 (Oct. 1967), 17.

43 Maurice Riel, "Septembre 1960: la fondation de la Maison du Québec à Paris," in *Le Québec 1967–1987: du général de Gaulle au Lac Meech* (Montreal, 1987), 44.

44 *Le Monde hebdomadaire*, no. 1069, 17–23 April 1969.

45 Gilles Houde, "10e anniversaire de l'OFQJ," *Le Devoir*, 29 Jan. 1977, 18.

46 Michèle Georges, "Ils étudient au Québec," *L'Express*, no. 2393, 15–21 May 1997, 97–8.

47 André Passeron, "Vers une profonde réforme de l'ENA et de la haute administration," *Le Monde hebdomadaire*, no. 1164, 11–17 Feb. 1971, 6.

48 Études internationales, (1970), 115–16.

49 Passeron, "Vers un profonde réforme de l'ENA," 6.

50 Claude Morin, Québec versus Ottawa: The Struggle for Self-Government, 1960–72 (Toronto: University of Toronto Press, 1976), 40.

51 Among its members were Gaston Cholette, Jean-Guy Laurendeau, and Jean Tardif. See Jean-Charles Bonenfant, "Les relations extérieures du Québec," Études internationales, 2 (1971), 136–7.

52 This does, indeed, seem to have been the prevalent idea in the Department of External Affairs. See Hilliker and Barry, Canada'a Department of External Affairs, II, 400.

53 NA, Cadieux Papers, Marcel Cadieux to Paul Tremblay, 29 Feb. 1968.

54 Morin, Québec versus Ottawa, 40.

55 Le Devoir, 28 May 1973, 11.

56 Jack Aubry, "Trudeau's Secret Quebec Plan: Classified Documents Show 1976 Cabinet Discussed Partition, Use of Army," Ottawa Citizen, 16 June 1997, A1, A2; 17 June 1997, A1, A15.

57 Such is the opinion too of Pierre Godin; Godin, La poudrière linguistique (Montreal: Boréal, 1990), 105. However, Eldon Black and Max Yalden both disagree with this interpretation and think of Couve as a sincere peacemaker, quietly in disagreement with the troublesome policies of his master.

58 Martin, A Very Public Life, II, 576.

59 NA, Cadieux Papers, file 4–7, Confidential memo from Paul Martin to Prime Minister Pearson in French (5 pp.), dated 16 June 1967, with covering letter of 19 June.

60 Ibid., vol. 13, file 13–4, Marcel Cadieux's memo of 15 March 1973 (2 pp.).

61 "Le Général a été rassurant au sujet de son voyage au Canada."

62 Martin, A Very Public Life, II, 597.

63 Cadieux Papers, "Compte-rendu d'un entretien entre le Premier Ministre du Canada et le Premier Ministre de France ... 30 Sept. 1968 de 3 p.m. à 4:40 p.m."

64 Mme Anita Cadieux assures me that Couve de Murville was generally hostile to the English-speaking world, partly as a result of his time as tutor to Harold Nicolson's children in summer 1928 when he was twenty-one years old; see Harold Nicolson, Diaries and Letters 1945–1962 (London: Collins, 1968), 349.

65 NA, Cadieux Papers, vol. 13, file. 13–6, memo of 14 Feb. 1974.

66 Ibid., vol. 11, file 11–14, a letter of 7 June 1976 enclosing an article from Le Soir of 3 June 1976 summarizing a lecture given in Antwerp by Couve de Murville.

67 "Je vous raconte tout cela car cela prouve tout de même qu'il n'est pas trop sous l'influence du 'grand patron.'" See NA, Cadieux Papers, file

4–6, confidential letter from Mme Pauline Vanier to Marcel Cadieux 15 Sept. 1967.

68 Sharp, *Which Reminds Me*, 191.

69 NA, Cadieux Papers, memo, 9 Feb. 1967 (4 pp.).

70 *Le Devoir*, 9 Nov. 1985, 11; Hélène Galarneau, "Chronique des relations extérieures du Canada et du Quebec," *Études internationales*, 17 (1986), 149.

71 *Le Devoir*, 9 Nov. 1985, A1, A11, and A12.

72. Lucien Bouchard, *À visage découvert* (Montreal: Boréal, 1992), 148ff.

73 Jack Aubry, "Federalists' 'Plan F': Flood Canada with Francophones," *Ottawa Citizen*, 18 Nov. 1997, A8.

74 Lucien Bouchard, *À visage découvert*, 221ff.

75 Christian Rioux, "Changement de garde à Paris," *Le Devoir*, 7 May 1997.

76 "Quebec's Bid for UN Status Quashed," *Globe and Mail*, 21 June 1997, A4.

77 François Brousseau, "Parizeau lance le ballet diplomatique européen," *Le Devoir*, 6 July 1993, A4.

78 Michel Vastel, "Parizeau aurait agi tout de suite," *Le Soleil*, 7 May 1997, A1 and A2.

79 Agence France Presse, "Bouchard se rendra en France cet automne," *Le Devoir*, 8 July 1997, A4; Christian Rioux, "Simard constate le maintien de l'intérêt de la France pour le Québec," *Le Devoir*, 9 July 1997, A4; Louis-Bernard Robitaille, "Paris déroulera le tapis rouge pour Bouchard," *La Presse*, 10 Sept. 1997, B1.

80 See, for example, a series of three articles by the editor of *Le Devoir*, Lise Bissonette, in late June and early July 1997; and Claude Bariteau, "Urgences en vue du prochain référendum, les souverainistes doivent réveiller au danger d'être les complices du Canada," *Le Devoir*, 8 July 1997, A7.

81 Christian Rioux, "Le Québec selon Jospin," *Le Devoir*, 9 July 1997, A1.

82 Jules Richer, "Un ambassadeur blessé," *Le Devoir*, 1-2 Nov. 1997, A7; Vincent Marissal, "Un ambassadeur 'meurtri': Jacques Roy n'a pas apprécié la façon dont il a été traité lors de la visite de Bouchard à Paris," *La Presse*, 1 Nov. 1997, B9.

83 See Hans Ravn (of Toronto), "France Plots with Quebec," *European*, 3–9 July 1997, 8.

CHAPTER NINE

1 "Diplomat's Remarks Seen as Challenge to Trudeau," *Telegram* (Toronto), 18 Sept. 1968, 59; author's interview with Max Yalden, 22 Jan. 1998.

2 John Ralston Saul, *Reflections of a Siamese Twin: Canada at the End of the Twentieth Century* (Toronto: Viking, 1997), 375–77.

3 Interview with John Starnes, 14 Aug. 1997.

4 Paul Martin, *A Very Public Life*, chap. 18, "A Tale of Three Cities"; NA, Cadieux Papers, MG31, E31, vol. 13, file 13–4, secret memo of Cadieux reporting a conversation with Francis Lacoste, 15 March 1973 (2 pp.)

5 Bernard Dorin, "Un combat de quarante ans pour la cause du Québec," *Les cahiers d'histoire du Québec au XXᵉ siècle* (Centre de recherche Lionel–Groulx), no. 7 (spring 1997), 27; Claude Morin and Paul Gérin-Lajoie describe Maillard as a "diplomate sympathique au Québec," "un allié et un collaborateur assidu et efficace pour le Québec" See Claude Morin, *L'art de l'impossible: la diplomatie québécoise depuis 1960* (Montreal: Boréal, 1987), 430; Paul Gérin-Lajoie, "De Gaulle et le Québec," *Espoir* (Paris), no. 86 (Sept. 1992), 105.

6 Pierre de Menthon, "Les activités du Consulat Général de France à Québec, 1967–1972," *Études gaulliennes*, 7 (1979), 91.

7 NA, Cadieux Papers, secret memo, 6 Sept. 1968 (5 pp.), 1.

8 Ibid., secret memo, 21 Aug. 1968 (7 pp.), 3.

9 Peter Worthington, "The Message in Trudeau's Message," *Telegram* (Toronto), 13 Sept. 1968, 2.

10 Reg Whitaker, "Apprehended Insurrection? RCMP Intelligence and the October Crisis," *Queen's Quarterly*, 100 no. 2 (summer 1993), 383–406.

11 NA, Cadieux Papers, secret memo, 19 Sept. 1968 (7 pp.), 1.

12 Confidential source.

13 Pierre Godin, *René Lévesque, héro malgré lui* (Montreal: Boréal, 1997) 719; Richard Cléroux, *Pleins feux sur les services secrets canadiens* (Montreal: Éditions de l'homme, 1990), 241.

14 Confidential source; testimony of Joseph Ferraris to the McDonald Commission, 14962–5, submissions to D.C. McDonald, et al., *Commission of Inquiry Concerning Certain Activities of the RCMP* (Ottawa: Queen's Printer, 1981).

15 Cléroux, *Pleins feux*, 230–2; John Starnes told me on 14 August 1997 that Trudeau and his government were never much interested in the French but wanted only to counteract the separatists in Quebec.

16 Nick Auf der Maur, "All the Signs of Some Very Weird Times in Quebec History," *Montreal Gazette*, 8 April 1992, A2.

17 Louis Fournier, *F.L.Q.: The Anatomy of an Underground Movement* (Toronto, NC Press, 1984), 26, 33, 59, 60, 78.

18 For example, Richard Gwyn says almost nothing about French influence or interference in his study, *The Northern Magus: Pierre Trudeau and Canadians* (Toronto: McCelland and Stewart, 1980), nor do William Johnson in *A Canadian Myth: Quebec, between Canada and the Illusion of Utopia* (Montreal: Robert Davies, 1994), Graham Fraser in *René*

Lévesque and the Parti Québécois in Power (Toronto: Macmillan, 1984), or Michael D. Behiels in *Prelude to Quebec's Quiet Revolution: Liberalism versus Neo-Nationalism, 1945–1960* (Montreal: McGill-Queen's University Press, 1985).

19 James Littleton, *Target Nation: Canada and the Western Intelligence Network* (Toronto: Lester and Orpen Dennys and CBC Enterprises, 1986); John Sawatsky in *Men in the Shadows: the RCMP Security Service* (Toronto: Doubleday, 1980).

20 This document was reprinted in the *Ottawa Citizen* on 17 June 1997, A15.

21 Marc Lavallée, *Adieu la France, salut l'Amérique* (Montreal: Stanké, 1982), 106ff.

22 Claude Morin, *Les choses comme elles étaient: une autobiographie politique* (Montreal: Boréal, 1994), 345; see also 198, 329, 330; Memorandum of 26 Aug. 1997 to the author by Peter Marwitz.

23 *Globe and Mail*, 14 Dec. 1976, 10.

24 Confidential source.

25 De Menthon, "Les activités du Consulat Général," 92.

26 Ibid., 91.

27 See below chap. 13.

28 Cléroux, *Pleins feux*, 267, 437.

29 This was not known in 1980 when John Sawatsky discussed Brunet's activities in *Men in the Shadows* (Toronto: Totem Books, 1983), 210–11, 213–25, 227–8.

30 Ibid., chap. 18; Louis Fournier et al. *La police secrète au Québec* (Montreal: Éditions Québec/Amérique, 1978), 40.

31 Louis Fournier et al, *La police secrète au Québec* (Montreal: Éditions Québec/Amérique, 1978), 15–40, "Dix ans d'opérations (1968–1978)."

32 Gilles Paquin, "Morin traitant avec le cerveau de l'escouade anti-séparatiste," *La Presse*, 3 May 1992; Gilles Paquin, "Pour s'y trouver dans l'affaire Morin," *La Presse*, 16 May 1992; Normand Lester, *Enquêtes sur les services secrets* (Montreal: Éditions de L'homme, 1998), chap. 7.

33 Morin, *Les choses comme elles étaient: une autobiographie politique* (Montreal: Boréal, 1994), 198–211, 325–45.

34 Sawatsky, *Men in the Shadows*, 247–51, 278–81.

35 Gilles Paquin and Denis Lessard, "La GRC aurait placé Louise Beaudoin et François Cloutier sous écoute," *La Presse*, 2 April 1992, 1–2.

36 *Montreal Gazette*, 7 March 1978, 1.

37 Jean-Claude Leclerc, "La gendarmerie politique du Canada," *Le Devoir*, 14 May 1976, 4.

38 Pierre Cloutier, "La Commission McDonald et l'Opération Ham: des faits troublants," *La Presse*, 13 April 1992, B3.

39 Confidential source.

40 Littleton, *Target Nation*, 141ff.

41 NA, Cadieux Papers. vol. 13, file 13–2, secret memo of 20 Nov. 1970 (12 pp.), 10. He seemed to have forgotten, however, the RCMP report that the department had received on 8 December 1966: Cadieux Papers, personal memo, 8 Dec. 1966 (3 pp.).

42 John Starnes, "Trudeau's Critical Judgment of RCMP Unfair and Unjustified," *Ottawa Citizen*, 28 Dec. 1993; Pierre Trudeau, *Memoirs* (Toronto: McClelland and Stewart, 1993), 130ff.

43 Lester B. Pearson, *Mike: the Memoirs of the Right Honourable Lester B. Pearson*, vol. III, *1957–1968* (Toronto: University of Toronto Press, 1975), 242–3.

44 Sharp, *Which Reminds Me ... A Memoir* (Toronto: University of Toronto Press, 1994),192–97.

45 George Bain, *Globe and Mail*, 23 Dec. 1971; Pierre Vallières, *L'exécution de Pierre Laporte: les dessous de l'opération essai* (Montreal: Éditions Québec/Amérique, 1977), appendix I, 177–184.

46 David Pugliese, "Military Feared FLQ Would Steal Nuclear Arms," *Ottawa Citizen*, 16 Feb. 1998, 1–2, citing John Clearwater, *Canadian Nuclear Weapons: The Untold Story of Canada's Nuclear Arsenal* (Toronto: Dundurn Press, 1998).

47 Confidential source.

48 Interview with John Starnes, 14 Aug. 1997.

49 Starnes, "Trudeau's Critical judgment"; Reg. Whitaker, "Apprehended Insurrection? RCMP Intelligence and the October Crisis," *Queen's Quarterly*, 100 no. 2 (summer 1993·), 383–406.

50 Interview with J. Gordon Robertson, 18 Feb. 1998.

51 Quoted in Littleton, *Target Nation*, 130–1, and in Robert Chodos and Nick Auf der Maur, eds., *Quebec, a Chronicle, 1968–1972* (Toronto: Lewis & Samuel, 1972), 50–51.

52 Sharp, *Which Reminds Me*, 195.

53 Interview with Inspector Joseph Ferraris, 26 Aug. 1997.

54 Michael Mandel, "Discrediting the McDonald Commission," *Canadian Forum*, 61 (March 1982), 14–17.

55 Cléroux, *Pleins feux*, 85.

56 Interview with John Starnes, 14 Aug. 1997.

57 Normand Lester, *Enquêtes sur les services secrets* (Montreal: Éditions de l'homme, 1998), 332–4.

58 Cléroux, *Pleins feux*, 243–4.

59 Littleton, *Target Nation*, 154.

60 *Report of the Royal Commission on Security* (Mackenzie Report) (Ottawa: Information Canada, 1969), 105–16.

61 Pierre de Menthon, "Les activités du consulat général de France à Québec, 1967–1972," *Études gaulliennes*, 7 (1979), 89–94.

62 Confidential source.

63 Cléroux, *Pleins feux*, 85.

64 Interview with John Starnes, 14 Aug. 1997.

65 Littleton, *Target Nation*, 156.

66 For an account of the CSE, see John Bryden, *Best-Kept Secret: Canadian Secret Intelligence in the Second World War* (Toronto: Lester Publishing, 1993), 2–3, 328–33.

67 Michael Frost, *Moi, Mike Frost, espion canadian: activités ultrasecrètes à l'étranger et au pays* (Toronto: Éditions de l'homme, 1994), 319.

68 Ibid., 320.

69 Ibid., 130, 191, 205, 322–3.

CHAPTER TEN

1 Dan G. Loomis, *Not Much Glory: Quelling the F.L.Q.* (Toronto: Deneau, 1984); and Loomis, *The Somalia Affair: Reflections on Peacemaking and Peacekeeping* (Ottawa: DGL Publications, 1996), see chap. 2, 15–40, "Lester Pearson's Strategy for Quelling the FLQ: Peacemaking and Peacekeeping Criteria in Civil Conflicts." The latter draws on the recollections of John Ross Matheson.

2 Éric Bédard, *Chronique d'une insurrection appréhendée: la crise d'Octobre et le milieu universitaire* (Silléry, Que.: Septentrion, 1998), 55; Gustave Morf, *Le terrorisme québécois* (Montreal: Éditions de l'homme, 1970), 31–6.

3 Georges Lefebvre, *Les paysans du nord pendant la révolution française*, thesis, two vols. in one, Paris and Lille: n.p., 1924; repr. Bari, 1959.

4 Georges Lefebvre, *La révolution française*, 3rd ed. (Paris: Presses universitaires de France, 1951).

5 Curzio Malaparte, *Technique du coup d'état*, trans. Juliette Bertrand, 1931, rev. ed. (Paris: Bernard Grasset, 1948), ix and 94.

6 Ibid., ix and 94.

7 John Shy and Thomas W. Collier, "Revolutionary War," in Peter Paret, ed., *Makers of Modern Strategy from Machiavelli to the Nuclear Age* (Princeton, NJ: Princeton University Press, 1986), chap. 27 and 839–48.

8 Clausewitz's famous treatise, *Vom Kriege* (1833), first translated into English in 1873 as *On War*, has appeared in several later translations. Other volumes of unpublished writings appeared subsequently. For an expert summary account, see Peter Paret, ed., *Makers of Modern Strategy from Machiavelli to the Nuclear Age* (Princeton, NJ: Princeton University Press, 1986), chap. 7.

9 Che Guevara, *Guerrilla Warfare* (1961), trans. J.P. Morray (New York: Vintage Books, 1969); and a revised third edition, ed. Brian Loveman and T.M. Davies (Wilmington, Del.: SR Books, 1997).

10 Che Guevara, *Revolution in the Revolution?* (New York: Monthly Review Press), 1967.

11 Pierre Vallières, *Nègres blancs d'Amérique* (Montreal: Édition Parti Pris, 1968), appendix 1, 509–26.

12 George Grivas, *General Grivas on Guerrilla Warfare*, trans. Agon Eoka Antarlopolemos (New York: Praeger, 1964).

13 Many editions, for example, Vancouver: Pulp Press, 1974. See Claire Sterling, *The Terror Network* (Berkeley, Calif.: Berkley Books, 1982), 19–20.

14 Griffith, *On Guerilla Warfare* (New York: Praeger, 1961), especially on Chinese insurgency methods; and Griffith, *The Chinese People's Liberation Army* (New York: McGraw Hill, 1967).

15 Peter Paret and John W. Shy, *Guerrillas in the 1960s* (New York: Praeger, 1962); Franklin M. Osanka, ed., *Modern Guerrilla Warfare* (1962) (New York: Free Press of Glencoe, 1966); Major John S. Pustay, *Counterinsurgency Warfare* (New York: Free Press, 1965); Lt. Col. John J. McCuen, *The Art of Counter-Revolutionary War: the Strategy of Counter-insurgency* (London: Faber & Faber, 1966); Lt.-Col. T.N. Greene, ed., *The Guerrilla and How to Fight Him* (New York: Praeger, 1966).

16 *Revolt in the Desert* (New York: Doran, 1927), and *The Seven Pillars of Wisdom*, new ed. (London: Jonathan Cape, 1940).

17 Sir Robert Thompson, *Defeating Communist Insurgency: The Lessons of Malaya and Vietnam* (New York: Praeger, 1966); Major Anthony Crockett, "Action in Malaya," James E. Doughty, "The Guerilla War in Malaya," and Paul M.A. Linebarger, "They Call'em Bandits in Malaya," all in Franklin M. Osanka, ed., *Modern Guerilla Warfare* (New York: Free Press of Glencoe, 1966), 293–322; Lucien W. Pye, *Guerrilla Communism in Malaya, Its Social and Political Meaning* (Princeton, NJ: Princeton University Press, 1956).

18 Peter Paret, *French Revolutionary Warfare from Indochina to Algeria: The Analysis of Political and Military Doctrine* (New York: Praeger, 1964).

19 Loomis, *The Somalia Affair*, 23; Standing Committee on National Defence, *Minutes of Proceedings and Evidence, No. 11 (Tuesday, 21 June 1966) Respecting Main Estimates 1966–67 of the Department of National Defence* (Ottawa: Queen's Printer, 1966), 269–306, 296.

20 Robert V. Daniels, *Year of the Heroic Guerrilla: World Revolution and Counterrevolution in 1968* (Cambridge, Mass.: Harvard University Press, 1989), 149ff.

21 Ibid., passim; and Sterling, *The Terror Network*, chap. 1.

22 Author's interview with John Ross Matheson, 6 April 1998; also quoted in Loomis, *The Somalia Affair*, 23.

23 Author's interviews with General Loomis on 20 March and 3 April 1998; Jean Victor Allard, *Mémoires du Général ..., en collaboration avec Serge Bernier* (Boucherville, Que.: Éditions de Mortagne, 1985), chap. 12.

24 Quoted in Robert Speaight, *Vanier, Soldier, Diplomat and Governor General: A Biography* (Toronto: Collins, 1970), 283.

25 Author's interview with John Ross Matheson, 6 April 1998.

26 Standing Committee on National Defence, *Minutes* (Tuesday, 21 June 1966), 269–306 (see NA, XC34–271/1–11); *House of Commons Debates*, 17 Oct. 1970, 260–1, 272–6. See also Allard, *Mémoires*, 362, but note that the date of the briefing is wrongly cited as 20 May 1966 instead of 21 June 1966.

27 Allard, *Mémoires*, 368. Jean Lesage was premier of Quebec until he lost the election of 16 June 1966 to Daniel Johnson *père*.

28 Ibid., chap. 12, "Commandant de la Force mobile."

29 Ibid., 353.

30 *Le Devoir*, 19 Oct. 1967, 8.

31 Bédard, *Chronique*, 34–100.

32 "Des chrétiens de l'U. de M. manifestent leur solidarité envers Gagnon et Vallières," *Le Devoir*, 28 Oct. 1966, 4. None of them was in the history or political science departments.

33 Dan G. Loomis, *Not Much Glory: Quelling the F.L.Q.* (Toronto: Deneau, 1984), 156–7.

34 Bédard, *Chronique*, 87; Loomis, *Not Much Glory*, 157.

35 Loomis, *The Somalia Affair*, 23–4.

36 Pierre Vallières, *L'exécution de Pierre Laporte: les dessous de l'opération essai* (Montreal: Éditions Québec/Amérique, 1977), chap. 2.

37 Quoted in Gérard Pelletier, *La crise d'octobre* (Montreal: Éditions du jour, 1971), 128. This book was written for Pelletier by Pierre Billon.

38 Bédard, *Chronique*, 108, 185.

39 Allard, *Mémoires*, 473.

40 Loomis, *Not Much Glory*, 160.

41 Ibid., 122.

42 Ibid., 143–5.

43 Pelletier, *La crise d'octobre*, 121–45.

44 Loomis, *Not Much Glory*, 65, 99.

45 Ibid., 146–7.

46 Juliet O'Neill, "Pearson Saved Hippie Youth Group," *Ottawa Citizen*, 4 April 1998, A7.

47 John Ross Matheson, *Canada's Flag: A Search for a Country* (Belleville, Ont.: 1986), chap. 8 and 198.

CHAPTER ELEVEN

1 P.J. Franceschini, "Essor et limites de la francophonie," *Le Monde heb-domadaire*, no. 1130, (18–24 June 1970), 6.

2 Alfred Grosser, *La politique extérieure de la Ve républic* (Paris: Seuil, 1965), 77.

3 Jean-François Bayart, "France-Afrique: aider moins pour aider mieux," *Politique internationale*, no. 56 (1992), 141; "Seeking Freedom from France," *Ottawa Citizen*, 20 May 1997, A1–A2; Patrick de Saint-Exupéry, "Afrique: la France à contre-pied," *Le Figaro*, 10 June 1997, A4; Eric Fottorino, "France-Afrique, les liaisons dangereuses," (a series of five retrospective articles), *Le Monde*, 22–26 July 1997; John Chipman, *French Power in Africa* (Oxford: Blackwell, 1989), passim.

4 Letter to the author dated 24 Aug. 1997.

5 A brief summary of this French empire, with a map, is to be found in Ieuan LL. Griffiths, *An Atlas of African Affairs*, rev. ed. (London: Routledge, 1985), 102–3.

6 Franck Petiteville, "Quatre décennies de 'coopération franco–africaine': usages et usure d'un clientélisme," *Études internationales*, 27 (1996), 572.

7 "CFA-Franc Zone: France Retreats from Its Empire," *Economist*, 330 no. 7846, (15–21 Jan. 1994), 45.

8 Marc Mertillo, "La coopération militaire de la France en Afrique," *Revue française d'administration publique*, no. 46 (1988), 91; "France in Africa: Mitterrand's Muddle," *Economist*, 326 no. 7800, 27 Feb.–5 March 1993, 42.

9 Griffiths, *Atlas*, 102.

10 Alec Russell, "More French Troops Sent to Embattled Brazzaville," *Ottawa Citizen*, 9 June 1997; *Le Devoir*, 11 June 1997, A1, A5; Arnaud de La Grange, "Renforts militaires français à Brazzaville," *Le Figaro*, 10 June 1997, A3.

11 See the columns of the French journal *Jeune Afrique*, in summer 1979, for example, 6 June, 16–17; 20 June, 14–15; 11 July, 17; 18 July, 27.

12 See above, chap. 10.

13 *Elf, l'empire d'essence* (Paris: Les dossiers du Canard enchainée, March 1998), 26, 61–4.

14 Jocelyn Coulon, "La langue française est en plein recul en Afrique," *Le Devoir*, 3 Sept. 1997, A1; Mireille Duteil, "La France va-t-elle perdre l'Afrique?," *Le Point*, no. 1297, (26 July 1997), 40–6.

15 *Le Monde hebdomadaire*, no. 2544, 9 Aug. 1997, 5.

16 See, for example, ibid., no. 2525, 29 March 1997, 6; Roger Faligot and Pascal Krop, *La Piscine: Les Services Secrets français depuis 1944* (Paris: Seuil, 1985); and Patrice Chairoff, *Dossier B. Comme Barbouzes* (Paris: Éditions Alain Moreau, 1975).

17 Philippe Gaillard, *Foccart parle: entretiens avec Philippe Gaillard*, 2 vols. (Paris: Fayard, 1997).

18 Douglas Porch, *The French Secret Services: A History of French Intelligence from the Dreyfus Affair to the Gulf War* (New York: Farrar, Straus and Giroux, 1995), 439–47. F.X. Verschave, *La Françafrique*, (Paris: Stock, 1998).

19 NA, Cadieux Papers, MG 31 E31, vol. 13, file 5–11, letter of Marcel Cadieux (Washington) to Paul Tremblay (Ottawa), 7 Jan. 1974. *The Délégué* apostolique in question was Monseigneur Jadot.

20 Cadieux pleaded prior engagements. (See ibid., vol. 9, file 9–4, Cadieux (Washington) to the President of the University of Vermont, Burlington, 27 April 1971 (1 p.).

21 *Le Monde hebdomadaire*, no. 1054, 2–8 Jan. 1969, 2.

22 *Les Amitiés acadiennes*, no. 13 (July 1980), 21.

23 See *Les Amitiés acadiennes*, no. 30 (4ᵉ trimestre 1984), 17.

24 Robert Gildea, *France since 1945* (Oxford: Oxford University Press, 1996), 223.

25 Jean-Louis Turlin, "TV5 USA: la grande chance de la francophonie," *France–Amérique, Edition internationale du Figaro*, 20–26 Dec. 1997, 41; James Baer, "Le rôle de TV5 dans le rayonnement internationale de la culture acadienne," in *Le congrès mondial acadien, l'Acadie en 2004, Actes des conférences et des tables rondes, 16–20 août 1994* (Moncton: Éditions d'Acadie, 1996), 114–18.

26 Eveline Bossé, *La Capricieuse à Québec en 1855: les premières retrouvailles de la France et du Canada* (Montréal: Éditions de la Presse Ltée, 1984), 46.

27 Ulric Barthe, ed., *Wilfrid Laurier on the Platform* (Quebec, n.p., 1890), 73.

28 Jacques Monet, SJ, *The Last Cannon Shot: A Study of French-Canadian Nationalism 1837–1850* (Toronto: University of Toronto Press, 1969), 393–9 and passim.

29 Fernand Ouellet, *Papineau, textes choisis et présentés*, 2nd ed., (Quebec City: Université Laval, 1970), 21–3.

30 Henri Bourassa, *Grande-Bretagne et Canada: Questions Actuelles* (Montréal: n.p., 1901), 15: part of a speech delivered on 20 Oct. 1901.

31 Henri Bourassa, *Patriotisme, Nationalisme, Impérialisme* (Montréal: n.p., 1923), 33–4.

32 Monet, *The Last Cannon Shot*, 399.

33 Claude Morin, "De Gaulle et l'émergence internationale du Québec," in *L'Action nationale* (March 1991), 419–31; see also André Patry, "Québec et les relations internationales," and Louise Beaudoin, "Les relations France–Québec," both in Claude Glayman and Jean Sarrazin, eds., *Dossier Québec* (Paris and Montreal: Stock, 1979), 377–95 and 397–413, respectively.

34 Mike Trickey, "Make 'Soft Power', Not War," *The Ottawa Citizen*, 13 April 1998, A4.

35 NA, Cadieux papers, vol. 13, file 13–4; memo 15 March 1973 (2 pp.).

36 *Le Monde hebdomadaire*, no. 1016, (4–10 April 1968), 6–7; and passim in 1970, especially 5 and 12 Feb., 8 Oct. and 10 Dec.

37 Léopold Genicot, ed., *Histoire de la Wallonie* (Toulouse: Privat, 1973), 463.

38 See *Le Point*, no. 1274, 56–61.

39 Claude de Groulart, De Gaulle: *"Vous avez dit Belgique?,"* suivi de *"petit discours insolent sur nous-mêmes"* (Lausanne: Favre, 1984), 41, in a chapter headed "Aide-toi, la France t'aidera."

40 Yves Cornu, "Wallonie, la tentation française," *Le Point*, no. 1274, 15 Feb. 1997, 56–61.

41 NA, Cadieux Papers, memo, 20 Oct. 1966 (4 pp.).

42 Black, *Direct Intervention*, 15, 26, 27; P.J. Franschesci, "La création d'une agence de coopération ... .," *Le Monde hebdomadaire*, no. 1130, 18–24 June 1970, 6.

43 *Québec libre* (Montreal), 1, no. 3 (June–July 1964), 8, a report from "Pierre Gravel, notre délégué permanent en Europe."

44 *Globe and Mail*, 14 Sept. 1968, 1–2.

45 Philippe Rossillon, "Coopération France–Acadie," in *Études gaulliennes*, 7, no. 27–8 (Sept.–Dec. 1979), 145.

46 André Patry, *Le Québec dans le monde* (Montreal: Leméac, 1980); Claude Morin, *L'art de l'impossible: la diplomatie québécoise depuis 1960* (Montreal: Boréal, 1987), 95–100.

47 Ibid., 69, 109, 112.

48 Morin, *L'art de l'impossible*, 96.

49 NA, Cadieux Papers, memos of 8, 9, 10, 11, etc., May 1967.

50 Serge Jaumain, "Le Centre d'études canadiennes (CEC), Université libre de Bruxelles (Belgique)," in *Cultures du Canada français*, 5 (fall 1988), 12–15. This is a publication of the *Centre de recherche en civilisation canadienne-française* at the University of Ottawa.

51 Gaston Cholette, *L'action internationale du Québec en matière linguistique: coopération avec la France et la francophonie de 1961 à 1995* (Quebec City: Laval University Press, 1997), 120–2.

52 *Études internationales*, 28 no. 1 (March 1997), 149.

53 John R.G. Jenkins, *Jura Separatism in Switzerland* (Oxford: Clarendon, 1986), 28.

54 *Les Amitiés acadiennes*, no. 5 (July 1978), 2.

55 Québec. Ministère des relations internationales, *Recueil des ententes internationales du Québec* (Quebec: Ministère des communications, 1984), 170.

56 Pichette, *L'Acadie par bonheur retrouvé*, 242; and see above, chap. 6.

57 *Acadie Infos*, no. 86 (nov. 1993), 3.

58 NA, Cadieux Papers, vol. 13, file 13–4, memo of 16 April 1973 (2 pp.).

59 Ibid., memo secret, 21 June 1973 (4 pp.), 3–4.

60 Rossillon, "Belgique et Acadie," *Les Amitiés acadiennes*, no. 2 (July 1977), 3; no. 3 (Nov. 1977), 14.

61 Philippe Rossillon, "Visite à Paris d'une délégation louisianaise," *Les Amitiés acadiennes*, no. 14 (Oct. 1980), 9.

62 André Maindron, "Quinze ans d'Amitiés acadiennes ou l'Acadie, vue de France," *Revue de l'Université de Moncton*, 27, no. 1 (1994), 294.

CHAPTER TWELVE

1 J.F. Bosher, *The French Revolution* (New York: Norton, 1988), chap. 11, "A New Leviathan," and 287–291, "The Bureaucratic Tradition"; Bosher, *French Finances 1770–1795: From Business to Bureaucracy* (Cambridge: Cambridge University Press, 1970), part 2, "The Bureaucratic Revolution"; and Bosher, "French Administration and Public Finance in Their European Setting," *The New Cambridge Modern History*, 12 vols. (Cambridge: Cambridge University Press, 1957–70), VIII, chap. 20.

2 For French abroad, see, for instance, Sanche de Gramont, *The French: Portrait of a People* (New York: Putnam, 1969), chap. 4, or Alain Peyrefitte, *Le mal français* (Paris: Plon, 1976), chaps. 28–34; and the observations of a Swiss who spent ten years in Paris, Herbert Lüthy, *France against Herself*, trans. Eric Mosbacher (New York: Meridian Books, 1957), 5–27. Adam Gopnik, "Papon's Paper Trial," *New Yorker*, 27 April–4 May 1998, 86–95. Alistair McAlpine, "Is Europe ready to be a French Colony?," *European*, 5–11 June 1997.

3 Eric Trottier, "Parizeau propose de commencer la rédaction de la future constitution du 'pays du Québec,'" *La Presse*, 24 May 1998, p. A6.

4 André D'Allemagne, *Le R.I.N. de 1960 à 1963: Étude d'un groupe de pression au Québec* (Montreal: Étincelle, 1974), 63; André Bernard, "Option Québec 1968–1997," in René Lévesque, *Option Québec*, new ed., (Montreal: Typo, 1997), 21; Graham Fraser, *René Lévesque and the Parti Québécois in Power* (Toronto: Macmillan, 1984), 59.

5 That calendar endured in France and was imposed throughout French-occupied Europe until Napoleon abolished it in An XIV (1806).

6 Jacques Godechot, *The Counter-Revolution, Doctrine and Action, 1789–1804*, trans. Salvator Attanasio, (Princeton, NJ: Princeton University Press, 1971), 217–20, 232–45; Colin Jones, *The Longman Companion to the French Revolution* (London: Longman, 1988), see index, 449; M.J. Sydenham, *The First French Republic, 1792–1804* (London: Batsford, 1974), 16, 20, 32, 37, 40, 305.

7 J.F. Bosher, *French Finances 1770–1795*, chap. 16 and 310–11; Michel
   Bruguière, *Gestionnaires et profiteurs de la Révolution* (Paris: Olivier
   Orban, 1986), 223–317; Thierry Pfister, *La république des fonctionnaires*
   (Paris: Seuil, 1990).

8 "Fonctionnaires : le trop plein," *France–Amérique*, 25 April–1 May
   1998, 8–9.

9 They are summarized in Bosher, *The French Revolution*, 137–8; their
   full texts are in, for example, Jacques Godchot, *Les constitutions de
   la France depuis 1789* (Paris: Garnier-Flammarion, 1970), 33–4,
   423–4.

10 Chantal Hébert in *Ottawa Citizen*, 24 June 1997, A11.

11 Pierre Arbour, *Quebec Inc.*, 146–8.

12 Keith Henderson, "Double Taxation System Costs Quebec $250 Million
    a Year," *Financial Post*, 8 April 1998, 17.

13 The current list runs to hundreds of pages. See Le Conseil de la vie
    française en Amérique, *Le répertoire de la vie française en Amérique,
    1997*, 31ᵉ éd. (56 rue St-Pierre, 1ᵉʳ étage, Québec G1K 4A1), 572.

14 Gérard Tougas, *La francophonie en péril* (Ottawa: Le cercle du livre de
    France, 1967), 122ff.

15 Frédéric Dumon, *La communauté franco-afro-malgache: ses origines, ses
    institutions, son évolution, Octobre 1958–June 1960* (Brussels: Université
    libre de Bruxelles, 1960), appendix 10: "Les [treize] constitutions des
    états membres de la communauté."

16 Anne Szulmajster-Celnikier, "Des serments de Strasbourg à la loi Toubon:
    le français comme affaire d'État," *Regards sur l'actualité*, no. 221 (May
    1996), see 49.

17 *Acadie Infos*, no. 117 (June 1997), 4.

18 Robert LeBidois, "Bilan de la deuxième biennale de la langue française à
    Quèbec," Le Devoir, 4 Oct. 1967, 5.

19 Norman Delisle, "Odette Lapalme dirigera la Commission de protection
    de la langue française," *Le Devoir*, 17 Aug. 1997, A5.

20 Diane Francis, "Artwork the Latest Target of Quebec's Tongue Troop-
    ers," *Financial Post*, 2 April 1998, 17.

21 Gaston Cholette, *L'action internationale du Québec en matière linguis-
    tique: coopération avec la France et la francophonie de 1961 à 1995*
    (Quebec City: Université Laval, 1997), 44; see also Arbour, *Québec Inc.*,
    chap. 6, "Québec Inc. et le dirigisme linguistique," and for a summary
    sketch, Xavier Deniau, *La francophonie* 3rd ed. (Paris: Presses universi-
    taires de France, 1995), 98–100.

22 See, for example, *Organisations et associations francophones: répertoire
    1989* (Paris: La documentation française, 1989), 107; Le Conseil de la
    vie française en Amérique, *Le répertoire*, 572 ; *Etat de la francophonie
    dans le monde: données 1994 et cinq enquêtes médités* (Paris: La docu-

mentation française, 1994), 543–7; Deniau, *La francophonie*, 59–88; Jean-Pierre Gomane, "Les institutions de la coopération française," *Études*, 342 (1975), 851–66; Michel Tétu, *La francophonie: histoire, problematique, perspectives* (Montreal: Guérin littérature, 1987), 303–15; *Le Québec international: repertoire descriptif* (Sainte-Foy: Québec dans le Monde, 1997); Jean-Michel Hercourt, "Les associations de la Francophonie au Canada," in *La francophonie et le Canada, actes du colloque de Grenoble des 2 et 3 mai 1990* (Grenoble: Association française d'études canadiennes, 1992), 119–34; Jean-Marc Léger, *La francophonie, grand dessein, grande ambiguité* (Montréal: Hurtubise, 1987), 200–4.

23 Cholette, *L'action internationale du Québec*, 191.

24 See Pierre Maillard, "Le Québec un quart de siècle après …," *L'Espoir, revue de l'Institut Charles-de-Gaulle*, no. 20 (Oct. 1977), 7–22.

25 Jean-Charles Bonenfant, "Les relations extérieures du Québec," *Études internationales*, 2 (1971), 138.

26 *Telegram* (Toronto), 12 Sept. 1968, 5; 13 Sept. 1968, 5.

27 Le Conseil de la vie française en Amérique, *Le répertoire de la vie française en Amérique, 1997*, q.v. "Institut de recherche … "

28 Louis-Jean Calvet, *La guerre des langues et les politiques linguistiques* (Paris: Payot, 1987); Lüthy, *France against Herself*, 210ff.

29 Beaudoin Bollaert, "Le royaume de la francophonie," France–Amérique, 15–21 Nov. 1997, 3.

30 Sylvie Guillaume and Pierre Guillaume, *Paris–Québec–Ottawa: un ménage à trois* (Paris: Éditions entente, 1987), 188.

31 Pierre Savard, "L'ambassade de Francisque Gay en 1948–1949," *Revue de l'Université d'Ottawa*, 44 (1974), 14–16.

32 *La politique étrangère de la France: textes et documents* (Paris), 1e semestre 1971, 125.

33. D.L. Hanley, A.P. Kerr, and N.H. Waites, *Contemporary France: Politics and Society since 1945*, rev. ed. (London: Routledge, 1984), 252–3.

34 Bollaert, "Le royaume," 3.

35 Christian Rioux, "La bibliothèque idéale" and "Du rêve à la réalité," *Le Devoir*, 14–15 June 1997, D1, D2.

36 Jean Lacouture, "L'assemblée des parlementaires francophones," *Le Monde hébdomadaire*, no. 1040, 26 Sept.–2 Oct. 1968, 6.

37 *La politique étrangère de la France: textes et documents* (Paris), 1er semestre 1971, 125; 2e semestre 1971, 343.

38 Szulmajster-Celnikier, "Des serments," see 43.

39 *La Presse* (Montreal), 11 April 1997; Laurence Oiknine, "Pour un nouvel élan politique," *France–Amérique*, 15–21 Nov. 1997, 2.

40 Luong Tûyen Nguyen, "La culture française a subi un flagrant recul au Vietnam," *Le Devoir*, 3 Nov. 1979, A9.

41 "Plaidoyer pour la langue: le président Chirac exalte la défense de la langue française," *Le Devoir*, 18 July 1997, B8.

42 Sylviane Tramier, "La Francophonie prend un tournant politique," *Le Devoir*, 15 Nov. 1997, A8; Denis Lessard, "Boutros-Ghali devient secrétaire général de la francophonie par défaut," *La Presse*, 13 Nov. 1997, 4; Laurence Oiknine, "Pour un nouvel élan politique," *France–Amérique*, 15–21 Nov. 1997, 2; Bollaert, "Le royaume," 3; Henri-Christian Giraud and Patrice de Meritens, "Boutros Boutros-Ghali: 'la francophonie est essentielle à la civilisation de l'universel," *Franc–Amérique*, 15–21 Nov. 1997, 4; and 7–13 March 1998, 3.

43 Colette Braeckman, "Une belle idée qui, en se politisant, a perdu tout son sens," *Le Soir* (Brussels), quoted in *Courrier international*, no. 368, 20–26 Nov. 1997, 14.

44 Deniau, *La francophonie*, 71.

45 *Acadie Infos*, no. 73 (Aug.–Sept. 1992), 4.

46 Le Conseil de la vie française en Amérique, *Le répertoire*, 1997, 246–7.

47 *Acadie Infos*, no. 105 (May 1996), 4.

48 Michel Lucier, *Délégué général* du Québec à Paris from 1 June 1997, replacing Marcel Masse, with whom Lucien Bouchard never got along and whom Parizeau appointed just before he resigned; Lucier is a former priest who worked closely with Cardinal Léger for about ten years; then he worked at the Université de Montréal and founded the faculty of education; in 1976 he became Jacques Léonard's *directeur de cabinet*; from 1983 he worked with *la francophonie* mainly in Paris; earlier the *Délégué général* had been Louise Beaudouin. Of Lucier, *Le Soleil* reports, "C'est un habitué du Quai d'Orsay ... et il possède, dit-on, ses entrées à Matignon et à l'Élysée. A Paris il cumulera les fonctions de représentant personnel du premier ministre pour la Francophonie et le délégué général (à l'image de Lucien Bouchard, qui était à la fois ambassadeur du Canada et 'sherpa' de Brian Mulroney)." See *Le Soleil*, 7 May 1997, A13.

49 The *Association acadienne de la région de Québec*, the *Association internationale francophone des aînés*, the *Centre internationale de documentation et d'échanges de la francophonie*, the *Centre international de recherche, d'échanges et de coopération de la Caraïbe et des Amériques*, the *Conseil de la vie française en Amérique*, the *Forum international des jeunes pour la francophonie*, the *Année francophone internationale*, the *Mouvement francité*, the *Fonds mondial pour l'enseignement du français*, and the *Richelieu international*. See *France–Amérique*, 4–10 April 1998, 24.

50 Jacques Cellard, "Canada: un débat à Paris à l'occasion de la présentation de l'ouvrage *Dossier Québec*," *Le Monde*, 13 Feb. 1980, 6.

CHAPTER THIRTEEN

1 "Il est bien acquis pour quiconque connaît les démarches des gaullistes
   que ceux-ci ne s'embarrassent jamais trop de légalité et de protocole. Au
   contraire, ils agissent avec brutalité et leurs méthodes sont plutôt celles
   de véritables gangsters que d'hommes d'état européens civilisés comme
   on pourrait le croire à prime abord." NA, MG31, E31, Cadieux Papers,
   memo of 25 Sept. 1969, 5.

2 Michael King, *Death of the Rainbow Warrior* (Harmondsworth: Penguin
   Books, 1986); Ramesh Thakur, "A Dispute of Many Colours: France,
   New Zealand, and the 'Rainbow Warrior' Affair," *World Today*, 42, no.
   12 (Dec. 1986), 209–14; Douglas Porch, *The French Secret Services: A
   History of French Intelligence from the Dreyfus Affair to the Gulf War*
   (New York: Farrar, Straus and Giroux, 1995), chap. 19; Peter Tweed,
   Dictionary of Twentieth-Century History, 1914–1990 (Oxford: Oxford
   University Press, 1992), 390.

3 *Le Monde*, 2 Sept. 1985, 7 and 17; 19 Sept. 1985, 1, 6–7; 19 Sept. 1985,
   1 and 7; 20 Sept. 1985, 1 and 8; and passim through that month.

4 Ibid, 4 March 1995, 8.

5 Edwy Plenel, "Dominique Prieur livre la vérité de l'affaire Greenpeace,"
   in *Le Monde*, 12 May 1995, 14.

6 Thakur, "Dispute," 209.

7 King, *Death of the Rainbow Warrior*, 119ff.

8 *Toronto Star*, Tuesday, 11 July 1995, A3; *Economist*, 336, (15–21 July
   1995), 25–26.

9 Vincent Jauvert, "Essais nucléaires: les archives interdites de l'armée"
   and "Sahara: les cobayes de 'Gerboise verte,'" in *Le Nouvel Observateur*,
   no. 1735, 5–11 Feb. 1998, 4–11.

10 Bertrand Goldschmidt, "Les origines du CEA [Commissariat à l'energie
   atomique]," in *Espoir, revue de l'Institut Charles-de-Gaulle*, no. 103
   (July 1995), 61–5; Robert Bothwell, *Nucleus: The History of Atomic
   Energy of Canada Limited* (Toronto: University of Toronto, 1988),
   4ff.

11 Thomas L. Neff, *The International Uranium Market* (Cambridge, Mass.:
   Harvard University, 1984), 240.

12 Robert Bothwell, *Eldorado: Canada's National Uranium Company*
   (Toronto: University of Toronto Press, 1984), 407–9; Earle Gray, *The
   Great Uranium Cartel* (Toronto: McClelland and Stewart, 1982), 70ff.

13 H. Basil Robinson, *Diefenbaker's World: A Populist in Foreign Affairs*
   (Toronto: University of Toronto Press, 1989), 111–12.

14 John Newhouse, *De Gaulle and the Anglo-Saxons* (New York: Viking,
   1970), 103–4.

15 Charlotte Girard, *Canada in World Affairs*, vol. XIII, *1963–1965*

(Toronto: Canadian Institute of International Affairs, 1980), 213–24;
Financial Post, Toronto, 18 Jan. 1964.

16 David Crane, "France Buys $1.5 Million in Plutonium from Canada,"
Globe and Mail, 1 Oct. 1968, B5; Pierre-C. O'Neil, "Accord Paris–
Ottawa pour la vente de $1.5 million de plutonium," *Le Devoir* (Mon-
treal), 1 Oct. 1968, 1.

17 John Hilliker and Donald Barry, *Canada's Department of External
Affairs*, vol. II, *Coming of Age, 1946–1968* (Montreal: McGill-Queen's
University Press, 1995), 393 – one brief, cryptic line about the trouble
over uranium sales. For a longer discussion of the issue, see below
chapter 13.

18 This was Mokta (Canada) Ltd. See Crane, "France Buys."

19 Philippe Decraene, "Le voyage de M. Pompidou en Afrique noire," in *Le
Monde hebdomadaire*, no. 1163, 4–10 Feb. 1971, 2.

20 In 1969 President Diori Hamani was in Paris apparently asking for aid in
return for uranium. (See Philippe Decraene, "Le Niger a besoin d'une aide
économique," *Le Monde hebdomadaire*, no. 1081, (10–16 July 1969), 5.)

21 *L'Express*, 10–16 July 1967, 22; Decalo, *Historical Dictionary of Niger*
(NJ: Scarecrow Press, 1989), 32, 227–8.

22 Neff, *The International Uranium Market*, 193–203.

23 Ibid., 240–1. By 1990 Canada was producing 27.7 per cent of the
world's uranium, Australia 11.2 per cent, the United States 10.8 per cent,
Namibia 10.1 per cent, and France 8.9 per cent. See Mel Hines, *Canadian Foreign Policy Handbook* (Montreal: Jewel Editions, 1996), 234.

24 For arrangements with the Soviet Union, see Paul Leventhal, "The
Nuclear End Run," *New York Times*, 145, 5 June 1996, A17 and A21.

25 Anthony Sampson, *The Arms Bazaar* (London: Hodder and Stoughton,
1977), 108–113, 299–305.

26 Samy Cohen, "Le lobby militaire, a-t-il gouverné la France?" *L'Histoire*,
no. 211 (June 1997), 62–5; for the diplomatic use of the *force de frappe*,
see Wilfrid L. Kohl, *French Nuclear Diplomacy* (Princeton, NJ: Princeton
University Press, 1971).

27 *The World Today* (London), May 1986, 78–9.

28 Jolyon Howorth, "France since the Berlin Wall: Defence and Diplomacy," *The World Today* (London), 46 (July 1990), 127.

29 Vincent Jauvert, "Quand la France testait des armes chimiques en
Algérie," *Le Nouvel Observateur*, 23–29 Oct. 1997, 4–10.

30 Messmer was minister for national defence from 1960 to 1969 and prime
minister from 1972 to 1974. See Pierre Messmer, "B2-Namous c'était
vraiment très secret," *Le Nouvel Observateur*, 23–29 Oct. 1997, 10.

31 David S. Yost, "France" in Fen Osler Hampson et al., eds, *The Allies and
Arms Control* (Baltimore, MD: Johns Hopkins University Press, 1992),
162–88.

32 Ibid., 168–9.

33 Andrew Knapp, *Gaullism since de Gaulle* (Aldershot: Dartmouth Publishing, 1994), 364–5.

34 *World Today* (June 1988), 103.

35 J.F. Bosher, *The French Revolution* (New York: W.W. Norton, 1988), 286–7.

36 Agence France Presse, "Tous les classiques y étaient, le char Leclerc en plus," *Le Devoir*, 15 July 1997, A4.

37 Bertrand Goldschmidt, "La politique de non-prolifération," in *Espoir, revue de l'Institut Charles-de-Gaulle*, no. 93 (Sept. 1993), 43–5.

38 Mireille Duteil, "Rwanda: La France face au génocide," *Le Point*, no. 1322, 17 Jan. 1998, 15; Pierre Rousselin, "La France et le Rwanda," *France–Amérique*, no. 1337, 24–30 Jan. 1998, 2; no. 1336, 17–23 Jan. 1998, 4; "Not our Business," *Economist*, no. 8053, 31 Jan.–6 Feb. 1998, 53–4; various articles in *L'Express*, no. 2432, 12–18 Feb. 1998, 46–59.

39 Vincent Hugeux, "Bosnie–Rwanda: l'embarras de Paris" and "Rwanda, pourquoi tant de gêne?," *L'Express*, no. 2432, 12–18 Feb. 1998, 46–51.

40 Marc Epstein, "Tribunal international: le blocage français," ibid., 58–9.

41 Porch, *The French Secret Services*, 441; Roger Faligot and Pascal Krop, *La piscine: les services secrets français, 1944–1984* (Paris: Seuil, 1985), 245–52.

42 Philippe Decraene, "Guinée An IV: voyage au bout de la nuit," *Le Monde hebdomadaire*, no. 689, 28 Dec. 1961–3 Jan. 1962, 3; no. 690, 4–10 Jan. 1962 3; no. 691, 11–17 Jan. 1962, 4; "Difficultés pour M. Sékou Touré en Guinée," *Le Monde hebdomadaire*, no. 1073,(15–21 May 1969, 5.

43 Pascal Krop, *Les secrets de l'espionnage français de 1870 à nos jours* (Paris: Lattès, 1993), 499.

44 Faligot and Krop, *La piscine*, 246–7.

45 See a summary and extracts of the Guinean documents, *L'impérialisme et sa cinquième colonne* in Krop, *Les secrets de l'espionnage français*, 501–6.

46 Philippe Gaillard, *Foccart parle: entretiens avec Philippe Gaillard*, 2 vols. (Paris: Fayard, 1997), I, 161–77.

47 Ibid., 341ff.

48 Faligot and Krop, *La piscine*, 262.

49 Ibid., 343–4.

50 Krop, *Les secrets de l'espionnage français*, 519.

51 Ibid., 518–9.

52 Faligot and Krop, *La piscine*, 261–2.

53 Ibid., 262–4.

54 J.L. Granatstein and Robert Bothwell, *Pirouette: Pierre Trudeau and Canadian Foreign Policy* (Toronto: University of Toronto Press, 1990), 276.

55 Mitchell Sharp, *Which Reminds Me ... A Memoir* (Toronto: University of Toronto Press, 1994), 207.

56 Mireille Duteil, "Rwanda: La France face au génocide," *Le Point*, no. 1322, 17 Jan. 1998, 15; Pierre Rousselin, "La France et le Rwanda," *France–Amérique*, no. 1337, 24–30 Jan. 1998), 2; no. 1336, 17–23 Jan. 1998, 4; "Not our Business," *Economist*.

57 Jan Palmowski, *Dictionary of Twentieth-Century World History* (Oxford: Oxford University Press, 1997), 531.

58 Vincent Hugeux, "Rwanda, pourquoi tant de gêne?" *L'Express*, no. 2432, 12–18 Feb. 1998, 48–51.

59 Patrick de Saint-Exupery, "Première audition de la mission parlementaire française," *France–Amérique*, 4–10 April 1998, 2.

60 "West 'Ignored' Rwanda Warning," *Ottawa Citizen*, 13 April 1998, B1.

61 Patrick de Saint-Éxupery, "Première audition de la mission parlementaire française," *France–Amérique*, 4–10 April 1998, 2.

62 Adnane Zaka, "La France s'interroge de sur son rôle au Rwanda," *France–Amérique*, 11–17 April 1998, 4; Francois-Xavier Verschave, *La Françafrique: le plus long scandal de la République* (Paris: Stock, 1998). 239–51, 280–1, 328–9.

63 *Le Monde*, 17 December 1998, 1, 2, 3, 15, and a 16-page supplement, "La France et le Rwanda."

64 "La France a secrètement aidé les Forces armées rwandaises (FAR) en 1993," *Le Devoir*, 22 May 1998, B5, quoting *Le Monde* and *Le Canard enchâiné*.

65 Rémy Ourdan, "Le rapport de la Mission Quilès suscite des critiques au Rwanda et en Belgique," *Le Monde*, 18 December 1998, 5.

CHAPTER FOURTEEN

1 Sarah Bennett Farmer, "Ouradour-sur-Glâne: Memory in a Preserved Landscape," *French Historical Studies*, 19 (1995), 27–47.

2 *New Cambridge Modern History*, vol. XII, 464ff.; P.M.H. Bell, *The Origins of the Second World War in Europe* (London: Longman, 1986), 20–1; for a French analysis of American motives, see Denise Artaud, "Le gouvernement américain et la question des dettes de guerre au lendemain de l'armistice de Rethondes (1919–1920)," *Revue d'histoire moderne et contemporaine*, 20 (1973), 201–29.

3 Richard Mayne, *The Recovery of Europe 1945–1973*, rev. ed. (New York: Doubleday, 1973), 144; Peter Tweed, *Dictionary of Twentieth Century History, 1914–1990* (Oxford: Oxford University Press, 1992), 296.

4 *Le Monde hebdomadaire*, no. 983, 17–23 Aug. 1967, 4; *La Presse*, 13 Aug. 1997, 1–2; 20 Aug. 1997, B1. The tragic Dieppe Raid took place on 19 August 1942.

5 *Canadian News Facts* (Toronto, 1967), 62. Prime Minister Pearson

assured the House of Commons on 12 April that the French government had been informed and consulted beforehand.

6 See, for example, Pierre Miquel, *La seconde guerre mondiale* (Paris: Fayard, 1986), 14. Even the fairer and better-informed study of André Kaspi, *La libération de la France, Juin 1944–Janvier 1946* (Paris: Perrin, 1995), is deficient in this respect.

7 Henry Rousso, *The Vichy Syndrome: History and Memory in France since 1944*, trans. Arthur Goldhammer (Cambridge, Mass: Harvard University Press, 1991), 17; Pierre-Louis Mallen, *Êtes-vous dépendantiste?* (Montreal: Éditions de la Presse, 1979), 150; Larry Collins and Dominique Lapierre, *Is Paris Burning?* (New York: Warner Books, 1965), 334. On the Gaullist myths in general, see the judicious comments of Brian Crozier, *De Gaulle, the Warrior, the Statesman*, 2 vols. (London: Eyre Methuen, 1973) II, 672–86, and Robert Gildea, *The Past in French History* (New Haven, Conn.: Yale University Press, 1994), 62, 80–1.

8 The last doubts about Vichy collaboration with the Nazis were removed when Pétain was photographed shaking hands with Hitler at Montoire on 24 October 1940; Kim Munholland, "Wartime France: Remembering Vichy," *French Historical Studies*, 18 (1994), 801–20; Philippe Gaillard, *Foccart parle: entretiens avec Philippe Gaillard*, 2 vols. (Paris: Fayard, 1995 and 1997), I, 38.)

9 Pierre Vennat, "Des Dieppois ont fait feu sur des Canadiens en 1942," *La Presse*, 13 Aug. 1997, 1–2.

10 See also Bernard Ledwidge, "De Gaulle et Churchill, les premières rencontres, juin 1940," in *Espoir, revue de l'Institut Charles-de-Gaulle*, no. 20 (Oct. 1977), 7–22.

11 Louis Héron de Villefosse, *Les îles de la liberté: aventures d'un marin de la France libre* (Paris: Albin Michel, 1972), 46ff. and passim; Jean-Louis Crémieux-Brilhac, *La France libre: de l'appel du 18 juin à la Libération* (Paris: Gallimard, 1996), 190ff, 474, 479; Robert Mengin, *De Gaulle à Londres, vu par un français libre* (Paris: La table ronde, 1965); Vice-Admiral Muselier, *De Gaulle contre le Gaullisme* (Paris: Éditions du chêne, 1946); Henri de Kerillis, *De Gaulle dictateur: une grande mystification de l'histoire* (Montreal: Éditions Beauchemin, 1945), 58 and passim.

12 General Pierre Koenig, *Bir-Hakeim, 10 juin 1942* (Paris: Robert Laffont, 1971).

13 D.C. Anglin, *The St. Pierre and Miquelon Affair of 1941* (Toronto: University of Toronto, 1966), 60, 93, 96, 120.

14 John Keegan, *Six Armies in Normandy: from D-Day to the Liberation of Paris* (London: Pimlico, 1982), chap. 8.

15 Martin Thomas, "The Discarded Leader: General Henri Giraud and the Foundation of the French Committee of National Liberation," *French History*, 10 (1996), 86–111; André Kaspi, "Les États-Unis et le problème

français de novembre 1942 à juillet 1943," *Revue d'histoire moderne et contemporaine*, 18 (1971), 203–36; Anthony Verrier, *Assassination in Algiers: Churchill, Roosevelt and the Murder of Admiral Darlan* (London, Macmillan, 1991).

16 "[De Gaulle] overstated his claims, overplayed his hand, dealt in tantrums, sulks, insults, postures, silences, Olympian detachment, political self-right-eousness, moral holier-than-thouery and, when it suited his book, double-dealing and backstairs intrigue characteristic of the Third Republic at its most underhanded"; Keegan, *Six Armies*, 296. Gerhard L. Weinberg makes a brief but similar denunciation in *A World at Arms: A Global History of World War II* (Cambridge: Cambridge University Press, 1994), 517.

17 Harold Nicolson, *The War Years 1939–1945, Vol. II of Diaries and Letters*, ed. Nigel Nicolson (New York: Atheneum, 1967), 138, 225, 279, etc. Max Egremont, *Under Two Flags: The Life of Major-General Sir Edward Spears* (London: Weidenfeld and Nicolson, 1997), 236–42.

18 David Dilks, ed., *The Diaries of Sir Alexander Cadogan, 1938–1945* (London: Cassell, 1971), 496, 628, 634–5.

19 François Kersaudy, *De Gaulle et Churchill* (Paris: Plon, 1981); Maurice Ferro, *De Gaulle et l'Amérique, une amitié tumultueuse* (Paris: Plon, 1973); Collins and Lapierre, *Is Paris Burning?*

20 For example, in James C. Humes, *The Wit and Wisdom of Winston Churchill: A Treasury of More than 1,000 Quotations and Anecdotes* (with bibliography) (New York: Harper, 1994), 151.

21 Crémieux-Brilhac records the anti-British feelings prevailing among French refugees in England: *La France libre*, 91.

22 Dilks, ed., *Diaries of Cadogan*, 72, 217, 302, 309–10, and see index entry for "de Gaulle," 850.

23 Alan Hamilton, "Old Rivalries Forgiven at the Statue de Gaulle Didn't Want," *Times*, 24 June 1993, 2.

24 Rousso, *The Vichy Syndrome*, 16–17.

25 *France–Canada, Organe de l'amitié franco–canadienne* (Trois-Rivières, Que.), 2 (1944) (see Ottawa University Library, per DC 397.A1.F72).

26 André Kaspi, "La bataille et le mythe," *Le Monde*, 25 Aug. 1994, a special supplement entitled "Paris libéré," I and II; Jacques Chirac, "Paris-symbole," *Le Monde*, 25 August 1994, 1 and 7.

27 Jean-Claude Lamy, "Libération de Paris: quand les écrivains racon-taient," *Le Figaro*, 24 Aug. 1994, 1 and 6; Rousso, *The Vichy Syndrome*, 10, 16–17, 71.

28 Agence France-Presse, "Un ancien ministre gaulliste pourfend le 'myth' de la France résistante," *Le Devoir* (18–19 Oct. 1997), A11; André Kaspi, *La libération de la France, juin 1944–Janvier 1946* (Paris: Perrin, 1995), chaps. 8, 15, 16.

29 Crémieux-Brilhac, *La France libre*; François Bédarida, "De Gaulle and the Resistance, 1940–1944," in Hugh Gough and John Horne, eds., *De Gaulle and Twentieth-Century France* (London: Edward Arnold, 1994), 19–34.

30 Ferro, *De Gaulle et l'Amérique*.

31 Crozier, *De Gaulle*, II, 670.

32 As Brian Crozier (ibid., 663) sums up de Gaulle, he was "a showman. The fame of de Gaulle outstrips his achievements. Those most susceptible to the charisma of his name find this impossible to concede; but the facts speak for themselves." This is the view, too, of Louis Héron de Villefosse and Robert Mengin, to mention only the best-known of the anti-Gaullists. The story of the liberation of Paris is told from a Gaullist point of view, however, in Collins and Lapierre, *Is Paris Burning?* 35.

33 Wolton, *L'histoire interdite*, 22–6.

34 John Hellman, *The Knight-Monks of Vichy France: Uriage, 1940–45*, 2nd ed. (Montreal: McGill-Queen's University Press, 1997), 252–3; Robert Gildea, *France since 1945* (Oxford: Oxford University Press, 1996), 64–70.

35 François Bédarida, "De Gaulle and the Resistance, 1940–1944," in Hugh Gough and John Horne, eds., *De Gaulle and Twentieth-Century France* (London: Edward Arnold, 1994), 28; Kaspi, *La libération*, 21–29.

36 James F. McMillan, *Twentieth Century France: Politics and Society 1898–1991* (London: Edward Arnold, 1992), 149.

37 David Stafford, *Britain and European Resistance, 1940–1945: A Survey of the Special Operations Executive with Documents* (Toronto: University of Toronto Press, 1983), 52–3.

38 Thierry Wolton, *L'histoire interdite* (Paris: Lattès, 1998), 204–21; Jean-Louis Crémieux-Brilhac, *La France libre*, 190ff., 474, 479; Maurice Diamant-Berger (alias André Gillois), *Histoire secrète des Français à Londres de 1940 à 1944* (Paris: Hachette, 1973), 37, 39, 53–4; Crozier, *De Gaulle*, I, 134–43. On André Labarthe, see Christopher Andrew and Oleg Gordievsky, *KGB: The Inside Story* (New York: Harper Collins, 1990), 446–7.

39 Robert Mengin, *De Gaulle à Londres vu par un Français libre* (Paris: La Table ronde, 1965), translated as *No Laurels for De Gaulle: An Appraisal of the London Years* (New York: Farrar, 1966), passim.; and Mengin, *La France vue par l'étranger* (Paris: La Table Ronde, 1971).

40 Louis Héron de Villefosse, *Les îles de la liberté: aventures d'un marin de la France libre* (Paris: Albin Michel, 1972), 82.

41 P.L. Thyraud de Vosjoli, *Lamia, l'anti-barbouze* (Montreal: Les Éditions de l'homme, 1972). "Lamia" was Vosjoli's secret-service code name.

42 Michael Pearson, *Tears of Glory: The Heroes of Vercors, 1944* (New York: Doubleday, 1978), 283; Kaspi, *La libération*, 27–29.

43 Martyn Cornick, "The BBC and the Propaganda War against Occupied France: The Work of Émile Delavenay and the European Intelligence Department," *French History*, 8 (1994), 316–54; see also Delavenay, *Témoignage d'un village savoyard au village mondial* (Aix-en-Provence, 1992); Crozier, *De Gaulle*, I, 135.

44 Cornick, "The BBC," 334–5; Raymond Aron, *Mémoires*, 2 vols. (Paris: Julliard, 1983), I, 182ff.

45 Crémieux-Brilhac, *La France libre*, 263–6; Crozier, *De Gaulle*, I, 183–207.

46 Thyraud de Vosjoli, *Lamia*, 113.

47 Kerillis, *De Gaulle dictateur*.

48 Pierre Viansson-Ponté, *Histoire de la république gaullienne Mai 1958–Avril 1969* (Paris: Robert Laffont, 1971); Kaspi, *La libération*.

49 Crozier, *De Gaulle*, II, 670.

50 Claude Galarneau, "Les étudiants québécois en France," in Centre de recherche Lionel-Groulx, *De Gaulle et le Québec* (Les cahiers d'histoire du Québec au XXᵉ siècle, Sainte Foy, Que.), no. 7 (spring 1997), 130–45; Pierre Savard, "Les Canadiens français et la France de la 'cession' à la 'révolution tranquille,'" in Paul Painchaud, ed., *Le Canada et le Québec sur la scène internationale* (Quebec City: Presses de l'Université du Québec, 1977), 471–95.

51 Marcel Fournier, *Les Français au Québec 1765–1865: un mouvement migratoire* (Sillery, Que.: Presses de l'Université du Québec, 1995).

52 Mallen, *Vivre le Québec libre*, 31 note.

53 "Vous êtes né Français, vous n'avez pas cessé de l'être." Hilda Neatby, *Quebec: The Revolutionary Age, 1760–1791* (Toronto: McClelland and Stewart, 1966), 174.

54 Ibid., 189.

55 J.F. Bosher, *The French Revolution* (New York: Norton, 1988), 167–8, 182–3, 196–7, 203–6, 273–4.

56 Joseph Chaballe, *Histoire du 22ᵉ bataillon canadien-français*, 2 vols., (Montreal: Chantecler, 1952), I, 352–84.

57 Keegan, *Six Armies*, 119.

58 Michel Grenon, ed., *L'image de la révolution française au Québec, 1789–1989* (Montreal: Hurtubise, 1989), 226.

59 Elisabeth de Miribel, *La liberté souffre violence* (Paris: Plon, 1981), 48ff. and chap. 3; see also Philippe Prévost, *La France et le Canada: d'une après-guerre à l'autre, 1918–1944* (Saint-Boniface, Man.: Éditions du blé, 1994), 339ff.; Sylvie Guillaume, "Les québécois et la vie politique française (1914–1969): parenté et dissemblance," thèse de doctorat de 3ᵉ cycle, Université de Bordeaux, 1975, 132–43; John Bryden, *Best-Kept Secret: Canadian Secret Intelligence in the Second World War* (Toronto: Lester Publishing, 1993), 207–9, 220–2; and J.F. Hilliker, "The Canadian

Government and the Free French: Perceptions and Constraints 1940–44," *International History Review*, 2 (1980), 89, 91, 98–9, 108.

60 André Laurendeau, *La crise de la conscription, 1942* (Montreal: Éditions du jour, 1962); C.P. Stacey, *Arms, Men and Governments: The War Policies of Canada, 1939–1945* (Ottawa: Queen's Printer, 1970), 424ff.

61 Only 25.69 per cent of men aged 18–45.

62 Stacey, *Arms, Men and Governments*, 422.

63 Esther Delisle, *Mythes, mémoire et mensonges: l'intelligentsia du Québec devant la tentation fasciste, 1939–1960* (Montreal: Robert Davies, 1998), pp. 9–20 and passim. Yves Lavertu, *The Bernonville Affair: A French War Criminal in Quebec after World War II*, trans. George Tombs (Montreal: Robert Davies, 1995); Pierre Savard, "L'ambassade de Francisque Gay en 1948–1949," *Revue de l'Université d'Ottawa*, 44 (1974), 20–5; Delisle, *Mythes*, 15–18.

64 Hilliker, "The Canadian Government," 87–108.

65 "... ce qui frappe dans cette affaire c'est que le Général se situait véritablement dans une perspective historique." *Espoir, revue de l'Institut Charles-de-Gaulle*, no. 20 (Oct. 1977), 9. Pérol worked as press attaché at the Élysée and was in charge of de Gaulle's texts when he came to Canada in 1967.

66 Charles de Gaulle, *Discours et messages, janvier 1966–avril 1969*, vol. V (Paris: Plon, 1970), 236–40 (press conference of 27 Nov. 1967).

67 Mallen, *Vivre le Québec libre*, 11.

68 For an analysis of the crisis on the basis of archival research, see J.F. Bosher, "Shipping to Canada in Wartime, 1743–1760," in Bosher, *Business and Religion in the Age of New France: Twenty-Two Studies* (Toronto: Canadian Scholars' Press, 1994), chap. 21; Bosher, *The Canada Merchants* (Oxford: Clarendon Press, 1987), chap. 10, "Merchants at the Conquest," reprinted in C.M. Wallace, R.M. Bray and A.D. Gilbert, eds., *Reappraisals in Canadian History: Pre-Confederation*, 2nd ed. (Scarborough, Ont.: Prentice Hall, 1996), 207–28; and Bosher, "The French Government's Motives in the affaire du Canada, 1761–1763," *English Historical Review*, 96 (1981), 59–78.

69 Reprinted in many places, such as Pierre-Louis Guertin, *Et de Gaulle vint ...* (Quebec City: Claude Langevin, 1970), 220–4; Centre Lionel-Groulx, *De Gaulle et le Québec*, 98–101; and de Gaulle, *Discours et messages*, V, 236–40.

70 André Lachance, *La justice criminelle du roi au Canada au XVIIIe siècle* (Quebec City: Presses de l'Université Laval, 1978), 75–96.

71 Bosher, *The French Revolution*, 176–82, 194–203, 224.

72 Alfred Leroy Burt, *The Old Province of Quebec* (Minneapolis: University of Minnesota Press, 1933), 56. Hilda Neatby did not contradict Burt's conclusion in her *Quebec*, chaps. 2–5.

73 Élisabeth Labrousse, *Essai sur la révocation de l'édit de Nantes* (Paris: Payot, 1985), chap. 8; André Zysberg, *Les galériens: vie et destins de 60,000 forçats sur les galères de France, 1680–1748* (Paris: Seuil, 1987), 54–6, 102–11, 172–93; Marc Vigié, *Les galériens du roi, 1661–1715* (Paris: Fayard, 1985), 99–103, 296–9; and see the many scholarly articles concerning French religious persecution in *Le bulletin de la société de l'histoire du protestantisme français*, published quarterly since 1855.

74 Rex Whitworth, *Field Marshal Lord Ligonier: A Story of the British Army, 1702–1770* (Oxford: Oxford University Press, 1958).

75 Bédarida, "De Gaulle and the Resistance," 21.

76 Naomi E.S. Griffiths, *The Contexts of Acadian History, 1686–1784* (Montreal: McGill-Queen's University Press, 1992), chap. 3.

77 This petition, ten pages in length, as aired at a conference held at Caen, France, under the title, "International Defence of Human Rights," rests on a nationalist view of Acadian history. See Warren A. Perrin, "Une pétition à l'Angleterre," in *Le congrès mondial acadien, L'Acadie en 2004, Actes des conférences et des tables rondes, 16–20 août 1994* (Moncton: Éditions d'Acadie, 1996), 47–51, and *Acadie Infos*, no. 50 (March 1990), 3; "Cajuns' Belated Counter-attack," *Economist*, no. 8053, 31 Jan.–6 Feb. 1998, 32–3.

78 See, for example, the details in Richard I. Melvoin, *New England Outpost: War and Society in Colonial Deerfield* (New York: Norton, 1989), 19–20, 213–14, 215–26, 234–43, 263–7.

79 Stephen E. Patterson, "1744–1763: Colonial Wars and Aboriginal Peoples," in Phillip A. Buckner and John G. Reid, eds., *The Atlantic Region to Confederation: A History* (Fredericton, NB: Acadiensis Press, 1994), 147; Francis Jennings, *Empire of Fortune: Crowns, Colonies and Tribes in the Seven Years War in America* (New York: Norton, 1988), 134–5.

80 "Memoire [de Louis XIV] pour servir d'instruction à Monsieur le comte de Frontenac sur l'entreprise de la Nouvelle-York," in *Le Rapport de l'Archiviste de la Province de Quebec, 1927–28*, 12–16; Marcel Trudel, "Louis XIV et son projet de deportation," *La Revue de l'histoire de l'Amerique francaise*, 4 (1950), 157–71.

81 A.F. Williams, *Father Baudoin's War: D'Iberville's Campaigns in Newfoundland, 1696, 1697* (St John's, Nfld.: Memorial University, Department of Geography, 1987), 63, 131 note 8, 184.

CHAPTER FIFTEEN

1 Jean Lacouture, *De Gaulle*, 3 vols. (Paris: Seuil, 1984), I, 10; Paul Robert, *Dictionnaire* (Paris: Société du nouveau Littré, 1970), 773.

2 The Nine Years War (or War of the League of Augsburg), 1689–97; the

War of the Spanish Succession, 1702–13; the War of the Austrian Succession, 1744–48; the Seven Years War, 1756–63; the War of American Independence, 1776–83; the French Revolutionary War, 1793–1802; and the Napoleonic War, 1803–15.

3 The issue is summarized with references in J.F. Bosher, "The Franco-Catholic Danger, 1660–1715," *History: Journal of the Historical Association* (London), 79 (Feb. 1994), 5–30.

4 John Carswell, *The Descent on England: A Study of the English Revolution of 1688 and Its European Background* (London: Barrie and Rockliff, 1969), 183. See also Jonathan I. Israel, ed., *The Anglo–Dutch Moment: Essays on the Glorious Revolution and Its World Impact* (Cambridge: Cambridge University Press, 1991), and Charles Wilson and David Proctor, eds., *1688: The Seaborne Alliance and Diplomatic Revolution* (London: National Maritime Museum, 1989).

5 This was François de Laval's successor, Jean-Baptiste La Croix de Chevrières de Saint-Vallier (1653–1727).

6 Dominic Aidan Bellenger, *The French Exiled Clergy in the British Isles after 1789* (Bath: Downside Abbey, 1986), 139–301.

7 Bruce Lenman, *The Jacobite Risings in Britain, 1689–1746* (London: Eyre Methuen, 1980); Bruce Lenman and John S. Gibson, *The Jacobite Threat: England, Ireland, Scotland and France* (Edinburgh: Scottish Academic Press, 1990).

8 Jonathan R. Dull, *The French Navy and American Independence: A Study of Arms and Diplomacy, 1774–1787* (Princeton, NJ: Princeton University Press, 1975).

9 Cedric Jennings, "Le Pélican de d'Iberville va reprendre la mer," *Seaports and the Shipping World* (1987).

10 Pierre-Louis Mallen, *Vivre le Québec libre* (Paris: Plon, 1978; Montreal: Presses de la Cité, 1978), 311; Gerald S. Graham, ed., *The Walker Expedition to Québec, 1711*, Navy Record Society, vol. XCIV (London, 1953), 24, 86, 102–3, 130, 220.

11 James Pritchard, *Anatomy of a Naval Disaster: The 1746 French Expedition to North America* (Montreal: McGill-Queen's University Press, 1995).

12 Claude Fohlen, "The Commercial Failure of France in America," Nancy L. Roelker and Charles K. Warner, eds., *Two Hundred Years of Franco–American Relations* (Newport, RI: French Historical Studies, 1978), 93–120; Fohlen, "La guerre de Sécession et le commerce franco–américain," *Revue d'histoire moderne et contemporaine*, 8 (1961), 259–70; J.M. Price, *France and the Chesapeake: A History of the French Tobacco Monopoly, 1674–1791, and of Its Relationship to the British and American Tobacco Trades*, 2 vols. (Ann Arbor: University of Michigan, 1973), II, 785–7.

13 Raymond C. Howell, *The Royal Navy and the Slave Trade* (New York: St Martin's Press, 1987); Christopher Lloyd, *The Navy and the Slave Trade: The Suppression of the African Slave Trade in the Nineteenth Century* (London: Frank Cass, 1968); W.E.F. Ward, *The Royal Navy and the Slavers* (London: Allen and Unwin, 1969).

14 For a brief review of the earlier invasion attempts, see J.F. Bosher, "The Franco–Catholic Danger, 1660–1715," *History: Journal of the Historical Association* (London), 79 (Feb. 1994), 5–30. On the later ones, see Dull, *The French Navy*, 143–59, and Édouard Desbrière, *Projets et tentatives de débarquement aux Isles Britanniques, 1793–1805*, 5 vols. (Paris: R. Chapelot, 1900–02).

15 G. de Berthier de Sauvigny, *La restauration* (Paris: Flammarion, 1955), chaps. 1 and 2.

16 F.H. Hinsley, *British Intelligence in the Second World War*, 5 vols. (London: HMSO, 1979–90), I, 149–54.

17 P.A. Gagnon, *France since 1789* (New York: Harper and Row, 1964), 191.

18 Mason Wade, *The French Canadians, 1760–1945* (London: Macmillan, 1955), 299.

19 Eveline Bossé, *La Capricieuse à Québec en 1855: les premières retrouvailles de la France et du Canada* (Montreal: Éditions de la Presse, 1984), 37.

20 Wade, *The French Canadians*, 300.

21 Bossé, *La Capricieuse*, 88.

22 Ibid., 42.

23 Wade, *The French Canadians*, 300.

24 Bossé, *La Capricieuse*, 46.

25 François-Edmé Rameau de Saint-Père, *La France aux colonies: Acadiens et Canadiens* (Paris: Jouby, 1859); and *Une colonie féodale en Amérique: l'Acadie 1604–1881*, 2 vols. (Paris: Plon, 1889).

26 Cécille Gallant, "L'engagement social de Georges-Antoine Belcourt, curé de Rustico, 1859–1869," *Les Cahiers, Société historique acadienne*, 2, no. 4 (1980), 316–39; Pichette, *L'Acadie par bonheur retrouvé*, 42–4.

27 Henry Rousso, *The Vichy Syndrome: History and Memory in France since 1944* (Cambridge, Mass.: Harvard University Press, 1991), 244.

28 Robert Gildea, *The Past in French History* (New Haven, Conn.: Yale University Press, 1994), 62; Kim Munholland, "Wartime France: Remembering Vichy," *French Historical Studies*, 18 (1994), 801–20.

29 "Le moment, n'était-il pas unique, où, lui, le vieil homme, mais souverainement puissant par le Verbe, pouvait encore répondre à un appel et redonner à ce peuple la confiance en lui dont il avait besoin." Pierre de Menthon, "Les activités du Consulat Général de France à Québec, 1967–1972," *Études gaulliennes*, 7 (1979), 89.

30 "Sa phrase," declares Maurice Druon of the Académie française, "a la somptueuse cadence de Corneille, de Bossuet, de Montesquieu, de Chateaubriand. Mais à regarder de plus près l'oeuvre, on y distingue des procédés de composition, des tournures de récit qui font songer, particulièrement pour les *Mémoires*, à Tacite et plus encore à César." De Gaulle (Paris: Hachette, Collection Génie et Réalités, 1973), 281–2.

31 Laurent Zecchini, "Les riches heures londoniennes du général de Gaulle," *Le Monde*, 24 June 1993, 12.

32 *Le Devoir*, 27 July 1997, A7.

33 Interview with Eldon Black, 15 July 1997.

34 Jean-Marc Salvet, "De quoi amuser de Gaulle," *Le Soleil*, 23 July 1997, A1–2; Alain Abellard, "Québec commémore 'Vivre le Québec libre!,'" *Le Monde*, 24 July 1997, 2.

35 Jean-Marc Salvet, "Huit plaques en l'honneur de Charles de Gaulle," *Le Soleil*, 25 July 1997, A8.

36 Michel Venne, "Guerre de clans pour le général," *Le Devoir*, 24 July 1997, A1, A8.

37 It was illustrated by a large photograph of the French group, including de Gaulle, who welcomed Daniel Johnson *père in* Paris in May 1967; see Jean-Marc Léger, "France-Québec, un destin commun," *Le Devoir*, 23 July 1997, A7.

38 He avoided any mention of Quebec's hostility to de Gaulle and the Free French during the Second World War; and he made six references to a "Pierre-Louis Mullen," natural perhaps in a province with so many Irish families, and had later to apologize for so naming Pierre-Louis Mallen. See Jean Chartier, "De Gaulle s'était adressé aux Québécois dès 1940," *Le Devoir*, 23 July 1997, A2.

39 Charles Halary, "Le Québec, dernier refuge pour le gaullisme mystique?" *La Presse*, 24 July 1997, B2.

40 William Johnson, "France Has Been a Secret Enemy," *Montreal Gazette*, 25 July 1997, B3.

41 Jack Aubry, "Liberal Leader Refuses to Attend Unveiling," ibid., 23 July 1967. These politicians were not relatives of the above-mentioned journalist.

42 Ingrid Peritz, "Rally Stirs Emotions," ibid., 25 July 1997, A1–2.

43 John B. Wolf, *Louis XIV* (New York: Norton, 1968), xii, 369–78

44 Peter Burke, *The Fabrication of Louis XIV* (New Haven, Conn.: Yale University Press, 1992), 93, 160.

45 J. Lucas-Dubreton, *Le culte de Napoléon* (Paris: Albin Michel, 1960); Adrien Dansette, *Louis Napoléon à la conquête du pouvoir* (Paris: Hachette, 1961), chap. 4; Gildea, *The Past*, chap. 2.

CHAPTER SIXTEEN

1 Pierre Savard, "L'ambassade de Francisque Gay en 1948–1949," *Revue de l'Université d'Ottawa*, 44 (1974), 5–31.

2 André Siegfried, *Le Canada, puissance internationale* (Paris: Armand Colin, 1937).

3 André Kaspi, *La libération de la France, juin 1944–janvier 1946* (Paris: Perrin, 1995); John Ralston Saul, *Reflections of a Siamese Twin: Canada at the End of the Twentieth Century* (Toronto: Viking, 1997), 241.

APPENDIX

Chronology of Events

1940	10–15 May	German armies invade France.
	4 June	British army's evacuation from Dunkirk ends.
	17 June	General Charles de Gaulle tkes refuge in London.
	18 June	De Gaulle makes first speech to France from London over the BBC.
	22 June	France and Germany sign armistice at Compiègne.
	3 July	French fleet at Mers el-Kébir, in the Mediterranean, is bombarded by Vice-Admiral Sir James Somerville's forces.
	5 July	the Vichy government of France breaks off diplomatic relations with Britain.
	22 Oct.	Hitler and Pierre Laval meet at Montoire showing Vichy's collaboration.
1941	7 Dec.	Japanese forces attack Pearl Harbour; the United States enters the war at last.
	24 Dec.	Free French forces of de Gaulle seize Saint-Pierre and Miquelon.
1942	10 June	First Free French encounter with German forces takes place at Bir-Hakeim in North Africa.
	24 Dec.	Jean-François Darlan is shot to death by Fernand Bonnier.
1944	11–12 July	Charles de Gaulle visits Ottawa, Montreal, and Quebec City.
	26 Aug.	De Gaulle makes triumphant march through Paris celebrating its liberation.
	9 Sept.	De Gaulle forms a government as prime minister.
1945		*École nationale d'administration* (ENA) is founded in Paris.

	22 Aug.	Charles de Gaulle visits President Harry Truman in Washington, DC.
	28–29 Aug.	Charles de Gaulle visits Ottawa.
	20 Oct.	Walloon congress in Liège votes in favour of joining France, but nothing ensues.
	13 Nov.	De Gaulle is elected president of provisional government.
1946	20 Jan.	Prime Minister Charles de Gaulle resigns from government.
	12 Feb.	*Association nationale France-Canada* is founded.
	13 Oct.	Constitution of the Fourth Republic is accepted in a national referendum.
1947	7 April	De Gaulle launchs *Rassemblement du peuple français* (RPF).
1953	6 May	De Gaulle disolves RPF.
1954	7 May	French imperial forces are defeated at Dien Bien Phu, Indochina (Vietnam).
	20 July	French rule in Indochina comes to an end.
	1 Nov.	Algerian War for Independence begins.
1958	13 May	Coup d'état takes place, and a Committee of Public Safety is formed.
	1 June	De Gaulle's government begins with majority vote in National Assembly.
	28 Sept.	Referendum gives popular approval for constitution of Fifth Republic.
	20–26 Aug.	De Gaulle visits Africa.
	4 Oct.	Constitution of the Fifth Republic is formally adopted.
	21 Dec.	De Gaulle is elected president of the republic.
1959	8 Jan.	Fifth Republic officially begins.
	7 March	French naval forces in the Mediterranean are removed from NATO command.
	6 Sept.	Premier Maurice Duplessis dies.
1960	13 Feb.	First French atomic bomb is exploded at Reggane, Algeria.
	18–22 April	Charles de Gaulle visits Ottawa, Toronto, Montreal, and Quebec City.
	22 June	Liberal Jean Lesage wins the Quebec provincial election.
	13 Sept.	*Le Rassemblement pour l'Indépendance Nationale* (RIN) is set up.
	Autumn	Pierre Dupuy, Canadian ambassador in Paris, tours ten French-speaking African countries.

	Autumn	Georges-Émile Lapalme visits André Malraux in Paris.
1961		Quebec's *Office de la langue française* is established.
	4 Oct.	*Délégation générale du Québec à Paris* Lesage formally inaugurates.
	17 Oct.	Paris police massacre some 200 people engaged in demonstration.
1962	3 July	France recognizes Algerian independence.
	28 Oct.	De Gaulle holds a referendum to win power over National Assembly.
	Oct.	Basson and Thorailler, from Foreign Affairs Committee of French National Assembly, visit Quebec.
	8 Nov.	Law in Belgium draws linguistic line between Flemish and French-speaking parts.
	Nov.	Special number of *Esprit* on "Le Français, langue vivante" appears. President Léopold Senghor of Sénégal praises French as marvellous tool, etc. (*Le Monde hebdomadaire*, no. 1130, 18–24 June 1970, 6).
1963		FLQ terrorists begin bombings and other attacks early in year.
	14 Jan.	De Gaulle applies first veto of British application to join Common Market.
	22 Jan.	Franco-German treaty of cooperation is signed.
	10 Feb.	*Comité international pour l'indépendance du Québec* is founded in Paris.
	May	Lesage makes second mission to Europe, especially France.
	21 June	Pierre-Louis Mallen arrives in Montréal for six-year posting for ORTF.
	Sept.	Jean Cathelin and Gabrielle Gray, *Révolution au Canada*, appears in Paris.
	7–15 Oct.	André Malraux visits Montreal to open technological exhibition.
	3 Dec.	OECD mission headed by Roger Grégoire, French *conseiller d'état*, visits Quebec.
1964	Jan.	Prime Minister Pearson visits Paris.
	7 May	Marcel Cadieux is promoted to under-Secretary of state at External Affairs.
	1 June	Jules Léger presents credentials to de Gaulle as Canadian ambassador.
	June	Xavier Deniau, deputy in French National Assembly, visits Quebec.

	13 July	French National Assembly's cultural commission visits Quebec.
	Nov.	Jean Basdevant, *Directeur général des Affaires culturelles et techniques* at Quai d'Orsay, visits Quebec.
1965	27 Feb.	Franco–Quebec agreement on educational cooperation is signed in Paris.
	27 Feb.	Order of Jacques Cartier is formally disbanded.
	29 Oct.	Ben Barka, Moroccan political figure, is kidnapped and murdered by French *barbouzes*.
	Nov.	President Habib Bourguiba of Tunisia, visiting Dakar, calls for "un Commonwealth à la française, une sorte de communauté qui respecte les souverainetés de chacun et harmonise les efforts de tous.".
	17 Nov.	Cultural agreement (accord-cadre) is signed at Ottawa by Paul Martin and French ambassador.
	24 Nov.	Broad Franco–Quebec cultural agreement is signed.
	1 Dec.	Second meeting of *Commission permanente de coopération franco–québecoise* takes place in Paris.
1966	27 Feb.	France–Quebec entente for promotion of French in world is signed.
	4 March	De Gaulle takes France out of command structure of NATO.
	March	President Senghor calls for "un Parlement francophone qui permettrait mieux encore de faire entendre la voix de l'Afrique dans le monde." Bourguiba says that France should not let its colonial past inhibit such a step.
	31 Mar.	De Gaulle creates *Haut comité pour la défense et l'expansion de la langue française*.
	May	Senghor and Bourguiba meet at Tunis and discuss project for francophone community.
	June	Heads of state of *Organisation commune africaine et malgache* (OCAM) meet at Tananarive (Madagascar) and ask President Diori Hamani of Niger to present project for *communauté francophone* to French government.
	17 June	Party of Acadians is welcomed at National Assembly in Paris.
	2 July	French atomic tests begin on Mururoa Atoll in Pacific.
	Sept.	Christian Fouchet, French minister of education, visits Quebec and Ottawa.

29–30 Sept.	Couve de Murville visits Canada and has private talk with Premier Johnson.
Oct.	Louis Joxe visits Quebec for opening of métro in Montreal.
26 Oct.	It was decided to move headquarters of Atlantic Council from Paris to Brussels.
Nov.	*Association de solidarité francophone*, promoted by French ambassador to Canada, is founded.
Nov.	Jean de Broglie, secretary of state in French Department for Foreign Affairs, expresses "sympathy and interest" of France for Quebec but hopes this will not give rise to unfriendly criticism.
7 Dec.	Department of External Affairs receives report from RCMP about French efforts to assist Quebec separatists.

1967	Jan.	President Diori Hamani confers with de Gaulle about *la francophonie*. InParis *l'Association de solidarité francophone* is developed.
	12–16 Jan.	Michel Debré makes official visit to Quebec.
	Feb.	President Sekou Touré of Guinea denounces *la francophonie* as "an attempt to betray African interests, expressing the old will to maintain the exploitation of countries that wish to free themselves from colonization" (*Le Monde hebdomadaire*, no. 1130, 18–24 June 1970, 6).
	9 April	De Gaulle refuses to attend fiftieth anniversary of Vimy Ridge.
	18 May	*Association [or Assemblée] internationale des parlementaires de langue française* (AIPLE) is founded.
	27 May	Agreement grants France B2–Namous, Algeria, for secret testing of chemical weapons.
	spring	Gilbert Pérol visits Ottawa about de Gaulle's coming visit.
	17–22 May	Premier Daniel Johnson visits Paris and sees de Gaulle twice, on 18 and 20 May.
	May	*Conseil international de la langue française* is set up in Paris, and *Association internationale des parlementaires de langue française* meets in Luxemburg.
	15 June	De Gaulle reassures Paul Martin in 35-minute interview in Paris.
	20–21 June	Georges Gorsse, French cabinet official, stops at Montreal.
	23–26 July	De Gaulle and party visit Quebec.

26 July	De Gaulle returns to Paris, but Xavier Deniau goes on to Ottawa.
3 Aug.	François Aquin, Liberal MPP for Dorion (Quebec) becomes a "Gaullist."
3–9 Aug.	Michel Habib-Deloncle's article, "J'étais à Montréal," appears in *Le Monde hebdomadaire*, no. 981, 3–9 Aug. 1967, 4.
Sept.	*Conseil international de la langue française* (CILF) is founded.
10 Sept.	Alain Peyrefitte, minister of education, visits Quebec.
26 Sept.	François Misoffe, *ministre français de la jeunesse et des sports*, visits Quebec.
30 Sept.	Couve de Murville assures Trudeau that France does not support Quebec separatism.
Oct.	First report comes from Royal Commission on Bilingualism and Biculturalism.
20 Oct.	Michel Bignier, director of public relations at French National Centre of Space Studies, visits Québec with party, without going to Ottawa.
23–26 Nov.	The Estates General (*États généraux*) meets in Montreal.
27 Nov.	De Gaulle makes hostile remarks about Canada in press conference.
27 Nov.	De Gaulle places second veto on British application to join European Community
Dec.	Pierre Trudeau tours six French-speaking African countries.
Dec.	Pierre Bourgault and Gille Grégoire, two Quebec separatist leaders, visit France.
11–16 Dec.	Quebec deputy ministers stay in France: Gélinet (Health) and Marier (Family and Social Welfare).
18–20 Dec.	Loubier and Charron, Quebec minister of tourism and his deputy, visit Paris.
31 Dec.	The Quebec provincial legislature is henceforth called *l'Assemblée nationale*.
1968 6 Jan.	De Gaulle instructs Pierre de Menthon, consul in Quebec, to aid separatist cause.
Jan.	Heads of state of OCAM at Niamey suggest making permanent institution of francophone meetings. Diori Hamani is asked to take this in hand.
6–20 Jan.	Four Acadians chosen by Philippe Rossillon spend week in Paris.
10–19 Jan.	Jean-Noel Tremblay, Quebec's minister of culturel Affairs, visits Paris and sees de Gaulle.

29 Jan.–4 Feb.	Quebec minister of natural resources visits France.
5–10 Feb.	France, Quebec, and 15 other states attend Libreville conference on education.
9 Feb.	*Office franco-québécois pour la jeunesse* (OFQJ), is founded with headquarters in Paris.
10 Feb.	Jean-Guy Cardinal, Quebec minister of education, on way home from Gabon, visits de Gaulle in France.
Feb.	Gabon invites Quebec to meeting of ministers of education of French-speaking countries at Libreville.
March	Jean-Daniel Jurgenson, director of American Division at Quai d'Orsay, visits New Brunswick.
April	Pierre Trudeau becomes prime minister of Canada.
27 April	French-speaking ministers of education meet in Paris, continuation of Libreville meeting.
20 July	*Conseil pour le développement du français en Louisiane* (CODOFIL) is founded at Lafayette.
12 Sept.	Prime Minister Trudeau denounces French interference in Canada.
16 Sept.	Jean de Lipkowski, French secretary of state, addresses 800 French-Canadian businessmen at meeting of Richelieu Club at Cannes, France.
23 Sept.	Report of Royal Commission on Security, chaired by M.W. Mackenzie, appears.
25 Sept.	Premier Daniel Johnson dies.
30 Sept.	Couve de Murville assures Trudeau that France does not believe in Quebec separatism.
Dec.	First Congress of French-speaking Youth meets in Tunis.
20 Dec.	Claude Morin gives a lecture in Paris, "Le passé et l'avenir du Québec."
1969 Jan.	French-speaking ministers of education meet at Kinshasa, Zaïre. Mauritius joins movement.
9 Jan.	*Association France-Québec* is set up; its journal is first issued on 11 Dec. 1968.
Feb.	First conference at Niamey, Niger, of French-speaking states approves a project for francophone cooperation.
19 Feb.	Canada suspends diplomatic relations with Gabon.
27 April	French referendum expresses hostility to de Gaulle; he retires next day.
23 Sept.	Federal commission of inquiry, the Mackenzie Commission on national security, gives Trudeau govern-

		ment report on two big threats: international communism and separatist movement in Quebec.
	1 Oct.	William Leonard Higgitt is named general commissioner of RCMP, and John Starnes, director of security and intelligence.
	7 Oct.	Canada resumes diplomatic relations with Gabon.
	9–16 Oct.	Jean de Lipkowski, *secrétaire d'État aux affaires étrangères*, visits Quebec.
	Autumn	French mission headed by Jurgensen visits New Brunswick; also Jean Basdevant.
	5 Dec.	*Conférence des ministres francophones de la jeunesse et des sports* (CONFEJES) first meets; it plans to meet annually.
	19 Dec.	Cabinet discusses Trudeau's memo, "Current Threats to National Order and on Québec Separatism," and gives rise to police inquiries about French interference.
1970	1 Jan.	John Starnes, first civilian head of Security Intelligence Branch of RCMP, takes up duties in Ottawa.
	5–15 Jan.	Marcel Masse, Quebec's minister of intergovernmental affairs, visits France.
	20 Mar.	During second conference at Niamey, Niger, 21 countries sign convention creating the *Agence de coopération culturelle et technique des pays francophones* (ACCT).
	June	Conference of ministers of education takes place in Paris.
	28 Aug.–1 Sept.	François Cloutier, Quebec's minister of cultural affairs, visits France.
	10–20 Sept.	Delegation of *Commission des Affaires culturelles, familiales et sociales de l'Assemblée nationale de France* visits Canada.
	23–28 Sept.	Philippe Malaud inaugurates new ENA in Quebec.
	5 Oct.	James Cross, British trade commissioner, is kidnapped by FLQ in Montreal.
	10 Oct.	Pierre Laporte, Quebec's minister of labour, is kidnapped.
	16 Oct.	War Measures Act is put into force in Quebec.
	18 Oct.	Pierre Laporte's body is discovered in trunk of car.
	9 Nov.	Charles de Gaulle dies.
	30 Nov.–4 Dec.	10th session is held of *Commission permanente de coopération franco–québécoise*.
1971	Feb.	*Agence de presse libre du Québec* (APLQ) is founded.

	March	Secret *Centre d'analyse et de documentation* (CAD) is charged with informing Quebec government on questions of national security and subversion, directly under Premier Robert Bourassa (Louis Fournier et al., *La police secrète au Québec* [Montreal: Éd. Québec/Amérique, 1978], 15–40).
	5 April	French film *Le chagrin et la pitié*, about wartime collaboration with Nazi Germany, is first shown.
	19–22 April	Bourassa visits Paris.
	22–3 Sept.	Maurice Schumann, French minister for foreign affairs, visits Ottawa.
	30 Sept.–1 Oct.	Maurice Schumann visits Quebec to confer with Bourassa.
	4–9 Oct.	Pierre Billecocq, *secrétaire d'état à l'éducation nationale*, visits Quebec.
	7 Dec.	*Association Québec–France* is founded at Quebec City.
1972	1–6 June	*Commission permanente de coopération franco–québécoise* meets.
	1 Aug.	French naval ship rams David McTaggart's *Vega*, near French atomic testing.
	6 Oct.	RCMP agents burgle documents at *Agence de presse libre du Québec*.
	29 Nov.–1 Dec.	*Commission permanente de coopération franco–québécoise* meets.
1973	Jan.	"Operation Ham" by RCMP steals a list of PQ membership.
1974		*Association francophone d'amitié et de liaison* (AFAL), president Xavier Deniau, is founded.
	17 May	French *Comité interministériel pour les affaires francophones* is set up.
1975	20 Jan.	*Radio-France internationale* is launched.
	1–6 June	Xavier Deniau visits Quebec.
	1–6 June	French parliamentary delegation visits Quebec.
	5 June	French underground atomic tests begin on Fangataufa Island in Pacific.
	8–13 June	Norbert Ségard, French secretary of state, visits Quebec, Ottawa and western Canada.
	3–8 July	Michel Poniatowski, minister of interior, visits Quebec, Montreal, and Ottawa.
	8–12 July	French *Délégation sénatoriale* visits Quebec.
	4–5 Oct.	Marcel Cavaillé, French secretary of state for transport, visits Canada on Concorde.

1976		*Les Amitiés acadiennes* is organized by Philippe Rossillon and Lucien Bertin.
	5 March	Maison de la francité (MDLF) is founded in Brussels.
	26–31 March	René Haby, French minister of education, visits Quebec.
	15–17 Oct.	Mme Christian Scrivener, secrétaire d'état d'économie et des finances, visits Quebec – her 24th visit (see *Le Devoir*, 18 Oct. 1976, 3).
	16 Oct. 1976	*Congress of the Association Québec–France* takes place at Quebec.
	8–10 Nov.	*Commission permanente de coopération franco–québécoise* meets.
	15 Nov.	Parti québécois wins election in Quebec.
1977	10–12 Jan.	André Rossi, French minister for foreign trade, visits Ottawa to preside over *Mixed Economic Commission* which had met annually since founding in 1974. He also visits Quebec to confer with René Lévesque, Claude Morin, and other officials.
	14 March	*France–Louisiane; France–Américaine* (FLFA), is set up in Paris.
	15 June	Quebec announces creation of Keable Commission.
	6 July	Federal government announces creation of McDonald Commission.
	Aug.	"The Charter of the French language" (Bill 101) is passed by Quebec legislature.
	8–14 Sept.	Alain Peyrefitte visits Canada.
	5–7 Oct.	Louis de Guiringaud visits Canada.
	22–25 Oct.	René Monory, minister of economy, visits Canada.
	2–4 Nov.	Premier René Lévesque pays first official visit to France, signs various agreements.
	3 Nov.	Lévesque is named *Grand Officier de la Légion d'Honneur* in Paris.
1978	4 May	Henri Curiel, aide to international terrorists, is shot dead in his Paris apartment.
	25–27 June	J.P. Soisson, from French Ministry of Education, visits Quebec.
	2–4 July	Jean-Philippe Lecat, leading member of UDR, visits Quebec.
	15–17 Sept.	Joël Le Theule, minister of information, visits Quebec.
1979	8–13 Feb.	PM Raymond Barre visits Quebec (and Ottawa pro forma) to make agreements; party includes Jean-Philippe Lecat (minister) and Olivier Stirn and

		Jean-Pierre Prouteau (both secretaries of state). French PM and Quebec premier agree to meet at least once a year.
	1 May	*Association internationale des maires francophones* (AIMF) is founded.
1980	20 May	First referendum is held on Quebec's sovereignty.
	6–7 Dec.	First congress takes place of Philippe Rossillon's organization, *Amitiés Acadiennes*.
1981	26 Jan.	McDonald report is submitted.
	6 March	Keable Report is submitted.
1982	April	PM Pierre Mauroy makes official visit to Quebec to sign agreements; he is at Moncton on 26 April.
1983	June	Lévesque makes official visit to Paris.
	1 July	At Porrentruy, Lévesque signs entente between Quebec and Jura.
1984	8 March	Place d'Acadie is inaugurated in Paris.
	12 March	*Haut conseil de la francophonie* is set up to advise President of France.
	21 June	Parliament passes law establishing Canadian Security Intelligence Service (CSIS).
	7–10 Nov.	PM Laurent Fabius pays official visit to Ottawa, and Quebec.
1985	4–5 May	Louise Beaudoin attends meeting of *Association France–Québec* at Cannes.
	2 July	Prime Minister Brian Mulroney appoints Lucien Bouchard ambassador in Paris.
	10 July	French secret service agents bomb and sink *Rainbow Warrior* in New Zealand.
	Aug.	Philippe Rossillon spends several days visiting towns in New Brunswick.
	19 Sept.	Article in *Le Monde* reveals French government's role in *Rainbow Warrior* affair.
	7 Nov.	Mulroney's government allows Quebec to take part in Francophone Summits.
1986	17–19 Feb.	First Francophone Summit meets in Paris.
	2 May	French establish *Secrétariat d'État chargé de la francophonie*.
	13 May	Mme Lucette Michaux-Chevry, *Secrétaire d'État chargé de la francophonie*, visits Quebec.
1987		PM Jacques Chirac visits Quebec for an *entente fiscal* with Bourassa.
	May and Sept.	President François Mitterrand pays official visit to Quebec.

	29 May	Mitterrand stops at Moncton and addresses crowd.
	2–4 Sept.	Second Francophone Summit meets at Quebec City.
	1 Nov.	René Lévesque dies; funeral is attended by three leading Gaullists, Jacques Chaban-Delmas, Xavier Deniau, and Pierre Mauroy.
1988	25–29 Jan.	Governor General Jeanne Sauvé visits Paris.
1989	24–26 May	Third Francophone Summit meets at Dakar.
	2 June	French establish *Conseil supérieur de la langue française*.
1990	7–11 Sept.	Alain Decaux, minister for *la francophonie*, visits Acadia.
1991	Nov.	Fourth Francophone Summit meets in Paris.
1992	7 May	Public announcement is made in Quebec that Claude Morin had been informing RCMP.
	23 June	House of Commons passes Bill C-81 in preparation for federal referenda.
1993	June	Statue of Charles de Gaulle is unveiled outside 4 Carlton Gardens, London.
	14 July	Constitutional revision converts Belgium into federal state.
	16–18 Oct.	Fifth Francophone Summit meets in Mauritius.
1994	11 Jan.	*Communauté financière africaine* is abolished; its franc is devalued by 50%.
	4 Aug.	"La loi Toubon" is adopted in France, laying down rules for use of French.
1995	Jan.	Jacques Parizeau is named to *Légion d'Honneur* in Paris.
	1 June	Jacques Chirac is elected president of Fifth Republic.
	[June]	Jacques Larché, président of French senate's *Commission des lois constitutionelle du sénat français*, visits Quebec in that capacity as one of eight members of Commission.
	9 July	*Rainbow Warrior II* is boarded, its crew seized, etc., by French forces in Pacific.
	30 Oct.	Second Quebec referendum is held on sovereignty.
1996	Feb.	Hervé de Charette, French foreign minister, visits Canada.
	26 March	Yves Galland, *Ministre délégué aux Finances et au Commerce extérieur*, visits Quebec, together with dozen French industrialists.
	8–11 June	PM Alain Juppé visits Quebec.
1997	19 March	Jacques Foccart (born Jacques Koch 31 Aug. 1918) dies.

	7 Apr.	Jean-Émile Vié, retired French police official, admits tapping telephones in the 1950s and 1960s.
	23–5 July	Philippe Séguin, representing President Jacques Chirac, and Pierre Messmer, for Institut Charles-de-Gaulle, visit Quebec City and Montreal for unveiling of de Gaulle's statue in Quebec and celebration of thirtieth anniversary of de Gaulle's visit in July 1967. Philippe Rossillon and about 40 others from France also come.
	6 Sept.	Philippe Rossillon (born 10 Aug. 1931) dies.
	28 Sept.–2 Oct.	Lucien Bouchard, Sylvain Simard, Bernard Landry, and Louise Beaudoin visit Paris to confer with Jacques Chirac, Lionel Jospin, Dominique Strauss-Kahn, Catherine Trautman, and Philippe Séguin. A score of businessmen travel with them.
	12–16 Nov.	Francophone Summit meets in Hanoi.
1998	3 Jan.	French-language television network TV5 USA reaches almost all of North America.
	10 Feb.	Maurice Schumann (born on 10 April 1911) dies.
1999		Eighth Francophone Summit is to meet at Moncton, NB.

Index